D0148405

WITHDRAWN

AYUB KHAN

PAKISTAN'S FIRST MILITARY RULER

Altaf Gauhar with Field Marshal Ayub Khan, Government Guest House, Nathiagali; 23 July 1967.

AYUB KHAN
PAKISTAN'S FIRST MILITARY RULER

ALTAF GAUHAR

Karachi
Oxford University Press
Oxford   New York   Delhi
1996

Oxford University Press, Walton Street, Oxford OX2 6DP

Oxford   New York
Athens   Auckland   Bangkok   Bombay
Calcutta   Cape Town   Dar es Salaam   Delhi
Florence   Hong Kong   Istanbul   Karachi
Kuala Lumpur   Madras   Madrid   Melbourne
Mexico City   Nairobi   Paris   Singapore
Taipei   Tokyo   Toronto
and associated companies in
Berlin   Ibadan

Oxford is a trade mark of Oxford University Press

© Altaf Gauhar, 1996

All rights reserved. No part of this publication may be reproduced,
stored in a retrieval system, or transmitted, in any form or by any means,
without the prior permission in writing of Oxford University Press.

This book is sold subject to the condition that it shall not, by way
of trade or otherwise, be lent, re-sold, hired out or otherwise circulated
without the publisher's prior consent in any form of binding or cover
other than that in which it is published and without a similar condition
including this condition being imposed on the subsequent purchaser.

First edition Sang-e-Meel, Lahore, 1993
Paperback edition Sang-e-Meel, Lahore, 1994
This edition Oxford University Press, 1996

Not for sale in Pakistan

ISBN 0 19 577647 X

Printed in Pakistan at
Mas Printers, Karachi.
Published by
Oxford University Press
5-Bangalore Town, Sharae Faisal
P.O. Box 13033, Karachi-75350, Pakistan.

DS
385
.A9
G4
1996

111197-4576X8

ZARINA

FOR ALL HER LOVE AND COURAGE

Contents

List of Photographs

Between pp. 160-1

11. Ayub Khan with Mr and Mrs Liu Shao Chi at Chaklala Airport; 26 March 1966.

12. President Ayub and Premier Aleksei Kosygin, President's House, Rawalpindi; 17 April, 1968.

13. Ayub Khan's last official act, decorating Altaf Gauhar with Hilal-i-Quaid-i-Azam. President's House, Rawalpindi; 25 March 1968.

14. President's farewell lunch for Altaf Gauhar and family (L-R) Raana, Naveed, Altaf Gauhar, Ayub Khan, Begum Ayub, Zarina, Humayun; President's House, Rawalpindi; 25 March 1969.

15. Altaf Gauhar with Manzur Qadir, coming out of High Court of Sindh and Balochistan after hearing a habeas corpus petition; Karachi 1972.

On a Personal Note

This book has been a long time in the making—some twenty-three years of isolation, research and reflection including long spells of sheer indolence. The compulsion to write never left me, not in the bleak days of solitary confinement, nor during the years of 'residence' abroad. When living in Pakistan became difficult, an invitation from the Institute of Commonwealth Studies in 1976 to use its facilities in London as a base from where to work on General Muhammad Ayub Khan's period of military rule in Pakistan (1958-1969), provided a way out. It proved a rewarding experience not only because colleagues in the Institute, and later in the community of journalists, showed great personal consideration, but because I learnt to write without fear. There is nothing like the freedom with which you can write when you don't have to look over your shoulder. In Pakistan, as in most other Muslim countries, that freedom remains an illusion. It was ratifying to receive the British press award within a year of working as co-editor of the *Guardian Third World Review* in 1978.

I became a journalist by force of circumstances having served the government first in India and then in Pakistan for over twenty-four years. In Pakistan bureaucrats can become prime ministers and presidents, but not journalists. In my case there was an added problem: I had been the head of the Ministry of Information and Broadcasting for more than five years under Muhammad Ayub Khan and, according to my critics, had kept the Press on a leash. It is true that I had not denounced the Press and Publications Ordinance, an instrument of control, even though I had nothing to do with its promulgation, and many newspapers had acknowledged at the time that I had persuaded Ayub Khan to put the Ordinance on hold after my appointment as Information Secretary. I remember that when I was trying to explain to Ayub Khan that many of the provisions in the Ordinance were harsh and not even practicable, he said, 'You have just come. You don't know what kind of a Press we have. These owners of newspapers are opportunists and money-makers.' I submitted, 'Mr President, whatever the nature of the Press, there are certain things a government cannot and must not do.' That clinched the argument and Ayub Khan agreed to repeal some of the more offensive clauses. But it was not until I was out of government service, following Ayub Khan's exit from office in 1969, and became the editor of *Dawn,* Pakistan's oldest English daily, that I became a poacher, turned inside out or outside in, and began to understand the workings of the Press.[1] The lesson I learnt was that the Press serving as a medium of official propaganda can have no credibility or influence under any circumstances. It can go on projecting the 'achievements' of the government, blocking out all criticism and dissent, without making the slightest impact on public opinion. The Press has only one purpose, only one responsibility, and indeed only one obligation to the people, and that is to keep the government under constant scrutiny and to hold it to account at all times. That lesson should have been obvious, but the obvious is the first casualty in and around the seat of power in any authoritarian system of government. Every step that brings you nearer the person in power puts another wrap of gauze around your eyes with the result that you cannot see what is visible to others, who watch the events from a distance, and it is only when you move out of the magic circle that the gauze-wrappings begin to wear off and you are confronted by the obvious.

My experience in *Dawn* was reinforced by my stay in England. The two publications I edited in London, the monthly magazine, *South,* and the *Third World Quarterly,* both of which built up quite a respectable circulation and acquired a degree of influence over a period of twelve years (1978-90), never endeared themselves to any Third World ruler. The Shahs, Amirs, Khalifas, and Generals, in the so-called Islamic states, who preside over the destiny of their people and regulate their lives, did not relish being exposed and called to account by publications edited by a 'brother'. Some of the Western academics and journalists initially treated *South*, an interloper in their preserve, with a great deal of scepticism but learnt to respect its independent and forceful editorial policy after the first one or two years. The two publications came to be seen as an important means of communication between North and South. *South* and the *Quarterly* had the support of the Third World Foundation which developed into a powerful forum for discussing the problems and aspirations of the people of developing countries. It was a great privilege to have been associated with the establishment of the Foundation and to have served as its Secretary General for more than fourteen years. The Foundation established the highly prestigious Third World prize which was awarded to eminent statesmen and scholars for outstanding contribution to the understanding of the problems of the people in the developing countries. Among the recipients of the prize were such eminent scholars and statesmen as Raul Prebisch, Nelson Mandela, Bob Geldof, Julius Nyereri, and Willy Brandt. It was during this period that I had the opportunity to travel extensively in Latin America, Africa and Asia and study different models of authoritarian rule, particularly in some of the Muslim countries. I came to meet some of the rulers and many dissenters and victims of despotic governments. It was a chastening experience which helped me to understand what the people must have gone through during the first spell of military rule in Pakistan when I was a close associate of Ayub Khan. More than that it enabled me to put Ayub Khan and his form of government in the broader perspective of a whole variety of personal forms of domination of the people. I realized with a sense of shock that people must have seen me operating more as an instrument than an adviser in Ayub Khan's scheme of personal rule.

Distance lends enchantment but if you are fortunate it also confers detachment on your appraisal of events in which you may have been involved as an agent or participant. The past is an immutable reality but it does get transformed in the process of reflection and recall. And because recall can never be total, and reflection is often subjective, no personal account of events can be relied upon as complete and objective. This is particularly true of events which may have caused public controversy and disapproval. Those who participate in the making of public policy are always vulnerable to the charge that they are prone to rationalize the causes and minimize the consequence of any unpopular decision. Participants seldom make good historians though their recollection and presentation of events often serves as a primary source of history. They are denied even the benefit of hindsight, a familiar instrument of historical analysis and judgement, because of the risk that they might employ it in their own cause.

Any participant has the option to say nothing and keep whatever he has witnessed to himself. Most of them choose to take their recollections to the grave. I happened to become a major participant in the affairs of government under Ayub Khan, and in his last six years in office (1963-9) I was his diarist, speech-writer, adviser, and one of his principal associates. I admired him for his grasp of problems and the firm and unambiguous manner in which he would convey his instructions and take full responsibility for the consequences. I was not happy with certain aspects of his system of government, particularly his scheme of elections, but my unhappiness never crossed the bounds of loyalty. Under any personal system of government, loyalty to the ruler becomes the highest value and the ultimate test of one's competence. Before you know it you become a courtier, if not a court jester. Since I had the pain and pleasure of participating in several important events during the Ayub regime, events which have left a lasting imprint on the course of Pakistan's history, I have always considered myself under an obligation to render an account of those events—perhaps the first 'insider' account of the period.

It took me some time to get over the anxiety to clarify my own position and justify the role I played during those years. Some of my friends thought I should explain my own role rather than write a history of the period. Fortunately for me, the problem was solved by the rulers who succeeded Ayub Khan. They brought a number of charges, ranging from misuse of power to treason, and kept me under detention for more than a year, when I was adopted as a prisoner of conscience by Amnesty International. All the charges levelled against me were found baseless, as were the grounds of my detention, by the courts. The proceedings which General Yahya Khan, Ayub Khan's immediate successor, started against me before a military tribunal turned into a farce because I refused to appear before the military tribunal. Yahya Khan had the pleasure of dismissing me from service without any regard even for his own arbitrary regulations but the nemesis came two years later when Yahya Khan was declared a usurper and all his actions were found unlawful by the Supreme Court of Pakistan, on a petition filed by Zarina, my wife, when I was under detention.

There were some unforgettable moments during this period of persecution and incarceration. On a humid morning in Karachi, Ijaz Hussain Batalvi, ever my friend and lawyer, caused quite a consternation in court when he threw up his hands and demanded, 'What Barrister Khoja and what tribunal?' I was at that time accused of trying to flee the country on a forged passport. I was nabbed before I could make good my escape together with a considerably amount of foreign currency and a bottle of whisky! A thoroughly subdued magistrate explained that in view of the gravity of the charge the government had decided to set up a special tribunal to try the case. That did not satisfy my lawyer because the magistrate could not give him any information about the location or the composition of the tribunal except that a Barrister Khoja had been appointed as its chairman. The police embarked on a long search during the course of which I was taken back to the gates of Karachi Central Prison only to be refused admission for want of a warrant of custody. Barrister Khoja was finally discovered in Sind Club, a popular haunt of businessmen, where he was having a relaxed lunch. When informed of his appointment Khoja could only manage a hoarse lisp, 'I know nosing. I'm going home to zleep.' The police pursued Khoja to his residence which was located in a block of flats near Gandhi Gardens. As we alighted from the police van we were greeted by a colourful string of laundry fluttering in the breeze, strikingly reminiscent of Kafka's *The Trial*. We waited in a dreary room while the chairman of the tribunal was pulled out of his bed by the superintendent of police. A bleary-eyed Khoja kept nodding while it was argued that the chairman, without the other members, did not constitute the tribunal and had no authority to pass any orders. The police superintendent respectfully placed a piece of paper in front of the chairman and told him where to sign and that was the end of the proceedings. I was taken back to prison and Khoja to his bed.

A more ennobling moment came during the hearing of my habeas corpus petition by Tufail Ali Abdul Rehman, Chief Justice of the High Court of Sindh and Balochistan, and Fakhruddin G. Ibrahim, an eminent young lawyer, who had just been elevated to the Bench. I was accused of anti-state activities and the major piece of evidence, which the Attorney-General, Yahya Bakhtiar, an old school fellow from Quetta, was urging with some flourish, was a statement I had made at a private party soon after the Pakistan Army went into action to brutally suppress a popular agitation in Dhaka. (Spelt Dacca at the time). A young officer, who had just come back from Dhaka, was narrating with great relish, the horrible story of a sniping spree in the heart of the city in which some twenty Bengalis were 'bagged' by a colonel of the frontier scouts. When I could not take it any more I said, 'I am ashamed of being a Pakistani.' That according to the Attorney-General was conclusive proof of my anti-Pakistan sentiments. I pleaded guilty to having made that statement and the Chief Justice held that only a patriotic Pakistani could have made that remark in a moment of anguish.

Fortunately all this is behind me and I do not have to burden this narrative with any explanation or justification on my own behalf. I figure in this book only by designation as Information Secretary, like the other officials, and that too only when it is necessary to identify the participants in any meeting or discussion. I have avoided narrating juicy stories and anecdotes because I did not want to divert the reader's attention from the hard facts of the period.

This is the place to acknowledge a debt of gratitude long overdue. Manzur Qadir, an outstanding constitutional and criminal lawyer whom Ayub Khan appointed as his first Foreign Minister, and who later became the Chief Justice of the High Court of West Pakistan, appeared on my behalf before the Supreme Court and the High Court of Sindh and Balochistan in a number of cases, which were instituted against me when Zulfikar Ali Bhutto came to power. Manzur Qadir did this without any financial consideration and at great inconvenience to himself. His health was failing and the government was harassing him in different ways, but having taken up a case, it was not his custom to let go until the matter was judicially determined. In the cases against me he not only vindicated my position but also exposed the government for acting in an unlawful and malicious manner.

Official documents and personal notes

I gained access to classified documents when Ayub Khan decided to write his political autobiography in 1964. The autobiography was published in 1967 under the title *Friends Not Masters.* He invited me to talk to him about his life and work for several days in Murree where he was convalescing after a hernia operation in 1964. These conversations developed into regular interviews resulting in a 1,500-page transcript. The transcript was entrusted to Tom Dawson, the London editor of *Scotsman,* who produced a manuscript after a couple of months which Ayub could not recognize as his own. He wanted his ideas to be expressed in his words, as close to the language of the transcript as possible. The task was then assigned to me but it took me nearly two years to complete the job because the book was overtaken by events which claimed all my time—the 1965 War between India and Pakistan and its fallout. All the official documents relevant to the period covered by the book were declassified, though not made public, and handed over to me along with a selection of Ayub Khan's personal papers and some of his diaries. It is these documents, along with my personal notes taken during official meetings and in private conversation with Ayub Khan, which form the documentary evidence on which I have relied while describing and analyzing the main events of the Ayub period. These records were carefully sifted, indexed, and chronologically arranged for me by Dr Maleeha Lodhi when she was working with me in London.

Manzur Qadir left me some of his personal papers from which I have greatly benefited in writing the chapter on the 1962 Constitution and in dealing with the Agartala Conspiracy and the round table conference in 1969. I have also had the opportunity to go through five other manuscripts. These are: (1) *Memoirs of Lt.-Gen. Gul Hassan Khan,* who was Director of Military Operations during the 1965 War (since published in an edited form); (2) *Recollections of the 1965 War* by Mr Nazir Ahmed, who was Defence Secretary under Ayub Khan, which he recorded in Washington just before his death; (3) memoirs of the late Sir Morrice James (later Lord Saint Brides), who was the British High Commissioner in Pakistan in 1965 and whose manuscript bears the title 'What we gave we have'; (4) a study of the 1965 War by some members of the Staff College, Quetta to which I gained access through the courtesy of Captain (Retd.) Saeed Malik, and (5) *From Agartala to Round Table Conference* by Dr Kemal Hosain, former Foreign Minister of Bangladesh.

I have also had the advantage of studying some of the official documents of the US State Department which have been declassified in recent years including the papers maintained in the libraries of Presidents Kennedy and Johnson. More recently I have had the opportunity to examine the US State Department papers in the National Archives, Washington, relating to the events preceding the declaration of martial law in Pakistan in 1958. I must thank Mr Carl Kaysen, who was Special Assistant under President Kennedy, for giving me a complete gist of two important letters, still partly classified, written by the Indian Prime Minister, Pundit Jawaharlal Nehru to President Kennedy during the India-China War of 1962. Mr B.K. Nehru who was India's Ambassador in Washington at the time was good enough to confirm Mr Kaysen's recollection of the contents of the two letters. He recalled that he had handed over the first letter to President Kennedy in the morning and found another letter waiting for him when he returned to the embassy. When the letter was deciphered the 'ground slipped from under my feet. We had put India and its security at the mercy of the Americans.'[2]

Dramatis personae

For the convenience of the reader the major players of the Ayub drama are introduced here before the curtain goes up. I came to know most of them during the course of my service starting as Finance Officer in the Government of India in 1946 and ending as Information Secretary in the Government of Pakistan in 1969. I never had the privilege of meeting Quaid-i-Azam Mohammad Ali Jinnah, the President of the All-India Muslim League, who led the struggle of the Muslims of India for an independent homeland of their own and became Governor-General of Pakistan in 1947, nor did I know Liaquat Ali Khan, the first Prime Minister of Pakistan, who was assassinated in 1951.

Soon after Independence I came in contact with Malik Ghulam Muhammad, Pakistan's first Finance Minister, who assumed the office of Governor-General after Liaquat Ali's assassination. I served in East Bengal (which was named East Pakistan after the four provinces in the western part of Pakistan were integrated into One Unit in 1955) for more than five years between 1951-6. It was during this period that I came to know many of the Bengali politicians, in particular Huseyn Shaheed Suhrawardy, who became Prime Minister of Pakistan two years before the military takeover in 1958. The Muslims of East Pakistan, who had played a pioneering role in the establishment of Pakistan, were deeply disillusioned and embittered because of persistent neglect and unfair dealings by an indifferent central government dominated by West Pakistanis located some twelve hundreds miles away in Karachi, the first capital of Pakistan. When Suhrawardy became Prime Minister in 1956 he selected me for appointment as District Magistrate of Karachi. A year later Suhrawardy was replaced by Malik Firoz Khan Noon, the last Prime Minister under the parliamentary regime, and I was appointed Deputy Secretary in the Prime Minister's Secretariat which put me at a vantage point to observe the intrigues and squabbles of politicians and the working of the federal cabinet in its dying days. My first encounters with some of the political players of the period left a lasting impression on my mind.

General Ayub Khan

It was a rainy afternoon in September 1948. Three men were sitting in a damp room in a rest house in Dhaka as I made my way through a cluster of stray cats fighting in the verandah. I entered the room in the wake of Zahid Hussain, the first Governor of the State Bank of Pakistan, who was on a visit to East Bengal to brief the officials about the difficulties he had faced in getting the Bank off the ground. One of the three men was the image of Hercule Poirot with an outstanding moustache hanging in the air and a serviette draped over his stomach; the second looked a little lost like an embarrassed host; and the third offered a commanding presence behind a flushed face sprinkled with beads of perspiration. Zahid Hussain had hardly said a few words when the flushed face interrupted him, 'But Mr Hussain, your bank has made no impression here.' Zahid Hussain, a man of peace but of caustic wit, retorted, 'General Ayub Khan, banks are not in the business of making impressions.' I have never forgotten the look of disdain on Ayub Khan's face. He was General Officer Commanding, 14 Division, with his headquarters in Dhaka, and from that position he could witness the antics of the politicians, running in circles in pursuit of personal power, and watch an inexperienced administration grappling with complex social and economic problems.

Malik Ghulam Muhammad

I was sitting with three of my colleagues in my room in the Sindh Assembly building, during the lunch break, when the door was pushed open and a tall, imperious figure, in a cocked Jinnah cap, strode in asking for me. We sprang to attention. The figure said, 'Why don't you fellows make a bridge four?' And then turning to me, 'And you! Go and get me all the information about this department of Economic Affairs the British are planning to set up. And don't come back without it.' That was Ghulam Muhammad, Minister for Finance, a man in a hurry, who would stand no nonsense. Formerly a member of the Indian Audit and Accounts Service, who had served as Finance Minister in the Indian state of Hyderabad, and was one of the directors in Tata's, a prominent industrial concern belonging to a Parsee family, just before Independence. He had come to acquire a dominant position in the government since he had the nation's purse-strings in his hands. He soon brought all the major sources of revenue under the control of the central government and reduced the provinces to the level of supplicants.

General Iskander Mirza

It was late in the evening in May 1954 when I was summoned to Manok House in Dhaka. I was Deputy Secretary in the Home (Political) Department. The Provincial Assembly and the elected Chief Minister, Fazlul Haq, had just been dismissed and the central government had appointed General Mirza as the Governor of East Pakistan. The news of Mirza's appointment hit the province like a tidal wave which swept all political activists and agitators underground. Mirza was known as a latter day Genghis Khan whom the British had transferred from the army to the Indian political service. The story was well known when, as political agent in the North-West Frontier Province, Mirza invited a group of stubborn tribal leaders to dinner and mixed a strong dose of *Jamal Ghota* (a vicious indigenous laxative) in their food. That was how Mirza managed to 'liquidate' his opponents at least for a few days.

I was conducted to the lounge next to the Governor's bedroom where the new Chief Secretary, N. M. Khan, and the Deputy Inspector-General of Police, Anwarul Haq, were waiting, it seemed, for some impending doom. I took my seat and watched the weight driven clock on the wall clicking away without remorse. Suddenly two hands drew the heavy grey curtains and Mirza appeared in the door in a red silk dressing-gown: 'I want all these *goondas* (rascals) to be rounded up at once. At least 1,500 by tomorrow morning.' And with that the red gown disappeared behind the curtain. Anwarul Haq immediately started dividing the figure of 1,500 by 17, the number of districts in the province, and didn't know what to do with the balance of four. N. M. Khan had a brainwave, 'Let us get the extra four from Mymensingh which, after all, is the largest district.' By next morning the police had rounded up every one they could get their hands on—rickshaw pullers along with their passengers, hapless vendors, and poor pedestrians. In less than three months Mirza, having subdued East Bengal, returned to Karachi where it did not take him long to persuade the ruling cabal to get rid of the ailing and disabled Ghulam Muhammad and invite him to assume the office of Governor-General.

Chaudhri Muhammad Ali

An intense person who had climbed to the top of the bureaucratic ladder in an incredibly short time through a combination of circumstances, but not without merit. Chaudhri Muhammad Ali, Secretary General of the Government of Pakistan, did not look up as I led a delegation of young Civil Servants into his office on the first floor of the Sindh Assembly building in May 1950. I had met him earlier in New Delhi when he was a relatively junior officer in the Government of India. Like Ghulam Muhammad, he too belonged to the Indian Audit and Accounts Service and would become Finance Minister before taking over as Prime Minister of Pakistan, all in a space of seven years after Independence. Even for a man of his ability, dedication, and integrity, it was a meteoric rise to the highest political office in the country. He had lived a life of isolation guided by rules and regulations framed by the British and knew little about the people or their problems. Faced with the reality of public pressures and demands he had a nervous breakdown and tendered his resignation. But he did give the country a democratic constitution despite its flaws.

He allowed the members of the delegation to take their seats before raising his head from the files. The young officers wanted their pay scales to be reviewed. They would be occupying positions of great responsibility for which a salary of Rs 350 per month (£40 at the time) was grossly inadequate. 'I started on less than that,' was Muhammad Ali's response. When I suggested that the exercise of power without adequate compensation could lead to corruption, he said, 'Wrong. Money has nothing to do with honesty. Most poor people are God-fearing and honest and many rich persons are thoroughly dishonest.' Chaudhri Muhammad Ali would not disturb the pay scales or indeed anything else Pakistan had inherited from the British. It was his faith in the British system of government which had won him the attention of his superior officers. G.E.B. Abell, Private Secretary to the Viceroy, Lord Wavell, had recommended Muhammad Ali for inclusion in the Viceroy's Executive Council when Jinnah and other Muslim leaders had declined the Viceroy's invitation to join the Council in 1946. The difficulty was that once he was appointed to the Council, Muhammad Ali would lose his lien on his permanent job, a risk he did not consider worth taking, given the vagaries of politics.[3]

Huseyn Shaheed Suhrawardy

I had gone to Calcutta along with Zahid Hussain in August 1948 when the managing director of an Indian bank took me to the race-course where he thought I had the best chance of seeing Suhrawardy who had been in the vanguard of the Pakistan Movement as Chief Minister of Bengal. Suhrawardy had opposed the partition of Bengal during the final phase of negotiations with the British which brought him into conflict with Jinnah. As a result, he decided to stay on in India after Independence. I saw him walking along the railings, a short, chubby man, with a large camera and couple of binoculars dangling over his stomach. He nodded when I was introduced to him, but the moment he learnt that I was Secretary of the State Bank of Pakistan he gave me a long sermon about why there should be no passport or visa restrictions between India and Pakistan or any exchange control: 'The borders between the two countries must remain open for free movement of capital and labour.' Suhrawardy soon discovered that he had no place in India and came over to East Pakistan where he had a considerable following.

I next met Suhrawardy in Dhaka in 1954 when he was leading the United Front of all opposition parties against the ruling Muslim League. My wife, when she was introduced to him, asked, 'What do you do Mr Suhrawardy?' 'I am a briefless lawyer, young lady,' replied Suhrawardy, and after finding out that she was a lecturer in geography, spent the whole evening talking to her about the mysteries of precipitation. A man of great charm and humour, he was equipped with an extraordinary intellect and power of persuasion.

Suhrawardy never slept except in Cabinet meetings when there was nothing of interest on the agenda. My bedside telephone would ring, 'Mr Magistrate, have you any idea what is going on in your domain?' 'No sir, I was fast asleep,' I would answer, not knowing what I had missed. 'Fiddling is better than snoring. Do you think you could take the trouble of coming over here at this unearthly hour.' I would rush to the Prime Minister's house—we were next door neighbours—only to be told that my presence was no longer required. The petitioner who had come with some complaint against the district administration had already been disposed of.

Twenty-fifth December marks Quaid-i-Azam's birth anniversary which every political party wants to celebrate in Jehangir Park, Karachi. The Muslim League applied first and I allotted them the coveted park which left the Prime Minister's Awami League without a suitable venue to celebrate the occasion. Suhrawardy decided to leave for Dhaka late at night on the twenty-fourth of December. I was standing in the reception line at Mauripur Airport but the Prime Minister ignored me, much to my embarrassment. A few minutes later I was summoned into the aircraft where I was confronted by the Prime Minister getting into his pyjamas. 'You know Mister Magistrate, I have to leave Karachi because you have given Jehangir Park to my opponents.' 'But they came first, Sir', I pleaded. 'A technicality, Sir, a technicality for which the Prime Minister must leave the city.'

Suhrawardy knew no fear. He would not yield to Ayub or any other general. A few months after the promulgation of martial law, Suhrawardy was reclining in a chair in the VIP room at Lahore Airport. I was standing in a corner, a mere Chief Controller of Imports and Exports, behind a cluster of two and three-star generals. Suhrawardy spotted me and shouted, 'Come here Altaf, and tell me how the army has become so corrupt in such a short time?'

Malik Firoz Khan Noon

A man of great dignity, Malik Feroz Khan Noon was the last Prime Minister in the parliamentary period 1947-58. He presided over a coalition of parties, each headed by a former prime minister or chief minister, who would disown him on a signal from Iskander Mirza. I was Deputy Secretary on his staff which meant being on call twenty-four hours. I came to be treated as a family member. The Prime Minister instructed me that if he made a mistake of fact during a discussion I should caution him by rubbing the lobe of my left ear. The ministers could never quite make out why I was always pulling my ear during Cabinet meetings. I would be called in the evening when the Prime Minister, locked in an animated discussion with one of his political associates, would reel off a series of commands—transfer that incompetent chief engineer, suspend that corrupt police officer, build a district road—and direct me to implement those orders immediately. I would quietly go home knowing that the whole thing was meant for the benefit of the person who was sitting with the Prime Minister.

Noon knew that Iskander Mirza was using the politicians as puppets and would call off the show if he was pushed too hard toward a general election. He also knew that his Cabinet was packed with Mirza's men and he particularly distrusted the Finance Minister, Syed Amjad Ali.

Noon was a political bird and could deal with problems in an objective manner when he was not under pressure. His visit to

India in 1958 was an outstanding success when he persuaded Nehru to transfer Berubari—an enclave in East Bengal under Indian possession—to Pakistan. He also negotiated the amalgamation of Gwadur, along the Mekran coast, into Pakistan.

Zulfikar Ali Bhutto

A nattily dressed mercurial young man came to see me when I was District Magistrate of Karachi with a request for a gun licence. 'Do you have any guns?' I asked. 'About thirty,' the young man replied. 'That should be enough,' I said and turned down the request. Zulfikar Ali Bhutto never forgot or forgave what he considered an act of rudeness on my part. When he became the Minister of Commerce under Ayub Khan and I was posted as Chief Controller of Imports and Exports he told me 'You have served in East Bengal but in our part of the world to refuse a gun licence is to deny the social status of a person.'

A man of phenomenal intelligence and courage he believed he could cut any knot, work his way out of any pinch and outwit any opponent. He was Ayub Khan's *alter ego* and gave a dynamic dimension to Ayub Khan's foreign policy. He disowned Ayub after the 1965 War and led the popular agitation against him which resulted in his abdication. Bhutto never trusted anyone, not even himself, and though we became close friends he rarely took me into confidence.

When I became Chief Editor of *Dawn* and wrote against military action in East Pakistan, Bhutto thought I was trying to topple his government and had me locked up in preventive detention. He summoned me when the High Court of Sindh and Balochistan declared my detention unlawful and told me, 'You must know that courts do not figure in my book.' Little did he know at the time that the courts would award him the death sentence in a highly controversial murder case and a ruthless military dictator would execute him in a cold-blooded manner. I was shocked. Apart from a deep sense of personal loss I knew that Bhutto's execution would hold the country in thrall for years to come.

A.K. Fazlul Haq

'Sher-e-Bangla' (the Bengal Tiger) was how the people of Bengal greeted Fazlul Haq. He had dedicated his life to the welfare of the peasants. Jinnah was addressing the historic Muslim League session in Lahore in 1940 where the Pakistan Resolution was adopted. The audience erupted into spontaneous applause when Fazlul Haq, at that time Chief Minister of united Bengal, entered the hall. Finding his voice drowned by the public outburst, Jinnah resumed his seat saying, 'Now that the tiger has arrived, the lamb must retire.'

Fazlul Haq led the United Front of opposition parties to victory in the 1954 election in East Pakistan and became the Chief Minister. I was appointed his Private Secretary in addition to my duties as Deputy Secretary in the Home Department. A few weeks after taking over as Chief Minister, Fazlul Haq went on a private visit to Calcutta where he declared, 'I do not believe in the political division of the country. I am in fact not familiar with the new words Pakistan and Hindustan. When I speak of India I mean both the countries.'[4] On his return I told him of the uproar that his statement had caused in the country. He looked at me and asked, 'Then why didn't you contradict the statement?' I was taken aback but soon realized that Fazlul Haq would say whatever he thought suited the occasion and then disown it. Most of the time I was drafting clarifications of the Chief Minister's statements, now contradicting some denial, only to deny the contradiction later.

The Bengalis knew their 'tiger' and loved him and he too had a genuine understanding of their problems and profound compassion for the poor. I remember a touching incident. He came, along with his wife, to see the house in which I was living in Dhaka—22 Hare Road. It was a large mansion dominated by a magnificent banyan tree standing majestically on the front lawn. The proposal was to convert it into the Chief Minister's residence. Fazlul Haq liked the house. As he was getting into the car he saw my children playing under the tree. 'Where will they play when you shift into an apartment?' he asked. Before I could answer,

Fazlul Haq had made up his mind not to deprive the children of their tree. He continued to stay in his old house at 27 K.M. Das Lane in Hatkhola. The house at 22 Hare Road was later turned into the President's House where Ayub Khan used to stay whenever he went to Dhaka.

Sheikh Mujibur Rahman

The 1954 election campaign was at its peak and a fiery student leader, Sheikh Mujibur Rahman, was stumping through Faridpur where I was serving as District Magistrate. In one of his speeches he threatened to peel off the skin of the Chief Minister, Nurul Amin, and turn it into a pair of slippers. 'That was most vulgar,' thought the Home Secretary and asked me to arrest the butcher. When Sheikh Mujib was brought to my office he denounced Punjabi bureaucrats and threatened to bring down the government. But why did he want to peel off the Chief Minister's skin? 'Because it is so thick,' was his spontaneous response. I agreed with him that he had not committed any offence and he immediately softened. A highly emotional person Mujib could be disarmed with a gesture of affection. Years later when he came to Rawalpindi during the last days of the Ayub government he came to my house and complained to my wife that in all those years he spent in prison I had never once enquired about his welfare.

Sheikh Mujib became the first President of Bangladesh in 1972, the state he had created, and was hailed as 'Bangla Bundhu' (Friend of Bengal). He was assassinated in a military *coup* three years later.

Manzur Qadir

I used to see Manzur Qadir in a study circle in Lahore in 1944. The circle was an informal affair where some officers belonging to the Indian Civil Service, Judges of the High Court, academics and lawyers used to meet once a month for dinner and discourse. I was an interloper, being still a student, but I used to enjoy getting into an argument with Manzur Qadir, which was easy. The difficult part was getting out of it. He was much admired for his intellect and his conduct, though his friends found him a little tedious because he was so completely above reproach. He came to be seen as a touchstone for others to test their conduct.

Manzur Qadir was a highly successful lawyer when Ayub Khan invited him to join his Cabinet in 1958. People were a little surprised that a passionate advocate of the rule of law should have joined a military regime. The American Ambassador in Pakistan, William Langley, thought he was like 'a goldfish in a government bowl.' Ayub Khan was deeply impressed by Manzur Qadir's range of knowledge and was fascinated by his obsession with words and ideas. He was the only person around Ayub who was not interested in personal advancement. Manzur Qadir was trained to argue, to plead, and then to accept the decision of the court. Ayub Khan would give him a patient, indeed respectful, hearing and then give a firm and clear decision. Ayub's only complaint against Manzur Qadir was that he was inflexible and would not allow him to deviate from a position that he had once adopted. Ayub distrusted politicians. Manzur Qadir drove him to the point where he decided to snuff out all political parties. Ayub disapproved of public demonstrations, whether of approbation or reprobation. Manzur Qadir convinced him that 'public opinion' was an instrument of political manipulation and not a reliable guide for policy-making. Manzur Qadir adopted Ayub's political plan as his brief, and devoted all his talent to presenting and expounding that plan in the most persuasive manner. The force with which public opinion asserted its supremacy by demolishing the entire political structure he had helped Ayub to raise, came as a shock as much to Manzur Qadir as to Ayub Khan.

Acknowledgements

I must thank Professor W.H. Morris-Jones who, as Director of the Institute of Commonwealth Studies invited me to work on the

Ayub period. After reading one chapter that I gave him after a few months he assured me that I was 'well-launched', though he had no suspicion of the long loop I had planned to follow. Professor Hugh Tinker and Dr Peter Lyon were most helpful during the few months I spent at the Institute. My son, Humayun, who fought a running 'wall-chalking' battle with the government when I was in prison, managed to save my papers and documents when the police was looking for them all over Karachi, and had them transported to London. He saw the manuscript at different stages and gave me valuable comments.

Professor David Taylor of the School of Oriental and African Studies read the manuscript in its original form and gave me some useful suggestions to re-arrange and condense the material. But it is to my friend Leslie Wolf-Phillips of the London School of Economics that I am particularly indebted for going through the manuscript like a professional editor. I must thank Mr Mushahid Hussain, former editor of *The Muslim,* who read the manuscript and made some incisive comments and corrected certain dates.

My brother Tajammul, who has been a constant source of strength in my life, never gave up on me. I have relied on many of his suggestions while revising the manuscript. I must also thank my friend M.H. Shah, former Commissioner, Rawalpindi Division, for his comments and suggestions. I cannot thank him enough for all the help he and his wife Sadiqa gave me, with great affection and courage, during the period that I remained in prison and subsequently under police surveillance. Mr Irshad Ahmad Haqqani was good enough to read the manuscript with great care and I found his comments most useful. Raana, my daughter, has acted throughout as a critical reviewer and is responsible for the exclusion of whatever material she considered redundant and unnecessary. Her husband, Dr Noman Sheikh, preserved the manuscript on hard discs and while guiding me through the mysteries of word-processing ended up typing a major part of the revised version.

My elder daughter Naveed and her husband Rumman Faruqi were most helpful in getting me some useful material from the US State Department files. My good friend Thomas Hexner in Boston arranged for me to meet with Professor Carl Kaysen and some other distinguished academics in Harvard. Mr Shuja Nawaz in Washington was good enough to obtain for me some useful information about the 1965 India-Pakistan War. I must thank Mr Nazir Ahmad, who was my Private Secretary in the Ministry of Information and later worked with me in London, for keeping the papers in safe custody during some difficult days.

Needless to say that none of the persons who helped me with the manuscript is in any way responsible for the views and opinions expressed in the book.

I would like to acknowledge the help I received from the staff of the India Office library, the Public Record Office, London, the Kennedy Library, the Johnson Library and the National Archives, Washington.

I must thank Mr Niaz Ahmad, of Sang-e-Meel Publications for the care and patience with which he supervised the publication of the book at different stages.

My wholehearted thanks to Tyaba Habib, Editor at the Oxford University Press, who was kind enough to go through the text with painstaking care. Her scholarly comments helped me to remove certain obscurities and clarify some points of detail. Also, in this edition certain spellings have been updated expect where in quotes.

I do not know how to thank my wife Zarina, who showed tremendous courage and fortitude during a difficult period, and my children for all their love and their interest in the progress of the book.

London:
24 April 1993

Altaf Gauhar

NOTES

1. 'He did not know that a keeper is only a poacher turned inside out and a poacher a keeper turned outside in.' Charles Kingsley, *The Water Babies*. Ch.1.

   The Press and Publications Ordinance was issued in 1960. It was amended on 2 September 1963, two weeks before the author took charge of the Ministry of Information. The amendments caused an uproar in the Press. As a result of negotiations between the author and the Press Committee several clauses were repealed. The contribution of the author was acknowledged by most newspapers. *Dawn,* 10 October 1963: 'Mr Altaf Gauhar, the Central Information Secretary, worked hard and often long into the night in exchanging views with and considering the objections as well as suggestions put forward by the Joint Committee of the Press.' *See* also *Nawa-e-Waqt,* Lahore, 11 and 15 October 1963; *See* also *Jang,* Karachi, 16 October 1963.

2. Conversation with the author in London in 1980.

3. Nicholas Mansergh (Editor-in-Chief) *Transfer of Power,* 1942-7, Vol. VII p. 495, May 1946; Her Majesty's Stationery Office, London, 1977.

4. *Statesman,* Calcutta, 4 May 1954.

Introduction

The story of General Muhammad Ayub Khan, who ruled Pakistan from October 1958 till March 1969, when he was swept out of office, should have disappeared without a ripple in the turbulent waters of Pakistani politics. Instead, it has become a story of compelling relevance and contemporary interest, not only for Pakistan but for all the Muslim countries where the tradition of dynastic and authoritarian rule continues to defy the growing demand for the establishment of some democratic form of government.

Ayub Khan stands out as the first Muslim ruler in South Asia who tried to put his country on the modern secular path without renouncing the fundamental principles of Islam. He tried to persuade his people to recognize the contemporary compulsions and realities and to respond to the challenge of the modern age instead of living in the past in the belief that all the problems of life that they may be called upon to address now or in the future had already been resolved for them in the light of the Holy Qur'an and Sunnah, the traditions of Prophet Muhammad (peace be upon him). They could not hope to progress if they continued to cling to the belief that their salvation lay in adopting the traditional formulations and solutions, as embodied in the Shariah, the Islamic code of life, and resisting the lure of any innovation.

Born in Rehana, a picturesque village in the North-West frontier province of what is now Pakistan, on 14 May 1907, Ayub Khan had an uneventful childhood. His father, who had retired as a non-commissioned officer in the Indian Army, had a large family and a small income from his army pension. He managed to save enough money to send Ayub to Aligarh in 1922, a famous Muslim university in the United Provinces of India. Ayub was conscious of his humble origin and would trace his lineage to the

Tarin tribe which ruled over parts of the North-West Frontier Province and fought against the Sikhs and the British.

While he was preparing for graduation he was spotted by General Skeen, Adjutant-General of the Indian Army, who had come to Aligarh looking for suitable soldierly material. He must have been struck by Ayub's appearance; tall, well-built, of fair complexion and appropriate mould. Ayub was chosen for training as a commissioned officer at Sandhurst. For a young Indian of rural background, that meant instant elevation to the higher strata of society. Ayub had found his vocation. He did remarkably well at Sandhurst securing the top position among the Indian cadets. Among his colleagues was General J.N. Choudhry, who later became Commander-in-Chief of the Indian Army. It was at Sandhurst that Ayub got into the habit of reading. Though military science was his special interest he read any book on history that came his way.

During the Second World War Ayub served first as a staff officer in the army headquarters in Delhi and later moved to the headquarters of 15 Corps at Barrackpore, where he witnessed the drawing up of plans for the defence of India against the threat of Japanese invasion. He was second-in-command of the 1st Assam Regiment and saw some heavy fighting in Burma.

The subcontinent was in turmoil when the British decided to quit India in August 1947. Ayub was then a Brigadier in the Indian Army and was attached to the Boundary Force, under Major General Rees, which had been organized to deal with the problem of communal rioting in the Punjab, a province where Muslims and Hindus were trying to exterminate each other. The Boundary Force was a British stratagem of no purpose and was swept off like a pile of sand by the rising wave of primitive passions. Ayub Khan came in for a great deal of criticism for his failure to come to the assistance of the Muslims who were trapped and massacred in East Punjab. Ayub's pleas of helplessness received no sympathy.

When the subcontinent was partitioned in 1947 the Indian Army too was divided. To Pakistan was allotted a badly-equipped and disorganized force without any training centre. The military stores that came to Pakistan's share were despatched in 160 trainloads, but the wagons that arrived at their destination were found packed with stones and damaged equipment. Ayub's first job in Pakistan was to withdraw a major part of troops from the volatile North-West Frontier belt where several army divisions, as well as scouts and levies, were tied up in futile intermittent campaigns against the tribesmen. He managed to bring his troops out without any major mishap.

In January 1948, five months after Independence, Ayub was posted as General Officer Commanding of 14 Division in East Bengal—the most populous and politically conscious of the five provinces of Pakistan. It accounted for fifty-six per cent of the population of the country and was separated from the four western provinces by 1,200 miles of Indian territory. The capital of the country was located in Karachi in the western province of Sindh and already the feeling was growing among the Bengalis that the ruling elite, largely composed of West Pakistani politicians and civil servants, was treating East Pakistan as a colony. Ayub witnessed the development of political strains between the two wings of the country which would lead to a bloody separation twenty-four years later and the emergence of the independent state of Bangladesh.

Ayub got to know most of the Bengali politicians, Khawaja Nazimuddin, Muhammad Ali Bogra, H.S. Suhrawardy, Nurul Amin and A.K. Fazlul Haq. The first three became prime ministers of the country in 1951, 1953 and 1956 respectively, and the last two were chief ministers of East Bengal in 1948 and 1954. An under-staffed and ill-equipped provincial government came to rely on the army for maintaining a semblance of order and this provided Ayub with an opportunity to study the working of the civil administration and the mind of the politicians who excelled in the art of wheeling and dealing. He could see the mental barriers rising against the western provinces of Pakistan, especially the Punjab. His encounters with H.S. Suhrawardy, Muhammad Ali Bogra and A.K. Fazlul Haq convinced him that politicians, as a class, could not be relied upon to give the country a good and strong government. More than their opportunism, Ayub was distressed by their duplicity and vacillation. Rhetoric and demagogy were their stock-in-trade and they had little interest in commodities like reason and pragmatism. He would recall the occasion when Chief Minister Khawaja Nazimuddin sought his aid to stop an angry crowd of students from storming the Assembly building in Dhaka. Inside the hall the Chief Minister, who had a precarious majority, was busy delivering the speech of his life to save his government, and outside A.K. Fazlul Haq and Bogra, both in the Opposition at the time, were working up an angry mob. When things seemed to be getting out of hand Ayub walked up to Bogra, tapped him on the shoulder and told him to buzz off unless he was looking for a bullet. In the meantime, he had arranged to smuggle the Chief Minister out of the hall. Ayub told the crowd, 'The bird has flown', and the announcement was greeted with a roar of laughter. That single incident was enough to convince Ayub that the politicians could work on the emotions of the people but they were utterly lacking in discipline and had no real principles.

Ayub stayed in East Bengal for about two years. He left his large family, four sons and three daughters, behind in Rawalpindi lodged in an annex of Bachan Nawas, a deserted mansion, its Sikh owner having fled to India during the communal riots.

Ayub would recall with pride the speech he gave at the GHQ about social and political conditions in East Bengal. He spoke with authority and his presentation made a great impression on his colleagues. Many of them saw in him their future leader.

Ayub becomes Commander-in-Chief

On his return from East Bengal in 1950 Ayub was posted as Adjutant-General in the GHQ at Rawalpindi. This made him responsible for recruitment, maintenance, and discipline of personnel—a formidable task given the lack of financial resources and the absence of any *esprit de corps* among army units. Ayub instilled a sense of discipline into a disorganized force by adopting some harsh methods, not excluding corporal measures to sort out the rougher elements. It was as Adjutant-General that Ayub came in contact with the Central Government in Karachi. He would go to the Ministry of Finance hoping to elicit a straight yes or no. All he would get was a promise of 'consideration', which meant endless procrastination. It was as Adjutant-General that Ayub got to know General Iskander Mirza who was then Secretary, Ministry of Defence. They grew to like each other and it was with Mirza's support that Ayub was selected for appointment as the first Pakistani Commander-in-Chief of the Pakistan Army in January 1951. Two senior generals had been killed in an air crash and that accident opened the way for Ayub's promotion. 'To fashion the army, to train it, to find the right type of officers and soldiers, to create a high standard of morale'[1] became Ayub's mission to which he applied himself with singular dedication. Within a few years he created 'an agile and effective army, capable of meeting any challenge'[2] but not without overcoming serious unrest caused by swift promotions resulting in the devaluation of higher posts. 'Perfectly sensible people, Brigadiers and Generals, would go about bemoaning their lot. Each one of them was a Bonaparte, albeit an unhappy one.'[3] At the root was the growing consciousness among army officers about the insidious 'malaise in the political and administrative life' of the country.[4] The Muslim League, the ruling party, was riven by factions, each trying to run down the other, oblivious of the fact that the people were getting demoralized and frustrated. Every time Ayub visited Karachi he would be distressed by the differences and disputes among the politicians which were seriously undermining the morale and competence of the administration. The government, after the initial excitement of Independence, was beginning to lose its sense of direction and purpose.

In 1951 a group of army officers was engaged in a plot to overthrow the government. The plot, which came to be known as the Rawalpindi Conspiracy, was discovered in time. A number of army officers and some civilians were involved. The officers were tried by a special tribune on the charge that they were planning to overthrow the civilian government under Pakistan's first Prime Minister, Liaquat Ali Khan, and set up a military dictatorship on the communist model. Four of the accused were found guilty. Ayub was much praised for the skilful manner in which he detected the conspiracy and firmly re-established the British tradition of complete loyalty and subordination of the armed forces to civil authority.

Liaquat Ali Khan fell to an assassin's bullet while addressing a public meeting on 16 October 1951. With that the politicians lost their hold on the government and the management of the affairs of the country passed into the hands of a group of Civil Servants, three of whom rose to the top in less than four years. First, Ghulam Muhammad became the Governor-General immediately after Liaquat Ali's assassination. Then came Iskander Mirza who made Ghulam Muhammad abdicate in his favour and appointed Chaudhri Muhammad Ali as his Prime Minister.

Ayub kept himself studiously aloof from the palace intrigues of the bureaucrats, though he was always on the side of the Governor-General in his tussle for power with Parliament. He would be summoned to Karachi whenever the government was facing a crisis. His presence in the capital would dampen the rancorous spirits in Parliament, which was functioning both as a sovereign constitution-making body and as a legislative assembly. Constitution-making had become an endless and seemingly futile exercise which had cost Parliament its credibility though it still retained a semblance of legitimacy. The Constituent Assembly was summarily dissolved by Ghulam Mohammed in 1954 and reconstituted under judicial pressure and advice. The Assembly adopted a Constitution in 1956 (Ayub called it 'a document of despair')[5] which enabled Iskander Mirza to change his title from Governor-General to President with the approval of a moribund Assembly. The government now had the cover of a Constitution but it still lacked any popular mandate or representative character. The ruling junta, whatever its internal disputes and squabbles, was agreed on one thing: the country must not be exposed to the hazards of a general election. They had seen the results of provincial elections, particularly in East Pakistan in 1954 where the ruling Muslim League was wiped out, and they had no intention of committing electoral hara-kiri on a national scale.

A prolonged game of combinations and permutations ensued. Governments would be sworn in and out of office at the command of Iskander Mirza, who seemed content to preside over the rising rubble of the institutions that the country had inherited at the time of Partition. It was only a question of time before he would ring down the curtain on the charade of democratic rule in the country.

Was Ayub Khan privy to Iskander Mirza's plan to abrogate the Constitution and promulgate martial law in Pakistan? There is conclusive documentary evidence that not only was Ayub in sympathy with Iskander Mirza's plan of action but on more than one occasion he urged him to save the country from the politicians who were leading it to ruin.

A background of political developments leading to the collapse of the democratic order in 1958 is provided in the first chapter of this book; all the evidence leading to the imposition of martial law and the emergence of Ayub as the first military ruler of Pakistan is pulled together in the second chapter. The point is brought out that Ayub, playing a covert collaborative role, wanted Iskander Mirza to be seen as the man who decided, in his own judgement, to abrogate the Constitution and was personally responsible for the imposition of martial law. An extremely cautious person, Ayub did not want to be accused of violating the Constitution which could be seen as treason. Perhaps he wanted to retain the option that if Iskander Mirza's plan failed and the people rose in revolt he should be able to denounce Mirza and deploy the armed forces to restore law and order in the country. If the plan succeeded it should not be difficult to jettison Mirza once he had lost the constitutional cover. A number of entries in Ayub's personal diary, cited in the second chapter, show that he was acting with the utmost circumspection. Not a devious man by nature he was moving toward his target employing whatever subterfuge and camouflage as was necessary to cover his flanks. Ayub was willing to go along with Mirza but not to go down with him. Above all he did not want the reputation of the army to be tainted in any manner. One of his major worries was the problem of extricating the army once it got involved in the political life of the country.[6]

Ayub was far more vulnerable than Iskander Mirza whose position as elected President under the Constitution seemed impregnable. Ayub was completing his second term of four years as Commander-in-Chief and the Government could designate his successor at any time in 1958 which would have knocked him out of the game. Mirza, an adroit intriguer and skilful planner, kept Ayub on tenterhooks. He would tell him that he wanted to give him an extension of tenure but Malik Firoz Khan Noon, the last Prime Minister under the parliamentary regime, was being difficult. Meanwhile he would advise the Prime Minister not to be in a hurry to decide the matter. By the middle of May 1958 Ayub was getting quite anxious. He urged the Prime Minister to visit Rawalpindi and stay with him as his guest. He wanted to give him a ceremonial reception complete with a resplendent guard of honour and a twenty-one gun salute. He got a two-year extension of service in June 1958 which made him deeply beholden to Mirza. Having made sure of Ayub's loyalty Mirza could now plan the end-game with full confidence.

The extent to which Ayub was driven by personal ambition to seize power is not easy to determine. He was certainly not behaving like a conspirator waiting to seize control of the government by force at the first opportunity. He knew his turn would come and he was prepared to wait for it.

On a warmish night in London in 1954, Ayub was pacing up and down his hotel room trying to figure out what was wrong with the country and what could be done to put things right. He had a premonition that the Governor-General might draw him into politics which he 'wanted, above all things, to avoid.'[7] Finally he settled down and drew up a document in military style: 'A short appreciation of present and future problems of Pakistan.'[8] He recognized that 'the ultimate aim of Pakistan must be to become a sound, solid and cohesive nation' for which it was necessary to evolve a Constitution suited to 'the genius of the people'. The cultural diversity of the people of different parts of the country should be recognized and they should be made 'to feel equal partners' in the government.[9] He knew the merits of democracy but warned that 'unfettered democracy can, therefore, prove dangerous, especially nowadays when communism from within and without is so quick to make use of its weaknesses.' He favoured a strong central government in which the President should be the final custodian of power 'able to put things right both in the provinces and the centre, should they go wrong.'[10] It was too late 'to resile from universal suffrage however great its shortcomings', but members of the provincial and central legislatures, should be elected by an electoral college composed of the representatives of the people to ensure that the legislative bodies do not become 'irresponsible'.[11] The document provides an insight into the working of Ayub's mind at the time but it was not a take-over plan drawn up in the darkness of the night. When Ayub was invited to join the Federal Cabinet as Minister for Defence in 1954, an invitation which he accepted on the understanding that he would retain his position as Commander-in-Chief of the Army, he circulated the document among his colleagues. It duly came up for consideration before the Cabinet. No one thought that the document contained anything startling— it certainly wasn't seen as a warning of things to come—and the Cabinet decided to consign it to the archives.

There is no doubt that eminent people like the Aga Khan and the widow of the first Prime Minister, Begum Liaquat Ali, were urging Ayub to 'do something to save this country', but he kept himself and the army scrupulously detached from all the political wrangling. He used to imagine that he was acting 'as a buffer between the politicians and the armed forces.' Four years before the imposition of martial law Ayub's impression was that 'the government was utterly confused and almost leaderless...the politicians had their eyes on the army in which they wanted to create their own pockets of support.'[12] Protecting the integrity of the army became Ayub's prime concern.

While most other instruments of government were getting blunted, the army was developing an edge. Ayub had introduced new methods of training and the army was acquiring greater mobility and firepower. Ayub had persuaded the Americans that Pakistan could serve as a bulwark against communism and the armed forces of the country, with their tradition of military service, could provide an effective deterrent against communist expansion in the region. The Americans entered into a military alliance with Pakistan in 1954 under which a substantial quantity of arms and equipment was provided to Pakistan on a regular basis. This was the beginning of a military relationship between Pakistan and the USA in which Ayub had a crucial role to play. By early 1958 the Americans had come to regard Ayub as their man in the area who could be relied upon to keep Pakistan on a stable course should the politicians fail to measure up to the requirements of the democratic system.

Several political scientists in Britain and the United States were advocating military rule in the former colonies as the most effective system of government which would guarantee their development and modernization. The armed forces were seen as the most disciplined and educated segment of post-colonial communities which, given their outlook and familiarity with sophisticated technology, could pull their economies out of the quagmire of under-development. Ayub had established contact with some senior US officials and he had close relations with Allen Dulles, the head of the Central Intelligence Agency. Ayub's diary shows that at his suggestion Allen Dulles interceded on behalf of Pakistan with the Secretary of State, John Foster Dulles, who was his brother.[13] Allen Dulles arranged for Ayub to meet the American Chiefs of Services where Ayub was able to impress upon them that India, which had adopted a neutralist stance in international affairs, would never prove a reliable partner whereas they could count on Pakistan for the preservation of the 'free world'. Ayub inducted Pakistan into CENTO (Central Treaty Organization), an American sponsored defence pact in the Middle East, and was responsible for persuading the government to provide military bases to the Americans in Pakistan.

The Americans had come to realize by 1958 that their friend, Iskander Mirza, the real architect of US-Pakistan alliance, was beginning to lose ground. While they continued to support him they were coming to rely on Ayub to look after their interests in Pakistan. They found Ayub articulate, persuasive and straightforward, a man who didn't mince his words, and was passionately opposed to communism.

Ayub Khan takes over as President

Iskander Mirza took the plunge on 7 October 1958. He dismissed the central and provincial governments and Assemblies, abrogated the Constitution which he had sworn to defend and preserve, promulgated martial law throughout the country and appointed Ayub Khan as the Chief Martial Law Administrator. All political parties were abolished and with that the political process came to a sudden halt. In the Presidential Order of the Day Iskander Mirza said :

> For the last two years, I have been watching with the deepest anxiety, the ruthless struggle for power, corruption, the shameful exploitation of our simple honest, patriotic and industrious masses, the lack of decorum and the prostitution of Islam for political ends....The mentality of the political parties has sunk so low that I am unable any longer to believe that elections will improve the present chaotic internal situation and enable us to form a strong and stable government capable of dealing with the innumerable and complex problems facing us today. We cannot get men from the moon. The same group of people who have brought Pakistan on the verge of ruination will rig the elections for their own ends....The Constitution which was brought into being on 23rd March 1956, after so many tribulations, is unworkable. It is full of dangerous compromises so that Pakistan will disintegrate internally if the inherent malaise is not removed...It is said that the Constitution is sacred. But more sacred than the Constitution or anything else is the country, is the welfare and happiness of the people.[14]

Iskander Mirza who had little credibility and even less public support knew that his rhetoric would have been of little avail if the army had not swung into action in his support. The people had no experience of martial law—the older generation could recall some horror stories under British rule when martial law was imposed in some towns and people were made to crawl on their bellies. There was not a ripple of protest in any part of the country. Even the most fierce opponents of Iskander Mirza, politicians, journalists and academics, meekly accepted the imposition of martial law in the hope that it would lead to the restoration of democracy. The decision to consign the Constitution to the dustbin was received by the people with relief, if not joy. The soldiers received plaudits as they went about rounding up smugglers and black-marketeers. Goods were disposed off at throw-away prices and soon the shops were empty.

While Mirza was celebrating his initial success, he did not realize that with the abrogation of the Constitution he had placed himself at the mercy of the armed forces. He could abrogate the Constitution but he could not abrogate martial law without the consent of the army. Military order was now its own source of law and the Chief Martial Law Administrator the fountain-head of that law. The army tolerated Mirza's presence on the scene for no more than three weeks. On the night of 27 October 1958 three generals walked up to Iskander Mirza's bedroom and asked him to sign a letter of resignation. That left Ayub in undisputed command and he immediately assumed the office of President. Ayub had earlier warned that 'while martial law will not be retained a minute longer than is necessary, it will not be lifted before the purpose for which it has been imposed is fulfilled.'[15]

Ayub went about his business in a systematic fashion. He had a forceful personality and an impressive presence. There was a general expectation that a spell of sanity and discipline would be good for the country. People heard Ayub with respect in the hope that he would be true to his word and restore the democratic order after introducing certain reforms which he had spelt out in his 1954 document. Some thirty commissions and committees were appointed to bring about radical changes in various fields. The ones that attracted public attention were the Land Reforms Commission, Law Reform Commission and the Press Commission. In less than three months Ayub was able to restore the confidence of the civil administration which started to function with reasonable efficiency; military courts were disbanded and the armed forces returned to the barracks.

Land reforms was the first item on Ayub's agenda. He had written in 1954: 'But nothing much will be gained unless we carry out reforms in a scientific fashion. Possession of vast areas of land by a few is no longer defensible nor is acquisition of land without compensation.'[16] All earlier attempts by the government to establish a more rational distribution of land were subverted by the landlords who were the dominant partners in the ruling junta. Ayub could see the link between land reforms and economic development and wanted to curtail the political power of the feudal classes. He decreed that no person would be allowed to own more than 500 acres of irrigated or 1,000 acres of unirrigated land. Tenants would have security of tenure and there would be no ejectment without compensation. An embargo was placed on rent increases; and exactions such as fees and free labour, were made illegal. The reforms were widely publicized and won considerable initial acclaim but they lost their initial impact in the course of implementation. Most of the landlords were able to transfer, on paper, their excess holdings in the names of their sons, brothers and close relations. The feudal aristocracy emerged from the threat of land reforms almost unscathed. The tenants and the landless classes were deeply disappointed and public interest and confidence in Ayub Khan's reforms in other fields dwindled quite rapidly.

Few military rulers, during the post-colonial period, have come to power under more auspicious circumstances that Ayub Khan. The political parties, which were mainly the splinter groups of the Muslim League, had lost all credibility and influence even before they were abolished. Except for the right wing Jamaat-i-Islami, under Maulana Abul A'la Maududi, originally a firm opponent of the concept of a territorial Muslim state, no party had any organization or manifesto. The Awami League, which was spearheading the demand for provincial autonomy and had a large following in East Pakistan, had gone into hibernation after the proclamation of martial law. Most of the prominent politicians who were charged with misuse of power and corruption thought it prudent to accept the offer of retiring from political life for a number of years under the Elective Bodies (Disqualification) Ordinance of 1959, instead of contesting the charges against them in a court of law. Even such distinguished figures as Khawaja

Nazimuddin, Maulvi Tamizuddin Khan, A.K. Fazlul Haq and H.S. Suhrawardy (who was put under detention in 1962) decided to abjure all political activities.

Academics, scholars, and writers, particularly in West Pakistan, welcomed Ayub's arrival on the scene and the Press too gave him considerable support. There was no English newspaper with country-wide circulation at the time, and Urdu and Bengali dailies too had restricted regional circulation. The more eminent publishers and editors were deeply enmeshed in partisan politics and with the retirement of their masters from political life they found themselves in a vacuum. Not until martial law was lifted in 1962 did the newspapers discover their bearings or purpose. In the meantime they accepted without demur whatever restrictions, including pre-censorship, which were imposed on them. There was no editorial protest against the abrogation of the Constitution or the dissolution of the Assemblies. Despite all this Ayub never trusted the Press. He thought that some of the newspaper owners earned 'their livelihood by resorting to blackmail'.[17] While he talked of building a healthy and responsible Press his main concern was to exercise control over the Press. He arranged the take-over of Progressive Papers which published several daily newspapers including *The Pakistan Times, Imroze* and *Mashriq,* which were eventually placed under the officially sponsored National Press Trust. After martial law was lifted in 1962 a section of the Press, particularly in East Pakistan, started asserting its independence. Ayub was frankly surprised by this turn around. In September 1963 he promulgated the new Press and Publications Ordinance which was widely condemned as a repressive instrument meant to curb the freedom of expression. As noted earlier the more oppressive clauses of the Ordinance were repealed and the rest of it was placed under a moratorium after prolonged negotiations much to the relief of the Press, but it continued to serve as a halter around the neck of the newspapers.

The genius of the people

The one problem Ayub had not anticipated was the problem of

legitimacy. His 1954 document was based on the assumption that once the accused politicians were removed from the field the people would rally round their benefactor and give him full support in establishing a simple and stable political order which did not suffer from the vagaries of parliamentary form of government. He recognized that 'our eventual aim must be to develop democracy in Pakistan, but of a type that suits the genius of the people.' He thought he had discovered the type of democracy that would work in Pakistan when he hit upon the idea that the country should be divided into small units, each composed of 1,000 adults, which should elect their representatives to an electoral college, and that college should elect the members of the central and provincial legislatures and the president. Such a system, he believed 'would be more easily manageable and would make for a good deal of responsibility.'[18] He had not worked out the details of how the system would be made 'manageable', nor who would determine 'responsibility'. He made a passing reference to Islamic democracy only to say that every body talks about it but no one has tried to define it. He concluded: 'Perhaps it is not possible to define it. Would it, therefore, not be correct to say that any variety of democracy when worked in the spirit of the Qur'an can be called an Islamic democracy.'[19] With that he left the subject which would haunt him for as long as he stayed in power.

The phrase 'genius of the people' was taken by Ayub as self-explanatory. Ayub had a highly patronizing, almost racist, attitude toward the Bengalis. He felt that the people in East Pakistan suffered from 'all the inhibitions of down-trodden races and [had] not yet found it possible to adjust psychologically to the requirements of the new-born freedom', while the people in West Pakistan represented a 'forced mixture of races [which had] brought about fusion of ideas, outlook and culture despite the linguistic variety....'[20] Ayub struggled for more than three years to formulate his version of democracy.

Ayub's first Cabinet, which consisted of three generals and six civilians, three from West Pakistan and three from East Pakistan, adopted the 1954 document as its political charter. Among the civilians there were two persons of outstanding ability: Manzur

Qadir from the Punjab, known for his independence of mind, who became the Minister of Foreign Affairs, and Zulfikar Ali Bhutto, a zealous young lawyer from Sindh, who was allotted the portfolio of Commerce. Manzur Qadir, who was committed by training and belief to constitutional rule, came to admire Ayub for his vigorous and decisive approach to problems, and Bhutto saw Ayub first as Pakistan's Abraham Lincoln and then adopted him as Salahuddin Ayubi, the Muslim crusader. We shall have occasion to see the contribution that Manzur Qadir and Bhutto made to the framing of the Constitution which was promulgated by Ayub in 1962. Here it is enough to note that it was Manzur Qadir who persuaded Ayub that public opinion was a hoax since it was often ill-informed and that he should not deviate from his belief that political parties were a menace to any democratic system, and Bhutto passionately and successfully argued in favour of Ayub retaining all power in his own hands and setting up a centralized authoritarian system of administration. He made Ayub abandon his idea of making the provinces equal partners in his constitutional scheme.

Bhutto was a complex personality. Handsome, articulate and ebullient, he could inject passion into mundane ideas. He treated everybody as a potential foe which kept him constantly on the alert, ever watchful, almost paranoid. He had no political experience when Ayub picked him up from anonymity, but within a few months he became a colourful player on Ayub's otherwise lacklustre side. He began to cultivate the right people, doing whatever job was assigned to him with vigour and imagination. He relieved the country's trade of all bureaucratic controls, as Ayub wanted, and later negotiated an oil-exploration deal with the Soviet Union. But it was in January 1963, when Ayub gave him the portfolio of Foreign Affairs that Bhutto's genius came into full play. The Boundary Agreement with the People's Republic of China had been negotiated by Manzur Qadir in 1959 and concluded by Ayub soon after the Indo-China War in 1962. Since the details of the agreement were made public only in 1963 it came to be seen as Bhutto's personal achievement. But there is no denying that Bhutto became a passionate supporter of Pakistan-China friendship. He introduced Pakistan to the Afro-Asian club, which was India's preserve until 1962, and was principally responsible for leading Pakistan into war with India in 1965. The war ended in a stalemate and when Ayub signed a peace agreement with India at Tashkent in January 1966, under the auspices of the Soviet Union, he was portrayed by Bhutto as the man who had lost at the negotiating table whatever the valiant armed forces of Pakistan had won on the battlefield.

Ayub asked Bhutto to resign in 1966 but by then Bhutto had come to be seen as a hero by the people, and as an ally by some of the generals, who blamed Ayub for losing heart and not fighting against India to the bitter end. Bhutto had been cultivating senior officers in the GHQ, particularly S.G.M.M. Peerzada, who was Adjutant-General, and Gul Hassan, Director Military Operations. They swallowed whatever stories of Ayub's 'cowardice' Bhutto told them. The younger officers and *jawans* already looked upon him as a man after their heart. This would prove a major asset three years later when Bhutto led a mass movement which resulted in Ayub's downfall. Bhutto was the most prominent actor in the rise and fall of Ayub: an eloquent advocate of a highly centralized and authoritarian system of government, Bhutto became a promoter of popular socialist ideas and a volatile opponent of all that Ayub stood for. Being a trusted insider he carried great conviction when he exposed the inner weaknesses and contradictions of the government. He could exaggerate, even falsify, the record to suit his purpose. He soon acquired the image of a man of courage who had the guts to defy and denounce a powerful dictator because he found his policies opposed to the interests of the people.

The international ring

Ayub was an adroit and far-sighted negotiator in international affairs. His principal asset was the straightforward manner in which he would analyse a problem and offer his solution. He would never exaggerate his own concerns nor understate the problems of his adversary. Always he acted more as a mediator than a partisan. He convinced the Americans of the strategic value of their alliance with Pakistan despite the influence of a powerful pro-India lobby within the US administration. The result was the Mutual Defence Agreement between the US and Pakistan in 1955. Despite Pakistan's close relations with the US, Ayub never lost sight of the fact that Pakistan was surrounded by powerful neighbours on all sides, India, China and USSR. Pakistan was locked in a major dispute with India over the future of the state of Jammu and Kashmir, and with the Soviet Union, Pakistan's relations were quite strained because of the existence of American military bases in Pakistan. Of particular concern to the Soviets was the highly sophisticated communications base at Badaber, near Peshawar, from where the Americans could carry out high altitude surveillance of Soviet territory.

With the People's Republic of China, Pakistan had relatively strain-free relations except for the question of undemarcated borders between the two states in the Sinkiang and Baltistan areas. Ayub suggested to the Chinese in 1959 that it would be to the advantage of both sides to demarcate the border. Soon after coming to power Ayub had set out his foreign policy objectives: 'Our relations with other countries would be determined by our requirements of national defence and development and must reflect the geo-political compulsions of our location. We would hold fast to those who were our friends among our neighbours.'[21]

Ayub knew that he did not have too much room for manoeuvre with the Soviet Union at the height of the cold war but he sincerely believed that he could normalize relations with India. Once that was done the region could be assured of peace. At his very first meeting with the Prime Minister of India, Pundit Jawaharlal Nehru, on 1 September 1960 at Palam Airport, New Delhi, Ayub proposed a joint defence arrangement between India and Pakistan which Nehru dismissed out of hand. He also suggested that the people of Kashmir should be allowed to exercise their right of self-determination in accordance with the United Nations resolutions. Nehru showed no enthusiasm for holding any kind of plebiscite in Kashmir and wanted that Pakistan should sign a 'no-war' pact with India. He was not impressed by Ayub's plea that a 'no-war' pact would serve no purpose so long as the Kashmir dispute, the *casus belli,* was not resolved. Ayub was disappointed. He did not see any evidence of 'idealism or starry-eyed thinking' often attributed to Nehru but he continued to explore the possibilities of settling Pakistan's differences with India in a spirit of accommodation. He was anxious that some rational 'plan of neighbourliness' should be followed instead of allowing relations between the two countries to be 'dictated by drift'.[22]

Partition in 1947 had left the headworks of some of Pakistan's major irrigation systems in Indian territory. Three of the major rivers whose waters flowed into Pakistan's canals originated and ran for long distances in Indian territory before they entered Pakistan. India wanted to divert the waters of these rivers for its own use and huge engineering works were being developed which would have turned large parts of West Pakistan into a desert. By 1958 the problem had assumed alarming proportions. Ayub took determined steps to work out a mutually acceptable formula for the division of waters between the two countries with the good offices of the World Bank. When Pundit Nehru came to Pakistan to sign what was called the Indus Basin Waters Treaty between 19 and 23 September 1960, Ayub took up the question of Kashmir again with him and again he drew a blank.[23]

The whole original situation was transformed in 1962 when border clashes between India and China developed into war. The United States rushed to the assistance of India providing it with massive arms without even consulting Pakistan. Ayub felt badly let down. He disagreed with the American reading of the Chinese intentions. The Americans had convinced themselves that the Chinese had embarked on an expansionist course and would gobble up large chunks of Indian territory, whereas Ayub believed that it was Nehru's unwillingness to come to any reasonable arrangement over certain remote and inaccessible border areas which had forced the war on China. Ayub had no doubt that once the Chinese had asserted their control over the areas which they claimed to be theirs the war would be over. Despite tremendous American pressure, including personal appeals by President John F. Kennedy, Ayub refused to provide even a formal gesture of support to India in its war against China. He showed equal foresight and courage in resisting strong domestic pressure to take advantage of India's vulnerability at the time and move his forces into Kashmir. Any adventurist action on Ayub's part would have completely alienated the Americans and exposed Pakistan to incalculable risks. Ayub knew that by resisting American pressure to come to India's support he had put the future of Pakistan-US relations in jeopardy but he had gained China's friendship which was to prove of lasting value. The details of US-Pakistan negotiations at the time are discussed in the chapter dealing with the India-China War of 1962 and the India-Pakistan War of 1965.

After his re-election as President in 1965 (Chapter 6), eight months before the war with India, Ayub went on a state visit to China where he received a rapturous welcome. The Chinese Prime Minister, Zhou Enlai, conducted him to various cities and historical sites. The Americans were upset by the anti-imperialist tone of some of Ayub's statements in China. President Johnson, who had succeeded Kennedy, conveyed it to Pakistan's Ambassador in Washington that 'I don't relish the sight of my friend Ayub breaking bread with my enemies.'[24]

Soon after visiting China, Ayub went on a state visit to Moscow. Ayub's meeting with the Soviet leaders brought about a fundamental change in Pakistan's relationship with the Soviet Union. Ayub gave Prime Minister Alexsei Kosygin an understanding that the lease for the American communications base at Badaber would not be renewed and the Soviets promised substantial military aid to Pakistan. President Johnson responded by cancelling Ayub's scheduled visit to Washington and the notice of cancellation was conveyed to Ayub while he was still in Moscow. The lines were now clearly drawn and Pakistan was seen to have opted out of the American orbit. Pakistan was taking decisive steps to cultivate friendship with the People's Republic of China and to normalize its relations with the Soviet Union because Ayub could see that 'in the event of India attacking us, it was most unlikely that the USA would honour its commitment and come to our assistance.'[25] Ayub had taken great care to develop his relations with the superpowers on a bilateral basis but he knew that no bilateral equation could exist in isolation. He endeavoured to keep these equations within the limits of tolerance, but for the Americans he had over-reached the limit when he started acting as a leader of the Afro-Asian movement locked in an alliance with China, and exploring areas of co-operation with the Soviet Union. Ayub stood his ground and insisted that if the Americans expected Pakistan to do something that was against the interests of another power 'we will have to decline because that would be going against the interests of Pakistan.'[26]

After the death of Pundit Nehru in 1964, Ayub became the most sought-after Asian leader. He had acquired enough international prestige and influence to be able to keep his domestic opposition under control and to contain the alienation of the United States. The question why Ayub embarked on a course of action in Kashmir, which led to war with India in 1965, has remained unanswered so far. An attempt is made to provide an answer to this question in chapters 9, 10 and 11 where some important new evidence is examined.

Whatever the causes of the 1965 War, the effects were highly destabilizing for Pakistan and devastating for Ayub. Not being a political animal he did not know how to make a scapegoat of his associates, though he knew that he had been grievously misled and deliberately kept in the dark about the course of Operation Gibraltar in Kashmir. He took all the blame on himself and agonized over every little miscalculation. He could not bring himself to criticize the armed forces, his own creation, for haphazard planning and grave miscalculations. His Foreign Minister, Bhutto, dissociated himself from the government to win the admiration of the people and the respect of the armed forces. Ayub was never the same man again. He seemed to have lost confidence and the power of decision. His principal worry was the threat of renewed hostilities as the forces of the two sides were still in their trenches along the battle front, while his generals were decorating themselves and their colleagues with medals of valour for imaginary victories, and his Foreign Minister was busy rousing the passions of the people by his anti-Indian rhetoric. An uneasy cease-fire arranged by the United Nations was followed by negotiations between Ayub Khan and Lal Bahadur Shastri, the Indian Prime Minister, through the good offices of the Soviet Union. India and Pakistan signed a declaration at Tashkent pledging themselves to abjure the use of force in the settlement of their disputes.

The Tashkent Declaration was received in Pakistan with great dismay. To popular indignation was added a sense of betrayal by a faint-hearted President who did not have the nerve to carry on the fight, which he had himself started, to the bitter end. The generals transferred the blame for their own incompetence and culpable negligence to Ayub whose reputation as the Supreme Commander of the armed forces was badly damaged. Ayub recovered enough to put down the popular demonstrations which were threatening to disrupt the domestic situation but he had lost all credibility.

Ayub had promised to give the country a democratic system suited to the genius of the people. What he managed to establish was a form of personal rule supported by a small college of 'Basic Democrats' which was systematically manipulated by the administration in Ayub's support. The people felt robbed of their right of franchise and Ayub's claims about the merits of the presidential form of government were dismissed as self-serving. His economic reforms too had run their course and while considerable industrial progress had been made the benefits had not trickled down to the common man. The main threat to Ayub's system was, however, beginning to develop in East Pakistan where the feeling of economic exploitation and political repression was taking the form of a secessionist movement.

The end came in December 1967 when Ayub suffered a serious heart attack. He survived the attack but the political system he had constructed began to quaver under the weight of its own contradictions. The Constitution provided that the Speaker of the National Assembly should take over as Acting President if the President was incapacitated, but nobody had the courage to invoke that provision of the Constitution. Some members of Ayub's family, particularly his son, Gohar Ayub, were accused of corruption. Ayub's personal integrity, which had been one of his strong points in the early years, became suspect. Gohar Ayub, who had retired as Captain from the Army, acquired a General Motors car-assembly plant in Karachi under highly questionable circumstances. He renamed the plant as Gandhara Industries and Gandhara became the symbol and proof of Ayub's corruption. Politicians used Gandhara as a whip to lash Ayub's government, and Habib Jalib, known as the poet of the masses, turned it into a refrain of popular denunciation of Ayub's Constitution. Ayub discovered too late that he did not have any agency to mediate on his behalf—his political party was a hand-maiden of the administration, his Basic Democrats a bunch of unscrupulous opportunists, and the government-controlled media an ineffective, partisan and oppressive instrument of propaganda.

Ayub took over the reins of power in 1958 when the country was plunged in political gloom. He pulled the country out of a morass of difficulties and confusion with infinite patience and realism inspired by the highest motives of pariotism and service. His reforms fell far short of the promise because they failed to secure the support and participation of the people. He worked for the welfare of the people but he never recognized their right to manage their own affairs. Ayub's rule which lasted for over ten years—1958 to 1969—remains a chapter of abiding interest in Pakistan's political history. This study should help to demonstrate that military rule is a wasteful and oppressive form of government. It cannot lead a country to political growth and economic development, regardless of the qualities of the military ruler. No individual, however accomplished, can replace the people who represent the supreme political reality to which a government must remain subservient and accountable at all times.

In order to grasp the full complexity of the social and political problems that Ayub inherited, and the struggle he went through to resolve those problems, it is important to understand the historical background of those problems. What were the social conditions which compelled the Muslims of India to demand a separate homeland of their own in the Indian subcontinent? And once Pakistan was established, how did the Muslims proceed to reconcile the concept of a nation-state with the Islamic ideal of Muslim brotherhood (Ummah)

which transcends all territorial divisions? What contribution did the
ulema and the judges make toward the resolution of these problems?
How did the elitist classes—the landlords, bureaucrats, generals, and
the *nouveau riche* come to dominate the political process? The debate
which these questions generated in the nineteen fifties continues to
influence the thinking of the intellectual classes in Pakistan even
today. The first chapter provides an outline of this debate, and in the
final chapter an attempt is made to strike a balancesheet of Ayub's
contributions and his failures, and some lessons are drawn which
have a direct bearing on the efforts that are being made in Pakistan
today to establish a democratic system of government in consonance
with the principles of Islam.

NOTES

1. Muhammad Ayub Khan, *Friends Not Masters,* Oxford University Press, Karachi, 1967, p. 21.
2. Ibid., p. 47.
3. Ibid., p. 38.
4. Ibid., p. 39.
5. Ibid., p. 54.
6. Ibid., p. 58.
7. Ibid., p. 186.
8. Ibid., pp. 186-91.
9. Ibid., p. 189.
10. Ibid., p. 190.
11. Ibid., p. 189.
12. Ibid., p. 190.
13. Ayub's personal diary, entries for April 1958.
14. *Dawn,* Karachi, 9 October 1958.
15. Ayub Khan, op. cit., p. 86.
16. Ibid., p. 190.
17. Ibid., p. 84.
18. Ibid., p. 189.
19. Ibid., p. 190.
20. Ibid., p. 187.
21. Ibid., p. 85.
22. Ibid., p. 123.
23. Ayub's diary.
24. Author's personal notes.
25. Ayub Khan, op. cit., p. 130.
26. Ayub's diary.

PART I

CHAPTER 1

With the Benefit of Hindsight

When Ayub Khan seized control of the Government of Pakistan in October 1958 he was immediately confronted with a number of social and political problems which had defied solution ever since the country became independent in August 1947. The parliamentary system of government had collapsed because the ruling elite refused to seek any mandate from the people or submit to the general will. They circumvented, manipulated and mangled every democratic norm and convention to maintain their hold on power which ultimately became the preserve of a coterie of landlords, bureaucrats, and generals. For eleven years the country remained under authoritarian rule, in one form or another, and a single individual, called either the Governor-General or the President, exercised absolute authority, even though a democratic government and a parliament were nominally in existence. The people were never given a chance to exercise their right of franchise in a general election. Elections were held at the provincial level on some occasions, but they were controlled by the administration and the ballot was blatantly rigged. Where a popular upsurge turned an election into a referendum, as happened in East Pakistan in 1954, and the party in power was obliterated, the rulers at the centre knocked out the elected representatives of the people and assumed direct control of the government of the province. The Provincial Election Commissions, supposedly independent bodies, watched these goings-on with great detachment, where they were not acting in collusion with the administration, which was the rule rather than the exception.

The country had a well-established judicial system, known for its independence and integrity, for all its alien features and colonial traditions. But it did not take the rulers long to co-opt the judiciary, particularly some of the more senior judges of the Supreme Court and the High Courts, into their scheme of power. Successive Law Ministers served as a means of liaison with the higher judiciary. They would play the game of carrot and stick with great skill without leaving any trace of their behind-the-scene operations. They would disown all responsibility for the laws and constitutional devices which they would work out to sustain authoritarian rule the moment they were relieved of their official responsibilities. By 1954, the rulers could rely upon the judges to pull their chestnuts out of the fire. But let it be said that there were some honourable exceptions to this unworthy arrangement.

The executive was consistent in its subservience to the ruling elite and the administration was at the beck and call of whichever political faction happened to be in command. They had been trained by the British to obey orders. They had the right to express their opinion, which they exercised with great circumspection, but once their opinion had been given due consideration and a decision taken, they were expected to implement the decision without question. The occasion never arose when a government servant resigned his job rather than carry out an order which he considered unconscionable or against the interests of the country.

The *ulema* (scholars of Islam), with a few exceptions, were the natural allies of the rulers and had no objection, in principle, to personal or authoritarian rule. It was part of their belief that power was the preserve of God Almighty, and he conferred it upon whomsoever he wished, and took it away whenever he deemed it necessary. Throughout Muslim history this belief has served the more pliable *ulema* to justify the seizure of power by some of the most tyrannical rulers. The role of the *ulema* in the constitutional controversies of Pakistan was negative, if not meaningless, in content and dubious in purpose. They would not recognize the fundamental rights and freedoms of the people, nor the democratic principle of the equality of all citizens in all respects regardless of differences of faith, class, or gender. Despite their eloquent and fervent advocacy of the Islamic system of government they failed to provide even a definition of the system.

In the early years the army was not a part of the ruling arrangement, but after Ayub Khan became the Commander-in-Chief in 1951 and built the army into a disciplined and well-trained instrument of defence, the rulers came to rely upon it for their own survival. By 1954 Ayub Khan had come to be seen by the people as a principal lever of power.

How was the state of Pakistan to be structured socially and politically? Who would run the country? Would Pakistan be a democratic state based on the Islamic principles of equality, justice and freedom, where people had the power to elect their representatives to administer the country on their behalf or would it be a theocratic state in which the *ulema* would determine the principles and mode of legislation and administration? These were among the most important questions that Ayub Khan inherited in 1958, and, for ten years, he devoted all the power and energy he possessed in resolving them.

In order to understand the complexity of the problems, which continue to haunt Pakistan even today, it is important to understand the process of their formulation in its historical perspective. The authoritarian form of government did not descend on Pakistan from the skies. It developed out of the colonial experience and was reinforced by the long tradition of dynastic and personal rule in Muslim history. Before undertaking a study of the problems that Ayub set out to resolve, and arriving at any judgement about the results he achieved, it is necessary to consider, however briefly, the emergence of Pakistan as an independent sovereign state; the important phases of experience that the people of Pakistan had to go through after Independence, while learning to govern a new country; the kind of administrative structure and traditions they inherited at the time of Independence; the composition and growth of the elitist classes; the role of the *ulema* and the judiciary and, above all, the working of the Constituent Assembly which was entrusted with the task of framing a Constitution for the country. Without this background the appearance of the phenomenon of military rule, and its recurrence in Pakistan, will not be fully understood. The emergence of Ayub Khan as Pakistan's first military ruler was not an accident but the inevitable sequel to the haphazard course of political developments in the country directed by a small coterie of self-centered individuals with no political vision or mass contact.

The British decide to quit India

Pakistan emerged as an independent nation-state on 14 August 1947 under traumatic circumstances. The British Prime Minister, Clement Attlee, announced on 19 February 1946 that a special mission consisting of three Cabinet ministers, Lord Pethic-Lawrence, Secretary of State for India, Sir Stafford Cripps, President of the Board of Trade, and A.V. Alexander, First Lord of the Admiralty, were being sent to India to devise a constitutional scheme for the transfer of power to the Indians. The Cabinet Mission arrived in Delhi on 24 March 1946 and embarked on a prolonged and strenuous round of negotiations with the political leaders of India, in particular, the heads of the two major political parties, the Indian National Congress and the All-India Muslim League. When the Mission failed to persuade the Congress and the League to 'reach agreement upon the fundamental issue of the unity or division of India', it presented, on 16 May 1946, its own solution which aimed at preserving India as a united country.[1]

The Muslim League had been demanding that the areas in which the Muslims were numerically in a majority, as in the north western zone (the Provinces of the Punjab, Sindh, North-West Frontier, and British Balochistan), and the eastern zone of India (the Provinces of Bengal and Assam) should be grouped together to constitute a separate state of Pakistan. The demand had crystallized out of the historic experience of Hindu-Muslim 'separateness' which had divided the two communities into opposing social groups. There was little that they shared with each other; they had conflicting beliefs, customs, and rituals, and there were no common cultural or educational institutions which could bring them together at any level. The two communities lived in different localities, even in the villages, and in the cities they rarely shared the same street. It was impossible for a middle-class Muslim to rent a house in the Hindu part of the town and the same convention isolated the Hindus from the Muslim localities. The beef-eating Muslim was a pungent presence in a vegetarian Hindu household where the cow was treated as *mata* (mother). Though there was greater social contact among the upper-class Hindus and Muslims, it was this fact of 'separateness' which governed the social behavior of both the communities. After the fall of the Mughal Empire, and the advent of the British Raj, communal segregation was further sharpened and the Muslims, as a minority, came to view the prospects of Hindu domination with growing distrust and alarm.

The Indian National Congress insisted on India's secular character and rejected the Muslim demand for Pakistan as a communal aberration, sustained by religious fanaticism, which could lead to the vivisection of India. The Congress wanted the British to leave them in power to deal with the problem of the Muslims and other minorities in India. The Muslims saw the Congress commitment to democracy as a sham and a self-serving device to seize power. Since the Hindus out-numbered all the ethnic minorities in India by at least four to one they had everything to gain by subscribing to the democratic principle of majority rule. It was common belief among the Muslims that the Congress was projecting itself as a modern and progressive political organization so that the British and Western political circles would see the Muslim League as a body dominated by obscurantists.

The Cabinet Mission recognized 'the very genuine and acute anxiety of the Muslims lest they should find themselves subjected to a perpetual Hindu majority rule and lest they should thus lose their independence and their culture.'[2,3] The Mission was convinced that the fear of Hindu rule amongst the Muslims could not be 'allayed by mere paper safeguards' and if there was to be internal peace in India 'it must be secured by measures which will assure to the Muslims a control in all matters vital to their culture, religion, and economic or other interests.'[4] But the Mission considered the demand for Pakistan as an untenable proposition for administrative, economic, and military reasons and rejected it on the ground that it could see no justification for including within a sovereign Pakistan those areas of the Punjab, Bengal, and Assam in which the population was predominantly non-Muslim. The Mission formulated a three-tier constitutional plan and suggested the convening of a Constituent Assembly and the 'setting up at once of an interim government in which all portfolios, including the War Member, will be held by Indian leaders having the full confidence of the people.'[5] The plan came under intense examination and dissection. If there was one thing in common between Hindu and Muslim political thinkers, it was their penchant for legal hair-splitting and disputation; nothing activated their grey cells more than the challenge of interpreting English words and phrases used in official documents. The first to start the dissection was Mahatma Gandhi. He wrote in his journal *Harijan* on 17 May 1946 that the Mission's plan was not an award: 'The proposed Constituent Assembly being a sovereign body could consider the recommendations of the Mission' and 'it would be open to that body to vary them, reject them or improve them.'[6] Muhammad Ali Jinnah, President of the All-India Muslim League, accepted the Mission's plan on 6 June and agreed to join the constitution-making body. He also agreed to discuss with the Viceroy the arrangements for the establishment of the interim government. Jinnah's understanding was that the plan, once it was accepted, would be binding on both sides. The Congress continued to insist on the sovereign character of the Constituent Assembly and never fully accepted or rejected the Mission's plan. The Working Committee of the Congress claimed that the continued presence of 'a foreign army of occupation is a negation of independence' and declined to give a final opinion 'because it found that the statement did not give a full picture.'[7] Nehru told the Mission on 10 June that 'the Congress was going to work for a strong centre and to break the group system and they would succeed. They did not think that Jinnah had any real place in the country.'[8] The Viceroy, Lord Wavell, was baffled by Gandhi, who kept changing colours like 'a king chameleon'.[9] Lord Pethic-Lawrence wrote to Attlee 'Gandhi is provokingly enigmatic and blows hot and cold.'[10] Wavell had written a detailed appreciation of the possibilities in India on 30 May 1946 in which he described Gandhi as 'a pure political opportunist, and an extremely skilful one.'[11]

The Mission was now left with one card which they could use both as a threat and a lure. They played this card on 16 June 1946 when the Viceroy invited fourteen Indian politicians, including Nehru and Jinnah, to serve as members of the Interim Government. To the invitation was added the proviso that if the two major parties, or either of them, declined the invitation the Viceroy would 'proceed with the formation of an Interim Government which will be as representative as possible of those willing to accept the statement of May 16th.'[12]

The Congress declined the invitation knowing that the British were in no position to form a government without its participation. The Mission departed in despair leaving the Indian politicians embroiled in a war of words. A fatal blow was given to the plan by Nehru when he announced at a press conference on 10 July that the Congress had made no commitment regarding the Constituent Assembly:

> It is true that by going into the Constituent Assembly inevitably we had agreed to a certain process—that is the election of the candidates to the Constituent Assembly. What we do there, we are entirely and absolutely free to determine. We have committed ourselves on no single matter to anybody.[13]

Jinnah naturally expected that since the Congress had declined to come into the Interim Government the Viceroy would call upon the League to form the government as he had promised in his formal statement of 16 June. When this did not happen he accused the Viceroy of bad faith and withdrew the League's acceptance of the Mission's plan and announced on 29 July that the time had come 'for the Muslim nation to resort to "direct action" to achieve Pakistan.'[14]

Toward the end of August, the Viceroy had a meeting with Gandhi and Nehru to obtain a definite assurance from them that the Congress meant to allow the Constituent Assembly to function in the way 'laid down'. It was not a pleasant meeting. At one point Gandhi said that 'if a bloodbath was necessary it would come about in spite of non-violence.'[15] The British succumbed to the pressure of the Congress and decided to establish an Interim Government leaving the Muslim League out in the cold.

The Interim Government, comprising twelve members, was sworn in on 2 September 1946. All twelve members were nominated by the Congress since the Muslim League had refused to join the government. Nehru, who had now taken over as President of the Congress from Abul Kalam Azad continued to insist that the Congress would enter the Constituent Assembly proposed by the Cabinet Mission 'completely unfettered by agreements and free to meet all situations as they arise.'[16] The League, finding itself outmanœuvered by the Congress and betrayed by the British, finally joined the Interim Government on 26 October 1946, when five Muslim League nominees were sworn into the Cabinet. The key portfolio of Finance was allotted to Nawabzada Liaquat Ali Khan, Secretary-General of the Muslim League. The Interim Government was expected to administer the affairs of the country while the Constituent Assembly would devise a constitutional plan for India.

The Constituent Assembly proved a 'sickly infant' and the Interim Government a 'still-born babe' in the words of Lord Wavell.[17] The unhappy experience of the Interim Government convinced the British that there was no hope of the two communities, Hindus and Muslims, living and working together under a common constitutional arrangement.

On 20 February 1947, Attlee announced the definite intention of the British government 'to take the necessary steps to effect the transference of power to responsible Indian hands by a date not later than June 1948.' Attlee added: 'We are, as a whole, committed to some form of central government for British India, or in some areas to the existing provincial governments, or in such other way as may seem most reasonable and in the best interests of the Indian people.'[18] The British had obviously decided to cut their losses and run. Winston Churchill said in the House of Commons, 'Let us not add—by shameful flight; by a premature hurried scuttle—

at least, let us not add to the pangs of sorrow so many of us feel, the taint and smear of shame.'[19]

The highly contentious and volatile business of dividing the subcontinent into two sovereign states, India and Pakistan, was entrusted to Rear-Admiral Viscount Mountbatten of Burma who took over from Lord Wavell as Viceroy on 22 March 1947. Mountbatten had come to India armed with a partition plan which he proceeded to execute with singular determination. Soon he was able to persuade Attlee that June 1948 was too distant a date and the timetable of the British departure from India could be brought forward by almost a year. To Nehru he had only to say that as the vision of Independence was within his reach he should grasp it without delay. Once the Congress had accepted it, Jinnah had no choice but to acquiesce in the new schedule of Partition. On 3 June 1947, Mountbatten announced that the Indian subcontinent would be divided into two independent states, India and Pakistan, which would come into existence as sovereign states on 15 and 14 August 1947 respectively.

Pakistan appears on the world map

Mountbatten's announcement instantly transformed the whole political landscape. An overwhelming feeling of suspense and uncertainty soon displaced the initial euphoria. Every official was provided with a tear-off calendar—'72 days to Independence', '71 days to Independence'—to instil the urgency of the situation into a war-weary and demoralized bureaucracy. The inexorability of the process was branded on the minds of the people who were being pulled towards an unknown future by some irresistible force. Every moment was a moment of no-return. Fear and anger, combined with a poignant sense of growing insecurity, led to clashes and rioting which triggered off a chain reaction of revenge. There were pools of blood on the streets, and in small towns and villages neighbours were no longer neighbours, only targets of suspicion and hatred. Political rhetoric and oratory ignited mass hysteria, inflaming old fears, reviving long-forgotten wars and unleashing atavistic passions.

Ayub Khan was a Brigadier in the Indian Army at the time and was attached to the Boundary Force under Major-General Rees to put down communal rioting in the Punjab, where villages were being put to flame, and men, women and children were being butchered in religious frenzy. It was a hopeless task.

The agony of Partition was compounded by total confusion and unpreparedness at the official level. Any problem that could not be solved was put on the back-burner, and every issue that proved intractable was kept under wraps or resolved by adopting some formulation capable of more than one interpretation. Many major political questions were deliberately allowed to remain unanswered in order to keep the tryst with freedom. Even the exact boundaries of the two dominions were not officially notified until a day *after* Independence. The Congress and the Muslim League agreed with Mountbatten that if the boundaries were announced earlier it might mar the Independence Day celebrations! But the fire was already consuming the subcontinent. The Congress and Muslim League leadership was under the illusion that the advent of Independence would be enough to harness the winds of hatred that were sweeping across the land. The great Calcutta killings (August 1946), the horrible Noakhali bloodshed, followed by the Bihar massacre (November 1946), and the Rawalpindi riots (June 1947), should have given some warning to the government that the subcontinent was hurtling toward an abyss of chaos, but Mountbatten remained unruffled. He assured the Indian leaders: 'I shall see to it that there is no bloodshed and riot. I am a soldier not a civilian. If there should be the slightest agitation I shall adopt the sternest measures to nip the trouble in the bud. I will order the army and the air force to act and I will use tanks and aeroplanes to suppress anybody who wants to create trouble.'[20] For Mountbatten the date of British departure took precedence over everything else. While millions of people were uprooted and blown away like dry leaves by a hurricane of hate and violence, Mountbatten stuck to his cold-blooded strategy of Partition.

Pakistan's political legacy

The demand for Pakistan was based on Jinnah's 'Two-Nation Theory' according to which the Muslims of India represented a separate nation and were entitled to an independent homeland of their own. Jinnah did not question the principle of majority rule, nor did he disagree with the western concept of democratic government. He rested his case on the claim, which was not easy to refute, that the principle of majority rule under one government could not apply to two separate nations. The fact of Hindu-Muslim 'separateness' was the critical point in Jinnah's argument which had a tremendous emotional appeal for the Muslim masses because it reflected so dramatically the reality of their social condition.

Once Pakistan was established, the sense of separateness and fear of Hindu domination which had provided the principal motivating force during the struggle for liberation disappeared. Free at last, the Muslims were called upon to establish a nation-state based on the principles of equality, justice, accountability to the people, and respect for fundamental human rights and freedoms. The only collective political concept with which the Muslims were familiar was that of the 'Ummah' (Muslim brotherhood). A democratic nation-state, governed by majority rule regardless of caste, colour or creed was something wholly novel, if not alien, to Muslim history. But in the euphoria of Independence, Islam and Pakistan had come to be treated as synonymous.

Jinnah recognized the problem and attempted to resolve it in his inaugural address to the Constituent Assembly on 11 August 1947. But there were fundamental conceptual contradictions which could not be resolved by appeals to national unity. The distinction between the nation and the state was not recognized; indeed the state was not even defined. With the establishment of Pakistan two lobbies began to assert themselves: the reformists, inclined towards secular democratic ideals, and the funda-mentalists, who favoured the revival of an authoritarian form of government dominated by civil-military bureaucracy. To the reformists, Islam was a dynamic force, a concept of life and not of law, a source of nourishment for the springs of creative thought and not an immutable code of do's and don'ts. They maintained that the Qur'an did not prescribe any form of government nor were any rigid rules or regulations laid down for organizing the institutional structure of the state. The Islamic state should be built on the principles of equality and justice as presented in the Qur'an and it must respond to the demands of time by providing full freedom to the creative spirit of the people. The principles of equality and justice were immutable but there was an ever expanding field available for innovation and progress in the intellectual, political and social spheres. The reformists asserted these principles quite forcefully, but when it came to giving them a concrete form, suited to the needs of the people, they could not think of any institutions other than the ones they had become accustomed to under the British.

The fundamentalists, on the other hand, insisted that the Holy Qur'an and the Hadith (sayings of Prophet Muhammad PBUH) provided all the laws that would ever be needed by mankind and those laws were applicable to all societies at all times. All fundamental questions of principle having been finally settled, there was no longer any room for innovation or dissent. All that was required was to *discover* those laws from the Qur'an, by following the judgements and decrees of authoritative Muslim jurists, not to *invent* new laws. The reformists had the support of the Western educated classes. The fundamentalists found their supporters among the conservative lower-middle classes. The reformists clung to the British institutions, the fundamentalists to the memory of the past. Paradoxically, both the reformists and the fundamentalists ended up by becoming the champions of *status quo* and allies of the ruling junta in frustrating the popular forces of change.

Chaudhri Muhammad Ali, who was Secretary-General in the Government of Pakistan, and later became Prime Minister, regarded the British institutions as 'the principal gift of the British to their colonies.'[21] The Western elite, and politicians, the civil servants, the judges and the lawyers believed that the future of the country, as much as their own, depended on the continuation of those institutions.

Among the fundamentalists there was much talk of introducing the Shariah (the Islamic code) and establishing Islamic institutions. But when it came to formulating any concrete proposals, the *ulema* could not go beyond making vacuous assertions and pious declarations. It took them years to decide whether sovereignty belonged to the people or to Allah. They never paused to reflect that sovereignty was a complex western concept based on 'the principle that the authority of law was derived from the community, and the law was supreme, not only over subjects but over rulers.'[22] In 1956 when the first Constitution was adopted, after nine years of political debate, all that was recognizable as Islamic in the Constitution was a directive principle of state policy that 'steps shall be taken to enable the Muslims of Pakistan individually and collectively to order their lives in accordance with the Holy Qur'an and Sunnah.' The rest of the Constitution was no more than a revised version of the Government of India Act 1935. Ayub Khan would later describe the Constitution as a 'document of despair'.[23]

The British-style institutions

Neither the reformists nor the fundamentalists understood that British institutions had been introduced to serve an imperial purpose which, after Independence, had ceased to be relevant. A new purpose—the progress and happiness of the people—had taken its place and existing institutions needed to be modified and adjusted, radically if necessary, to suit the needs of an independent nation. The 'principal gift'[24] of the British to their colonies should have been examined a little more closely: the evolution of the original institutions through the democratic process should have been compared to the working of their fake replica in India and the values, conventions, and customs which had sustained their growth in Britain should have been distinguished from the form in which they were transplanted in the colonies. The British came as conquerors with a set of liberal ideas which they found difficult to transmit to the natives in India. The concept of sovereignty of the people had been established in England after a long and bitter struggle. The British considered the Indians too backward to understand such a concept. They had to be educated and trained to govern themselves but it would be a long time before they would qualify as a people capable of exercising the right of self-determination. In the mean time education and property were the only standards available to the rulers to judge whether an individual was civilized or not. Sovereignty of the people was recognized as an ideal, as was the need for free and fair elections, but the British would decide when and how a subject race should be allowed to organize its social and political life according to that ideal.

The British left behind an institutional structure which was neither representative of British liberal values nor reflective of Indian culture and traditions. Instead of developing a representative parliament through free and fair elections, the Indians were introduced to a game of electioneering and politicking. The right of franchise was limited and circumscribed by a variety of means. The electoral process was controlled and manipulated by the officials. The people were exposed for the first time to political harangues, bribes, and threats, all intended to secure their support in election. Every local rift, sectarian difference and family dispute was exploited by the candidates to advance their prospects. There was corruption at every step from the recording of names in the electoral rolls to the counting of votes. Forgery, impersonation, and casting of bogus votes were all part of the game. Politics soon became a profession of skill and strategy and only losers talked of principles and programmes. The British succeeded in creating a class of politicians and political workers well-versed in the art of election management.[25]

The rule of law was sacrosanct in England and an independent judiciary was the pride of British society. In India the power of courts was severely circumscribed. The executive could curtail the liberty of a citizen without having to disclose the grounds of detention and torture of political prisoners and witnesses was accepted as a routine part of the investigative procedure. The legal system established by the British was as oppressive as it was incomprehensible for most people in the country.

A free Press was another cherished British institution, but in India freedom of expression was curtailed on the plea that freedom must not be allowed to degenerate into licence. Newspapers and journals could be published only under a certificate granted by the district magistrate. Two copies of all publications (newspapers, books journals, posters, and even leaflets) were required to be submitted to the district magistrate, and errant writers, journalists, and poets, were swiftly seized and punished. Publications were subject to strict censorship and special laws were enacted to regulate the freedom of expression.

The institutions which Pakistan inherited from the British proved highly oppressive in their working. They could operate only if the people were kept subdued by administrative officers trained to manipulate and control them. The leadership in Pakistan, unfortunately, chose to align itself with those institutions and not with the people.

The elite

The principal beneficiary of the British system was the Pakistani elite. It was, and remains, a self-generating and self-perpetuating class. Government servants, landlords under the patronage of the British, army officers, lawyers favoured by the district administration, and government contractors, were the original members of this class. Their sons and grandsons (women being ineligible) were a fertile source of recruitment and a guarantee for the continuation of the class. It was this class which provided all the politicians, bureaucrats, lawyers, doctors, engineers, teachers and commissioned officers for the armed forces under the British.

Members of the Indian Civil Service (ICS) donned European dress and aped British manners, cheerfully accepting all forms of discrimination. The judges wanted their wigs and robes, and the lawyers their silk and Halsbury's *Laws of England*. After Independence members of the ICS agreed, not without persuasion, to suffix the letters 'ICS (Pakistan)' after their names. They prided themselves on the fact that they were entitled to have their pension in sterling and their 'home' leave in England. They were the first living specimens of what Lord Macaulay had set out to create. In his now famous Minute of 1835, Macaulay wrote: 'We must at present do our best to form a class who may be interpreters between us and the millions whom we govern; a class of persons Indian in blood and colour but English in taste, in opinions, in morals and intellect.' As Macaulay had forecast, members of the superior services became the main advocates of the British system of administration and devoted their careers to the retention and consolidation of British institutions in the form in which the British had bequeathed them to India and Pakistan.

Pakistan's constitutional quest

The concept of Pakistan found its first formal expression in the Pakistan Resolution adopted by the Muslim League in 1940. The resolution envisaged the grouping of areas in which the Muslims were numerically in a majority, as in the north-western and eastern zones of India, into 'independent *states* in which the constituent units shall be autonomous and sovereign.' This position was reconsidered by the Muslim League in the Legislator's Convention held in Delhi between 7 and 9 April 1946. In his speech to the Convention, Jinnah said:

> We are a nation of 100 million, and what is more, we are a nation with our own distinctive culture and civilization, language and literature, art and architecture, names and nomenclature, sense of values and proportion, legal laws and moral codes, customs and calendar, history and traditions, aptitudes and ambitions; in short, we have our own distinctive outlook on life and of life. By all canons of international law we are a nation.

In the resolution that was adopted by the Convention on 9 April it was demanded that 'the zones comprising Bengal and Assam in the north-east and the Punjab, North-West Frontier Province, Sindh and Balochistan in the North-West of India, namely Pakistan zones, where the Muslims are in a dominant majority, be constituted into a sovereign independent *state*.' On 12 May 1946 the Muslim

League endorsed the President's memorandum of the minimum demands of the Muslims according to which the six Muslim provinces (Punjab, NWFP, Balochistan, Sindh, Bengal and Assam), named as the Pakistan Group would deal with all subjects and matters 'except foreign affairs, defence and communications necessary for defence'. A separate constitution-making body would be established for the six Muslim provinces to 'frame constitutions for the Group and the provinces in the Group' and to determine 'the list of subjects that shall be provincial and Central (of the Pakistan Federation) with residuary sovereign powers vesting in the Provinces.' While the subjects were not identified the memorandum provided that: 'After the *Constitutions* of the Pakistan Federal government and the Provinces are finally framed by constitution-making Body, *it will be open to any province of the Group to decide to opt out of its Group,* provided the wishes of the people of that Province are ascertained by a referendum to opt out or not.' [Emphasis added].[26] The provinces were thus given a pledge that they would have full control over all subjects except the three which were allocated to the central government under clause I of the memorandum. It is true that the memorandum was adopted while the Muslim League was still engaged in negotiations with the British and the Congress in the hope of establishing a confederation in India composed of two federations and, therefore, the powers of the confederal authority were being restricted to the minimum possible extent. But even a plain reading of the April resolution, and of all the earlier resolutions, leaves one in no doubt that the Muslim League did not envisage at any time the establishment of a federal state of Muslim provinces in which the constituent units would be wholly subservient to central authority.

In his Presidential address to the Assembly on 11 August 1947 Jinnah said: 'The Constituent Assembly has got two main functions to perform. The first is the very onerous and responsible task of framing our future Constitution of Pakistan and the second of functioning as a full and complete sovereign body as the federal legislature of Pakistan.'[27] Referring to the first function, he made a momentous declaration, saying:

Pakistan could be made happy and prosperous if the government were to concentrate on the well-being of the people and especially of the masses and the poor. If you change your past and work together in a spirit that every one of you, no matter to what community he belongs, no matter what relations he had with you in the past, no matter what is his colour, caste or creed, is first, second and last a citizen of this state with equal rights, privileges and obligations…you may belong to any religion or caste or creed—that has nothing to do with the business of the state.

He concluded with the words:

Now, I think we should keep that in front of us as our ideal and you will find that in course of time Hindus would cease to be Hindus and Muslims would cease to be Muslims, not in the religious sense, because that is the personal faith of each individual, but in the political sense as citizens of the state.

When Jinnah's speech appeared in the newspapers it caused a great consternation among the orthodox classes since Jinnah was clearly advocating a secular model of democratic government for Pakistan. The question arose 'What will be the position of Islam in Pakistan?' Almost immediately the *ulema* who had, at best, played a subsidiary role in the struggle for Pakistan began to assert that they alone had the authority to define the place of Islam in the future Constitution of Pakistan. The Lahore Resolution contained no reference to Islam. Nor was there anything to suggest that Pakistan had been established to revive old Islamic institutions. The Resolution only talked about the areas where the Muslims were in a numerical majority and required that such areas should be grouped to constitute independent states. It was a secular demand based on the western secular concept of the people exercising their right of self-determination. Thus were sown the seeds of a major conflict between those who shared Jinnah's vision of Pakistan as a democratic state, where all citizens would have equal status and rights, and the fundamentalists who wanted to convert Pakistan into a model Islamic state governed by the Qur'an and Sunnah.

The Constituent Assembly of Pakistan, consisting of some sixty-nine members, comprising politicians, landlords, retired bureaucrats, lawyers and businessmen, few of whom had any knowledge of Islamic law or history, was overwhelmed by the rhetoric of the *ulema*. They had been elected to the Constituent Assembly not directly by the people but by the provincial assemblies before Independence. In March 1949 the Assembly adopted what was called the Objectives Resolution.[28] The Resolution proclaimed: 'Whereas sovereignty over the entire universe belongs to God Almighty alone and the authority which He had delegated to the State of Pakistan through its people for being exercised within the limits prescribed by Him is a sacred trust.' The concept of sovereignty was not defined nor was any indication given of the limits prescribed by Allah. The Resolution required the Assembly to frame a Constitution for 'the sovereign independent State of Pakistan'.

A Basic Principles Committee and a Board of Talimaat-i-Islamia was appointed to advise on matters arising out of the Objectives Resolution. The Committee submitted an interim report in September 1950. It proposed that the Objectives Resolution should be incorporated in the Constitution as a directive principle of state policy. The Committee also suggested that 'steps should be taken in many spheres of governmental activities to enable the Muslims, as laid down in the Objectives Resolution, to order their lives in accordance with the Holy Qur'an and Sunnah'.

The growing differences of opinion among the representatives of the different sects of Islam compounded the problem of providing an agreed definition of the Islamic State and the fundamentalists began to fear that the Islamic Constitution might come to be seen as 'a riddle, wrapped in a mystery, inside an enigma'.[29] Stung by this fear the *ulema* held a convention in Karachi in January 1951. Thirty-one religious scholars 'representing all the schools of Islamic thought' unanimously formulated what they called 'the fundamental principles of the Islamic State'. The document containing these principles provided, *inter alia* that 'ultimate sovereignty over all Nature and all Law vests in Allah, the Lord of the universe, alone' and 'the Laws of the Land shall be based on the Qur'an and the Sunnah and no law shall be enacted nor any administrative order issued in contravention of the Qur'an and Sunnah'; that 'the State shall be based not on geographical, racial, linguistic, or any other materialistic concepts but on the principles and ideals of Islamic ideology'; that 'the Head of the State shall always be a male Muslim in whose piety, learning, and soundness of judgement the people or their elected representatives had confidence'; and that 'no interpretation of the Constitution which is in conflict with the provisions of the Qur'an or the Sunnah shall be valid'. The *ulema* made no attempt to define 'the principles and ideals of Islamic ideology' on which the state was to be based nor did they suggest any institution or procedure for the interpretation of the Qur'an and Sunnah. They did not recognize universal franchise and there was no mention of any legislature. They talked about the body empowered to elect the Head of the State but did not suggest how that body was to come into existence. The provinces were to be reduced to the level of 'administrative units' under the 'supremacy of the Centre'. The whole document was a farrago of archaic, contradictory, and self-serving recommendations aimed at establishing an authoritarian form of government in which the *ulema* would have the ultimate authority to interpret the Qur'an and Sunnah and prescribe the scope and limits of legislation. In other words the *ulema* would act as a supra-parliament body with the power to overrule the legislature. Not surprisingly the unanimous endeavours of the *ulema* did not advance the cause of the Islamic state.

The final report of the Basic Principles Committee was published in December 1952 and another convention of the *ulema* met in Karachi in January 1953 and proposed a number of amendments to the recommendations made by the Committee. At last the *ulema* mustered the courage to address the problem of defining Islamic ideology. They held that: '…it was not enough to say in the Constitution that no law should be enacted which was repugnant to the Qur'an and Sunnah. What is required is that it should be laid down as a matter of principle that the dictates and directives of the Qur'an and Sunnah should be the chief source of legislation.'[30]

Before giving assent to any bill, the Head of State must consult 'a Board consisting of not more than five persons well-versed in

Islamic laws', and if the Board unanimously found the bill repugnant to the Qur'an and Sunnah the bill should be referred back to a joint sitting of the two houses of the federal legislature. For a member of the Board it was enough to have been a *mufti* for ten years or a *qadi* or a teacher in any religious institution, but to be a member of the legislature a Muslim must be known to observe all the Islamic duties and desist from all that was forbidden. Most of the amendments proposed by the *ulema* were as vague as the principles formulated by them.

Dismissal of the Constituent Assembly

It was in this environment of confusion and absence of agreement on any of the fundamental political issues that the Constituent Assembly continued to grapple with the problem of framing a Constitution for the country. On 15 September 1954 Prime Minister Muhammad Ali Bogra announced that 'the last hurdle' in constitution-making had been crossed and the house could now go ahead and adopt a Constitution.[31] The Assembly felt that the time had come to curtail the powers of the Governor-General, Ghulam Muhammad, who had been dismissing Federal and Provincial Governments according to his whims. The legislators decided to discipline the wayward Governor-General and assert the supremacy of Parliament. A bill was moved by a member seeking to amend Sections 9, 10, 10-A and 10-B of the Government of India Act, and to replace them with a new Section 10 under which 'the Parliament shall exercise its executive authority through the Prime Minister who commands the confidence of the majority of the Parliament'. This would give the Prime Minister the right to choose his ministers, making the government collectively responsible to Parliament. The bill provided that the 'Governor-General shall be bound by the advice of the Prime Minister.' The Press hailed the bill as a triumph of democracy.[32] The Governor-General, who was away from the capital having a holiday in Gilgit, cancelled his programme and immediately returned to Karachi.

The Prime Minister had, in the meantime, taken off for London, *en route* to Washington, ostensibly for important negotiations but principally to avoid any confrontation with Ghulam Muhammad, whose reactions were not always predictable. He had earlier dismissed a Prime Minister, who enjoyed majority support in the Assembly, on the plea that his government 'had proved entirely inadequate to grapple with the difficulties facing the country'.[33] Ghulam Muhammad was furious and felt that Bogra, whom he had recalled from the wilderness, had stabbed him in the back. Rumours were rife in Karachi that the Governor-General was about to dismiss the government and dissolve the Assembly. Several political leaders came out with statements urging Ghulam Muhammad not to take the extreme step. The central executive of Jamaat-i-Islami declared that the proposed Constitution 'was to a very great extent Islamic in character and demanded its adoption forthwith.' The central executive condemned the move for the dissolution of the Constitution Assembly, and urged the people 'to closely watch the activities of the people at the helm of national affairs who appeared determined to deprive them of the fruits of seven years of their struggle for an Islamic Constitution'.[34] The Jamiat-i-Ulema-i-Islam also declared the proposed Constitution to be 'in consonance with the requirements of Islam'. The move to dissolve the Assembly was condemned by the Jamiat as 'mischievous'.[35] Undeterred by all the fuss that the politicians and the *ulema* were creating the Governor-General dissolved the Assembly and dismissed the Federal Government on 24 October 1954. A proclamation was issued in which the Governor-General announced 'with deep regret' that the constitutional machinery in the country had broken down, the Constituent Assembly had lost the confidence of the people and could no longer function. He recognized that the ultimate authority vested in the people 'who will decide all issues, including the constitutional issues, through their representatives to be elected afresh.'[36]

The Governor-General's action, however arbitrary, was not entirely incomprehensible in the political context. The Constituent Assembly had been locked in a futile constitutional debate for over seven years and had little to show for its labours and the people had lost all faith in its ability to produce a Constitution. But it was when all the Bengali members of the Constituent Assembly lost their seats in the East Bengal Assembly, from which they derived their mandate, in the 1954 election that the position of the Assembly became completely untenable. Few people were, therefore, surprised or unhappy when the Governor-General knocked it off the stage. Having lost its representative character the Assembly was trying hard to adopt some constitutional formula to regain its credibility. In the process the Assembly overreached itself and passed a bill curtailing the powers of the Governor-General which brought about its downfall.

The dissolution of the Assembly was followed by a most bizarre development. Bogra, who had just been dismissed as Prime Minister, accepted 'the gracious invitation of the Governor-General to reform the government with a view to giving the country a vigorous and stable administration'.[37] It was well known in official circles that the Prime Minister had been ordered by the Governor-General to cut short his stay in Washington and return to Karachi. This the hapless Prime Minister did with great anxiety but without the slightest delay. All he wanted was to be assured of personal safety on his return. Ayub Khan, who happened to be with the Prime Minister, reassured him, and in fact accompanied him to Karachi by a chartered flight from London. Ayub later described how he, along with Iskander Mirza and Chaudhri Muhammad Ali, went to see Ghulam Muhammad to plead on behalf of Bogra:

The Governor-General was lying in his bedroom. He had very high blood-pressure and an agonizing backache which compelled him to lie flat on hardboard. He was bursting with rage, emitting volleys of abuse which luckily, none understood. Chaudhri Muhammad Ali ventured to say something and received a volley; then Iskander Mirza said something and got another. We were pleading with him to give another chance to Muhammad Ali [Bogra]. His only reply was an angry growl, 'Go, off you go.' All he wanted was to shoo us off. We marched out of the bedroom in single file. Iskander Mirza at the head, Chaudhri Muhammad Ali following, and I bringing up the rear. I was about to step out of the room when the nurse attending the Governor-General tugged at my coat. I turned and found myself facing a different man. There he was, the sick old Governor-General, who a moment ago was insane with anger, now beaming with delight and bubbling with laughter. I said in my heart, 'You wicked old man!' He beckoned me with a peculiar glee in his eye. 'Sit down on the bed.' He then pulled out two documents from under his pillow. On one was written something to the effect: 'I, Ghulam Muhammad, so and so, because of this, that, hand over such and such authority to General Ayub Khan and command him to produce a Constitution in three months.[38]

It was Ayub's refusal to accept this offer which left the Governor-General with no choice but to bring Bogra back.

Within hours of the swearing-in ceremony Bogra said in a nation-wide broadcast that:

…certain actions of the Constituent Assembly have provoked a storm of indignation throughout the country. Recently, by far the majority of you have seriously questioned its competence to speak for you, with the net result that its decisions have ceased to command that general acceptance by people which is the *sine qua non* of a workable and stable Constitution.

To this the Prime Minister added that 'Constitution-making is important but more important by far is the security and stability of our country.'[39] The people were completely stunned by this public grovelling by their Prime Minister, but it took the Governor-General no time to persuade several political leaders to endorse his action. Even Suhrawardy announced from Zurich, where he was undergoing medical treatment, that by dissolving the Assembly the Governor-General had accepted his contention 'that the Constituent Assembly was not a representative body'.[40]

The Press had been put under censorship. For the first two days there was no evidence of any public reaction, but by 27 October most newspapers had come round to the Governor-General's point of view, and even those papers which had been campaigning against the dissolution of the Assembly were able to say that 'the interests of the people have been well-served now than they were being served by the intrigue and provincialism-ridden democratic hotch-potch which has been ended.'[41]

Ayub Khan was now recognized as the man behind the throne. He was getting disenchanted with the working of the government which he found 'utterly confused and almost leaderless'.[42] The

Governor-General invited him to join the new Cabinet as Minister for Defence to which he agreed on the condition that he would continue as the Commander-in-Chief. General Iskander Mirza, the most powerful member of the Cabinet, became the Home Minister.

Iskander Mirza lost no time in condemning democracy and the mess it had made in the country. The masses, he said, were illiterate: 'they are bound to act foolishly sometimes, as they did in East Pakistan, and again, their elected leaders did in the Constituent Assembly.'[43] Mirza elaborated his theme by asserting that the administration had gone to pieces: 'You cannot have the old British system of administration and at the same time allow the politicians to meddle with the Civil Services.'[44] A foreign correspondent said that the right to make mistakes was conceded in a democracy and the people had also the right to elect even the wrong kind of leaders. Mirza's reply was categorical: 'No, I do not concede that luxury to the people. There should be somebody always to correct them.' What the people of Pakistan needed, Mirza declared, was 'controlled democracy'.[45]

The Provincial Governments

While the Constitution was in the making the four provincial governments were going through their own unpredictable game of combinations and permutations leading to the emergence of a variety of short-lived coalitions.

As early as April 1948 the Punjab Cabinet 'presented a spectacle of petty squabbles, sordid intrigues and all other accompaniments of an internecine war between the factions.'[46] Jinnah tried to sort out the ministerial tangle and even he threw up his hands in disgust.[47] Finally, in the beginning of 1949 the ministry was dismissed; the Assembly was dissolved; and Governor's rule was imposed under Section 92-A of the adapted Government of India Act 1935.[48] This was the first time that the constitutional process was suspended in Pakistan. After this, the suspension of the constitutional process in the centre, as in the provinces, was to become the norm.

In the North-West Frontier Province there was strong opposition to the Muslim League government and there was talk of starting a civil disobedience movement in August 1948. The Muslim League was in a minority in the Provincial Assembly elected in 1946 but with the support of members of the Opposition, who defected to the Muslim League, it had converted itself into the majority party. Jinnah went to the province in 1948 and appealed to the people 'to avoid domestic controversies and provincialism'. He warned that the government, the province and the Civil Service were being watched: 'It is under our searchlight and there is no doubt we shall soon be able to X-ray it and throw out the poison from our body politic.'[49]

The province of Sindh was notorious for its shifting alliances. At the time of Partition a Muslim League ministry was in office but the Chief Minister soon found himself involved in a public controversy with two of his ministers, each accusing the other of corruption and maladministration. The Governor dismissed the Chief Minister in April 1948, although he had majority support in the Assembly. The communiqué issued at the time stated that a *prima facie* case had been made out against the Chief Minister on charges of maladminisration, gross misconduct in the discharge of his duties, and corruption. A tribunal consisting of two Chief Judges of the High Courts found the Chief Minister guilty on a number of charges. The new Chief Minister did not last long. He was accused of harbouring criminals and was disqualified from holding any public office. His successor survived for a few months but toward the end of 1948 the Assembly was dissolved, and Governor's rule was imposed under the dreaded Section 92-A of the Government of India Act of 1935.

In East Bengal the Muslim League remained in a relatively comfortable position for the first two years. Its popularity was gravely undermined when the popular demand that Bengali should be recognized as one of the state languages was resisted leading to rioting and bloodshed in Dhaka in February 1952. The party did not feel confident enough to hold any by-election. The opposition parties combined in 1954 to fight the provincial elections. Of the 310 seats in the Assembly the ruling party lost all but nine seats.

The United Front, with an overwhelming majority in the Assembly, was allowed to assume office with A.K. Fazlul Haq as the Chief Minister, but the popularly elected government was dismissed after two months on charges of maladministration and the province was placed under Governor's rule. Iskander Mirza was appointed as the Governor to discipline the province and bring it back into the orbit of the Central Government. Mirza carried out his assignment with characteristic zeal.

The Emergence of One Unit

Perhaps the most significant administrative development during this period was the merger of all the provinces and states in the western wing of Pakistan into what was called One Unit in 1955.[50] The Punjabi politicians had been advocating that all the four provinces in the western wing of Pakistan should be brought under a single administration. Malik Firoz Khan Noon had made a plea in the Constituent Assembly in March 1949 for the merger of the provinces in the interest of 'efficient administration'.[51] It was not efficient administration but a mixture of political motives which was behind the demand for the merger of the provinces of West Pakistan. The smaller provinces, Sindh, NWFP, and Balochistan had become deeply resentful of Punjabi dominance in the administration and were demanding greater autonomy. East Bengal was a natural supporter of their cause. But there was a much more fundamental question which was worrying both the Federal Government and Punjab: the question of representation. The Muslim League had fought against the democratic principle of majority rule in India on the ground that the principle could not apply to two separate nations yoked together under a single government. It was now faced with the problem of having to concede the principle of majority rule within Pakistan where the Bengalis represented fifty-six per cent of the population. If representation in Parliament was determined according to population, Punjab would lose its pre-eminence and the Bengalis would come to govern the country. The problem might have been resolved if the provinces had been granted full autonomy as envisaged in the Lahore Resolution. But the Central Government had taken control of the provinces and was unwilling to part with any of its powers. It was to circumvent the principle of majority rule that the Federal Government devised the formula of parity of representation between the two wings of the country. Such a formula could only be implemented if the provinces of West Pakistan were all merged into a single political and administrative unit. Thus was born the new province of West Pakistan. It was an unholy arrangement, brought about through a great deal of political skulduggery, which only aggravated the tensions and distrust between the provinces and the centre. The smaller provinces of West Pakistan, robbed of their identity, found that the new dispensation had placed them in double jeopardy: having been exploited by the Central Government for eight years they were now to suffer the additional penalty of Punjabi domination. East Bengal too was unhappy because even after having sacrificed its legitimate claim of representation on the basis of population it was being denied its share in services and in the resources of the country on the basis of parity.

The judiciary gets into the act

The first Prime Minister was assassinated, the second dismissed, and their successors relieved of office at the pleasure of the Governor-General. The Government of India Act 1935 was used to dismiss the Federal Cabinet in April 1953 when Khwaja Nazimuddin was the Prime Minister. Nazimuddin was replaced by Muhammad Ali Bogra who was not even a member of the legislature. The new Cabinet contained eight ministers from the previous Cabinet which had been dismissed for incompetence. Bogra himself was dismissed a year later when the Constituent Assembly was dissolved by the Governor-General.

The only person who challenged the action of the Governor-General was Maulvi Tamizuddin Khan, Speaker of the National Assembly, who filed a writ petition in the Chief Court of Sindh in which he alleged that the Governor-General had acted without lawful authority. The court declared the Governor-General's action illegal. The Chief Justice of Sindh, Sir George Constantine, decided that the dissolution of the Assembly was 'a nullity in law'.[52] The two other Judges on the bench agreed. One of them observed that:

> ...the supreme prerogative to amend and repeal existing laws and to frame and bring into force a new Constitution which was the essence of Her Majesty's sovereignty had been granted solely to the Assembly and as the grant was without any limiting words the Assembly could exercise it as fully as Her Majesty could.

The other Judge dismissed the Governor-General's claim that he was the Queen's representative in Pakistan on the ground that he was only a symbol because the Queen 'reigns but does not rule'. The matter was taken up in appeal before the Federal Court of Pakistan.[53] The Chief Justice, M. Munir, did not go into the merits of the case and allowed the appeal on the technicality that the Chief Court of Sindh had no jurisdiction to issue the writs. He gave no ruling on the question whether the Governor-General had the power to dissolve the Constituent Assembly.

Fortified by the decision of the Federal Court, the Governor-General proceeded to promulgate an Ordinance to validate a number of laws which had been passed by the Constituent Assembly but had not been submitted to him for his assent. The Ordinance was declared invalid and in sheer helplessness the Governor-General appealed to the Federal Court to advise him about his powers and responsibilities in respect of the government of the country.[54] Here was the Chief Executive pleading with the highest court in the country to provide him with some legal cover to continue with his authoritarian style of government. After some further judicial manœuvring a second Constituent Assembly was convened in 1955. Chaudhri Muhammad Ali, who had become the Prime Minister, presented the fourth draft of the Constitution in 1955. The draft was adopted by the Assembly and the Constitution of the Republic of Pakistan was finally promulgated in March 1956. General Iskander Mirza was sworn in as the first

President of Pakistan. Mirza took a solemn oath to defend and preserve the Constitution.

The *ulema* in eclipse

The *ulema* who had been vociferously demanding the establishment of an Islamic system in the country accepted, indeed welcomed, the adoption of the 1956 Constitution, which was in every respect a secular document, and did not recognize any of the recommendations made by successive conventions of the *ulema*. The *ulema* pretended that the struggle between the Islamic and anti-Islamic trends had been 'finally and unequally settled' in favour of the former.[55] The truth was that the *ulema* had lost whatever political influence and credibility they had in 1953 when they launched a politically inspired agitation against the Ahmedis in the Punjab. The agitation spread like wildfire resulting in indiscriminate killings, arson, and rioting in several major towns of the Punjab. Lahore, the capital of the province, had to be placed under martial law. The Ahmedi sect was established by Mirza Ghulam Ahmad who claimed to be a *nabi* (prophet). The sect was regarded by the Muslims in general as a community of heretics who had misappropriated the title of Islam in order to create dissensions and confusion within the ranks of the Muslims.

The government appointed a court of enquiry under Justice Muhammad Munir. Almost all the leading *ulema* of the country appeared before the court to explain why they regarded the Ahmedis as heretics. The main demand of the *ulema* was that the Ahmedi community be expelled from the general body of Muslims and be put on a separate electoral roll along with other minority communities. They also insisted that the Ahmedis should not be associated with the affairs of state and demanded the expulsion of Chaudhri Zafarulla Khan, then Foreign Minister, from the Cabinet. Naturally, the court required that the *ulema* must first give their definition of a Muslim before it could be decided who should, or should not, be considered a Muslim. The report of the court of enquiry noted:

What is Islam and who is a *Momin* or a Muslim? We put this question to the *ulema* and we shall presently refer to their answers to this question. But we cannot refrain from saying here that it was a matter of infinite regret to us that the *ulema*, whose first duty should be to have settled views on the subject, were hopelessly disagreed among themselves....Keeping in view the several definitions (of a Muslim) given by the *ulema*, need we make any comment except that no two learned divines are agreed on this fundamental. If we attempt our own definition as each learned divine has done, and that definition, differs from that given by all other, we unanimously come out of the fold of Islam.[56]

The demand that the Ahmedis should not be associated with the affairs of the state, struck at the very root of the concept of common and equal citizenship. The court referred to Jinnah's statement in the Constituent Assembly of 11 August 1947: 'We are starting with this fundamental principle; that we are all citizens, and equal citizens, of one state.' The *ulema* rejected the concept of state presented by Jinnah and a member of the Jamaat-i-Islami said: 'A state based on this idea is the creature of the devil.' The *ulema* claimed that Jinnah's concept of a modern nation state was superseded by the Objectives Resolution of 12 March 1949. It was freely admitted before the court that this Resolution: '...although grandiloquent in words, phrases, and clauses, is nothing but a hoax, and that not only does it not contain even a semblance of the embryo of an Islamic state, but its provisions particularly those relating to fundamental rights, are directly opposed to the principles of an Islamic state.'

The court examined the definition of an Islamic state 'of which everybody talks but nobody thinks.'[57] Most of the *ulema* recalled the form of government which prevailed between AD 632-61, a period of less than thirty years, and relied on the verses of the Qur'an and *Hadith* (sayings of the prophet) to explain their concept of an Islamic state. The court stated categorically that 'accordingly to modern law of evidence, including our own, the *Ahadith* are inadmissable of *Sunnah* because each one of them contains some links of hearsay, but as authority on law, they are admissable *pro prio vigore*.'[58] The *ulema* emphasized:

...that Islam is the official religion revealed by God, complete and exhaustive in all respects, and that God will not abrogate, detract from, or add to this religion (*din*) any more than He will send a fresh messenger. The *din* having been perfected (Sura V, verse 3) there remains no need for any new code repealing, modifying, or amplifying the original code; or for any fresh messenger or message.[59]

The *ulema* conceded the principle of consultation and consensus *Ijma*. The authority of *Ijma* rests on the belief in divine protection and is based on the prophet's tradition 'my people will never agree in error'. But the court noted the *Ijma* represented the agreement of the *ulema* who by virtue of knowledge could claim the right to form a judgement of their own, and consultation with the people, or securing their agreement to any position, was expressly excluded from the process. The court concluded 'indeed if the legislature is a sort of *Ijma* the masses are expressly disqualified from taking part in it.'[60] The legislature in its present sense was unknown to the Islamic system: 'The law had been made and was not to be made. The only function of those entrusted with the administration of law being to *discover* [emphasis added] the law for the purposes of the particular case, although when enunciated and applied it formed a precedent for others to follow.'[61]

The enquiry report conclusively demonstrated that the *ulema* did not have an agreed answer to any of the fundamental questions like the rights and status of a citizen, the role of the people in the political process, nor indeed did they have any clear understanding of the concepts of sovereignty or state. The court acknowledged the agitational prowess of the *ulema* and conceded 'that provided you can persuade the masses to believe that something they are asked to do is religiously right or enjoined by religion, you can set them to any course of action regardless of all considerations of discipline, loyalty, decency, morality, or civic sense.'[62] The court concluded that, 'If democracy means the subordination of law and order to political needs—then Allah knoweth best and we end the report'![63]

The performance of the *ulema* before the court of enquiry eroded their credibility as exponents of Islam and exposed the hollowness of their claim to exclusive knowledge of the Qur'an and Sunnah. For a while, at least, they were driven to the margins of political life where they took to wheeling and dealing without any loss of zest. That was the real reason why they acclaimed the 1956 Constitution as Islamic.

The end game

The period 1957-1958 was one of suspense. The Federal Government had no political base or legitimacy and the provincial governments were in limbo. The legislative Assemblies had degenerated into theatres of factional fights. Like a latter day Oliver Cromwell, President Iskander Mirza was looking for some pretext to banish the noisy rabble and proclaim, 'What shall we do with his bauble? Take it away.'

Mirza had waited for a long time to pull down the curtain on the democratic pantomime and assume direct control of the affairs of the country. What he did not know was that General Ayub Khan too was waiting in the wings.[64]

NOTES

1. Nicholas Mansergh, Vol.VII, op. cit., p. 387.
2. Ibid.
3. Ibid., p. 304.
4. Ibid.
5. Chaudhri Muhammad Ali, *The Emergence of Pakistan*, Nafees Printers, Lahore, 1973, p. 57.
6. Nicholas Mansergh, Vol. VII, op. cit., p. 614.
7. Ibid., pp. 679-82.
8. Ibid., p. 855.
9. Ibid., p. 654.
10. Ibid.
11. Ibid., p. 731.
12. Ibid., pp. 954-5.
13. Ibid., Vol. VIII, pp. 25-31. Maulana Abul Kalam Azad who, as President of the Indian National Congress, had given full support to the Mission's plan found Nehru's statement 'astonishing'. About Jinnah's reaction Azad said: 'Jawaharlal's statement came to him as a bombshell'. *See*, Azad, *India Wins Freedom*, Sangam Books, London, 1968, pp. 164-5.

14. Ibid., Vol. VII, pp. 138-9.
15. Ibid., p. 313.
16. Ibid., Nehru's Press Conference in Bombay on 10 July, p. 67.
17. Penderel Moon(Editor),*Wavell: The Viceroy's Journal;* Oxford University Press, 1974, p. 496.
18. Chaudhri Muhammad Ali, op. cit. p. 98.
19. Parliamentary Debates, House of Commons, 1946-7, Vol. CDXXXIV, Cols. 503-5.
20. Maulana Abul Kalam Azad, *India Wins Freedom,* Orient Longmans, 1959. p. 190.
21. Chaudhri Mohammad Ali, op. cit., p. 98.
22. Carlyle, *A History of Medieveal Political Theory in the West* (1950), p. 133, cited by Arthur Larson in *Sovereignty within the Law,* Dobbs Ferry, New York, 1865, p. 24.
23. Ayub Khan, op. cit., p. 54.
24. Chaudhri Muhammad Ali, op. cit., p. 379.
25. Ibid., p. 372; 'As public support for the idea of Pakistan gathered strength, Muslim politicians who were in training under the British in the art of contesting elections and in capturing such crumbs of power as the British allowed to fall, turned more and more toward the Muslim League. They were shrewd and hard-headed men, capable of being infected temporarily by mass enthusiasm but never forgetful of their own advantage.'
26. This and the preceding quotations in this section are from Sharifuddin Pirzada, (Editor) *Foundations of Pakistan,* Vol. II, National Publishing House, Karachi, 1970, pp. 505-33.
27. *Jinnah Speeches,* Sang-e-Meel Publications, Lahore, 1989, p. 14.
28. G.W. Choudhury, (Editor) *Documents and Speeches on the Constitution of Pakistan,* Green Book House, Dhaka, 1967, pp. 23-4.
29. Abul A'la Maududi, *The Islamic Law and Constitution,* Islamic Publications, Lahore, 1955, pp. 320-5. They were probably recalling Winston Churchill's description of the Soviet Union.
30. Ibid., pp. 327-51.
31. *Dawn,* Karachi, 16 September 1954.
32. Ibid., 22 September 1954.
33. M.A. Chaudhri, *Government and Politics in Pakistan,* Puthighar Ltd., Dhaka, 1968, pp. 168-9.
34. *Dawn,* 15 October 1954.
35. Ibid.
36. *Dawn,* 25 October 1954.
37. Ibid.
38. Ayub Khan op, cit., p. 52.
39. *Dawn,* 25 October 1954.
40. Ibid., 27 October 1954.
41. Ibid., editorial: 'After the Fourth Night of Crisis'.
42. Ayub Khan, op. cit., p. 53.
43. *Dawn,* 31 October 1954.
44. Ibid.
45. Ibid.
46. Choudhri Muhammad Ali, op. cit., p. 367.
47. Ibid.
48. Section 92-A was added by the Pakistan Constituent Assembly giving the Provincial Governors the power to dissolve the Assembly.

49. Choudhri Muhammad Ali, op. cit., p. 368.
50. The West Pakistan (Establishment) Order 1955, G.G.O. No. 4, 27 March 1955. Basic Constitutional Documents, Printing Corporation of Pakistan Press, Islamabad, 1979.
51. Inamur Rehman, *Public Opinion and Political Development in Pakistan,* Oxford University Press, Lahore 1982, pp. 66-7.
52. Justice (Retd.) Masud Ahmad, *Pakistan - A Study of its Constitutional History (1957-1975),* Research Society of Pakistan, Lahore, 1978, pp. 235-67.
53. Sir Ivor Jennings, *Constitutional Problems in Pakistan,* Cambridge University Press, 1957, pp. 259-349 (PLD 1955 F.C. 240).
54. Governor-General's Reference No.1 of 1955 (PLD 1955 F.C. 435).
55. K.K. Aziz, *Party Politics in Pakistan,* National Commission on Historical and Cultural Research, Islamabad, 1976, pp. 150-1.
56. *Report of the Court of Enquiry into Punjab Disturbances of 1953,* Government Printing Press, Lahore, 1954, pp. 205, 218.
57. Ibid., p. 203.
58. Ibid., p. 207.
59. Ibid., p. 208.
60. Ibid., p. 210.
61. Ibid., p. 211.
62. Ibid., p. 231.
63. Ibid., p. 387.
64. Evidence is now available that Mirza had been planning to abrogate the Constitution and impose martial law since the middle of 1957. He was dissuaded by the US Secretary of State John Foster Dulles who sent the following message to the American Ambassador in Karachi:

Embtel 3052. Department shares Embassy's concern over indication Mirza continuing consider some form authoritarian rule as solution present unsatisfactory situation. However Department reluctant take any action which could be construed as interference in internal political affairs Pakistan and thus would prefer at present not make suggested presentation to Mirza. Appreciate Embassy continuing follow situation closely and reporting fully.

Dulles Department of State 790.00/5-957 dated 23/5/57.

CHAPTER 2

Man on Horseback

By the end of 1957 the politicians in Pakistan had played out all the possible combinations and permutations—some fifty individuals forming and reforming the government only to keep themselves in power. Despite all their public professions and protestations they had no intention of exposing themselves to the uncertainties and perils of a general election. They knew too well that people would reject them the moment they got an opportunity.

Iskander Mirza had tightened his grip over the administration. Ayub Khan, Commander-in-Chief of the Army, whose term of office had been renewed for four years in 1955, was looking for another extension. Mirza recognized that Ayub, more than anybody else, had been responsible for securing American military aid and had come to the assistance of the civil government in some extremely difficult moments. He relied on Ayub, as much as Ayub relied on him, for continuing support.

Ayub Khan's ambition was to build a powerful Muslim army. It was his belief that Muslim power in India had declined because the Mughals failed to build a powerful military force under a central command in India. After appointment as Commander-in-Chief in 1951 Ayub Khan devoted himself to the task of organizing the Pakistan Army. He came in contact with senior American military and intelligence officers and it was largely through his efforts that the US gave a firm commitment in 1954 to provide substantial military assistance to Pakistan.

While General Ayub Khan remained in the background, Iskander Mirza came to dominate the political scene. He was a member of the Indian Political Service under the British and had served mostly in the North West Frontier Province. As noted earlier, Ghulam Muhammad appointed Iskander Mirza as Home Minister and Ayub Khan as Minister of Defence in 1954. After a brief stint as Governor of East Bengal Iskander Mirza returned to the Federal Cabinet as Home Minister. He dominated the proceedings of the Cabinet and became Governor-General in 1955.

Ayub wins American support for the *coup*

Mirza and Ayub Khan were not in a commanding position. Mirza held Ayub Khan in high esteem and warmly commended his contribution as Commander-in-Chief of the Army. Mirza knew that it was Ayub Khan who had persuaded the US government to assume a long-term commitment of military aid to Pakistan and had been responsible for getting Pakistan into the regional alliances which the US government had sponsored: the Central Treaty Organization (CENTO—known as the Baghdad Pact) and the South East Asia Treaty Organization (SEATO).

Mirza openly ridiculed the idea of elections: angels won't be flying out of the ballot-box, he would say to anyone who brought up the question of elections. The same politicians who had brought the country to ruin would return to exploit the people. He made no secret of his contempt for the Constitution and the political process; for him these were luxuries that Pakistan could ill afford.

Mirza's problem was to convince the Americans that Pakistan was not yet ready for the parliamentary system of government. An army take-over was still a novelty in developing countries. He left it to Ayub Khan to impress upon the Americans that if general elections were held in Pakistan the socialists would grab power and frustrate the American plan of building Pakistan into a bulwark against communism. In April 1958 Mirza deputed Syed Amjad Ali, who was Finance Minister in the last civilian Cabinet, to assist Ayub Khan in this task and to keep him informed of developments.

The American attitude towards Pakistan had undergone a change since 1956. A powerful group within the US administration was suggesting that Pakistan was becoming a demanding ally. For them India was a better bet which could be projected as a model democracy in Asia to stem the tide of communism and contain the influence of the Soviet Union and the People's Republic of China. Naturally, the growing understanding between the United States and India was beginning to cause great concern in Pakistan. The Indian attitude, too, was hardening toward Pakistan. The Indians had warned that the canal waters from the five rivers of undivided Punjab (Indus, Jhelum, Ravi, Chenab and Beas whose sources were under Indian control) would be diverted for Indian use after 1962. In the Pakistan National Assembly the US-Pakistan alliance now came under severe attack. The Prime Minister, Malik Firoz Khan Noon, made a passionate speech in Parliament on 8 March 1958 in which he declared that, faced with the threat from India, Pakistan would delink itself from its alliance with the Americans: 'Our people, if they find their freedom threatened by Bharat, will break all pacts and shake hands with people whom we have made enemies because of others. Let there be no mistake about it.'[1] The Prime Minister's statement was widely acclaimed by all sections of the people which came as a great surprise to the Americans.

The Americans were disturbed by the growing criticism in Pakistan of US policy toward India. The US Ambassador, Horace A. Hildreth, had persuaded the State Department and the Pentagon that a highly competent pro-western group was in command in Pakistan and the United States could rely on that group to maintain a positive and friendly attitude towards it and to keep Pakistan stable. Among this group the Americans counted Ghulam Muhammad, Iskander Mirza, Ayub Khan, Mohammad Ali Bogra, Chaudhri Muhammad Ali and Syed Amjad Ali. By the end of 1956 two of the three Alis were out and Ghulam Muhammad was dead. So the membership of the group had dwindled to three, of whom two were connected with the armed forces and the third, Syed Amjad Ali, was a genial and pliable representative of big business who relied on his brother Syed Wajid Ali, a prominent Punjabi businessman and a close confidant of Mirza.

In 1957 the Americans persuaded General Mirza to admit H.S. Suhrawardy to the ruling group. Suhrawardy was Chief Minister of Bengal in 1946 and had decided to stay on in India after Independence. When he came to Pakistan in 1948 he was treated with great suspicion by the Government, but because of his popularity in East Bengal he soon built a large following. He became Law Minister in the Central government in 1954 and this gave him an opportunity to build a base in West Pakistan. By 1956 he had established close and friendly contacts with British and American diplomats in Pakistan. In September 1956 Suhrawardy was appointed Prime Minister and became the most articulate supporter of the Pakistan-American Alliance.[2]

Suhrawardy did not last long as Prime Minister. It was unfortunate that a man of his calibre, who was quite a popular figure and a democrat by temperament, failed to realize that general elections were what the people wanted more than anything else and offered the only way to ensure the continuation of civilian rule in the country.

It was under these circumstances that Ayub's visit to the United States in April 1958 to secure military aid on a long-term basis assumed critical importance. He had to assure the US that Pakistan's security and stability depended on its defence forces. He had also to persuade the Americans that while democracy might be the ideal to which Pakistan must aspire, elections in the prevailing political climate would not necessarily be the best means of achieving that end. Ayub and Syed Amjad Ali succeeded in convincing the Americans that Pakistan would be destabilized if left-wing politicians came to power through election. The Americans were told that time was of the essence: the politicians were conspiring to hold the election in February 1959 and a large number of persons with dubious antecedents and socialist leanings would get themselves elected by exploiting the electoral procedures and rigging the polls.

Ayub Khan went to New York on 27 April where he had a discussion with Prince Aly Khan, Pakistan's Permanent Representative to the United Nations. Ayub learnt that the US government was becoming lukewarm about the regional defence pacts, CENTO and SEATO, though they continued to support the North Atlantic Treaty Organization (NATO). Ayub concluded that 'the cold war will in future be fought more in the realm of economics and psychological infiltration.'[3] He felt that:

> Americans have obviously decided to support India economically, despite considerable opposition in the country, to present India as a show-piece of development under a democratic set up and thus stop the spread of communism in South Asia. This change of policy should be a matter of great concern to us as India will gradually get stronger and become a bigger menace and greater threat. As long as this policy is operative I do not foresee India coming to any settlement with us over Kashmir or even the division of waters in West Pakistan.

The following day Ayub had a meeting with Allen Dulles, the Director of US Central Intelligence Agency, and recorded in his diary:

> Allen Dulles happens to be an old friend of mine. I particularly wanted to see him in the early round of my tour as obtaining his support for our point of view and getting him to work on his brother [John Forster Dulles, US Secretary of State] can be of decisive effect. During the interview I told him all thinking people in Pakistan were worried because Indian attitude on Kashmir had hardened to the extent of flouting world opinion [expressed] through the UN and India was now openly threatening to cut off the waters in the canals between Sutlej and Ravi in 1962.

Ayub told Allen Dulles that most people in Pakistan were attributing Indian stubbornness to the recently promised American aid and this was weakening the hands of the 'friends' of America who were in control in Pakistan. This would become an election issue and may well result in the victory of a majority of politicians hostile to the United States. The answer was to make American aid to India contingent on an equitable settlement of the Kashmir dispute and a fair distribution of Indus Basin Waters.

Ayub Khan and Syed Amjad Ali had a meeting with William M. Rowntree, Assistant Secretary of State, on 29 April 1958. The meeting was attended by the former Prime Minister, Mohammad Ali Bogra, who had become Pakistan's Ambassador to the United States; Rufus Burr Smith, Officer-in-Charge, Economic Affairs; and Garrett H. Soulen, Officer-in-Charge, Pakistan-Afghanistan

Affairs. The minutes of the meeting were recorded by Mohammad Ali Bogra.[4]

Ayub, having lobbied Allen Dulles, left the talking to Syed Amjad Ali who argued that American economic aid to India had enabled her to divert her own resources to large scale purchases of armament. Many prominent politicians were attacking the government for its foreign policy and

> ...a definite ground swell was developing against alliances which, the people felt, were not taking Pakistan anywhere. If this tendency continued it will turn into a turbulence and would affect the next elections. It would weaken the hands of the present leaders in Pakistan because the supporters of the present foreign policy were definitely finding themselves on a sticky wicket.

Amjad Ali identified three elements which were definitely hostile to the alliances; the Bhashani Group in East Pakistan, Ghaffar Khan and his 'Red-shirters' in West Pakistan and the entire Hindu population of the country. William Rowntree appreciated the free and frank manner in which the Finance Minister had presented Pakistan's problems. He said that he would not deny the surprise and disappointment of his government over the statement made by the Prime Minister of Pakistan in the National Assembly on 8 March 1958. The most disquieting aspect of the statement was the widespread acclaim it received in Pakistan. He realized that the policy of every government must be based on self-interest, but sometimes enlightened self-interest was more important. One had also to consider whether transitory interests should take precedence over more permanent ones. Pakistan had joined the Baghdad Pact and SEATO for self-defence and collective security and this had been warmly welcomed in the United States. Any weakening of Pakistan's determination to adhere to these pacts would be regretted by the United States. Rowntree assured the Finance Minister that there was no weakening in his government's desire to support Pakistan and he would find in the United States the same sympathetic consideration of Pakistan's problems as before. Rowntree pointed out that American economic assistance to Pakistan far exceeded what was being given to India given the proportions of the two countries. He added, 'Even if India and Pakistan were on the best of terms India would nevertheless be carrying out the military programme which she has undertaken and would build up a sizeable organization in order to counter any threat which China might pose against her.'[5]

Ayub Khan, Amjad Ali, and Mohammad Ali Bogra called on John Foster Dulles on 30 April 1958 at 12 o'clock. Also present on the occasion were William M. Rowntee and Frederick P. Bartlett, Deputy Assistant Secretary of State. They went over the same ground and tried to convince the Secretary of State that American aid to India was weakening the position of the government of Pakistan which was firmly committed to regional alliances. Dulles said he was impressed with the sincerity of Pakistan's leaders in their attempt to resolve disputes with India and their determination to follow a policy based on high principles. He felt that well-informed people in Pakistan should know that the US was friendly and loyal to Pakistan 'in a sense totally different to the United States' relationship with India'. The US respected India and her large population, her cultural influence in the world, as in the case of China, and, therefore, the relationship was on an intellectual level 'compared to the relationship with Pakistan which was more from the heart'. Dulles said that what was being done for India hurt the Americans more than it hurt Pakistan because it was their money. They would rather give it to Pakistan but they were forced to help India because it was part of their overall plan, because they had to see the world as a whole. The aid that US was giving to the 'neutralist' countries was actuated by a conviction that it was in the ultimate interest of the 'free world' including Pakistan and the whole of Asia.

Dulles promised to 'try to influence India as tactfully and diplomatically as possible' and indicated that the whole situation regarding assistance to India may be reviewed. Ayub Khan said Pakistan was tied to the United States by definite commitments and, therefore, Pakistan would stand by her friends and allies, whereas India was under no commitment and could adopt a free-wheeling policy and choose sides as and when it suited her.

Later that day Ayub Khan informed President Mirza and Prime Minister Noon (Cable No. C-218, 30 April 1958) that the Pentagon had agreed to supply twenty B-57 light bombers in 1959 and might supply some aircraft in advance for training purposes. He mentioned that Air Marshal Asghar Khan, Commander-in-Chief of the Pakistan Air Force, was 'not all that pleased as he would like to have B-66.' Ayub promised to persuade the Americans to reconsider their decision but he advised that if the Americans did not change their mind 'it will be unwise to refuse these aircraft'. He also mentioned in the cable his meeting with Allen Dulles who had 'promised to do what he could to influence his brother.'

Ayub Khan also reported to Mirza the results of his meeting with John Foster Dulles (Cable C-224, 1 May 1958). He said the Indians had:

> ...very cleverly convinced top-ranking Americans that their military build up is [directed] towards checkmating China. This is a palpable lie but somehow the Americans believe it to be true. I told Mr Dulles that I am amazed at their ignorance and gullibility when the best part of the Indian Army is either concentrated along the Pakistan border or is within ten days' call of the border. I think he was impressed with this argument.

On 1 May 1958 Ayub Khan joined General Nathan Twining and General Omar Bradley (former Chairman, Joint Chiefs of Staff) for a game of golf at the Burning Tree Golf Course. General Twining mentioned that he was puzzled by the State Department's policy towards India and felt 'there were still far too many communists in the State Department'. Twining told Ayub Khan that he had arranged a lunch for him on 5 May with all the service chiefs to enable him to talk to them informally about Pakistan's problems saying, 'I would like you to be as frank and forthright as possible.'

Ayub Khan received instructions from the government that failing a firm promise for B-66 bombers he should accept twenty B-57 light bombers but he must 'continue to press strenuously for B-66 which could ultimately replace B-57 and make up full strength of promised bombers'.

Ayub Khan met the US service chiefs at lunch on 5 May. Among other things he talked about the need for providing 'family accommodation in Kharian, issue of more M-47 tanks, issue of APCs (Armoured Personnel Carriers), issue of light aircraft to carry small parties to operate in and around the battle zone'. He did not ask for an immediate decision because 'the general trend in America seems to be to cut down aid commitments as much as possible.' At the end of the lunch he had the feeling that the Americans 'were sympathetic to [Pakistan's] requirements and will do what they can to support our demands.'

During the lunch Ayub Khan mentioned that 'the present aid only gives [Pakistan] an army that will have to be kept in Pakistan for its own defence, but if given further assistance to organize an army corps or so we can certainly provide an expeditionary force either in Iran or elsewhere in the Middle East.'

In the evening Ayub went to see Allen Dulles again to thank him for putting his brother in the picture. Allen Dulles assured him that he 'will do all he can on Pakistan's behalf'.

The following day, 6 May, Ayub Khan addressed the House Foreign Affairs Committee. Some eight members turned up and listened to him 'with rapt attention'. Ayub analysed the causes of trouble in the Middle East and advocated the need for strengthening the armed forces of Baghdad Pact countries, in particular the Pakistan Army. He argued against the United States giving any aid to India without first obtaining a guarantee of good behaviour and an undertaking from her to solve her disputes with Pakistan in a peaceful manner. He dismissed the suggestion that India faced any threat from China and noted in his diary: 'They asked me very searching questions. For instance, they questioned the recent statement of the Prime Minister and also stated that we looked like wanting military strength more against India than against communism. These doubts were satisfactorily removed.'

Later that night Ayub Khan flew to El Paso, Texas (Fort Bliss) and

…saw anti-aircraft guided missile demonstration. It was very impressive. It was obvious that anti-aircraft artillery is no longer of any use. The correct answer is to have these missiles which are 100 per cent effective against anything that flies in the air at any speed. We shall continue to agitate with the Americans to give us some of these, failing which we may even have to buy them out of our own resources.

On 8 May Ayub went to New York where he met Henry Cabot Lodge, US Representative at the United Nations, whom he considered 'the man mainly responsible for swinging America in favour of aid to India. I had a long discussion with him. I think at the end he felt very doubtful of the wisdom of his recommendations to his government.'

Ayub Khan informed (Cable 89: 8 May 1958) Mirza and Noon: 'As no other suitable aircraft available finally decided to accept B-57. They will be twenty-four in all. Four to six to be delivered in 1959, and the balance in 1960. It will take the Air Force that long to be ready to handle them. Asghar Khan agrees. American authorities anxious that this matter be kept secret.'

Ayub Khan left New York on 9 May and returned to Karachi on 18 May. On his way back he went to the Hague to see Begum Liaquat Ali Khan, Pakistan's Ambassador to the Netherlands:

Thought she might still be sulking about the manner in which enquiry in her husband's murder was carried out. Was glad to find that she had got over that and seemed relaxed. She was, however, very worried about the political situation in the country. Thought that only solution was tight rule in the country for about ten years.

He also went to Brussels to see the World Fair for a couple of hours.

The Russians were showing all sorts of machinery including Sputniks to convince the people how they were catching up with America. It is obvious that they are making tremendous strides in the technical field and will be second to none in a few years. They may not have freedom, but they have the element of greatness in them.

Back in Pakistan Ayub Khan felt reasonably pleased with the results of his mission. He told Mirza that the Americans may not review their programme of aid to India but they had understood the risks involved in pushing Pakistan toward the uncharted ocean of general elections in the hope of consolidating the democratic process in the country. With a major hurdle thus removed, Mirza found the path clear to swing his plan into action.

Ayub Khan left Karachi by train for Rawalpindi on 20 May. He stopped at Jhelum to see General Azam: 'He mentioned to me something about a rumour emanating from Abbottabad that General Umrao Khan and Brigadier Effendi had been arrested. I just laughed it off as being absurd and in any case if there was any truth in it the Chief of Staff, whom I rang up from Karachi, would have mentioned it to me.'

Ayub reached home and was sitting with his wife and children,

> …when a young sapper officer of 1 Armoured Division staff rang up to say that it was vital that he sees me at once. I thought it was some complaint about his promotion etc. However, when he came he looked out of breath and said that he had heard a terrible thing that I was arrested for having written something to a foreign power. I told him that there was no truth in it and he had no cause to worry. He said: Sir, if need be he and many others like him would be prepared to give their lives for me.

Ayub's wife too had heard some rumours but did not want to bother her husband. According to the version that reached her, Ayub, Yahya, Musa and some other generals were suspected of being Indian spies and Ayub had gone to America to collect his cheque from Nehru's agents. Ayub was furious as the entry of 21 May in his diary shows:

> It then dawned on me the extent some people in this country were prepared to go to for their selfish ends or out of sheer jealousy. They probably know what I have done for this country and the army but little realize that by showing malice to me in this manner they will cause this army to be rendered ineffective, and once that happens, the country would go back to Hindu or communist slavery in no time. Further, I was astounded at the credulity of our people. They seem to be prepared to swallow anything even against their greatest benefactor.[6] This surely is the sign of a people who are still in a state of decay and immaturity. I am an optimist by nature and I can stand a lot but this incident really shook my confidence in the future of this country. What if we were engaged in war and things started going badly and the enemy

started such rumours about the army in the back areas? The result would be disastrous. We would lose the war without firing a shot. It seems to me that there is a great need for character-building in this country.

The next day Ayub talked to General Musa about the rumour: 'He told me that these rumours came to his notice some time ago. On enquiries it transpired they had been started by some disgruntled politicians.' Ayub's reaction was,

The elections, of course, are coming near. The politicians have worked themselves into a state of hydrophobia, especially the dismissed ones. They are dying to get back into power by hook or crook. And having got there they know they will have nothing to show for themselves except further disrupting the country. In which case they will come face to face with me and the army. Hence I am regarded by them as Enemy Number 1 for doing my duty and trying to save the country. Their conscience is so deadened that in order to obtain a monetary gain, they will not even stop at destroying this army, the only shield they have. I am one of those who had saved democracy so far, as I believed that there is nothing like it if we can at all work the system. For instance, I refused to take over the country when offered by the late Mr Ghulam Muhammad on several occasions. Then I had hopes that some amongst the politicians might show patriotism, selflessness and the urge to get the country moving. But having tested them all, I am now certain that if left to them the country has nothing to expect except ruination. How else can it be when you do not have the corrective of public opinion and when eighty-five per cent our people are illiterate? It seems that we shall have to have a system of government for a generation or so which prepares the country for democracy and lays the foundation for the solution of our major problems like excessive population, education, judicial system, land reforms and a host of other things. Under the present Constitution no one seems to have any power except to destroy discipline and do harm, how can even an attempt be made to begin to resolve these problems. Under it the politician is jolly lucky if he can hang on to his seat, let alone do any good. Even if he wants to do any good, his supporters, demanding all sorts of selfish things, would ensure that he is not allowed to do any good and behave justly.

Meanwhile, certain actions have been put into operation to counter these rumours. These measures are proving effective. We shall continue with them. I was surprised that no counter action was taken before I returned. The people concerned at GHQ seem to have been paralysed until I pushed them. They seem to be very good when I am around but something happens to them in my absence.

These rumours finally convinced Ayub that the parliamentary system must be scrapped and the people given a strong dose of discipline. Who started these rumours was never discovered. The astonishing thing was that nobody in the Prime Minister's office or the President's Secretariat appeared to have heard of these rumours. Nor was there any such hint in the newspapers, some of which thrived on the most sordid kind of gossip. The possibility cannot be ruled out that these rumours, which remained restricted to a few army centres, were planted by military intelligence to help Ayub Khan make up his mind.

Once Ayub's mind was made up he proceeded to mobilize his constituency. On 27 May he called all the station officers and talked to them about his trip to the United States. He first told them how he had tried to alert the Americans about the danger of giving military and economic assistance to India, and then turned to the situation at home. What was going on in the political field, Ayub said, amounted to an attack 'on the country's existence'. He identified two threats: the Indians and the Communists. The Indian aim was expansion and domination and Pakistan's aim must be to 'attain a measure of co-existence with India'. This depends on having the capability to neutralize the Indian Army. Pakistan must have a deterrent force to fight a 'short sharp war' and for this reason American assistance was of fundamental importance. The Indians had isolated Pakistan in the Muslim world and the British too had not been particularly friendly. An important element in Pakistan's strategy was to recognize that the defence of East Pakistan lay in West Pakistan and that Pakistan's army must be 'a selective army', highly trained and professional. Pakistan must devise original tactical doctrines and techniques to develop a force 'capable of inflicting crippling damage to the enemy'. All this required internal stability which had been seriously undermined by the politicians. The point was not lost on young officers whose sole duty and ambition was to be prepared to repel any threat to the country's security.

Ayub Khan participated in a conference on 1 June presided over by Prime Minister Noon and wrote in his diary:

There were three other ex-prime ministers. They could have collected two more if they had waited a bit longer. I thought the setting was made to enable them to score off points against each other, but instead they listened to me intently and with understanding. They asked me what we should do about Kashmir and the threat of canal waters by India. Emotionally, of course, the answer is to go for the Hindu right away, but wisdom dictates a different course which I explained and which is indicated in my talk to the officers at Rawalpindi on 27 May. Prime Minister Noon offered me extension of my tenure. He started talking about consulting other senior officers in the army which I thought would be fatal for the discipline of the army. I told him that I was not fishing for a job but for the stability of the army it was imperative that the decision about the future Commander-in-Chief must be made. Noon is a nice man, means the country well, but he is very impetuous, lacking in ability and has no guts. He has a very bad memory, can't read anything. So, it is very difficult to do any serious business of life with him. But I am used to dealing with a galaxy of morons starting from Khwaja Nazimuddin downwards.

A few days later Ayub called the corps commanders and the divisional commanders 'nearer at hand' to discuss the origin of the rumours and the method to combat them. The minutes of the conference show how army officers at different levels were being put in a state of alert by their Commander-in-Chief:

Due to the coming general elections the tempo of political activity naturally has increased in the country. In this process some politicians have lost their balance completely and are stopping at nothing to gain power by means fair and foul. So far the army was kept out of politics but not so this time as the hyper-ambitious politicians know it that as they can only come into power and retain it through disruption, the army will at once come in their way. Attempts are, therefore, being made to malign the senior army officers in the eyes of the juniors so that they are isolated, and by that contrivance the army rendered ineffective in saving the country from their ravages. So the army in general and the Commander-in-Chief in particular is Enemy No.1 in their eyes. The object being to disrupt the army by elimination of the C.-in-C. In order to gain this end they have carefully analysed the weaknesses of this army and have tried to further their ends by playing on them. The following are some of the weaknesses that they have tried to exploit:-
(a) Use the disgruntled elements in and outside the army; whisper into the ears of their associates in the army and by and large tell a saucy story through subtle means to the soldier who, being honest, is naturally unwary and gullible.

(b) Unfortunately some of us are still influenced by provincialism, class and sectarian distinctions. These, too, have been subtly exploited. While the C.-in-C. was still in the United States trying to arrange the supply of aircraft under the MDAP, a fantastic rumour was started in Abbottabad saying that he was recalled and arrested at Karachi because he [C.-in-C.], in league with the GOC 14 Div [Maj-Gen. Umrao Khan] had accepted rupees two crore from the Indian Government in return for the withdrawal of troops from the Surma River disputed area. This rumour became widespread in different versions but the main theme remained the same e.g. serious allegations of anti-state activities against high ranking army officers.

The above four entries in Ayub Khan's diary (21 May, 22 May, 1 June, 6 June) show the working of Ayub's mind during this period. His claim that Ghulam Mohammad invited him to take over the government in 1954 rests on his own statement. But Ayub, a man of great prudence and patience, was not given to boasting. One should accept his statement that he declined the invitation because he still hoped that some 'patriotic politician might yet come to rescue the country'. Another reason could be that Ayub, unsure of public reaction, wanted to wait for the right moment to strike. To some of his generals he might have given the impression that he was dithering—waiting and wavering—while the country was going to the dogs. There was no doubt that the more vocal classes were thoroughly disenchanted with the performance of successive governments and were urging the army to come in and restore some semblance of order. Some of the politicians, too, were urging senior military officers to act. But Ayub Khan took his time to formulate his strategy. He also needed the government to extend his term of office because he had never considered staging a *coup d'etat* asking his troops to capture all the key buildings and packing off Mirza along with the rest of the political cabal. In Ayub's plan, Mirza would hold the stage while he would give him all the support. He had no doubt that the Constitution was not workable and would have to be abrogated but the job must be done by Mirza who must 'assume full responsibility for his decision'.[7] After all Mirza was the man 'who used the Constitution to promote political intrigue and bargaining'.[8] One of Ayub's problems was to keep Mirza propped up 'who was feeling insecure and had lost credit with the people'. Ayub would later recall that Mirza 'worked and thrived in an atmosphere of intrigue. He talked to me on several occasions those days and I could sense that he was feeling desperate and cornered. I would tell him that he would have to give a constructive lead if the country was to be saved'.[9]

By the middle of 1958 Ayub was fairly confident that there would be no public resistance to military intervention but he was not sure how the army, once it was drawn into politics, would extricate itself from the situation. It took Ayub quite some time to abandon the army tradition of 'complete subordination to civil authority'. To plunge the army into politics was 'like exposing my own child to unpredictable hazards'. What sustained him was the belief that the people 'seem to have blind faith in me'.[10]

Ayub, unlike Mirza, believed that 'there was nothing like the democratic system of government, if one knew how to work it'. But as he wrote in his diary on 22 May 1958, the democratic system cannot work 'when you do not have the corrective of public opinion and when eighty-five per cent of our people are illiterate'.[11] Ayub obviously believed literacy to be a vital ingredient of public opinion and it was this belief which strongly influenced his formulation of a new political system for the country and his attitude toward the Press.

The government finally decided to extend Ayub's tenure of service by another two years instead of the customary four. Ayub received a telegram from the Prime Minister on 9 June saying,

I am very glad that you have agreed to stay on as Commander-in-Chief of our armies for another two years. You are still very young, being fifty-one years of age, though very ripe in experience and ability. Pakistan at this juncture cannot afford to lose your services and I am confident that the defence [forces] of this country are safe in your hands as they have been in the past.

Ayub Khan replied:

Grateful for your message of appreciation and encouragement on my extension of tenure. Personally I would have been just as happy to retire as I would be in further serving this magnificent army, the building of which has been my

lifelong ambition. In any case I have eaten its salt for thirty-one years and
everything in me is due to it and belongs to it. So you can rest assured that
I shall continue to give my best to the army and through it to the country.

Ayub Khan then recorded his reactions:

In October '57 Mr Suhrawardy offered me a four-year extension but as he
was dismissed the next day it remained unannounced. Again, Mr Chundrigar
made a similar offer but he, too, went. Noon kept on evading the issue. I think
he was influenced by his wife who had been got at by people like Sher Ali,
recently removed from the army. He was also resisting to show a sort of
defiance to the President. A stupid idea subsists in the politician's mind that
I make or break 'Kings', little realizing that it is my duty as the head of the
army to carry out the lawful orders of a constituted authority, whoever it may
be. I can't help feeling sorry for the politician in giving me an extension, as
I am rather an uncomfortable bed-mate and I do not ask for favours. He would
rather do without me, but his trouble is that he cannot find a suitable
replacement yet. So, the situation is not without its comic side. However the
army should be, by and large, happy at this decision.

On 14 June Ayub Khan decided to go to Kaghan Valley for a
little rest. He 'spent the night at Shogran, a beautiful place with
lovely views. Went out for walks. Climbed about 1,200 feet one
afternoon. Took it very easy as it was my first day out on heights.'
The next day Ayub reached Naran and stayed there for four days.
He was accompanied by General Azam:

Did some fishing, but spent most of the time reading *The Men who Ruled
India* by an ex-ICS officer, Philip Woodruff.[12] I found it fascinating. Some of
the problems early Britishers had to solve were not dissimilar to what we
have to face today, except that they had a much freer hand in dealing with
them. Today our administrator is hamstrung and neutralized by the politicians.
They have killed his conscience, sense of justice and initiative by using him
for their ends.
Climbed to Lake Saif-ul-Muluk (12,000 feet high) one morning. It took me
two hours and fifteen minutes to climb 2,500 feet in four miles. It was the
stiffest thing I have known, but the art is to move on slowly. However, the
grandeur of the scenery was well worth the trouble. It was fascinating and I
could not take my eyes off it. I did the return journey in one hour and fifteen
minutes. It was the first time I had been with General Azam for any length
of time. He is very kind, affectionate, untiring and very loyal, thoroughly

patriotic but quite uneducated and limited. Also, it is very difficult to converse with him as half the time he does not hear what is said and then he has the habit of cutting one short and interrupting. So I found it rather trying to keep him amused.

On his return from Kaghan on 21 June Ayub Khan learnt that Azad Kashmir was in the grip of disorder because Chaudhri Ghulam Abbas was threatening to walk across the cease-fire line into Indian-held Kashmir along with a large band of supporters. His plan was to storm the Valley with 'freedom fighters' who would have full support of the oppressed people of Kashmir groaning under Indian tyranny. President Iskandar Mirza, who was resting in Nathiagali, was authorized by the government to discuss the matter with Abbas and recommend some course of action.

I found, to my utter horror, that he had recommended that no action be taken against Abbas and his people until they reached the cease-fire line. Then the army was to arrest them without any use of force. I at once rang up the President and the Defence Secretary protesting against this amateurish decision and demanded that if any action is to be taken, it should be taken by the civil authorities in Pakistan territory or Azad territory—the army only coming in support of civil power, if needed. A Cabinet meeting took place on this and I was told that my recommendations were accepted. The problem of my job is that not only do I have to run the army but I also have to keep a watch on so many other things concerning the security of the country. This would not be necessary if we had men of character and principle manning the government.

Ayub Khan went to see Mirza at Nathiagali where he also had a discussion with Nawab Muzaffar Ali Qizilbash, Chief Minister of West Pakistan, regarding the future of the border police.

There are some 58,000 men in East and West Pakistan worth about three divisions. My contention is that they should remain a civil force but officered by army officers like the Scouts so that they can be trained tactically. In that case they will give better service to the civil administration in time of peace and be available for use by the army in time of war. This is the obvious solution in the higher interest of the country but Qizilbash, having once agreed, had gone back on his promise. So, I had to be quite blunt with him and told him a few home truths. His worry is the disposal of some fifty or so police officers who will become surplus. So, to resolve this problem it was agreed that a committee consisting of the Defence Secretary, Chief Secretary and a representative of GHQ should go into this matter. Incidentally, I am having a similar problem with the East Pakistan government. However, I am determined to see that they do the right thing in the end. Pakistan cannot afford to lose the use of its manpower in time of war. In fact they may well prove to be a decisive factor.

Ayub was now spending a good deal of time reading books.

Lately I have been doing some interesting reading. Apart from *The Men who Ruled India,* I have read Gunther's *Inside Russia Today,* another fascinating book, and Captain Wynne's articles on *Pattern for Limited (Nuclear) War: the Riddle of the Schlieffen Plan* published in RUSI Journal. These articles have started our minds thinking and have led us to doubt our organizational concept and tactical doctrines. Certain ideas have emerged in mine and my associates' minds. I think very soon we shall be able to present something concrete which should be basic and of real value. I have to waste a lot of time in answering greeting messages on Eid days and other occasions but I do so not wanting to hurt people's feelings. Some of these messages are touching. They seem to have a blind faith in me. This makes me feel very humble and I pray to God to give me strength to come up to their expectations.

Ayub Khan attended a meeting at Government House, Lahore, on 4 July 1958. President Iskander Mirza, Prime Minister Noon, and the West Pakistan Chief Minister Qizilbash with his Cabinet colleagues were present. Ayub Khan wrote in his diary:

The Chief Minister called this meeting to get clarification over Abbas's move to cross the cease-fire line with volunteers, the mounting irresponsibility of the political parties to stir up trouble in the country to do down the government and increasing sectarian tension. I was interested in the decision about Abbas' move as that finally affected the army. It was decided that we should deal with Abbas more firmly and not allow him to create turmoil in the country.

Ayub Khan studied the planning papers of the Baghdad Pact with General Yahya, his Principal Staff Officer, on 8 and 9 July. The Baghdad Pact Planners had recommended nine divisions for Pakistan but the Americans had reduced them to six 'on spurious grounds'. Ayub Khan was anxious to get the original figure restored: 'The trouble is that the Americans are trying too hard to save their money. The fools don't realize that our strength one day will be of immense value to them.'

Ayub presided over a meeting of the Joint Chiefs of Staff on 13 July 1958:

Several important things came up for discussion. Admiral Choudhri raised the question of the concept of defence of Pakistan again over which the decision had already been given by the defence committee of the Cabinet, and he had agreed with the rest of us during the previous meetings. A heated discussion followed in which he continued to show stupidity and obstruction. The attached copy of my letter to the government explains the affair and my views of him. There is no doubt about it that this man is unworthy of his position.

Ayub's letter to the Defence Minister about Choudhri said:

I have to regretfully report to you that as long as Vice-Admiral H. M. S. Choudhri remains the Commander-in-Chief and a member of the Joint Chief's Committee, no tidy and speedy deliberations, planning and execution of inter-services nature is possible. He neither has the brain, imagination or depth of thought to understand such problems nor the vision and ability to make any contribution. Judging from his performance over a long period, I am surprised that the government should have first of all appointed him as the head of the Navy and then given him an extension for four years…. My belief is that as long as he stays where he is, not only no good can come out [of it] but a lot of harm would be done in the sphere of getting the country ready for war which is the function of the three services. I also firmly believe that such a joint services organization is vital, but full value cannot be obtained of it if power of command and control over the three services is not given to the headman, as it is done in Turkey. Temperamentally and otherwise we people are not built to run organizations composed of equals. In that case the organization for one thing just would not run but if it did, it would run at the pace of the weakest link amongst them as has been demonstrated in this case.

Ayub accompanied Iskander Mirza in the President's Viscount to Istanbul to participate in a conference of Baghdad Pact Heads of State on 14 July. They had a stop-over in Teheran where Ayub had a meeting with General Hedayat, Chief of Staff of the Iranian Armed Forces. During this meeting General Hedayat was called

out by a staff officer and told that news had come through from
their commander in Khanikin that a *coup d'etat* had taken place
in Iraq.

A Colonel, supported by pro-Nasser and Communist elements, had taken
over the country. Prince Abdul-Ala, the King's uncle, was murdered and his
body dragged through the streets of Baghdad. The palace was gutted and so
was the British Embassy. The crowds were jubilant and Nasser's photographs
were on display everywhere. The news about the fate of the King and Nuri-
el-Said were conflicting, but it looked as if Nuri had escaped, though his
house was burnt and the King was held as a prisoner. This was very serious
and sad news. With a heavy heart, we took off for Istanbul. As we were
approaching Istanbul, we were told to go back and land in Ankara. There we
were received by the President and Mr Menderes. The meeting was just like
a mourning. The Turks were very upset by the news from Baghdad. They
confirmed more or less what we had heard in Tehran. Their Ambassador in
Baghdad had a transmitter and kept them well-informed. But his reports were
also vague as he and his staff could not go out to check the details, there being
so much confusion in the city. Had dinner with President Bayar. It was a very
informal affair at which the Shah of Iran, our President [Mirza], the Turkish
Prime Minister, Menderes, and his Foreign Minister, Zorlu, were present. A
meeting was arranged after dinner in which the situation in Lebanon, Iraq and
the future of Baghdad Pact was discussed. The weak-kneed American policy
came in for a great deal of criticism. We dispersed at one a.m. deciding to
meet again tomorrow. There is no doubt about it that the Turks are most
anxious to help if they can find somebody who is prepared to resist in Iraq.
They think the King of Jordan might do that. I am still hoping that one of the
generals like Arif or Daghistani might put up a fight, though there are some
indications that they have been taken into custody. I was impressed with the
Shah's grasp of the situation and analysis. He seems to be very worried about
Arab hegemony, perhaps based on the experiences of their history during the
early period of Islam and Arab conquests. We, on our part, would welcome
such a hegemony if it was not brought about by Russia through Nasser.

The following day, that is, on 15 July 1958:

The three delegations met at the Presidential palace in Ankara at 1200 hours
in an atmosphere of gloom. A strong *démarche* was drafted urging the
Americans to honour the Eisenhower doctrine [The Americans were required
to come to the assistance of their allies in the 'free world' under this
Doctrine]. Later in the evening an American official of the State Department
told the Shah that 5,000 marines had landed at Beirut at 1515 hours. This

brought a ray of hope and everybody was happy. Later the American Chargé d'Affaires met Zorlu and asked the Turkish government for permission to land 60 aircraft carrying American troops from America through Germany at Aderna. Also they intend basing about 100 fighters and bombers at Aderna. The Turkish President and Prime Minister and the Foreign Minister went into a huddle for five minutes and agreed to give this permission. I can't picture such a decision taking less than weeks at Karachi! News came through that Nuri-el-Said was murdered and that his body was dragged about in Baghdad. This is the way these Arabs treat a man who had done so much for them! After dinner, the Shah took me aside and said, 'Have you any knowledge of the idea that I have in my mind?' I said I had heard that he was thinking of having a federation of Iran and Pakistan. He said the gainer in this case would be Pakistan as in a very few years Iran's oil revenues would rise to $1 billion a year and he would not know what to do with it. I said, I could help him spend it usefully. He said nowadays small countries don't count for much. A combination of Iran and Pakistan would, however, command respect. I forgot to mention that it would be a good thing to draw Afghanistan in too. The Shah said we could then barter East Pakistan for Kashmir. I said no, we shall retain East Pakistan and one day, Insha Allah, take Kashmir as well. He said what about your Constitution. I don't like it. I said nor do I. The damned thing would have to be sensibly altered, I said, but there is one thing we must recognize that except for the Shah there was nobody else in Iran who commands respect or had any calibre. So we have to federate in a manner that will cause the least possible friction and strain. He said yes we should run our two separate governments and federate on defence, foreign affairs and finance. He insisted that we must have one army. This is going to cause headaches but probably can be managed in some fashion. The Iranians may find it difficult to work up to our standard.

Ayub Khan returned to Pakistan on 30 July and gave the army officers an account of his visit to Turkey. The Shah of Iran had gone round the world and had invited heads of the four Muslim states in the Baghdad Pact to a meeting in Istanbul. He wanted to tell his friends about his discussions with the Americans and give his impressions of how the problems of the Middle East were seen in the different parts of the world. The Iraqis were keen on this meeting because they wanted the Lebanese situation to be discussed. According to Ayub's account:

The Lebanese situation was boiling, and a certain amount of fighting had gone on there. This was a source of great concern for the old regime of Iraq, considering the trouble was externally inspired. In Lebanon, the situation is abetted by Colonel Nasser, assisted by his secular [Radio] Voice of the Arabs, a powerful network consisting of talented people who are the most artful liars in the world. They have been fomenting trouble in the Middle East, especially in countries which do not line up behind Egypt. That undoubtedly and inevitably caused worry in the minds of rulers in Iraq, because they are the target of this subversion. The news of the *coup d'etat* in Baghdad came as a great shock. One would have expected General Daghistani, being the commander of a division, stationed about fifteen miles north of Baghdad and one of the brightest chaps in the Iraqi Army to react to the situation. The Iranian commander who had sent the first report of the *coup d'etat* to Tehran had shown commendable initiative and the Turks were particularly lucky to have a retired army general as their Ambassador in Baghdad, who sent information every half hour.

The Turks regarded the Russians as their eternal enemies. Their greatest obsession was being encircled by the communists. Nuri-el-Said and the King had no other aim in life but to make Iraq a secure and happy country. The Turkish leaders felt that the Iraqi high command had paid a high price for their membership of the Baghdad Pact. And frankly we all felt that if the Americans had not interfered in Suez Canal, the very root cause of this curse would have been eradicated. Doesn't matter what anybody does in Lebanon or Iraq or Syria the problem [of regional security] cannot be solved until you do something in Cairo and that is what the British wanted to do, but the Americans prevented them. From that point deterioration started and the sequence of events occurred.

The Shah of Iran was specially worried. His worry was that if the Arabs got together under the banner of communism, the next target would, undoubtedly, be Iran. I have talked to many Iranians and they say that the Arabs, some 1,300 years ago, at the time of early Islam, invaded their country. Apparently, the effect of that invasion is still felt by the Iranians. Arab hegemony is going to be dangerous for Iran, and that is another source of worry for them. From our point of view we would welcome the hegemony of the Arabs, and the stronger it is the better for us. But if this hegemony comes through communism, the whole of the Middle East, which is the heart of Islam, would come in the grip of communism. The Arabs say they gave us our religion. I say we are most thankful to them for giving us one religion, but we are afraid they are now going to give us another religion—communism. Arab nationalism is in a state of savagery and it is prepared to destroy itself in a most reckless manner. The pity is that none of the generals of the Iraqi Army had the courage to fight out the situation. Even with a couple of battalions, things could have been brought under control but apparently nobody reacted.

Jordan's King Hussein is a tough little chap but he could only be effective in Iraq if the Iraqis would accept his leadership. The Turkish leaders had approached the King but he had expressed his inability to act unless there was support for him in Iraq. Jordan would be the next target. Lebanon was in a very difficult situation despite the presence of American marines. So far as Saudi Arabia was concerned, King Saud had left 45 sons and Ibne Saud had got 25 sons and a number of close relatives. It will take a long time to kill all of them but Nasser had certainly succeeded in disturbing the whole area emotionally. The atrocities committed by the Arabs were alarming; I would have acted myself to take revenge on behalf of Pakistan's friends in Baghdad, but unfortunately one cannot indulge in private wars. The problems in the Middle East are fomented by the big powers. The whole of the Middle East is but an arena of politics among the major powers. The leaders of Iran, Turkey and Pakistan want the three countries to get closer but their co-operation would have meaning only if they are properly supported by America. It is unfortunate that a powerful lobby in America is in favour of disengagement. The Americans have two vital interests in the Middle East, the oil and the security of the region. They want to protect these two interests but there is great hesitancy and lack of resolution on their part to join the Baghdad Pact.

The Shah of Iran wants a confederation between Iran and Pakistan. He would provide financial support if Pakistan would agree to have one army for the Pakistan-Iran confederation. The Shah's aim is to get Pakistan to accept him as the King of the confederation. I gave the Shah no definite answer but it is clear that Pakistan must help Iran to strengthen its army and to prevent it from getting contaminated. The Baghdad Pact can function even if the Americans do not join the Pact provided it received adequate support. In the meantime, Pakistan, Turkey and Iran must work together. The situation in Iran was uncertain and if Iran fell the whole of Asia would go to the communists.

The *coup d'etat* in Iraq might have persuaded Mirza and Ayub to reconsider their plans of overthrowing the government, though Ayub's comments in his diary show how divorced he was from the real conditions and popular sentiments in the region. Ayub regarded Nasser as a menace and deeply regretted American intervention in the Suez crisis which had put Nasser in a commanding position in the region. Nasser had emerged as a popular hero and Arab rulers were seen as usurpers and despots. That was the reason the people of Baghdad acted in such a brutal manner when Nuri-el-Said was overthrown. The chaos that was unleashed in the streets of Baghdad after the popular revolt must have served as a warning that they must not take it for granted that there would be no public resistance to a military take-over in Pakistan.

Ayub's diary shows how he spent the whole of August watching military exercises at home. He had an interesting meeting with M. Sharif, West Pakistan's Education Secretary, on 11 August. Sharif had called on Ayub to discuss the organization of cadet corps in schools and colleges:

> He [Sharif] was very depressed and painted a gloomy picture of the running of the civil administration which was deteriorating rapidly through the perfidy of the politicians. He felt that a majority of the civil servants also lend themselves to such misuse. About the future he was of the view that because of weak and divided governments, the communists and neutralists will spend big money to prepare the people in Pakistan to force the government to adopt a neutralist policy. Once that happened all sorts of calamities will follow. He did not think that we can find solutions to our problem through democracy of the present type.

On 15 August Ayub met Qizilbash in his office. He agreed to allot land to those army officers who had been given gallantry awards and also for cattle breeding. He blamed Syed Wajid Ali for getting Mirza involved in political intrigues and creating confusion in the country.

The Defence Secretary, along with some officers from GHQ, discussed the problem of training the border police with the Chief Secretary of West Pakistan, and representatives of the police department. When Ayub was informed of the results of the discussion he wrote in his diary:

> The policeman is naturally trying to raise all sorts of objections and obstacles. The politician, too, is chary of making any hard decision which will annoy the police, as he probably expects a lot from him during the forthcoming elections. I believe the policeman is regarded as the real election-winning factor. A further meeting is arranged between our [officers] and police representatives on the 4th of September. My instructions to our fellows are to patiently keep relentless pressure until the right thing is done. It may take time, but the security of the country demands that this force would be militarized. I am receiving very depressing reports of economic distress and maladministration through political interference, frustration and complete loss of faith by the people in political leaders inclusive of the President. The general belief is that none of these men have the honesty of purpose, integrity and patriotism to root out the evils of the country, which will require drastic

action. The general belief is emerging that even I and the army are failing to do our duty and save them from these tyrants. This dangerous belief is obviously based on the ignorance of the function of the army, but when people become desperate they are apt to seek escape through any means. I wonder if they realize that if it were not for my keeping aloof from politics they would not have had this army and if this type of army was not there they would have lost their independence by now.

Ayub was now becoming more and more critical of the government. He was also getting worried that if he did not act, people would lose confidence in the army. All his civilian contacts were urging him to intervene and save the country from the perfidy of the politicians. His despair seemed to grow with every passing day. A statement by Abdul Qadir, Governor of the State Bank of Pakistan, so annoyed him that he sent a strongly worded message to the Prime Minister on 24 August:

I see from the Press that Mr Abdul Qadir, Governor State Bank of Pakistan, is going about saying that the way to check inflation in the country is to cut expenditure on the army and reduce America's military aid as it leads to inflation. Is this man saying these things with the approval of the Government, if not, does he realize the amount of harm he is doing to our stand with the Americans and encouraging our enemies to take greater liberties with our security? I believe that this man is talking through his hat but in a highly irresponsible manner, and if the government likes to be considered in command of the country, it should take steps to curb his nefarious activities. At any rate ask him how does he propose this country to be defended? I would request that this signal is shown to the President and the Prime Minister as from several sources I am told that the army is fed up to the teeth with this man's fulminations.

So far Ayub had studiously avoided attacking any official, but his patience was running out and he was now openly questioning the authority of the government.

Ayub went to Karachi on 5 September and stayed there till 9 September. There is no entry in Ayub's diary to show that he had any meeting with Mirza but it is reasonable to assume that the plan of action was given its final shape during these four days. This is borne out by the fact that on his return to Rawalpindi he gave instructions to some of his senior colleagues in GHQ to examine

the legal aspects of the army providing support to the President.
The record of Ayub's meeting with his officers is marked 'sacred',
and bears the title 'Scheme for Aid to Civil Power'.

Having made all the arrangements and assigned their duties to
the generals closest to him, Ayub Khan left for the northern areas
on 18 September. He was accompanied by Brigadier Effendi and
Colonel Gardezi. He was received by the Political Resident and
Political Agent. He was in Gupis on 19 September where he spent
a good deal of time fishing in the Gupis River. He returned to
Gilgit on 21 September and left for Hunza on 22 September.

It was on 24 September, when he was having lunch with the Mir
of Nagar at Chalt, that he received a message from his Chief of
Staff that he was moving to Karachi. He sent him instructions that
no major commitment should be made 'without his prior consent'.
He returned to Rawalpindi on 25 September, ten days before the
Constitution would be abrogated and the country placed under
martial law.

The trip to the northern areas was clearly intended by Ayub to
get as far away as possible from Mirza's reach. He had left it to
his Chief of Staff to maintain liaison with Mirza and keep a close
watch over the situation. Ayub knew that Mirza had lost all
credibility and he obviously did not wish to be seen associated
with him during the days immediately preceding the imposition
of martial law. The two officers he took with him, Brigadier
Effendi and Colonel Gardezi, were wholly unconnected with the
planned action. His choice of companions was designed to create
the impression that he had really gone on a holiday.

The final moves

During this period several politicians were in touch with Mirza and
he was encouraging them to organize demonstrations against the government. A long march was planned from Peshawar to Karachi to bring
down the government. Ayub Khan's Chief of Staff, and two or three
other generals in his confidence, remained in daily contact with Mirza
as he planned his final moves in what had become a devious and

tortuous game of chess between the politicians, the army, and the bureaucrats. Ayub allowed Mirza to proceed with his game plan in the belief that he enjoyed the unqualified support of the armed forces.

The curtain was rung down on the night of 7 October 1958. Brigadier Nawazish, who was Military Secretary to Iskander Mirza at the time, provided an account of the events of the fateful day.[13] President Mirza told him on the afternoon of 7 October that there would be a lot of work during the night and a trusted secretary should remain on duty to type out a number of letters. The Military Secretary had no knowledge of what was being planned. His office was chosen as the venue for the *coup d'etat* and it was arranged that General Yahya Khan, Chief of General Staff, would meet him at 7 p.m. President Mirza, General Yahya Khan and Brigadier Nawazish dined together at 10.15 p.m.; Nawazish was given a sealed envelope containing the proclamation that the Constitution was abrogated, the country placed under martial law and the civilian government dismissed; he was asked to have it delivered to the Prime Minister.

By 11 p.m. the contents of the proclamation and been communicated to all the corps commanders. The Commonwealth Secretariat and CENTO headquarters were also informed. Noon, the officer who had been deputed to deliver the sealed letter to Prime Minister, telephoned to say that the Prime Minister was asleep. He was told to wake him up. Noon read the letter and wanted to speak on the telephone to the West Pakistan Chief Minister, Nawab Qizilbash. This was not allowed.

At 11.30 p.m. members of the diplomatic corps were called to the President's House. Ayub Khan who had come to Karachi by train a day earlier, and was staying in his saloon, now emerged from the background and sat beside Mirza as he briefed the ambassadors. Mirza assumed full responsibility for the promulgation of martial law and the abrogation of the Constitution.

Mirza had informed US Ambassador Langley of his intention four days before the take-over and had asked him for an assurance that the new government would not have to seek diplomatic recognition by the US and other nations. While Ambassador Langley had full information about the coming of martial law,

Ayub and two of his generals were 'informed only in part as to the President's plans' at the time. The most significant thing that Mirza told Langley was that he was taking the proposed action to 'prevent the army seizure of power in Pakistan'.[14]

The new Cabinet was sworn in the next day. Zakir Hussain, a former Inspector-General of Police, who happened to be in Karachi, attended the Cabinet meeting and was deputed to take over as Governor of East Pakistan. Mirza appointed Ayub as the Chief Martial Law Administrator. While Mirza issued a special proclamation to explain the circumstances under which he had decided to abrogate the Constitution, Ayub broadcast a personal message to the people on 8 October at 7 p.m. He started by saying that he was going to speak on solemn matters: 'It is vital that you should listen to them carefully, understand them correctly so as to be able to act constructively.'

The first thing that Ayub wanted the people to know was that with his appointment as Chief Martial Law Administrator all the armed forces had come under his command. Martial law has been imposed 'with great reluctance but with the fullest conviction that there was no alternative to it except the disintegration and complete ruination of the country.' The previous civilian governments were 'week and irresolute' and they 'looked on with masterly inactivity and cowardice and allowed things to drift and deteriorate and discipline to go to pieces'.

Ayub Khan said that the armed forces were as sick and tired of the politicians as the people, but there were good reasons why he had not intervened in the political process earlier. He had wanted to build the army into a truly national force 'free from politics, a model of devotion to duty and integrity, imbued with the spirit of service to the people and capable of effectively defending the country'. He recalled how on several occasions Ghulam Muhammad had asked him to take over the country but he had declined to do so in the belief that he could serve Pakistan better from where he was, and he had 'a faint hope that some politicians would rise to the occasion and lead the country to a better future'. Events had falsified those hopes: 'A perfectly sound country has been turned into a laughing stock.'[15] There was not a word of appreciation for Mirza in Ayub's speech. Millions of Pakistanis who listened to Ayub recognized the voice of authority.

Having vanquished the fractious politicians, Mirza proceeded to set up what he called 'a two-man regime which makes policy together for the army to carry out.'[16] He did not suspect for a moment that, along with the politicians, he had dealt himself out of the new order. The two-man regime did not even speak with one voice. Bursting with confidence, Mirza told a group of journalists two days after he had pulled off the *coup d'etat:* 'My authority is revolution. I have no sanction in law or Constitution. I saved the country from a disaster which would have been a bloody revolution.' Sitting beside him, Ayub described by one correspondent as 'a handsome graduate of Britain's Sandhurst military academy', intervened to say that,

> In the final analysis it must always be the army's responsibility to protect the rights of the people. We both came to the conclusion that the country is going to the dogs. I said to the President, 'Are you going to act? It is your responsibility to bring about change and if you do not, which heaven forbid, we shall force a change.'[17]

The message was clear: from now on the army would be calling the shots. Ayub, having remained in the background so far, keeping himself severely aloof from the President and his plans to abrogate the Constitution, was now telling the people of Pakistan that in the final analysis their rights could be protected only by the army, and if the President had failed to act the army would have forced the change. The mask was off and people could see the full flame of power flowing from the barrel of the gun.

The next day Ayub reinforced the point: 'A time had come where the constitutional responsibility of the President demanded that he should call a halt, otherwise it would have been the duty of the armed forces to act.'[18] Later that afternoon Mirza and Ayub appeared together for a joint interview with four foreign correspondents and Ayub gave what amounted to a blunt public warning when he told Mirza that henceforth the army will exercise the ultimate authority: 'If the President does not react to a situation or his successor does not, I would act if something goes wrong, heaven forbid, if he does something senseless and joins politicians I will act and the decision will be mine.' Mirza had now been publicly put on notice. In a desperate attempt to retrieve his position Mirza announced a few days later: 'I shall run martial law for the shortest duration possible. Then we shall have a national council of not more than twelve to fifteen persons and run on that basis for some time to clear up the country.'[19] Ayub responded at once: 'Let me assure everyone that whereas martial law will not be retained a minute longer than is necessary, it will not be lifted a minute earlier than the purpose for which it has been imposed has been fulfilled.'[20]

On 18 October Ayub gave an interview to three British journalists and talked about his economic and educational reforms. He dismissed all rumours about desertions in the army 'as false and unfounded'. The army, he said, was 'already in the process of reverting to its parent jobs. There was no question of any politics in the army because the foremost thing for a soldier is his profession.'[21] Soon after that he announced the appointment of a land reforms commission, a pay commission, and an organizations and methods commission.

In less than a fortnight tensions had begun to develop between civilian and army officers: the civilians, relying on the announcement made by Ayub, expected the army officers to return to the barracks without delay and the army officers were put out by the statement of their own Commander-in-Chief that the armed forces should not remain involved in civil administration for too long. A directive was issued to the Governors of East and West Pakistan 'to devise ways and means to improve social contacts by way of mutual invitations, social functions, etc. Every attempt should be made to break the psychological barrier, if any.'[22]

Ayub went to Dhaka on 20 October and stayed there for three days. Zakir Hussain, the Governor of East Pakistan, introduced the Chief Martial Law Administrator to the citizens of Dhaka at a public reception. The Governor said that Ayub had lived in East Pakistan and was familiar with the agonies and aspirations of the people of the province. The fact that he had 'dashed' to East

Pakistan only twelve days after 'his assumption of power' showed his love for the province.[23] The phrase 'assumption of power' must have rung alarm bells in the President's House in Karachi. The Governor was the first to use the word 'revolution' for what took place on the night of 7 October and he gave Ayub full credit for ushering in the revolution. The Governor did not make even a token reference to President Mirza.

Mirza was getting desperate as he saw power slipping out of his hands. With the help of the Chief Commissioner of Karachi, he drummed up a labour rally in his support. The rift between Mirza and Ayub was now a subject of gossip in government offices. How long would they stick together? Who would get whom first? With Aziz Ahmed appointed as Secretary General and Deputy Martial Law Administrator (the first civilian to hold such an office) the Civil Servants had become partners in the *coup d'etat*. They did not quite anticipate that several senior civil officers, among whom were some men of ability and experience, would be summarily expelled from service.

Events of the last few days of Mirza-Ayub partnership are not documented. Brigadier Nawazish recalled Ayub asking him whether he could use the President's plane for his visit to Dhaka. Mirza allowed this. Nawazish noticed that Mirza had started smoking heavily and did not look his usual self. His wife looked even more unhappy.

The day before Ayub left for Dhaka he invited Mirza to a meeting which was also attended by Justice Munir, Chief Justice of the Supreme Court of Pakistan, and Colonel Kazi, Judge Advocate-General in GHQ. Under discussion was the question of defining the respective powers of the President and the Chief Martial Law Administrator. When Justice Munir, who was close to Mirza and was known in official circles as his adviser, was explaining the legal position in a sedate manner, Colonel Kazi interrupted him and said that with the abrogation of the Constitution the President had lost all the powers he enjoyed under the Constitution and the Chief Martial Law Administrator was now the only lawful authority in the country. Justice Munir was a little put out by that and Ayub asked Kazi not to press the point any further. The meeting came to an abrupt end but the young Colonel had conveyed the army's message to Mirza.

Ayub returned from Dhaka on 23 October and was shown an intelligence report that Mirza had telephoned Air Commodore Rabb of Pakistan Air Force, in charge of Mauripur Airport, and instructed him to arrest three army generals, Yahya, Sher Bahadur, and Hamid. Ayub immediately got in touch with Mirza and warned him that he was playing with fire. Mirza denied having given any instructions to arrest anyone and tried to assure Ayub that he had been misinformed. But the report had served its purpose. Like the earlier rumour about the arrest of some his generals, this intelligence report helped Ayub make up his mind to get rid of Mirza. Ayub was not a ruthless person and used to go through spells of hesitation and indecision before taking action against anybody with whom he had close personal relations. The generals close to him knew about this and always found some way of providing Ayub with the justification for taking an unpleasant decision.

On 24 October Ayub went to offer his condolence to Mumtaz Hassan, Secretary, Ministry of Finance, whose young daughter had died. There he told the President's Military Secretary that he was willing to work with anybody but in his own way, and he wanted vigorous action. The next day Ayub was invited to accompany the President on a duck shoot but Ayub declined the invitation on the plea that he had sprained his ankle and the shoot was cancelled.

On the evening of 27 October there was a TV interview with foreign correspondents on the lawns of the President's House. Ayub arrived at 4.30 p.m. and walked around in the garden with Brigadier Nawazish, telling him that the army was most unhappy with the present arrangement and wanted that 'all politicians must go'. Mirza and Ayub answered the correspondents' questions during the interview, which lasted for forty-five minutes. At the end of the interview, Mirza said to Ayub, 'You are a good actor.' Brigadier Nawazish left his office at 9.30 p.m. and went home. He was woken up by his ADC at 10.30 p.m. and asked to come to the office at once. He took a taxi and hurried to the President's House where he found an army officer stationed at the gate. Brigadier Bahadur Sher was occupying the Military Secretary's office. He informed him that President Mirza had resigned and would be leaving for Quetta in three hours.

Brigadier Nawazish went to Mirza's bedroom and knocked on the door. Mirza, in a red dressing-gown, was walking up and down, smoking a cigarette. As he entered the room Mirza said, 'You know what has happened now.' Begum Mirza was packing her things. She walked up to Brigadier Nawazish and said: 'Is this what we deserve?' They jammed their stuff in six boxes and left the keys for the rest of their belongings with Brigadier Nawazish who had received instructions that Mirza should be given every possible assistance. The President's House was surrounded by the army; the whole operation was under the control of Brigadier Bahadur Sher who was going around with a pistol in his hand. Mirza changed into a bush-shirt and left a golden pen for Q.U. Shahab, his Private Secretary, and some money for a servant whose wedding had been arranged earlier. He told Brigadier Nawazish that if he owed anybody any money he should be informed. Brigadier Bahadur Sher conducted Mirza and his wife to Mauripur Airport. Mirza and his wife boarded a plane and departed for Quetta without any ceremony. Next morning Brigadier Nawazish was called to the Prime Minister's House where Ayub, now President, was having breakfast with four of his generals, Burki, Shaikh, Yahya, and Azam. He learnt that the entire diplomatic corps had been summoned to the Prime Minister's House the previous night and informed of the change. Brigadier Nawazish was asked to deliver Mirza's belongings to Hassan Isphahani, who was Pakistan's first Ambassador to the United States after Independence.

Mirza stayed in Quetta for about a week. From there he sent 70,000 rupees for payment of personal bills. Ayub took time off for a shoot and then went to Rawalpindi to bring his family. Brigadier Nawazish did not know when it was decided to deport Mirza from Pakistan. Mirza and his wife were brought one night to Mauripur and put on a BOAC plane for London. Nawazish met them at the airport and found Begum Mirza in a state of collapse.

The plane took off but returned to the airport after a little while. The Mirzas were deeply disturbed by this. Nawazish tried to reassure them that the plane had returned because of some mechanical defect and they would soon be flying to London. That was the last he saw of President Iskander Mirza and Begum Nahid Mirza.

Ayub was now in undisputed command. There was not a ripple of protest nor any sign of agitation. Miss Fatima Jinnah, the revered sister of Quaid-i-Azam, issued a statement:

> The exit of Major-General Iskander Mirza from the political scene has brought a general sense of relief to the people of Pakistan....A new era has begun under General Ayub Khan and the armed forces have undertaken to root out the administrative malaise and the anti-social practices to create a sense of confidence and stability and eventually to bring the country back to a state of normalcy. I hope and pray that God may give them wisdom and strength to achieve their objective.[24]

Ayub lost no time in setting in motion all the reforms he had in mind by setting up a series of commissions to examine the country's educational, social and administrative problems. His most significant step was to suspend military courts throughout Pakistan and order the withdrawal of troops. Aziz Ahmed issued a message to senior civil officers on 12 November 1958 saying that the President, by ordering the withdrawal of troops and the suspension of military courts, had 'proclaimed his confidence in the ability of the civil machinery of government to tackle effectively the great economic and social tasks that face the country today.' He counselled the Civil Servants to be worthy of the President's trust.[25] As Secretary-General, Aziz Ahmed alienated the civil services by his overbearing manner, and as Deputy Martial Law Administrator he came to be distrusted by the defence services. He soon departed from the scene and took up the post of Pakistan's Ambassador in Washington.

NOTES

1. *Dawn,* 9 March 1958.
2. *Foreign Relations of the United States (1955-57),* Vol. VIII; South Asia; Department of State Washington; US Government Press, Washington 1987; pp. 411-90, especially pp. 52-3, 148, 421. The US Ambassador in Pakistan had come to be known in diplomatic circles as 'real Pak. Prime Minister'; p. 480.
3. All quotations in this section, unless specified otherwise, are from Ayub Khan's diary to which the author had access when he was working on Ayub's autobiography, *Friends Not Masters.*
4. The extracts that follow are taken from the minutes recorded by Mohammad Ali Bogra and kept by Ayub Khan in his papers.
5. The US State Department record of this meeting is contained in memorandum of Conversation M-559 dated 29 April 1958, Secret File 790.00/4-2958. According to this Amjad Ali pointed out that 'the new President of the Muslim League, Qayum Khan, was violently attacking the foreign policy, criticizing the President personally and eulogizing Nasser.' He said there were three main groups opposed to collaboration with the west: the Bhashani group, the Hindus, and the Ghaffar Khan elements. He excused Prime Minister Noon's 8 March speech as having resulted from harassment and as having been made 'off the cuff'. He added that had he been Prime Minister, he would have chosen different words and phrases. Amjad Ali reassured Mr Rowntree that Prime Minister Noon was definitely western oriented; his education and background as well as his convictions did not allow him to be otherwise. He stated that Noon did make snap judgments—some good, some bad—and that often his frankness and bluntness worked against the interest which he basically supported.
6. Ayub Khan, op. cit., pp. 60-1. The words 'greatest benefactor' were changed to 'their most devoted servant' in *Friends Not Masters.*
7. Ibid., p. 59.
8. Ibid., p. 54.
9. Ibid., p. 59.
10. Ibid., pp. 39, 58, 65.
11. Ibid., p. 61.
12. Philip Woodruff, *The Men Who Ruled India:* The Guardians: St. Martin's Press, New York 1954.
13. Conversation with the author in Karachi in 1966.
14. The US Ambassador Langley in Karachi sent a 'Night Action' message (requiring the recipient to be woken up) at 2 p.m. on 4 October 1958 which was received by the Secretary of State at 6.42 a.m. According to this Mirza confirmed to Langley that:

> ...he would take over the Government of Pakistan probably within a week and simultaneously proclaim martial law. The Constitution will be suspended, a commission created to write a new Constitution, and elections now scheduled for February 15 will not be held. General Ayub Khan will be Administrator of Martial Law, with General Umrao his Deputy in East Pakistan. These two and General Musa, Chief of Staff, are the principal individuals informed in part as to the President's plans at the moment. Ayub arrives in Karachi October 6 and will participate in preparations of the proclamations, his own and that of the President.

The take-over will occur at night. Troops already are being deployed, in Karachi and elsewhere. In East Pakistan, where troops have for some months been dispersed on the border, anti-smuggling duties are being reassembled to handle martial law. Mirza says he is taking over to prevent any army seizure of power in Pakistan. The pressures within the army come from officers below Ayub, both generals and brigadiers. Mirza says the army will fully support his take-over, despite previous reservations by Ayub that seizure of power by the President could only be possible if preceded by violence. Mirza thinks Ayub has revised his judgement in view of recent political events in Pakistan....

Top Secret File Karachi 775-790d.00/10-458. National Archives, Washington.

15. *Dawn,* 9 October 1958.
16. Ibid., 10 October 1958.
17. Ibid.
18. *The Pakistan Times,* Lahore, 11 October 1958.
19. *Dawn,* 16 October 1958.
20. Ibid., 17 October 1958.
21. Ibid., 19 October 1958.
22. Author's personal papers.
23. *Pakistan Observer,* Dhaka, 22 October 1958.
24. *Dawn,* Karachi, 29 October 1958.
25. Author's personal papers.

CHAPTER 3

Search for Legitimacy

The man on horseback was home and dry—his principal rival having fallen at the last fence. It had been a long and steep climb but Ayub knew 'the art of moving on slowly'.[1] The Ayub regime, heralded as a successful revolution, was recognized by the Supreme Court of Pakistan as 'a basic law-creating fact'.[2] Members of the United Nations did not take long to recognize the military regime. Public opinion in the West had been persuaded by sociologists and political scientists to treat Third World armies as instruments of modernization and economic development. The emergence of Ayub as the first military ruler of a developing country was a major test for the World Bank model of economic growth based on what was known as the 'trickle-down' theory—creating wealth at the top in the hope that some of it would trickle down to the common man.

Domestically Ayub could not have asked for a more propitious climate. The politicians had thoroughly blotted their copy book and few, if any, among them had an unblemished record. Political parties were but labels which could be changed at convenience. A number of politicians were debarred by the military regime from taking part in politics; the rest voluntarily withdrew from the field. Scores of Civil Servants were summarily retired from service to instil, as was said at the time, the fear of God into the bureaucracy. A few traders were arrested on charges of black marketing which was enough to strike terror into the heart of big business. The Press, which had played a highly parochial and partisan role in the parliamentary saga, forgot all about freedom of expression and quietly submitted to martial law regulations governing the Press. The media surrender was so complete that the government did not have to resort to any kind of censorship. Not one newspaper or journalist uttered a word of criticism against the imposition of martial law. Indeed, most newspapers acclaimed the advent of military rule as a blessing and many of the press barons became willing tools of the regime. *Dawn,* the leading English daily, an eloquent supporter of parliamentary government, took two days to comprehend the full implications of the imposition of martial law in the country and then proclaimed in an editorical that 'the way things were going, so much more damage would have been done to the country in the next few months that it might have been too late to save it from total collapse.' The editorial welcomed the Chief Martial Law Administrator's assurance that the aim was to restore democracy but cautioned that there was no need to hurry: 'Now that a break has been made with the past system and a new one has been ushered in, under which it is much more easy to take quick decisions on the country's urgent problems, it may not be desirable to make another early change.' Concluding on a triumphant note the editorial disclosed that the 'peaceful revolution' of 7 October might have been the 'answer from heaven'.[3]

Ayub was soon able to create an atmosphere of order. Discipline, according to him, was what the country needed most, and discipline was what he proceeded to introduce into the political, social, and administrative streams. After a few weeks he found it unnecessary to keep military courts in operation. Troops were withdrawn to the barracks and civil life returned to normal within three months of the imposition of martial law.[4]

Ayub included in his Cabinet three lieutenant generals, a former bureaucrat, and an industrialist from East Pakistan. None of the known politicians was invited to join the Cabinet. The most surprising person to join the Ayub government was Manzur Qadir, an eminent lawyer from Lahore, known for his ability and integrity and his unorthodox views. He was given the portfolio of Foreign Affairs. Another surprise inclusion was Zulfikar Ali Bhutto from Sindh who was virtually unknown at the time. He had been selected by Mirza but Ayub retained him after Mirza's exit and gave him the portfolio of Commerce.

Once his team was in position Ayub proceeded to set up a number of commissions to carry out social and economic reforms. But the problem uppermost in his mind was legitimacy. Martial law could not last for ever; more than anything else Ayub needed some constitutional cover to run the government. But legitimacy, to Ayub, meant little more than finding some means of keeping the government in touch with the people to help establish a competent and efficient administration, capable of solving the social and economic problems of the country. Legitimacy derived from the mandate of the people to establish a political order sustained by their full and free participation in the process of decision-making was a concept alien to Ayub's mind. He just did not believe that an uneducated mass of people possessed either the right or the competence to deal with the affairs of the state. He promised to promulgate a Constitution based on 'my knowledge of the people and soil of Pakistan'. There was nobody around Ayub who could speak for the people. Indeed both the West Pakistani lawyers in the Cabinet, Manzur Qadir and Bhutto, became eloquent supporters of a highly centralized and authoritarian form of government. Ayub had once suggested that the failure of parliamentary form of government was due to the absence of 'the corrective of public opinion'.[5] Manzur Qadir convinced him that 'public opinion' was a dangerous myth which must not be encouraged and that there must be no place for political parties in the future constitutional order. Ayub wanted the provinces to have full autonomy 'leaving Defence, Foreign Affairs and Currency in the hands of the centre', but Bhutto advocated a highly centralized form of government where provinces should have no legislative assemblies and heads of provincial governments should act as 'agents' to the President who must have the ultimate authority in all matters.[6]

Ayub had the option to call for a referendum, on the basis of universal franchise, to obtain a mandate from the people to rule the country until such time as general elections were organized. This would have given him the mandate to carry out the reforms he had in mind. But Ayub proceeded on the assumption that what the people wanted most was a strong man at the helm of affairs

who could give them a sense of security. He had no doubt that he
had found the answer to all the social and political questions
which the politicians had deliberately avoided addressing and he
could proceed to implement his ideas without associating the
people in the process of decision-making. It was for him to cut the
Gordian knot; he alone had the responsibility to devise and
establish the proper form of government suited to the genius of the
people, determine the place of Islam in the state, and decide the
powers of the provinces and their relationship with the central
government.

On 2 December, 1958 Ayub announced that he intended to
'consult the best brains and ascertain the feelings of the people in
order to draw up a Constitution suited to the needs of our country.'
He advised the people to 'have patience' and promised that the
future Constitution would be 'a very good Constitution indeed'.[7]
Addressing the Karachi Bar on 15 January 1959, he indicated that
a 'Constitution Commission would be set up and its recommendations put before the country, after which, if they were
accepted, free and unfettered elections would be held.' His
estimate was that the whole process might take 'a couple of
years'.[8] The Law Minister, Muhammad Ibrahim, said in Dhaka
that 'the present situation could not continue forever'.[9] Zulfikar
Ali Bhutto advocated a unitary form of government, which he
claimed would be the best for Pakistan. In March 1959, Manzur
Qadir undertook a tour of various districts along with the Home
Minister, General Sheikh, to ascertain whether the people were
really anxious to have a Constitution. During this tour he said that
steps would be taken to give a Constitution to the country 'as soon
as the views of the people were ascertained'. He gave the assurance
that 'only elected representatives of the people were to work out
details of the future Constitution.'

Manzur Qadir's impression was that the people were not
unduly worried about the delay in the introduction of the
Constitution though questions were being asked about the manner
in which the Constitution would be framed. Would the Constitution
be drafted by experts and then submitted to the people through a
referendum? Would it be debated by an elected assembly before

its adoption? Authoritative official pronouncements continued to strengthen the impression that the Constitution would be discussed and adopted by the elected representatives of the people.

On 23 March 1959 Ayub said that he had come to certain conclusions about the Constitution and when the draft was ready 'it would be put to a vote of the people in a suitable manner, and then put into effect.'[10] He hinted that there could be a two-stage plebiscite for the adoption of the Constitution. General Burki declared in London on 3 July 1959, that a referendum would be held about the new Constitution.[11]

When Ayub said that he had come to certain conclusions about the Constitution he did not disclose that he had actually put down those conclusions in the form of a presidential directive on 15 March 1959, bearing the title 'Outlines of our Future Constitution'.[12] The next day copies of this directive were given to all the cabinet ministers and the two provincial governors. The outline said, 'that for very good reasons we cannot yet work straight universal franchise, at the same time we cannot divorce the broad mass of the people from the affairs of the state.' The answer was 'to allow the broad mass of people to elect an electoral college, who will then in turn elect the legislatures, district boards and municipalities, and if we want to have a presidential form of government, the president as well.' This should

> …give everyone an opportunity to have his say in level with his horizon and power of understanding, and help build a democratic system from below— simple and cheap, capable of filling a gap between the government and the people, which now is very often filled by demagogues, whose sole purpose seems to be agitation for the sake of it and disruption.

Regarding the shape of the central government, it was Ayub's opinion that 'Pakistanis are a mixture of races, riddled with parochialism and linguistic differences, and do not make a team easily without a strong leader on top.' The only thing on which Pakistanis were all united was 'the fear of Hindu domination'. Having drawn what he called 'a sombre and dismal picture' Ayub assured his associates that the situation was not 'irremediable'. What was required was resolution and courage, and that had to be 'provided by the top leadership—ME'. Ayub saw it as his moral and spiritual duty 'to guide the thinking of the people' and to build them gradually into a united, progressive and strong nation: 'I firmly believe that this can be done. So I would like my associates and comrades to understand the spirit of what I am saying and guide their thinking and those of people towards the objectives I am outlining.' A strong central government, he said, was 'an absolute MUST' and a strong government meant a strong executive, not dependent for its existence 'on the whims of the legislature'. The parliamentary government was 'out with us once and for all'. Pakistan should have the presidential system, which meant 'an elected President free to choose his Cabinet, preferably outside the legislature, a legislature consisting of one or two houses, but not unduly large, because of the paucity of the type of manpower required, for the sake of economy.' His preference was for the French or the Egyptian model. The President in Pakistan should have 'wide powers, much more than even the American President'. The type of executive he was recommending appeared to him to be the same as existed in the days of the early caliphs. 'So, here you can see [the] essence of Islamic Constitution emerging'! Ayub could not understand the clamour for an Islamic Constitution: 'Everyone seems to have a different concept.' Ayub thought it should be enough 'to express and practise the spirit of Islam in the language of educated men, which is the language of science, history, economics and world affairs, and above all the language of nationalism.' Islam should, of course, be declared as the state religion, and in the preamble to the Constitution all Muslims must be enjoined 'to work the Constitution in the spirit of Islam in the light of modern requirements.'

Ayub recognized that in his scheme the nation would be dependent entirely 'on one man—the President'. It would, therefore, be a 'great blessing if we can arrange his election on non-party basis'. The President should represent the nation as a whole. How would the Constitution be framed and promulgated? In the light of past experience, it will be highly dangerous to talk about people's representatives formulating the Constitution.

This was Ayub's decision contrary to what some of his ministers were telling the people. Ayub 'wanted to formulate and start a Constitution with as little controversy as possible'. He told his colleagues that 'this may sound a bit undemocratic, but if a bit of lack of democracy is going to do a lot of good to the country, then we have to do it.' This benevolent end would be secured through the appointment of a 'fairly large Constitution Commission which could invite suggestions, discuss controversial points with people, and if need be, do a bit of canvassing to guide the people round to a sensible point of view.'

This directive represented a radical departure from Ayub's appreciation of Pakistan's problems which he had presented to the Cabinet as Defence Minister in 1954.[13] In 1954 Ayub was still a liberal, and thought in terms of the government 'exercising executive powers as voted by the legislature, subject to some effective control by the President, who should be elected'. Five months in office had turned him into a highly authoritarian and self-centered ruler who had come to see himself as the answer to all the problems of the country.

Ayub's constitutional plan was discussed and adopted at the Governors' Conference in Karachi on 1 May 1959. A month later a detailed programme of action to create 'Basic Democracies' (BDs) was approved by the Governors' Conference in Nathiagali on 12-13 June 1959. The question to which Ayub had not found an answer was how to put his plan to the people to secure their agreement without too much debate. He thought it could be processed and adopted by a Constitution commission which 'could do a bit of canvassing to guide the people round to a sensible point of view'.

On the morning of 4 August 1959 Ayub convened a meeting at the President's House, Karachi, to discuss the programme of introducing and implementing his constitutional plan. Invitations were issued to a carefully selected group of officials: the judiciary was represented by M. Munir, Chief Justice of Pakistan, and Justice Shahabuddin (who would later be appointed Chairman of the Constitution Commission); the central government by the Ministers of Foreign Affairs, Finance, Industries, Education and

Commerce (the most significant omission was that of Muhammed Ibrahim, the Law Minister); the Civil Service by the Cabinet Secretary, the Information Secretary and the Secretary to the President, and the politicians by Sir Muhammed Yamin Khan, an elderly figure who had long retired from politics.[14]

The participants were each given a copy of a memorandum called 'points for discussion'. The memorandum bore the signature of Ayub Khan and the date, 4 August 1959. These points of discussion read remarkably like a presidential directive to the participants who were given a few minutes to read and absorb the contents of the memorandum. They learnt that the government had decided to establish 8,000 units of Basic Democracies (BDs) by the end of the year. Each unit would elect ten members on the basis of adult franchise and together these 80,000 BDs would 'act as an electoral college for the Presidential election and the election to the parliament'. There would be no provincial legislatures and provinces would be run by governors appointed by the President as agents of the central government 'so by the end of this year we would have had the electoral college for the election of the President and for any form of reference to the people ready.' The question was 'how to go about framing a Constitution and at what stage the people's acceptance should be obtained'. The alternatives were: (1) to ask the people to elect the President and give him the powers to have a Constitution framed (2) to frame a Constitution and put it to the people for approval, and (3) frame the Constitution, hold Presidential elections first and elections to parliament a few months later. The memorandum required the participants to keep in mind that discipline within the country must not be impaired nor must the process of reforms be interrupted or reversed. Pakistan's bargaining position with India must not weaken nor should 'our credit with the friendly countries on whom we depend for a lot of support' suffer a setback during the period of constitution-making.

The memorandum required that the ideology of Islam should be defined 'in [a] tangible form and [we must] admit to ourselves as to what extent we can live by it in the context of the fast moving world of today.' There was need for protecting the fundamental rights of the individual but it should not be 'forgotten that unless the state is given certain protection and made strong' it will not be able to protect the rights of the individual. The memorandum concluded: 'In a country like ours one thing which under no circumstances must be allowed to happen and tolerated is the weakening of discipline. Any form of loose or starry-eyed thinking on our part on this subject will lead us to disaster.'

After a brief discussion it was decided that 'a commission to *draft* emphasis added a new Constitution should be appointed by the President at a time which he determines to be appropriate.' It was also decided that the 'Presidential elections should be held after the recommendations of the commission had been finalized and approved. Elections to the parliament should be held after a suitable interval determined by the elected President.' It was understood that the Constitution would be framed and the first elections held under martial law. There was some discussion about the size and composition of the commission and it was decided that it should have five to seven members, including the Chairman. For appointment to the commission, the names of Justice Muhammad Munir, Akhtar Hussain (Governor of West Pakistan), Justice Sharif, Altaf Hussain (Editor of *Dawn*), and Azizuddin (of East Pakistan) were mentioned, but the meeting was told that the President 'will look for other suitable talent in both wings of the country and finalize the composition of the commission at the appropriate stage.' The President suggested that 'younger blood' should be associated with the work of the commission. This was welcomed. The terms of reference of the commission should embrace 'the suggestion that the Constitution should be founded on the Islamic principles of equality, liberty, tolerance and justice.' It was recognized that 'the fundamental rights of the individual could not be ensured at the cost of the fundamental rights of the state. The two should be balanced in a spirit of realism.'

The meeting was not told that Ayub had already indicated to Justice Shahabuddin, who was present in the meeting, that he intended to appoint him as the Chairman of the proposed commission. Both Justice Munir and Justice Shahabuddin participated in the discussion and endorsed the ideas contained in the Presidential memorandum. The commission would be required to draft a Constitution based on the memorandum but that task too had already been assigned to the Foreign Minister, Manzur Qadir, a competent draftsman in his own right, which was the reason that the Law Minister was excluded from the meeting.

The meeting was a formality. Its real purpose was to acquaint the Chief Justice of Pakistan and his senior colleague, Justice Shahabuddin, with the constitutional order which Ayub was in the process of establishing in the country. Ayub's points for discussion made it absolutely clear that the President would be elected by an electoral college before the end of the year. The decision taken at the meeting that 'Presidential elections should be held after the recommendations of the commission have been finalized and approved' was intended to enable Justice Shahabuddin to claim, at least on paper, that the commission was an independent body not subservient to Presidential instructions.

The way was now clear for Ayub's ministers to propagate his constitutional thoughts and for the provincial governors to establish the system of Basic Democracies and secure a mandate for Ayub to promulgate his Constitution. The governors impressed on Ayub not to underestimate the risks involved in seeking a mandate even from a small electoral college. The spectre of politicians still haunted the administration and the view was urged on Ayub that there was a real risk that members to the electoral college would come under the influence of the 'old rogues' if they were not properly instructed by their area magistrates and police officers.

Manzur Qadir and Zulfikar Ali Bhutto had by now completely identified themselves with Ayub's thinking. Manzur Qadir took Ayub's constitutional scheme as his brief and proceeded to provide it with a philosophic and juridical base. Bhutto, the skilful politician, devised the operational strategy for the execution of Ayub's plans. Elections of the Basic Democracies were held in January 1960. Ayub wanted to obtain a vote of confidence from the newly-elected BDs, who formed the electoral college. Manzur Qadir conceded the need for the President to go to the electoral college for a mandate but only with the right kind of question. If a person did not understand the question to which he was required to give an answer, he could not be relied upon to cast his vote in a positive manner. Less than fifteen per cent of the people were literate and could hardly be expected to recognize any national issues; all they were concerned with were their local problems and personal difficulties. Anything other than that was beyond their comprehension. It was, therefore, essential, argued Manzur Qadir, that voting must remain a strictly localized affair. After a prolonged philosophic debate the question was finally formulated: 'Have you confidence in the President Field Marshal Muhammad Ayub Khan, Hilal-i-Pakistan, Hilal-i-Jurat?' This question was finally put to the members of the electoral college on 15 February 1960 and 75,283 of them, representing 95.6 per cent of the BDs, replied in the affirmative. Ayub was sworn in as the first elected President of Pakistan on 17 February and on the same day he announced the appointment of the Constitution Commission under Justice Shahabuddin, with five members from each province.

The timing of the commission's appointment and its terms of reference evoked a great deal of public criticism and ridicule. What was the object of setting up a commission, unless it was to endorse a draft already in existence? Since the President had already got himself elected would the commission be in a position to question his mode of election? Neither the government nor the commission could provide an answer to these questions. Addressing the Pakistan Bar Association, a day before the commission issued its questionnaire, M.R. Kayani, Chief Justice of the High Court of West Pakistan, who would become the first outspoken critic of the Ayub regime, mockingly welcomed the assurance given by the Chairman of the commission that the Constitution had not already been drafted!

The terms of reference required the commission to advise how best a democratic system could be established in the country 'adapted to changing circumstances and based on the Islamic principles of justice, equality, and tolerance; the consolidation of national unity; and a firm and stable system of government'. The commission was 'to examine the progressive failure of parliamentary government in Pakistan leading to the abrogation of the Constitution of 1956, and to determine the causes and the nature of the failure' and 'to consider how best the said or like causes may be identified and their recurrence prevented'.

The commission issued a questionnaire in the form of a booklet, spread over seventy-five pages, first in English, and, after public protests, in Urdu and Bengali. The questionnaire looked like an examination paper for postgraduate students in political science. Not surprisingly few people either saw the questionnaire or considered themselves sufficiently unoccupied to undertake the gruelling exercise of answering the questions.

Among the people who responded to the commission's questionnaire was the former Prime Minister, Chaudhri Muhammad Ali. His response created quite a sensation, not so much for its import but for the fact that the full text of his answers was first published by *The Pakistan Times* which was under the control of the government. The editor was immediately removed from his job and Ayub rebuked Muhammad Ali for his hypocrisy. By then several other newspapers had reproduced Muhammad Ali's reply which was seen as a powerful attack on the martial law regime. Muhammad Ali asserted that it was misleading to talk of the failure of parliamentary system when the Constitution was abrogated by Mirza, the very man who had taken the oath to protect and defend it. Mirza had taken this action because he had come to realize that 'however much he might juggle with various political elements, he had little chance of being re-elected after the first general elections.' Muhammad Ali also blamed 'a great many political leaders and other humbler politicians who in their scramble for power considered no means too ignoble.'[15]

Before the commission had recovered from Muhammed Ali's attack it compromised itself further by receiving a delegation of senior Civil Servants led by G. Ahmed, Secretary of the Ministry of the Interior, for evidence and discussion. The country was under martial law and all authority vested in the President and Chief Martial Law Administrator. The Civil Servants could act only as his servants and were in no position to express any views other than those approved by Ayub. The delegation had been formally instructed to impress upon the commission the need to adopt Ayub's constitutional plan. The commission did not consider it improper to discuss its ideas with Civil Servants or to elicit information from them about the government's likely response to its own constitutional ideas which were still in the process of formulation.

What were the causes of the failure of democracy in Pakistan? In the commission's view 'the real causes of the failure of the parliamentary form of government in Pakistan were mainly the lack of leadership, resulting in lack of well-organized and disciplined parties, the general lack of character in the politicians, and their undue interference in the administration.' The commission having decided to treat the effects as their own cause, did not want to hold 'an inquisition against the former President or his predecessor or the ministers who held office during the years preceding the revolution.' The commission rejected the argument that parliamentary democracy failed because of 'lack of proper elections and defects in the late Constitution'. The bureaucracy too, was exonerated as the statistics, worked out by the commission, showed that only two and one-half per cent of the persons who had responded to its questionnaire blamed the services for the failure of the parliamentary form of government. It did not occur to the commission that the answers to its questionnaire, in some cases at least, might have been provided by the administration itself. The commission absolved successive heads of state and governments of all blame because they 'could have done nothing to disrupt the democratic process, if the politicians had not been concerned more with maintaining their own position than that with working the Constitution'.

Why did the politicians act in such a selfish manner? Because they were such a selfish lot. The commission stated:

> The defects we have discussed in the preceding chapter are but a reflection of the indiscipline, lack of sense of duty and want of spirit of service and accommodation in an average member of society, noticeable particularly in countries which have emerged into independence before attaining universal education and a minimum level of economic development.

Lack of discipline, according to the commission, was caused by indiscipline, and lack of sense of duty was occasioned by its absence. The cure? Something must be done to educate the people: 'We are not experts on education', the commission confessed, but impelled by a strong sense of duty the members made such recommendations as occurred to them. Their first priority was that stories of service to noble causes should be 'narrated to children of tender age by their mothers in whose laps they initially acquired knowledge about God, religion and the world'! As an afterthought, the commission cautioned that such stories should not be based on 'exaggeration or superstition' since stories told to children make 'an indelible impression on their tender minds'. There was also need for courses of practical training, such as boy scout and girl guide activities. According to the commission this was how the recurrence of the causes which had led to the failure of parliamentary democracy in Pakistan could be prevented.

The commission disregarded the argument that people in Pakistan preferred the parliamentary form of government because of their familiarity with the system. The parliamentary form had succeeded in India because of the availability of trained leadership, which was lacking in Pakistan.

The commission decided 'that we should have a form of government where there is *only one person* [emphasis added] at the head of affairs, with an effective restraint exercised on him by an independent legislature, members of which, however, should not be in a position to seriously interfere with the administration by exercising political pressure for their personal ends.' The commission thus committed itself to the political principle of 'only one person' to control and direct the affairs of the state. Having placed a single individual in a commanding position, the commission proposed an independent legislature to exercise 'effective restraint' on that person, provided the members of the legislature were not in a position to 'seriously interfere' with the administration. The obvious contradiction between an independent legislature and a legislature with limited powers in respect of the executive escaped the attention of the commission.

How would the Presidential system work, when the character of politicians remained what it was according to the commission's own analysis? The answer was that when ministers were not utterly dependent on their supporters, they would act on the right lines! The need for political support, it seemed to the commission, was at the root of all evils: it was the dependence on political support which was responsible for the gradual fading of all the bright qualities of a politician. Once he was relieved of this pernicious necessity he would begin to act as a selfless and dedicated servant of the people. The commission argued itself into a position where all the essential elements of the political process, namely political support, political accountability, and political pressure came to be seen as malevolent influences, repugnant to the interests of the people. Having discarded the requirements of the political process, the commission found no difficulty in putting its trust in the authority of a single individual who should be left free, as far as possible, to run the affairs of the country. The commission argued that under the parliamentary system, a Prime Minister 'may not be a man of great merit, nor can he, in his turn, select his ministers on merit', but a President would have the freedom to select his team 'from amongst the ablest of men available and not necessarily from amongst the members of the parliament.' The possibility that even a President might sometimes suffer from human frailties did not occur to the commission.

Having faithfully adopted Ayub's constitutional scheme, the commission thought it politic to demonstrate its independence. It did that by sounding a 'note of warning'. The Presidential form should not be regarded as foolproof: the commission had recommended it after careful consideration of 'the possibilities and the probabilities of the situation'. One was left wondering about 'the possibilities and the probabilities of the situation' which had weighed with the commission. Did it mean there was no possibility of any system, other than the Presidential form of government, being accepted by Ayub, and if any other form was recommended the probability was that the commission would find itself disbanded and consigned to oblivion?

The commission studied the question whether the President, the Vice-President, and members of the legislatures should be elected by universal or restricted suffrage, and whether this should be done directly or through an electoral college. The commission advanced the view that the President should be elected directly, but on the basis of restricted franchise, considering his great responsibilities and the conditions in Pakistan. Because of the low level of literacy 'amongst the people, whose passions can easily be inflamed' it would be unwise to extend franchise to all the adult citizens. The franchise should be restricted to those who had attained a minimum standard of literacy or those who possessed 'sufficient property, or stake in the country'. The commission raised no objection to Ayub's election as President through the BDs for the first term of three years.

Regarding the Islamic character of the Constitution, the commission relied mainly on the provisions of the 1956 Constitution. The commission took an occupational interest in the subject of judiciary, and argued in favour of extending the age of retirement of the judges, increasing their emoluments and pension, and even urging the state to utilize 'the experience and ability of retired judges, especially in these days of dearth of talent'.

Two other documents deserve mention: one was drafted by Manzur Qadir on 26 May 1960 and the other entitled 'Thoughts on Constitution' was submitted by Zulfikar Ali Bhutto on 10 October 1959.[16] Manzur Qadir's paper was based on two assumptions (1) it was impossible for all the people 'to participate in the process of government', and (2) all the people 'are not qualified to form opinions on matters like fiscal policies, legal technicalities, scientific developments and the like'. Manzur Qadir argued that the breakdown of democratic institutions in Pakistan since Independence was due to the disregard of conventions and inadequate understanding of their real purpose:

The Constituent Assembly succeeded in perpetuating its position as a regent because there was no machinery to control the regent. Nor was there any process to select the men to run the institutions. To prevent the recurrence of events, which enabled the Constituent Assembly to prolong its life, restraints should be placed upon the sovereign power, and a substantial section of the people should be made aware of the need for those restraints so that they may be able to act as guardians of the sovereign power against the possible violations of it.

Bhutto started his paper by quoting Alexander Hamilton that if the representatives of the people betrayed their constituents, 'the citizens must rush tumultuously to arms without concern, without system, without resource, except in their courage and despair'. He defended the abrogation of the (1956) Constitution and said that, in 1954, there was still 'a dim hope for democracy to survive and succeed', but in the following four years 'the degeneration and decay reached uncontrollable dimensions'. Bhutto urged Ayub to give the country a fundamental law true to the genius and requirements of the people: 'A basic law without harmful compromises that render the structure into a weak and unworkable legal edifice.' Such an arrangement, he recognized, might invite unfavourable reactions from the West, but 'let us not be too sensitive to the reactions of democratic countries.' Bhutto suggested that the Constitution should mention the ideology of Islam in the preamble but 'the crusade for uniting the nation into an indivisible entity through the great force of Islam is to be mainly carried out by political, economic and social objectives, outside the Constitution.' The Constitution should, therefore, contain 'minimum reference to ideology'. Bhutto lauded the work that had already been done to implement

...the great and bold experiment of Basic Democracies [which] will form the base of the pyramid. By the beginning of next year, the foundation would have been well laid. Certain constitutional developments up to the level of the provincial advisory committees will automatically emerge from the womb of Basic Democracies. No new or separate *device* [emphasis added] is required up to this level. The *mechanism* [emphasis added] up to the governor's advisory councils is the logical sequel of Basic Democracies. The President's feeling is that election of the President and that of the parliament should be achieved through an electoral college constituted from the elected members of the Union Panchayts. This then is the combination of direct and indirect elections.

Bhutto was merely echoing Ayub's ideas but employing more sophisticated language. He thought it 'imperative for the executive to be independent of the legislature'. The President must not be subject to any legislative control:

> The President who is to be elected separately by the people through the indirect franchise of the electoral college, formed under the Basic Democracies, must be free and unhampered to act in the national interest without any interference. His remaining in office must not in any way be dependent on the authority of legislature.

Bhutto supported Ayub's view that there was no room for provincial legislatures or autonomous provincial government in the proposed constitutional plan: 'If we are to have a unitary government, the provinces would not exist as we have them today. Authority will not be divided. All policy will be determined by the central government and administered, wherever necessary, by the regions at different levels.' He saw the provinces acting as agents of the central government. But there must be no 'decentralization of policy'. If the regions were to be the agents of the central government, they must have only 'the powers of an agent'. Under no circumstances must the agent become 'more powerful than the principal'.

Bhutto was prepared to admit that some of his views could be considered 'undoubtedly unorthodox' and there might be many points 'needing improvement and even contradiction' but, on the whole he was convinced of the soundness of his constitutional proposal. Bhutto's ideas did not strike Ayub as unorthodox since they were in such close conformity with his own thinking.

While Manzur Qadir's brief strengthened Ayub in his opinions, Bhutto's opinion encouraged him in his tactics. It was interesting how everyone around Ayub, particularly those whom he chose to consult, arrived at the same conclusion as Ayub, though they did not always follow the same route. Ayub was greatly impressed by this and came to believe that his ideas had the power to convert his associates to his point of view. 'It is surprising', he would often say, 'how people who are totally opposed to me, begin to understand my ideas, once I have talked to them.'[17]

Ayub was flooded with unsolicited letters offering him advice about the kind of Constitution he should give to the country. Some of his correspondents were innocent folk, others had a definite axe to grind. In 1959 Ayub had written a paper on the 'Islamic Ideology in Pakistan' which was circulated to army officers among others. One of them, Brigadier M. Rafi Khan, who later became his Military Secretary, suggested to Ayub that Islam should be interpreted rationally and blind imitation of tradition should be abandoned. In his reply, Ayub said that the misfortunes of the Islamic world were due to the inability of the Muslims to evolve sound political, social and economic institutions based on the principles of the Qur'an. As a result tyrants, vested interests, and priesthood combined and took charge of the people and kept them backward, resulting in total stagnation: 'In order to develop a dynamic and creative society, people must be assured of a reasonable measure of freedom and equality.' They should be encouraged to inculcate 'the habit of scientific thinking and free enquiry' so that the country can 'move with the time, and perhaps, ahead of time.'[18]

Ghulam Ahmad Parwez, editor of a religious journal and author of several books on Islam, wrote to Ayub on 18 June 1959. He recalled an earlier meeting with him in August 1959, when he had explained 'how the 1956 Constitution was un-Islamic, how its abrogation, and the military revolution were justified, how a progressive Islamic Constitution could be framed, and how the reactionary forces working actively in the country could be neutralized.' According to Parwez, Ayub had been 'pleased to accept' his views, 'and decided to go ahead'. The immediate provocation for this letter was the publication of Chaudhri Mohammad Ali's reply to the Constitution Commission's questionnaire. Parwez had read Mohammad Ali's answers and could see a serious danger threatening the 'solidarity of Pakistan, the future of Islam in Pakistan, as well as your own position for which, due to your love for Islam, I possess immense respect and regard.' Parwez claimed that he had suggested a military takeover in October 1957, and reminded Ayub that when the 'revolution' came a year later 'everyone acclaimed you as Pakistan's saviour.'

Parwez referred to what he thought had been 'agreed' during his meeting with Ayub: the *ulema* must not be allowed to exploit religious sentiments, and an atmosphere should be created 'gradually and imperceptibly' to educate the people to accept:

(1) That the 1956 Constitution was un-Islamic and unworkable and deserved to be scrapped;

(2) That the parliamentary system was unsuited to Pakistan's conditions;

(3) That political parties and religious sects were anti-Islamic;

(4) That a Constitution on Islamic lines, progressive, dynamic and rational, was the only solution for Pakistan's problems.

Parwez stated that he belonged to no religious sect or political party, having never formed any: 'To me the establishment of parties is *shirk*' [meaning 'associating equals with God'—the gravest sin for a Muslim].

Ayub replied to Parwez on 2 July 1960 conveying his appreciation of the views expressed by him but, more important, he issued on 4 July 1960, a directive to the Governors of East and West Pakistan, asking them to put down with a heavy hand 'any attempt at irresponsibility' by former politicians and political *ulema*, who were trying to rehabilitate themselves, using the Constitution Commission's questionnaire as a means of creating disaffection against the government. A copy of the directive was endorsed to the Commander-in-Chief of the Pakistan Army with the remark, 'I hope to discuss these matters further with you and others on 14th.' This directive further damaged the reputation of the Constitution Commission and demonstrated the limits of public debate on the Constitution that Ayub was prepared to allow.

The report of the Constitution Commission was presented by the Chairman of the Commission to Ayub on 6 May 1961, at a solemn ceremony.[19] The report was not released to the Press. Ayub immediately recorded his comments on the report in a twenty-three-page memorandum. Ayub said he was 'most struck by the report's sobriety and balanced approach and presentation.' He thought it was 'a monumental document worthy of the highest consideration and respect', but the eulogy ended on the note 'so, whilst commenting on the report I do not wish to convey the impression that I, in any manner, mean to belittle the quality or excellence of the report.' Ayub explained:

> My comments are in the nature of basic differences in some places, the need for re-check of certain recommendations, and removal of doubts in others. And all these emerge from the peculiar experience and advantages I [have] enjoyed since the inception of Pakistan. If there is anyone who should have an overall view of the conditions and problems of Pakistan, it is me.

Recounting his advantages, he mentioned first that as Commander-in-Chief of the Pakistan Army, he had 'seen every inch of Pakistan, mostly from [the] ground, and met and exchanged views with all manner of people.' Then he had witnessed 'the functioning of different governments from very close quarters and gone through the mental torture of seeing chicanery and inefficiency on a perilous scale. A stage came when even my faith in the future of the country began to shake.' Finally, he understood the strategic problems of the country, and had acquired during the last three years 'the experience of running the country'.[20]

Given all these advantages, Ayub had come to the conclusion that

> ...politically, our people are immature. They are in the process of emerging from the tribal and feudal state. By and large, their horizon and thinking is still individualistic, tribal and parochial. However, there are signs that after a couple of generations are reared in an atmosphere of freedom and suitable education on which we have launched, a national outlook will emerge. Until then we shall have to be continually on our guard, and may even have to do things to *save people against themselves* [emphasis added].

On the question of ideology he felt that 'the true spirit of Islam has missed us'. If the Muslims of Pakistan failed to develop this spirit they 'are sure to disintegrate'.

Ayub rejected the commission's suggestion that it might be useful to set up a franchise commission:

> What can a commission tell us? Franchise on property or educational qualifications basis or adult franchise as in the past? The two former bases,

if accepted, will wreak havoc in the country. The effect will be disenfranchisement of a large number of people, especially in the rural areas where some eighty-five per cent of our population lives, and complete imbalance in power between the rural and urban population, creating a great schism in our society. About direct adult franchise, of course, I need not say much. It will be the undoing of every good that has been done and perhaps laying the foundation of disintegration of the country. I am, therefore, totally opposed to any such proposal, which seems to have been put forward to satisfy those who are brought up on the textbooks of English and American liberalism, without any sense of realism or practical common sense.[21]

Ayub insisted that in Basic Democracies the country had at last found

...a system which gives the broad masses of people satisfaction to choose representatives from their knowledge who, in turn, will have wider horizon to elect the President and the members of legislature. To condemn them merely because a small proportion of Basic Democrats are uneducated is nothing but pedantry. I have met a large number of them and have been most struck by their appearance, sound and healthy outlook.[22]

Having categorically rejected direct elections on the basis of universal franchise, Ayub directed that no one must belittle the importance of Basic Democrats in any manner. As representatives of the people they enjoyed a position of equality with government officials, at different levels, and must have a direct say in the running of the country.

A Cabinet sub-committee was appointed to examine the report of the Constitution Commission under Manzur Qadir's chairmanship. Other members of the committee were Zulfikar Ali Bhutto, M. Shoaib, A.K. Khan and Muhammad Ibrahim. The Cabinet Ministers and the Governors of East and West Pakistan were each given a copy of the commission's report, along with the observations recorded by Ayub. Notable among the other recipients of the report was Sir Muhammad Zafarullah Khan, a prominent member of the Ahmadiya sect, known for his legal and political experience.

Governor Kalabagh, a feudal lord who ran West Pakistan with an iron hand, had no time for 'intellectual theorists who live in a

world of their own and who would like to swim above the current.'
Sir Muhammad Zafarullah Khan attacked the commission's
recommendation that political parties should be allowed to
function. This recommendation, he said, was based on the hope
that as a result of the experience of the last three or four years
'political parties will emerge washed clean of all the elements that
had made the working of the old Constitution impossible'. That
hope was 'bound to prove vain and illusory'. It would require a
generation or so 'before the people of Pakistan could be trained in
the running of a representative form of government'. He agreed
with the Commission that 'it was a mistake for us to make a
sudden jump to universal adult franchise for the purpose of
electing representatives to our provincial and central legislatures'.
He recalled that his 'was the only voice raised against this step in
the Cabinet when the matter came up for discussion before us.'[23]
He thought it would be 'wise to start with a somewhat restricted
franchise, and then work by stages towards universal adult
franchise.' Zafarullah was 'in complete accord' with Ayub's
electoral arrangement which provided 'both a system of training
and a safeguard against the dangers of which we already have had
experience'.

Supporting the Presidential form of government Zafarullah
acknowledged with approval that

> ...the President will necessarily be the lever and mainspring of the whole
> system, and it is inevitable that he must exercise and bear full responsibility
> in respect of the government and administration of the state. That is a very
> delicate position. There are dangers inherent in it, but it is also capable of
> yielding great and lasting benefits. We have to take a risk on the former in the
> hope of gaining the latter.[24]

There was a stream of letters from Pir Ali Muhammad Rashdi,
Pakistan's Ambassador to the Philippines. During his state visit
to the Philippines Ayub asked Rashdi for his views on the
Constitution and gave him some papers on the subject. Rashdi
returned those papers to Ayub with a letter on 19 December 1960,
and volunteered to come to Pakistan to undertake 'a hurried
confidential survey of the home scene from the angle of a

discerning politician.' He could discover the Opposition's plans
and 'suggest how to forestall them, and to take the wind out of
their sails in advance so that when the Constitution comes into
force they find that the ground has been already completely cut
from beneath their feet.'[25]

Rashdi claimed that having investigated 'the causes of rise and
fall of the various ancient Moslem states,' he had arrived at a
'sensational conclusion'. The conclusion was that

> ...if we have to cut ourselves completely and permanently off from our recent
> unhappy past, if we have to put an end to all fissiparous tendencies,
> uncertainties, and conflicts, if we have to maintain Pakistan's unity and
> vitality as a state, we must provide a spectacular human symbol of our
> combined nationhood, an enduring pivot, a visible centralizing and balancing
> magnetic pole—permanent, unshakeable, and above the day-to-day conflicts
> and controversies—through the establishment of monarchy.

Despite Rashdi's eloquence, Ayub did not embrace the temptation
of monarchy.

Ayub did not have much direct information about the views and
reactions of the intelligentsia in East Pakistan. He was not conversant
with the Bengali language and what little appeared in the vernacular
newspapers and journals of Dhaka rarely reached him, except in the
form of translated excerpts. In any case he had little time for the
Opposition Press which he had come to treat as mischievous and
subversive. His personal contact with East Pakistan was limited to
official contacts and meetings with pro-government East Pakistani
politicians and academics. Ayub did not receive a single letter from
any Bengali who was not a government official, about the future
Constitution, which showed how distant and alien he must have
appeared to the people of East Pakistan. Despite the lack of personal
contact with the people of East Pakistan, Ayub was well-served by his
intelligence agencies and some of his East Pakistani Ministers. An
assessment given to him by the Intelligence Bureau towards the end
of July 1961 cautioned him that

> A good deal of the political and other activities would depend on the form of
> the future Constitution.... The people in this province will not be satisfied

unless the Constitution ensures them in reality equal and effective participation in the management of the affairs of the country, equal share of development resources and, in particular, full control over the administration of this province. The intelligentsia would also like to see a directive principle in the Constitution to increase speedily East Pakistan's share in the defence services as well as equal representation of East Pakistanis in the central services.

Muhammad Ibrahim, Minister of Law, wrote to Ayub on 6 May 1961:

> The first and foremost thing is the solidarity and strength of Pakistan.... But solidarity depends on the willing consent of the people to live together. These things are fundamental and must be secured and safeguarded. In order to do that it is essential that there should not be mutual suspicion, distrust, fear of domination and wide economic inequality between the East and West.

He referred to the widening economic gap between the two wings and recommended that 'the responsibility for their economic development should be cast respectively on the provinces themselves and for that end each province should be recognized as a separate economic entity'. 'This is sound', was Manzur Qadir's comment on this suggestion, but Ibrahim's next suggestion that 'the central government should have only Defence, Foreign Affairs, Inter-wing Communications and Currency; all the remaining subjects should be the concern and responsibility of the provinces' was dismissed by Manzur Qadir as unsound. Ibrahim's personal preference was 'for parliamentary government based on adult franchise, subject to such provisions as may be appropriate for strict party discipline, and for restricting eligibility for membership'. Manzur Qadir's reaction was 'this again will bring about chaos.'

Ibrahim suggested that if it was decided to adopt the presidential form of government then the provincial governors should be elected. 'How can this work?' asked Manzur Qadir, though he was inclined to agree with the suggestion that 'the governor must always be a man of the province.' Ibrahim then made a recommendation which must have appeared outrageous, if not treasonable: 'As regards the provincial subjects the provincial

Constitution may be made by the President in consultation with representatives of the respective provinces.' Was the Law Minister contemplating one Constitution for the centre and another for the provinces? Neither Ayub nor Manzur Qadir made any comment on this. Ibrahim proceeded to demand that 'there must be some law or convention that the post of President and Vice-President shall rotate between the two wings alternately.' He also asked for equal representation for the two provinces in the central Cabinet, and wanted the permanent seat of the central legislature to be located in Dhaka.

A.K. Khan, a Bengali industrialist, who was Ayub's Minister for Industries, wrote him a letter from Chittagong, on 15 July 1960, informing him of his meetings with Nurul Amin and Maulvi Tamizuddin Khan in Dhaka. 'Both of them had expressed themselves in favour of the federal and parliamentary system of government before the Constitution Commission.' A.K. Khan reported that they believed that the geographical position of the country demanded a federal parliamentary system of government; the unitary form of government could only work in a country composed of contiguous regions. When A.K. Khan asked Maulvi Tamizuddin Khan about the safeguards to prevent the repetition of the chaotic conditions of the past regimes, Tamizuddin suggested that the Constitution should require an elected member to resign his seat before changing his party affiliation.

A.K. Khan suggested that Ayub should meet these two gentlemen when he next visited Dhaka: 'I believe they will welcome such an opportunity. We are arranging for a few selected men to see you, both at Dhaka and Chittagong.' Ayub had this meeting a few days later which developed into a fierce exchange between him and Tamizuddin Khan. The latter maintained, despite Ayub's impatient interruptions, that the parliamentary system was the only form of government suitable for Pakistan. Ayub gave up in frustration.

The Cabinet sub-committee which had been appointed to examine the report of the Constitution Commission was deeply divided: the Bengali ministers demanded greater autonomy for East Pakistan particularly in the sphere of economic development and their West Pakistani colleagues insisted on maintaining a powerful central government under the presidential system. Bhutto continued to advocate the unitary form of government where the provinces would act only as agents of the centre and there would be no provincial legislature.

Manzur Qadir had by now drafted the Constitution on the basis of the outline prepared by Ayub which had been formally approved by the Governors' Conference in May 1959. He treated the Constitution Commission's report as a helpful document which he could draw upon for support wherever he found it consistent with Ayub's plan. The Law Minister, having stated his point of view, studiously avoided taking any further part in the deliberations of the government. The Industries Minister, A.K. Khan, too, was disappointed by Ayub's lack of response to his proposals. The Commerce Minister, Hafiz-ur-Rahman, was a quiet but intense man by temperament. He would often say that the whole constitutional exercise was aimed at establishing a highly centralized system of government which he feared would prove disastrous for East-West Pakistan relations. These three Bengali ministers would be dropped from the Cabinet after the promulgation of the new Constitution.

The advice which Ayub was receiving from the West Pakistanis and the Bengalis differed in quality, as in character. The main concern of the West Pakistanis, particularly the Punjabis and the Muhajirs,[26] was to save Ayub Khan from the machinations of politicians and to establish an all powerful and dominant central government. For them the question of regional autonomy was irrelevant. Even such luminaries as Sir Zafarulla Khan favoured the Presidential form of government. None of the West Pakistanis whom Ayub consulted had any faith in the democratic process or favoured an unfettered exercise of the right of franchise. Fundamentalists like Ghulam Ahmed Parwez and secularists like Manzur Qadir were both agreed on one point: there was no need or place for political parties in Pakistan. However, no one had the originality of Rashdi, who urged Ayub to become a monarch because Pakistan had been fortunate enough to discover in Ayub and his family the most suitable dynasty to rule the country.

Ayub was convinced that most of the politicians, though debarred from politics, had not given up their old ways and were busy creating confusion in the public mind about the Constitution. He did not realize that by using the Basic Democrats as an electoral college to get a vote of confidence for himself, and then converting that vote into a mandate for assuming the office of the President, he had already defeated the purpose for which he had set up the Constitution Commission. It was with some impatience that Ayub decided that he had had enough advice and the time had come for him to give a verdict on all contentious matters. About the ideology of Islam, he decided that it should be left to the members of the legislature to interpret all questions relating to the Qur'an and Sunnah. He was not prepared to entertain the claim of any group of religious scholars to interpret and decide matters pertaining to Islam. About the form of government, Ayub decided that the country needed the Presidential form under which the centre should have powers over all subjects. He was convinced that he had given sufficient recognition to the principle of universal franchise by allowing the people to elect their representatives at the local level. He was firmly opposed to direct election of the President or members of the national and provincial legislatures. Ayub had no doubt in his mind that whatever he was doing was in the interest of Pakistan. He was profoundly conscious of the difficulties of ordinary men and women, particularly in the rural areas, and wanted to alleviate those difficulties by all means at his disposal. But the people as the sovereign authority, to whom he was answerable, did not figure in his political plan. He viewed the people as a collection of uneducated and inexperienced groups of persons who needed help, guidance and protection which it was his duty and responsibility to provide. In this he was encouraged by Manzur Qadir and Bhutto. The former was convinced that the doctrine of the will of the people, if not fundamentally flawed, was inapplicable to the prevailing conditions in Pakistan, and the latter saw the people as useful pawns in a grand game of statecraft which could be moved and manipulated to serve any political purpose.

It was in this atmosphere of official confidence that Ayub promulgated his Constitution on 1 March 1962. Announcing the Constitution he said it was 'a blending of democracy with discipline'. The public rejection of the Constitution was instantaneous and unanimous. It was seen as an elaborate design to perpetuate one-man rule in the country. The only thing that provided some relief was the fact that martial law was lifted with the promulgation of the Constitution. Ayub saw the country 'behaving like a wild horse that had been captured but not yet tamed'.[27] He thought his critics were trying to break his will: 'They wanted me to feel that I would not be able to run the country without them. That was their game.'[28] Taming the wild horse now became Ayub's principal concern and the whole machinery of government was mobilized to suppress political dissent. What annoyed Ayub most was the behaviour of the Press: servile proprietors, submissive editors and pliable journalists, who had been at his beck and call so long as martial law was in force, suddenly assumed the role of rebels and liberators. The provincial governors carried out Ayub's instructions to the letter and within a few months the country was reduced to a state of sullen subservience. Ayub's Constitution did not resolve any of the major political problems, it merely swept them under a heavy authoritarian carpet.

Fortunately for Ayub the international situation took a dramatic turn in the second half of 1962. India's relations with China had been getting strained because of India's refusal to recognize China's claim to certain territory along the McMahon Line. The Indian Prime Minister, Pundit Jawaharlal Nehru, extended Indian administration through the North-East Frontier Agency (NEFA). He refused to believe that the Chinese would have the courage to go to war with India, the largest democracy in the world. Brandishing his stick in the Indian Parliament, Nehru said that if the Chinese made any move across the border, Indian forces would drive them back. Nehru's miscalculation drove the two countries to war in October 1962. That provided the Americans with a great opportunity to wean India away from her much trumpeted policy of non-alignment by rushing arms to India in response to her desperate appeals for help, much to the disappointment and alarm of Pakistan. Neither Ayub nor the Chinese knew that on 19 November 1962, forty-eight hours

before the Chinese declared a unilateral cease-fire, Pundit Nehru
had made a hysterical plea to Kennedy to save India from the
incoming Chinese soldiers who had demolished the Indian forces
and morale in less than two weeks, and were threatening to run
over the whole of India. Nehru urged Kennedy to bomb a number
of strategic sites on the Chinese mainland which, he thought,
would force the Chinese to retreat. As a result of these pleas India
and USA came to a formal military arrangement against China on
a long term basis.[29]

The Americans expected Ayub to fall in line with their plans
and give full support to India in her war against China. This Ayub
refused to do. He dismissed the whole American plan as unrealistic
and proceeded to settle Pakistan's boundary dispute with China
through direct negotiations. The US and its allies were alarmed by
this development because they could not understand how Pakistan,
the most 'allied ally' of the US, could take an independent line and
subvert their whole regional strategy. The Chinese responded
positively to Ayub's overtures, which further alarmed the
Americans. They began to exercise pressure on Nehru to enter
into negotiations with Pakistan to settle the Kashmir dispute.
India's swift and humiliating defeat in her war with China and
American disenchantment with Ayub propelled Pakistan on a
course of conflict with India.

As relations between India and Pakistan worsened and serious
strains began to develop in Pakistan's alliance with the US, the
constitutional and domestic problems, which were beginning to
threaten Ayub's position, receded into the background.

NOTES

1. Ayub Khan, op. cit., p. 30.
2. State Vs Dosso, 1958-see PLD 1958 Supreme Court 533. It is interesting to recall that
   on an earlier reference made by President Iskander Mirza, the Supreme Court had
   given a ruling that the President did not have the power to dissolve the National
   Assembly during the transitional period under the Constitution; Special Reference
   No.1 of 1957.
3. *Dawn*, Karachi, 10 October 1958.

4. On 28 February 1959, new regulations were promulgated giving military courts sole jurisdiction in offenses against martial law and authorizing the re-establishment of summary and special military courts throughout the country. The measure, it was claimed, was designed against black marketing and crime.

5. Ayub's diary, 22 May 1958.

6. Ayub Khan, op. cit., p. 190.

7. *Dawn*, 3 December 1958.

8. Ibid., 16 January 1958.

9. *Pakistan Observer*, Dhaka, 22 February 1959.

10. *Dawn*, 24 March 1959.

11. Ibid., 4 July 1959.

12. Ayub Khan's personal papers.

13. Ayub Khan, op. cit., pp. 187-92.

14. A barrister and landholder from the United Provinces, India; Leader of the United India Party in the Legislative Assembly; nominated to Council of State, 1935. Brigadier F.R. Khan was Information Secretary and Q.U. Shahab was Secretary to the President.

15. Chaudhri Muhammad Ali, *The Task Before Us,* Research Society of Pakistan, 1974, pp. 61-85.

16. Author's personal papers.

17. Ibid.

18. Ayub's letter to Brigadier Muhammed Rafi Khan, dated 28 September 1959.

19. Report of the Constitution Commission, Government of Pakistan, 1961.

20. Ayub's personal papers.

21. Ibid.

22. Ibid.

23. Sir Muhammad Zafarullah Khan was Minister for Foreign Affairs between 1947 and 1954.

24. Ayub's personal papers.

25. Ibid. When the US Embassy in Karachi reported the appointment of Rashdi as Ambassador to Philippines an officer of the State Department wrote on the embassy telegram: 'Rashdi is one of the most unscrupulous of Pakistani rascals; a power seeking man who would have his own brother's throat slit for profit.' G.K. Soulen, Department of State 790D.00/8-2157 Dated 21 August 1957.

26. Muslim refugees who migrated from India after 1947 and were mostly settled in Karachi and other towns of Sindh.

27. Ayub Khan, op. cit., p. 217.

28. Ibid.

29. *The Nehru Letters,* Appendix 1.

CHAPTER 4

The International Tightrope

Ayub was the architect of Pakistan's friendship and formal alliance with the United States. He was deeply conscious of the geo-political situation of the country surrounded as it was by three big neighbours: USSR, China, India, and a hostile Afghanistan. Ayub was fond of saying that in the field of foreign affairs he was constantly walking on a quadrangular tightrope—the art was not to lose one's balance. He did maintain a semblance of balance for a considerable time but keeled over in the end as the ropes intertwined and the trapezium collapsed.

Pakistan's relations with the US were based on the Mutual Security Defence Support Assistance Agreement signed in Karachi on 11 January 1955. The 1955 Agreement recognized mutual interest in 'the development of Pakistan's capacity to maintain its independence and security' and committed the US to 'furnish the Government of Pakistan such commodities, services, or such other assistance as may be requested by it and authorized by a Government of the US'. After this a pact of mutual co-operation was signed at Baghdad on 24 February 1955, 'to maintain their collective security and to resist aggression direct or indirect'. The Government of the US affirmed that it 'regards as vital to its national interest and to world peace the preservation of the independence and integrity of Pakistan'. This was followed by a bilateral co-operation agreement signed at Ankara on 5 March 1959, relating to CENTO. The Americans maintained that this agreement was limited by the Eisenhower Doctrine to cases of communist country aggression against Pakistan. But the US gave Pakistan an *aide-mémoire* on 5 November 1962, which clearly stated that '...the United States reaffirms its previous assurances that it will come to Pakistan's assistance in the event of aggression from India against Pakistan.'[1]

Pakistan joined the regional military pacts, SEATO and CENTO, which alienated her from the socialist countries, particularly the Soviet Union, and made her suspect in the eyes of the Afro-Asian community. These regional pacts were meant to secure Western strategic interests in the Middle East and South Asia but to Pakistan they provided a powerful deterrent against India. Pakistan allowed the Americans to establish a highly sophisticated communications base at Badaber near Peshawar which was of great strategic value to them. The Soviets saw that as a direct threat because the base allowed the Americans to maintain constant aerial surveillance over Soviet territory. When Pakistan's relations with the US became strained after 1962, Ayub started to worry about the risks Pakistan was incurring by letting the Americans operate from the Badaber base. In March 1965 when Ayub went to Moscow, the first visit by a Pakistani head of government to the Soviet Union, he came to an understanding with the Soviet leaders that the lease of the base, which was due to expire in 1969, would not be renewed. That laid the basis for normalization of relations with the Soviet Union and opened the possibilities of economic and military co-operation between Pakistan and the USSR.

Ayub's great disappointment was India. He offered India joint defence arrangements against foreign aggression in April 1959, within six months of coming to power. Nehru spurned the offer.[2] Why did Ayub make the offer? The Americans wanted Pakistan to establish friendly relations with India, and they had, perhaps, foreseen the possibility of India-China border dispute developing into a conflict, but Ayub genuinely believed, at the time, that India and Pakistan locked in joint defence could forestall any external aggression. Such an arrangement, he was convinced, would be in the interest of both countries. There were two major disputes between India and Pakistan: Kashmir and the division of Indus Basin waters. The Indus, with its five tributaries, is a great river on which the British developed a vast system of irrigation. When the subcontinent was partitioned in 1947, the province of Punjab

too was divided right across the Indus system of rivers. Pakistan
became the downstream riparian, leaving India in possession of
two major head-works, Madhupur and Ferozepur, which controlled
the supply of water to over 1.7 million acres of land in West
Pakistan. The rivers supported a large proportion of the population
of India and Pakistan. As the upper riparian India could deprive
Pakistan of the water flowing through its territory. India had given
an assurance to the Boundary Commission, which had demarcated
the boundaries of the two parts of the Punjab, that 'any arrangement
existing at the time of Partition as to sharing the waters of the
canals, or otherwise, would be respected by whatever government
acquired jurisdiction over the head-works concerned until new
arrangements were made.' India cut off the flow of water early in
April 1948 in all canals that came from India into West Pakistan.
For five weeks a million and half acres of land in West Pakistan
received no water and thousands of farmers were exposed to
starvation. Better sense prevailed and the supply of water was
restored but India continued to use the stoppage of water supplies
as a major lever of negotiations with Pakistan. The World Bank
offered its good offices in September 1951, to help resolve the
dispute, but it was not until Ayub came to power that an agreement
was reached to separate the water supplies of the Indus Basin
according to a plan drawn up by the World Bank.[3] This was quite
a breakthrough in Indo-Pak relations and Ayub hoped that he
might be able to persuade Nehru to resolve the Kashmir dispute
also in the same spirit, but he drew a blank.[4]

India-China relations

In the early 1950s friendship with China had been the cornerstone
of India's foreign policy, and the Chinese response to Indian
gestures of friendship was warm and enthusiastic. This great
relationship, dramatized by the much-chanted slogan *Hindee
Cheenee bhai-bhai* (Indians and Chinese are brothers) was a little
soured when Nehru discovered at the Bandung Conference, the
first ever get-together of Afro-Asian leaders in 1955, that Zhou

Enlai, whom he regarded as a protégé, was in fact a formidable rival. It was Zhou Enlai, soldier, poet and scholar, who outshone all the other luminaries and came to dominate the conference. Nehru, the great pundit, who was seen as a shining symbol of anti-imperialism, was completely eclipsed. By 1959 the two countries were squabbling over desolate Himalayan peaks. A summit meeting between Zhou Enlai and Nehru in April 1960 ended in frustration and ill-concealed recrimination. Thereafter, the two sides continued to exchange protest notes, as the Indians tried to establish an improved communications network along the border. The Indians also set up a number of posts and pickets in the western sector running from the Karakoram Pass to Demchok on the Indus while lodging protests against Chinese intrusions in the area. However, nothing much of significance happened and as a result of Soviet mediation the two countries agreed to enter into formal talks following the summit meeting. These talks, too, ended in a stalemate in December 1960. The Indian President, in his address to the budget session of the Indian Parliament in February 1961, announced that the Government of India was alert to the 'problems of aggression on and incursions into the sovereign territory of the Union'. During the debate on the President's address in the Upper House, Nehru said: 'The major advance of the Chinese forces into Indian territory took place in the summer of 1959. Ever since then there has been no advance anywhere.' The Chinese wanted that the border should be delimited and marked. Nehru rejected any suggestion of sitting down with the Chinese to define the border.

The situation was transformed when Ayub Khan suggested to the Chinese in November 1959 that the Pakistan-China border should be demarcated to eliminate any possibility of misunderstanding or dispute in the future. Ayub's move caused a stir not only in India but also among its Western allies and in the Soviet Union. Pakistan had introduced a wholly unexpected dimension into the strategic situation in the region.

The Indian leadership was positively cocky about their military prowess. Had the Indian forces not captured Goa in October 1961? The conquest of Goa 'had thrilled his people', Nehru claimed.[5] In January 1962, Nehru, while campaigning for Krishna Menon's election to Lok Sabha announced: 'I say that after Mr Menon became Defence Minister our defence forces have become for the first time a very strong and efficient fighting force. I say it with a challenge and with intimate knowledge…it is for the first time that our defence forces have a new spirit and modern weapons.'

India and China had signed a trade agreement covering the Tibet region in 1954 which was hailed by the two sides as a model for peaceful co-existence in Asia and elsewhere. Six months before the expiry of the agreement the Chinese suggested that negotiations should be taken up to renew the agreement. India declined to have any negotiations on a new agreement until China withdrew from the territory claimed by India. Two border incidents, one in Chipchap Valley and the other in Galwan Valley, resulted in the serious clash between Indian and Chinese forces, but on both occasions the Chinese withdrew and this confirmed the Indian belief that in the event of a real showdown 'the Chinese would do no more than huff and puff' and that if Indian troops remained resolute the Chinese would 'swerve away before the impact'.[6] But India pressed on with its forward policy in the Western sector to push the Chinese out of the territory claimed by India. It was in the Eastern sector, however, where the Chinese were not in occupation of any territory claimed by India that the Indian action of setting up a new post north of the McMahon Line invited swift retaliation. Diplomatic exchanges between India and China continued during August and September 1962. In October the Indians announced that a special force had been created to 'oust the Chinese'. When Nehru was asked by a reporter what orders had been given to the special force, he replied: 'Our instructions are to free our territory.' The reporter pressed: 'When?' and Nehru replied: 'I cannot fix a date, that is entirely for the army.'[7] With that the date was set and the war was on. The Chinese troops opened a heavy barrage on Indian positions leading to a full-scale war in October 1962.[8] Within less than thirty days the Indian forces along the front were encircled and routed and the entire disputed border area was captured by the

Chinese. Quite unexpectedly, the Chinese declared a unilateral cease-fire on 21 November and announced that their frontier guards would withdraw to positions behind the line of actual control that had existed between India and China on 7 November 1959. The Chinese decision astonished the world and turned India's military defeat into a national humiliation. This brief war transformed the security situation in the Indo-Pakistan subcontinent and fundamentally altered Pakistan's relationship with the United States.

President Kennedy had urged Ayub during the war to give India an assurance that it would do nothing to create any difficulties for her during her confrontation with China. Ayub declined to do that, and instead, used the opportunity provided by the war to conclude a boundary agreement with China, which caused consternation in India.

American interpretation of Chinese objectives

The US regarded the Chinese 'invasion' of India as part of the global communist strategy to overwhelm 'the free world'. Just when Kennedy had called the Russian bluff over Cuba, the Chinese, it seemed, were trying to enact a similar drama in the Indian subcontinent. For more than a decade the Americans had been trying to wean India away from communist influence. The Chinese action in the Himalayas gave them the opportunity they had been looking for and they immediately proceeded to extract the maximum advantage, regardless of their other commitments in the region. John Kenneth Galbraith, the US Ambassador in New Delhi, persuaded Kennedy that India should be given full military assistance including, if necessary, the protection of the nuclear umbrella, and that nothing should be done to encourage India formally to forsake its policy of non-alignment or to settle its differences with Pakistan. Galbraith made the India-China conflict his war and expressed great impatience with Pakistan's insistence that the US should exercise some pressure on Nehru to resolve the Kashmir dispute. To Galbraith such an approach smacked of blackmail. There were the Chinese grabbing Indian territory and the Pakistanis wanted the US to ask Nehru to hand over Kashmir to them. Since Dean Rusk, the US Secretary of State, and Robert McNamara, the Defence Secretary, were both engrossed in the Cuban Crisis, Galbraith could approach Kennedy directly, ignoring the State Department and the Department of Defence.

At the height of the crisis, Walter McConaughy, the US Ambassador in Islamabad, sought an interview with Ayub to deliver a letter from President Kennedy to him only to discover that Ayub was away hunting in Gilgit. Had he left the capital to make himself inaccessible? In desperation, the Ambassador barged into the residence of the Foreign Minister, Muhammad Ali Bogra, late at night, where a large dinner party was nearing its end. He impressed upon the Foreign Minister the urgency of giving some sort of assurance to Nehru so that he might be able to withdraw his forces from Pakistan's borders and deploy them against the Chinese. Such a gesture, he said, would soften India's attitude towards the Kashmir dispute and would be greatly appreciated by the US and other Western countries. Bogra told the Ambassador that Pakistan had to contend with two hostile neighbours, India and Afghanistan. There was no reason for her to incur the hostility of China. However, if the Americans would underwrite India's pledge to hold a plebiscite in Kashmir, the American request could be considered. McConaughy told Bogra that Nehru would react strongly against any such proposal. The American Ambasador continued to press the urgency of the situation and suggested that any indication given by Pakistan to India on the lines of the Kennedy proposal would remain in the strictest confidence. Bogra said he understood the American argument that in the long run it would be against Pakistan's interest to permit China to have a foothold in the plains of India but he emphasized that the feelings of the people would not allow Pakistan to make a unilateral gesture of friendship to India. Bogra presented Kennedy's letter to Ayub with the comment, 'God has given us a wonderful opportunity to get the Kashmir matter solved, provided India gets embroiled further. We should try to cash in on it.'[9]

At about the time that the US Ambassador was discussing President Kennedy's letter with Bogra in Islamabad, Aziz Ahmad, Pakistan's Ambassador in Washington, was summoned by Phillip Talbot, US Assistant Secretary of State, and told that the US had decided to give military assistance to India. Talbot did not give any details of the arms which the Indians had asked for but mentioned that Nehru had seen Galbraith and had asked for US arms aid against the Chinese. Galbraith, on the authority of the US Government, had informed Nehru that the US would give arms aid to India and it was up to Nehru to ask for what he wanted. Galbraith's account of his meeting with Nehru, as given in his *Journal* under the entries for 28 and 29 October, differs from Talbot's version. Galbraith met Nehru on 28 October to ask him whether he would welcome an assurance of no embarrassment from Pakistan. He found Nehru frail, brittle and desperately tired. Galbraith struggled to get a helpful word out of him. Nehru started by saying that he would have no objection to the Americans telling Ayub that he (Nehru) would welcome such an assurance. Could the Americans say that he would warmly accept such assurances? To this Nehru said of course the Americans could say that. There was no talk of arms aid during this meeting and Galbraith assured Nehru that the US was 'adhering to the policy of a quiet, steadfast friend'. Galbraith noted that even though no request for arms aid had been made, relations between his military attaché and the Indians had become extremely intimate. Galbraith had already summoned from Washington an American specialist in guerrilla operations. 'A week ago, of course, all this would have been unthinkable,' Galbraith noted with satisfaction. He assigned two colonels to draw up a movement table for elementary weapons for the Indian Army: 'I want to know how quickly and from where we can get such basic requirements as automatic rifles, mortars and shells. Once we are asked for aid, if we are asked, I hope we can have something come here within a matter of three or four days.' Under the entry for 29 October Galbraith described how he managed to secure an interview with Nehru so that the request for arms should come from him rather than from anybody else.

The Prime Minister, when I saw him, looked well and received the President's letter, an exceedingly good one, with gratitude. He told me that he had that morning addressed a letter to the President and Khrushchev congratulating them on the Cuban settlement. I then told the Prime Minister that if the President's letter produced a request for aid, as I gathered it would, I hoped it would come from him. I told him I was not playing on his vanity—but was not above doing so—but he must know he is loved in the US as no one else in India. The American people would respond to a request from him as they would not to anyone else.

Nehru told Galbraith that the Soviets had indicated that they would have no objection to India receiving arms aid from the US. He also said that such aid would not mean any military alliance between the US and India and Galbraith hastened to assure him that the US 'insisted on no such thing'. Galbraith later persuaded the Indian Foreign Secretary that the Press should be told that the request for aid had come from the Prime Minister. It is clear from these two entries that the request for aid was being extracted from Nehru as gently as possible.[10]

Aziz Ahmad told Phillip Talbot that the US had offered military aid to India without fulfilling the 'assurance of prior consultation' personally given by Kennedy to Ayub when they met in Washington in July 1961. Aziz Ahmed recalled what Ayub had told the Joint Session of the Congress of the United States on 12 July 1961

> …the only people who will stand by you are the people of Pakistan provided you are prepared to stand by them. So, I would like you to remember that, whatever may be the dictates of your commitments, you will not take any steps that might aggravate our problems or in any fashion jeopardize our security. And as long you remember that our friendship will grow in strength.[11]

Talbot explained that events had moved too rapidly and Kennedy had wanted to act without wasting any time; the US had been too preoccupied with the crisis in Cuba, and Ambassador McConaughy had found it difficult to reach Ayub Khan.[12] In response, Aziz Ahmad said that Ayub's temporary absence from Rawalpindi should not have prevented the US government from consulting the Pakistan Government.[13] Talbot grumbled about Ayub's inaccessibility and Aziz Ahmad maintained that simply informing Pakistan of the US decision to provide arms aid to India did not amount to consultation. An exasperated Talbot said that Pakistan's Foreign Minister had, in fact, been consulted on the subject during his recent visit to Washington. This was not in the knowledge of the Pakistan Ambassador. Galbraith noted in his *Journal* 'That Muhammad Ali [Bogra] had told Duncan Sandys in London that they would not make India's path more difficult, that India was in no danger of attack from Pakistan.'[14] McConaughy's meeting with Ayub on 20 October 1962, did not amount to consultation. At one point in the discussion Aziz Ahmed made the astonishing, and wholly unauthorized statement, that the Indian forces tied up on Pakistan's borders would be free to deal with the Chinese threat if there was an understanding between India and Pakistan on Kashmir. The full implications of this suggestion were not grasped by Talbot who merely remarked that 'there would be some dramatic changes in the subcontinent.'

Galbraith treated Talbot as one of the 'minor bureaucrats—who is unable to react.'[15] Galbraith noted, with unconcealed glee, the Indian request for transport aircraft:

In further modification of the non-alignment policy, the Indians also wish [American] pilots and crews to fly the aircraft. However, old habits die hard. When we went back at seven o'clock to work out details and get information on the need to support the request, all of the senior Air Marshals were unavailable. It was Saturday evening.

Three days later Galbraith noted:

The Indians at all levels are in a state of shock. Not one but two pleas are coming to us, the second one of them, still highly confidential. The non-alignment I was asked about at lunch is far out of date; *the Indians are pleading for military association* [emphasis added]. They want our air force to back them up so that they can employ theirs tactically without leaving their cities unprotected.[16]

Galbraith considered it unwise for the Indians to initiate any air action, but proposed all the same 'that we ask that elements of the

Seventh Fleet be sent into the Bay of Bengal, although this violated my rule that we do nothing that Indians did not request.'[17] The same day a message from President Kennedy brought 'the promise of airlift, air movement of spares for Indian transport planes of American origin which are urgently needed and proposals of three teams to help the Indians run the war'.[18]

Aziz Ahmad reported his meeting with Talbot to Islamabad and asked for permission to meet Dean Rusk and convey to him the point about the deployment of Indian troops against China once there was a firm understanding about Kashmir, which, he feared, had not been fully appreciated by Talbot. When Ayub saw the minutes of the Ambassador's meeting with Talbot he was extremely annoyed that Aziz Ahmad should have suggested to the Americans, without his approval, that if a firm undertaking were given by India for the settlement of the Kashmir dispute, Indian forces could be withdrawn from Pakistan's borders to fight the Chinese, leaving the defence of Kashmir to Pakistan. Ayub realized that the Americans would take this as an offer by Pakistan to engage the Chinese should the Indians agree to make a helpful commitment on Kashmir. On the Ambassador's despatch Ayub noted: 'This man gets quite excessive at times. Someone should tell him to get off the line.' The Ambassador was instructed not to mention, either directly or by implication, that Pakistan wanted a Kashmir settlement in order to be able to take over the defence of Kashmir against the Chinese to enable India to fight the Chinese elsewhere. Thus rebuked, Aziz Ahmad decided not to seek an interview with Rusk.

Ayub was playing a lone hand. He had a divided Cabinet. A group of ministers, led by the Finance Minister M. Shoaib, who had come on deputation from the World Bank with the good wishes of the US State Department,[19] was urging him to follow the American line, as were the CENTO heads of government, particularly the President of Turkey, who had promised to provide military hardware to India, and some of Ayub's close associates were urging him to move his forces into Kashmir. Ayub knew the risks of annoying the Americans but he was not prepared to expose Pakistan to the distrust and hostility of the Chinese which could have disastrous consequences. He understood better than anyone else in his government that any adventurous move in Kashmir would invite a massive retaliation from the Americans which Pakistan could ill afford. He did not want to alienate the Americans but he also wanted to use the opportunity that the Indo-China War had offered Pakistan to get closer to the People's Republic of China. He played his hand with great dexterity and skill though he lost the personal trust and support of the Americans in the process. He would pay a heavy price for that but Pakistan gained the friendship and support of China. That was Ayub's finest moment.

Ayub spent a great amount of time studying the Indo-China conflict and its repercussions on Pakistan's security. His personal view, as recorded on 28 October 1962, was that the scope of the conflict, because of the terrain, would perforce be limited. If the Chinese had larger objectives, the contest would have started much earlier. October was not the month to launch an invasion in an area where weather conditions would bring military operations to a halt by December. He was worried that the large amount of military equipment, which was being rushed to India by the US and the UK, would eventually be used against Pakistan. Ayub's assessment that the Chinese intentions did not extend to the conquest of vast chunks of Indian territory proved to be correct. To the surprise and relief of the world, the Chinese, having asserted their control over the territories claimed by them, declared on 21 November 1962[20] that their forces would cease fire in another twenty-four hours, and in another nine days begin to withdraw to positions twenty kilometres behind the actual line of control as it existed on 7 November 1959. This was exactly what Zhou Enlai had offered to Nehru in November 1959.[21]

The day after the cease-fire, Ayub addressed a special session of the National Assembly. A large crowd put up a vigorous demonstration outside the assembly building demanding the withdrawal of Pakistan from SEATO, CENTO and the Commonwealth. The crowd forced its way into the building and had to be dispersed by the police. Inside the House, Opposition members criticized the government for its failure to take advantage

of the India-China War to force a settlement of the Kashmir
problem. A member from Balochistan demanded the resignation
of the Cabinet for incompetence. The Opposition also demanded
the restoration of adult franchise and fundamental rights. It was
Ayub's unusually strong criticism of Western powers which
pacified the members. The Foreign Minister, Bogra, who was
known to be under American influence, announced that 'if Pakistan
were to find that its membership of SEATO and CENTO was no
longer in the national interest, it would quit both pacts without a
moment's hesitation.' To lend weight to this he disclosed that
'border negotiations [with China] were proceeding satisfactorily.'
Bhutto intervened at one point and advised caution 'in making
new friends and rejecting existing ones'. But he assured the
House that Pakistan's friendship with China was not only
unconditional, it was a fundamental principle of her foreign
policy.[22]

Ayub had jotted down in his own hand, the main points of his
speech on 19 November which shows that he must have known of the
Chinese decision to declare a unilateral cease-fire at least forty-eight
hours before its announcement. Ayub told the National Assembly
that Pakistan was placed in a difficult situation. Although India had
been defeated, it was not 'down and out'. For Pakistan 'the time to
march had not yet come'. The Americans had taken full advantage of
this and 'bagged' India. The Russian policy toward India might
change as a result of this and 'we should be ready to take advantage
of such an opportunity'. Ayub explained why Pakistan must not leave
the Western pacts even though these had not served Pakistan's
interests but he warned: 'If we find these pacts against our interest,
we shall not hesitate to give them up.' In the meantime, Pakistan
should continue to cultivate the Chinese 'without expecting the
Chinese to come to our assistance in time of need.' About Kashmir,
Ayub counselled the Assembly: 'We need Kashmir for the sake of
Pakistan. Calculated risks yes, but taking rash risks for Kashmir
would be a betrayal of Pakistan [which was] a place of refuge for the
Muslims of the subcontinent.'[23]

During his speech Ayub explained that one of the Chinese
objectives was the insulation of Tibet from Indian influence. The

route from Kashgar to Yarkand follows the traditional mule track into Tibet which the Chinese needed to develop into a road. If public opinion in India allowed Nehru to come to an agreement, the Chinese would perhaps give up their claim in other areas in exchange for their position in Ladakh. It was vital for the Chinese to protect their only line of communication between Sinkiang and Tibet. If the Chinese had any intention of waging a major war against India, they would have started their campaign in April or May when the snows begin to melt. Another limiting factor was the continuous Soviet pressure on China. The USSR did not want to lose India to the West. Ayub's address went down well with the Assembly.

The kind of pressures which Ayub was facing at the time are best illustrated by the conflicting positions his Ambassador in Washington was taking. Having failed in his attempt to sell the idea of relieving the Indians of any pressure from Pakistan, if there was an understanding on Kashmir, Aziz Ahmad had swung to the other extreme. He convinced himself that the Chinese would make a major move into Assam in order to secure the territory gained by them in the NEFA area. He wrote to Ayub on 8 November 1962, that the Chinese would do this by moving southwards through the wedge of Tibetan territory between Sikkim and Bhutan, to cut off Assam's link with the rest of India at its narrowest point. It would then become easier for them to take over the whole of Assam, which would give them control over territory adjoining the NEFA, apart from providing them with much needed oil. Aziz Ahmad suggested that Pakistan should forestall the Chinese advance by taking over the Lushai Hills (adjoining Chittagong Hill Tracts), the Tripura State, the Muslim majority areas of Cachar (which were unjustly separated from the Sylhet district and given to India under the Radcliffe Award) and other territory adjoining Sylhet (including the source of raw materials of Chatak Cement Factory), possibly up to and including Shillong. Having seized all this territory Pakistan could come to some understanding with the Chinese at the appropriate time. Aziz Ahmad thought that all this territorial acquisition could be easily explained to India: 'India need not consider this a step directed against her since she would have lost that territory in any case!' Ayub advised Aziz Ahmad to calm down: 'In spite of India's song and dance she still has the force to cover us as well as contain the Chinese.' Ayub explained: 'My reading is that in the desire to rush forward to help India with arms and ammunition, the Westerners, and especially the Americans, are almost in a state of madness and are not open to conviction. If they were, they would be telling Mr Nehru the sort of things they are telling us.'

Ayub was so confident about his analysis and assessment of the Chinese objectives that he freely offered it to any American official or journalist who came to see him. This infuriated the US State Department. Kennedy regarded Ayub as an obstructive and pompous fellow who had the temerity to hector his administration on foreign policy and defence strategy. Ayub, on the other hand, thought that Kennedy had lost all sense of proportion and was acting in a highly emotional manner. The problem for the Americans was that they could not afford to alienate Pakistan at the time. Pakistan, threatened by the enormous build-up of the Indian armed forces, would be forced to woo China, a possibility which the Western world could not but regard with alarm. The Americans and the British knew that by temperament, tradition and discipline, Ayub would not go too far with the Chinese, but he might go far enough to upset the balance of power in the region. Much as the Americans wanted India, whatever the price, they did not want to let go the bird in hand. The Indian bush was, after all, quite a murky and intertwined affair. Something had to be done to keep Ayub in good humour for the time being, but equally, India must not be put under any pressure. US pressure should be employed as a 'restraining influence' on Pakistan to India's advantage as far as possible.[24]

With the Indian administration in complete disarray Galbraith appointed himself as the custodian of India's interests against Pakistan. He openly expressed his disappointment that Pakistan, a member of SEATO and CENTO, should be 'forming some kind of axis with Peking'.[25] Any suggestion that the US should take a strong stand with India on Kashmir annoyed him: 'It would be seen that the Americans and Pakistanis were working together to seek the surrender of territory just as the Chinese were grabbing land. All would seem to be grabbing.'[26] Constant pressure was maintained on Ayub through commonwealth Heads of Government and member countries of CENTO to fall in line with US policy toward China, but Ayub refused to yield.

Why did Kennedy want that Ayub should 'signal to the Indians in a quick but effective way' that they need feel no concern on account of Pakistan? India had shown no anxiety about Pakistan. There was no direct or indirect Indian approach to Pakistan, except the letter which Nehru had addressed to all Heads of Government. The US State Department asked Galbraith to find out if Nehru would welcome an assurance that there would be no embarrassment from Pakistan and Galbraith approached Nehru as an anxious disciple approaches a failing guru:

> I was asked to seek an interview with Nehru to obtain this *assurance*. This I succeeded in getting at 6.45 p.m. Nehru was frail, brittle and seemed old and small. He was obviously desperately tired. The habit of a commanding role, the man who gives or refuses, is almost automatic, and when I asked him if we could tell Ayub that he, Nehru, would welcome these *assurances* he said in effect that he would have no objection to our saying so. I then moved in very hard on saying this would not be sufficient, that we must be able to say that he would warmly accept such *assurances*. He looked a little stunned, then said of course we could say it and went on to add that such a gesture from Pakistan would be important not only in the present situation, but in the future harmony of the two peoples. Taking advantage of a strong position, I then asked if I could be *assured* that he would respond to such *assurances*. He said on some appropriate occasion he would, and then I pressed that this was a time for generosity and he should be immediately forthcoming. Again he agreed.[27]

The Galbraith-Nehru meeting took place when the Indian forces had been routed in all sectors. Nehru knew that he had lost the war and any assurance from Pakistan at that time was of little military relevance. A day before the Chinese declared cease-fire the Americans sent twelve C-130 military transport planes to India. The planes were operated by US crew.[28]

Ayub had seen with growing distress the Americans wooing India regardless of their alliance with Pakistan. Public opinion in

Pakistan blamed Ayub for his failure to take advantage of what was considered a great opportunity to resolve the Kashmir problem. His critics blamed him for relying on America to persuade Nehru to come to terms with Pakistan when the Americans had told him that India should not be put under any pressure at a time when she was 'seeking, however ineffectively, to stand off a Chinese communist invasion'.

The Chinese must have been impressed by Ayub's resistance to American pressure. They now responded positively to Ayub's suggestion for the demarcation of the boundary between Pakistan and China not only as a token of appreciation of Pakistan's attitude during the India-China conflict but also because it was consistent with China's general policy of peaceful demarcation of disputed or undefined borders.

America was now pursuing two objectives in the region: to convert her military alliance with India into a permanent long-term arrangement and simultaneously restrain Pakistan from developing any further relations with China. The first enjoyed a higher priority since it was viewed by the Americans as of vital strategic importance to advance American interests in the region. Pakistan could harm American interests in India and it could also provide China with an opening to the world and this the United States was determined to forestall. They thought they could do this by arranging an elaborate exercise of India-Pakistan negotiations to resolve the Kashmir dispute through British mediation despite Galbraith's opposition.

Grasping the Kashmir nettle

The Indo-Pakistan talks about Kashmir ran parallel to Pakistan's negotiations with China to demarcate the border. Duncan Sandys, British Commonwealth Secretary, arrived in India along with President Kennedy's special envoy, Averell Harriman, after the Chinese cease-fire. The primary purpose of his mission was to lay the groundwork for providing substantial military assistance to India over the next three years. Averell Harriman and Duncan

Sandys had meetings with Nehru and other Indian ministers between 24-27 November 1962.[29] Duncan Sandys then flew to Rawalpindi on 27 November for a meeting with Ayub. He was joined by Harriman the next day. On 29 November 1962, the Governments of India and Pakistan issued a joint statement:

> The President of Pakistan and the Prime Minister of India have agreed that a renewed effort should be made to resolve the outstanding differences between their two countries on Kashmir and other related matters, so as to enable India and Pakistan to live side by side in peace and friendship. In consequence they have decided to start discussions at an early date with the object of achieving an honourable and equitable settlement. This will be conducted initially at the ministerial level. At the appropriate stage direct talks will be held between Mr Nehru and President Ayub.[30]

The joint statement was signed by Ayub and Nehru on 29 November 1962, and Nehru put the time 7.10 p.m. with the date under his signature. The statement contained the words 'discussions' and 'talks' instead of 'negotiations'. Nehru emphasized the distinction when he said that one could always talk even when there was no basis for negotiations. The day after signing the joint statement, Nehru said in Lok Sabha that during his talks with Averell Harriman and Duncan Sandys,

> The question of Kashmir was referred to, and we explained to them our position in regard to it, and pointed out that anything that involved an upset of the present arrangements would be very harmful to the people of Kashmir as well as to the future relations of India and Pakistan. We were, however, always ready to discuss this, as other matters, with representatives of the Pakistan Government at any level desired.

Nehru specifically denied the suggestion that Duncan Sandys or Harriman had put forward any proposals for partition or a plebiscite in Kashmir and added that 'it was not for Mr Sandys or anyone else to suggest what kind of talks we should have.'[31] One has only to compare the text of the joint statement signed late in the evening of 29 November, and the clarification given by Nehru in Parliament the next morning, to see that what was described as a renewed effort 'to resolve the outstanding differences' on Kashmir was meant to be no more than 'a friendly discussion'. Nehru wanted to clarify that there was nothing novel about entering into discussion with Pakistan on any problem. India was always ready to discuss Kashmir, as other matters, with Pakistan and had suggested meetings at various levels in the course of the last few months.[32] The issue was not India's willingness to talk, but Pakistan's failure to make a positive response to India's repeated offers. According to Nehru, Harriman and Sandys understood that the existing arrangements in Kashmir could not be upset, but still suggested that 'a friendly discussion about these matters between India and Pakistan might be helpful'. A Pakistani spokesman exclaimed in utter frustration that this made 'complete nonsense of the proposed talks'.[33]

Duncan Sandys saw Nehru's statement in Karachi while he was returning to London from New Delhi, having accomplished a particularly difficult mission. He cancelled his onward journey and flew back to Delhi. He released a statement to the Press on the morning of 1 December in which he said that he had returned to Delhi to meet Nehru in order to clear up the matter.[34] On 3 December Duncan Sandys reported to Ayub the results of his meeting with Nehru:

> I drove straight from the airport to his house and caught him just as he was going to bed. He was tired and not unnaturally irritated by my return. At first he genuinely did not seem to understand what all the fuss was about. He said that he had made his statement as he always does without a prepared text. His remarks had been made in answer to a question of which he had little notice, about a rumour on the BBC which suggested that the idea of partitioning Kashmir was already under discussion. He added that it was wrong to read too much into particular phrases. His statement should be read as a whole. He naturally did not like the idea of making any statement which could be interpreted as a retraction. However, at my insistence, he agreed that I should work out with Foreign Secretary Desai some statement which, while not involving any eating of words, would put a more favourable interpretation on what he had said and would help to allay some other doubts which his statement in Lok Sabha had aroused.[35]

Duncan Sandys feared that despite the corrective statement, Nehru's remarks in the Lok Sabha would strengthen the doubts of those who questioned his sincerity. But he thought that the incident had produced a favourable by-product to set on the credit side. Nehru had given a positive and public commitment to enter the talks without preconditions and not to exclude the consideration of any solution which Pakistan might decide to put forward. Nehru's explanatory statement was regarded in Pakistan as no better than a reassertion of India's familiar stand on Kashmir.

While the US government wanted to placate Ayub, Nehru too had an interest in creating the impression that bilateral talks between India and Pakistan held the promise of some solution of the Kashmir dispute. Such a prospect might deter Pakistan from pursuing boundary negotiations with China, which were clearly a threat to India.

Indo-Pakistan talks

The American Ambassador called on Ayub on 8 December 1962 and delivered a letter from President Kennedy saying that Harriman had fully briefed him about his talks with Ayub and some of his ministers. Kennedy appreciated that a start was being made on Kashmir and congratulated Ayub on his statesman-like approach. He added that a quick and easy solution to the problem was not possible. He singled out a remark Ayub had made to Harriman that a settlement of the Kashmir issue would cause dissatisfaction among many in India and Pakistan. But notwithstanding the dissatisfaction that any settlement might cause among his people, Ayub was still prepared to move in that direction with determination. The coming months, Kennedy added, would be a test of patience, perseverance and goodwill of both countries. He promised appropriate support and assistance in the search for a solution. He also mentioned what Ayub had told Harriman, that the Chinese aggression against India posed a threat to Pakistan and with the settlement of Kashmir there would be a long-term need for a combined plan for the defence of the subcontinent. Kennedy said that Ayub's discernment in this matter, going beyond the passions of the moment, was of the highest importance for Pakistan and the whole free world. Kennedy expressed his appreciation that Ayub had understood the need for the US and the UK to give military assistance to India to the extent necessary to make it possible for India to contain and defeat a renewed Chinese attack. This essentially was the purpose of the emergency military aid provided by the US to India and this would guide the US government in consideration of longer-term programmes. He promised to keep in touch with Ayub about further developments in US military aid to India and concluded on the note that this was a time not only of challenge but also of hope.

The American Ambassador, while delivering this letter, told Ayub that he had been called to Washington for consultation along with Galbraith, the US Ambassador in India. He wanted to know whether there was anything in particular Ayub wished to convey to Kennedy. Ayub said that the US would come under severe criticism if the volume of US aid to India were to put Pakistan at a serious disadvantage. Common sense demanded that the US, in its own interest, should insist on disengagement between India and Pakistan before making any definite commitment to India. This was, of course, entirely dependent on a just solution of the Kashmir problem. Should India fail to respond, the Americans must refuse aid until such time as a settlement was reached. There was no risk in following this line of action as the need for urgent supply of arms to India had vanished with the declaration of a cease-fire by the Chinese. Ayub also suggested that it might be a good thing to revive the idea of inducting Eugene Black (the World Bank President who had helped in resolving the Indus Basin Water dispute) or someone like him into India-Pakistan negotiations as an observer or arbitrator. In the meantime, it might be helpful if a 'sympathetic American' from the US embassy in Pakistan were attached to the American embassy in India to 'condition their thinking on the right lines'.[36] In conclusion, Ayub told the American Ambassador that if the US assessment about the subcontinent coming under renewed military pressure from China was correct then the first thing they should do was to bring Pakistan's military capacity to a level comparable to that of India. He did not visualize enlargement of Pakistan's manpower in arms, but there was need for modern arms so that Pakistan could ensure the security of her part of the subcontinent. Such support should be given along with long range support to India, and made contingent on India-Pakistan disengagement after the solution of the Kashmir problem.

Morrice James, the British High Commissioner in Pakistan, paid a short visit to India under instructions from Duncan Sandys. On his return, he tried to reassure Pakistan's Foreign Secretary, S.K. Dehlavi, that the forthcoming talks were not just a device by India to gain time and could produce positive results. He had seen Nehru in excellent health and almost rejuvenated. His assessment was that public opinion in India was ahead of Nehru's thinking on Kashmir and favoured a settlement. In fact, Nehru was under strong pressure to bring about normalization of relations with Pakistan. His meeting with the Indian Foreign Secretary had given him the clear impression that the Indians were coming with a sincere desire to discuss Kashmir 'thoroughly and down to the bottom'. James also said he had found Galbraith 'very interesting though he is not always a very practical person'. He mentioned that the midnight rush on the part of Sandys to obtain a clarification of Nehru's statement had slightly annoyed the Indians but that did not mean he had expended his usefulness. James was a little taken aback when Dehlavi told him that the Indians were coming only for three days, which were hardly enough to discuss the Kashmir problem threadbare. He had not been given any indication in Delhi that the Indians had put a three-day limit on the talks.[37]

Foreign Minister Bogra was unwell and Ayub decided that the Pakistan delegation should be led by Bhutto, who was then Minister for Industries and Natural Resources. A few days before the talks, the US Ambassador met Ayub and delivered a message from Kennedy dated 22 December. He also gave Ayub the particulars of the US-UK programme of military assistance to India. Kennedy agreed with Ayub that a settlement of the Kashmir problem would contribute more than anything else to the security of the subcontinent, but he made it plain that the programme of US-UK arms assistance could not be made contingent on the resolution of the Kashmir dispute.

Ayub replied to Kennedy after the first round of talks (2 January 1963). He admitted to being 'alarmed' by the scope of military assistance that Kennedy and Macmillan were proposing to provide to India:

> While the quantum of military support to India, which you have decided to extend in the Nassau meeting, may appear to be frugal in the context of your global strategy, we fear that it is sufficiently massive to alter the present ratio of military strength as between Pakistan and India and aggravate the danger to our security...Only a speedy and just Kashmir settlement could give Pakistan any assurance that the contemplated increase in India's military power would not be deployed against Pakistan in the future. No single step could contribute as much to the security of the subcontinent as the resolution of the Kashmir problem.

A message from Harold Macmillan was delivered to Ayub at about the same time (24 December 1962) by the British High Commissioner.[38] In his reply (2 January 1963), which was more explicit in some respects than the one he had sent to Kennedy, though both replies bear the same date (showing, incidentally, how much more relaxed Ayub felt with Macmillan than with Kennedy), Ayub said that the extent of assistance decided at the Nassau meeting had given Pakistan cause for great concern:

> The Nassau decision based on the assessment of your military experts, may seem, in the context of your global strategy, to be the minimum aid necessary to enable India to defend itself from attack through NEFA and Ladakh. We, on the other hand, find it hard to believe that any invasion of the subcontinent is likely to occur from these directions and consequently the quantum of military support to India, quantitative as well as qualitative, which you will be extending, is fraught with serious consequences to the maintenance of the present ratio of military strength in the subcontinent and hence to the security of Pakistan.

Ayub repeated that the disengagement of the armed forces of India and Pakistan was the key to the defence of the subcontinent. Ayub felt that 'if India sincerely desires an end to the dispute, and given goodwill on both sides, there is no reason why the two countries should not be able, with the assistance of Britain and the United States, to reach an equitable and honourable settlement within the next month or two'. Ayub said: 'While I am willing to exercise due patience, I will find it extremely difficult to convince the people of the virtue of this quality, if one round of discussion after another does not open the way to a solution.'[39]

The day before the talks formally opened, the Government of Pakistan announced that it had reached an agreement with China, in principle, on the common border between Kashmir and China. India expressed surprise at this announcement and felt that its timing was meant to bring pressure on India. The Americans, too, were a little perturbed. Ayub told the leader of the Indian delegation that the agreement had been under consideration for over two years, and the communication from Beijing about the time of the release of the text of the agreement had been received only a few hours after the Indian leader had called on Ayub the previous day. An official spokesman of Pakistan said there was 'nothing sinister' in the timing of the announcement.

Undeniably the announcement of the agreement between Pakistan and China cast a shadow on the talks. Pakistan had little to expect from the talks, and the intention must have been to signal to the Indians that Pakistan was not closing all its options when India had no intention of pursuing the talks in a constructive spirit. The signal was also intended to convey to the Western world that Pakistan would not be lured by talks with India to deny itself Chinese friendship and support. The opening speeches on the first day of the talks followed the familiar pattern of Pakistan inviting attention to United Nations Resolutions of 13 August 1948 and 5 January 1949. These provided for a cease-fire in Kashmir, the withdrawal of all troops from the state, and a plebiscite to determine the wishes of the people. The Indians, on the other hand, reiterated their familiar position that Kashmir was an integral part of India. The next two days were devoted to the discussion of the plebiscite proposal during which the Indian delegation continued to assert that any plebiscite in Kashmir would only result in a large-scale migration of the Hindu minority in Kashmir, leading to an upheaval throughout India and Pakistan. The communiqué issued at the end of the first round of talks consisted of a joint appeal to politicians, officials, and the media in the two countries 'to help in creating a friendly atmosphere for resolving the outstanding differences on Kashmir and other related matters and to refrain from any statements, criticism or propaganda, which might prejudice the success of these negotiations or tend to create discord between the two countries'.

Bhutto's view was that the Indians were coming on a probing mission to ascertain the thinking of senior officials in Pakistan. Western diplomats, too, would be busy contacting high official sources, to find out whether Pakistan would be receptive to a 'moderate' Kashmir solution. Instructions were, therefore, issued to all ministers, service chiefs and secretaries and joint secretaries to government, to refrain from entering into any discussion on the subject of Kashmir with the Indians or with foreign diplomats and Press correspondents. The Pakistani Press representatives and editors were also briefed by the Foreign Secretary and formally advised by the Information Ministry to maintain a 'sympathetic position' toward India. At least one editor, Altaf Hussain of *Dawn* flatly refused to follow the advice and stated that if the Indian attitude remained what it was he would be unsparing in his criticism of the Indian government.[40]

Muhammad Ali Bogra died on 24 January 1963. Bhutto was appointed Minister for Foreign Affairs, a portfolio he had been longing to secure. He had been to New Delhi for the second round of talks (16-19 January) at which the Indians ruled out the idea of a plebiscite in Kashmir as something that would only inflame communal passions and endanger the stability of the subcontinent. The Pakistan delegation reserved its position on plebiscite, but agreed to consider alternative solutions put forward by India. The Indians gave the outlines of a proposal for a political settlement that included the partition of Kashmir, military disengagement, adoption of a no-war declaration and demarcation of the international boundary in a way that took account of geographic and administrative considerations, and 'the need to ensure the minimum disturbance to the life and welfare of the people of Jammu and Kashmir'. The Pakistan delegation suggested that in determining the boundary it was necessary to take account of the composition of the population, defence requirements, control of rivers and the acceptability of any agreement between India and Pakistan to the people of the State. On 19 January Bhutto mentioned that in Pakistan's view mediation by a third party would help towards a settlement and that it would be possible to find mutually acceptable candidates.[41]

Before the third round of talks in Karachi (8-10 February), Kennedy wrote a long letter to Ayub, giving him his assessment of the situation. India, he said, would be unwilling to part with the whole of the Kashmir Valley under any circumstances and no amount of pressure from any quarter would change the Indian attitude. Any proposal that gave Pakistan the Valley would not provide a viable basis for compromise. Indeed any settlement likely to succeed would have to get around the basic irreconcilability of Indian and Pakistani positions on the Valley. However difficult this might be, Kennedy said, there would never be a better opportunity to resolve the issue. Whether or not the current Chinese communist attack on India was over, the threat remained, and this had a profoundly sobering effect on India. It had compelled the Indian government to realize the importance of reconciliation with Pakistan and to embark upon talks to that end. Kennedy admitted that the Indians had not yet shown their hand but there were indications that they genuinely desired compromise.

India's desire for US and UK military aid was also an incentive since the USA had made it clear to the Indians that their attitude towards Pakistan must inevitably be a factor in the US government's long-term military aid. However, if the threat were to increase or Sino-Indian fighting were to flare-up again, the US government would again be faced with the problem of providing substantial help to India. If India were forthcoming in further talks, it would appear to be greatly in Pakistan's interest to respond similarly. Once again Kennedy recalled Ayub's 'prescient remark' to Harriman that any settlement would be highly unpalatable to many on both sides. Kennedy expressed the fear that for either side to fail to recognize this would simply foreclose the possibility of fruitful negotiations and it was difficult to see how or when they could be reopened under such favourable circumstances. Further recourse to the UN would certainly accomplish little. Thus, however one looked at the problem, it was for Pakistan to do everything possible to achieve an immediate compromise settlement. He assured Ayub that the US would do everything it could within the limits of what it considered helpful to bring about such a settlement. The US government had not been idle so far and Ayub should know that. Nevertheless, Kennedy did not believe that a direct US government role in the talks would be immediately productive, it could be more helpful behind the scenes. He expressed the hope that during the next round of talks in Karachi both parties would consider the possibility of an international boundary running through Kashmir. This could only be achieved through substantial compromise. Even if this proved impossible to achieve in the third round, an agreed date in the future for a fourth round of talks should be fixed in order to maintain the momentum of the negotiations. Kennedy felt that Ayub was overestimating the amount of influence the US could exercise. The US and the UK could not force a solution on either India or Pakistan. Their influence could help if statesmanship on both sides managed to bring matters to the point where the gap remaining was sufficiently narrow for third party efforts to help close it. At present they were too far apart, but it should be possible from the current round of talks to move toward a settlement.

Kennedy thus made it clear that the US government had no intention of either proposing a solution or forcing India to accept UN resolutions on Kashmir. The only answer was for Pakistan to forget about the Valley and accept the existing cease-fire line as an international boundary subject to minor adjustments. While the US would certainly advise India that it was in her interest to come to a settlement with Pakistan, additional military assistance would be made available to her should there be a renewal of fighting between India and China. When he delivered Kennedy's letter, the American Ambassador informed Ayub that the US administration believed that the Chinese did not intend to decrease their pressure on Tibet, and there was a possibility of renewed flare-up. He also mentioned that active defence of Ladakh was a necessity—one that had been recognized by Ayub in his letter to

Kennedy. Whoever held Ladakh had to reckon with the general military build-up in Tibet, especially in the south-west.

Ayub was annoyed by what he called 'a deliberate distortion' of something he had mentioned in conversation to Harriman. He had allowed it to pass when Kennedy referred to it in his first letter but now reacted to it (11 January 1963):

American authorities and even their President keep on quoting my partial statement to Harriman that 'no negotiated settlement can be popular on either side'. But they omit to mention the rest of my statement: 'However, people will accept it provided they feel they can live with it and provided it safeguards their honour, security and economic interests.'

He directed the foreign office to 'take steps to disabuse American minds of this faulty notion'.

The third round of talks opened on 8 February in Karachi. The discussion concentrated on the delineation of a boundary line in Kashmir. The Indians suggested that it should broadly follow areas of control conceding bits of territory west and north of the Kashmir Valley to Pakistan. India would not surrender control of the Valley under any circumstances. The precise Indian suggestion was that India and Pakistan should forget about self-determination and divide the area by converting the cease-fire line into an international boundary subject to minor adjustments. The Indian delegation, knowing it had US support for its proposal, was adamant. The talks virtually broke down on 10 February 1963, but after a private meeting between the leaders of the two delegations, it was announced that they would resume discussion in Delhi.

In a press statement, Bhutto said that the position of the two sides was almost 'irreconcilable'. He stressed that the Kashmir Valley was 'the heart of the problem' and said that the future of the Valley could be discussed at a later stage, while the boundary for the rest of the state should be agreed as a first step. All this would be subject to India making a declaration that it had an open mind on the future of the Valley and recognizing that Pakistan had an 'interest and an involvement' in it. Sardar Swaran Singh, leader of the Indian delegation, said there were 'quite considerable differences' on the 'concrete terms' and mentioned that 'maps were referred to by both parties in the course of the discussion'.[43]

The American and the British initiative was running out. Pakistan was convinced that India would neither agree to plebiscite nor to any compromise arrangement regarding the Kashmir Valley. The Americans made it clear that they would not exercise any pressure on India to settle the Kashmir problem on any other basis than the existing cease-fire line. Since Pakistan was not prepared to accept that, the US considered herself absolved of any obligation towards Pakistan which had become a tiresome and unhelpful ally. The US considered herself free to proceed with her plans to help India. A spell of firm indifference would get Pakistan out of her sullen frame of mind. Unknown to Ayub Khan, President Kennedy had by now given a formal undertaking to Pandit Nehru to come to India's assistance in the event of any aggressive move by the Chinese.[44]

In New Delhi (15-16 May) the two sides reverted to square one. Pakistan swung back to the plebiscite proposal with some modifications. The wishes of the people of the Kashmir Valley should be ascertained after all the Indian troops had been pulled out of the area and replaced by forces of other countries after a period of six months. During the interim period the Valley should be placed under international administration. The Indians suggested a no-war declaration which would bind the two countries not to resort to force to alter the *status quo* in Kashmir. On 7 May 1963, Nehru announced that the partitioning of the Kashmir Valley, suggested to him by Dean Rusk and Duncan Sandys, was an 'extremely harmful idea' which would not be acceptable to India. Bhutto reiterated (9 May 1963) 'categorically and without equivocation' that Pakistan was 'firmly opposed' to any idea of converting the cease-fire line into international boundary. The possibility of a meeting between Ayub and Nehru was ruled out: 'the differences are very wide, there is no point in a summit meeting.'[45]

Ayub's proposal to introduce Eugene Black as a mediator had drawn some initial support in US circles, but India rejected the idea. Thus ended six rounds of futile talks which left Indo-Pakistan relations deeply strained and embittered.

Pakistan-China relations

The development of Pakistan's close relationship with China fundamentally altered the nature of the US-Pakistan alliance and deepened its differences with India. Pakistan recognized the People's Republic of China in 1950. Pakistan refrained from condemning the Chinese invasion of Tibet in 1950 and abstained from voting on the US draft resolution in the UN branding China as the aggressor. When Pakistan joined CENTO and later SEATO, an element of strain was introduced in Pakistan's relations with China. The *Peking Review* criticized Pakistan for the 'double-dealing tactics of extending recognition to China while at the same time ignoring China at the United Nations'. In May 1956, Pakistan entered into an agreement for the purchase of 300,000 tons of Chinese coal and in June the Sino-Pakistan Friendship Association was established in Beijing. Pakistan had meanwhile been trying to explain to Chinese officials at different levels that Pakistan's membership of SEATO was not directed against China.

Two important events took place in 1956: the visit to China of the Prime Minister of Pakistan, H.S. Suhrawardy, and the return visit of Zhou Enlai. The joint statement issued at the end of Suhrawardy's visit stated that talks had ranged widely and 'contributed greatly to the strengthening of friendly relations already existing between the two countries'. Zhou Enlai's visit was an occasion of great excitement in Pakistan. The Chinese Prime Minister was received enthusiastically and the people of Pakistan looked forward to the development of closer ties with China.[46] On 23 October 1956, Zhou Enlai told Pakistani newsmen that there was 'no reason why China could not be friends with Pakistan', thus indicating that Pakistan's membership of SEATO did not present an insurmountable hurdle to the growth of friendly relations. During his visit to Pakistan, Zhou Enlai was asked at a press conference to comment on the right of self-determination for the people of Jammu and Kashmir. He paused and then replied that the question needed careful study, but that he would advise India and Pakistan 'to settle this question directly between themselves'. To normalize the situation on the border with China,

Pakistan withdrew its frontier police from the border between Hunza and Sinkiang during 1955-7 to avoid the possibility of a clash with the Chinese.

Ayub was conscious of the geographical situation of Pakistan in Asia; in his meetings with Heads of State he would always point out that Pakistan had common borders with three major powers— the USSR, China and India, and a part of its border was with Afghanistan. He would indicate the size of these countries to emphasize the threat to Pakistan's security. In the proclamation issued on 7 October 1958, when Ayub took over power, it was declared that Pakistan wanted to have friendly relations with all nations and that its foreign policy would have to conform to the dictates of geography.

The growing strain in China's relations with India opened a window of opportunity for Pakistan. As noted earlier, Ayub initiated a tentative proposal for negotiations with China to demarcate the boundary between China and Pakistan. The Chinese responded with caution. There had been Chinese infiltration in Ladakh, but the Government of Pakistan played down the incident. As early as 23 October 1959, Ayub had drawn attention to events in Tibet and the roads being built in Afghanistan by the Soviet Union and had forecast that within five years the subcontinent would become 'militarily vulnerable and facilities will have been provided whereby a major invasion can take place and armies from Central Asia can march to the subcontinent'. He had also indicated that Pakistan should, in due course, approach China 'for a peaceful settlement of the border question by demarcating the northern frontiers'.

In March 1961, Pakistan's Foreign Minister, Manzur Qadir, announced that Pakistan had taken the initiative to negotiate a boundary agreement with China in 1960 and China had asked for time to consider the matter. He explained that there were two aspects of the problem that required careful consideration: first, the constitutional position of the northern areas, and, second, Pakistan's desire to be certain of the line beyond which Pakistan should not go, and across which the Chinese should not come. The US did not approve of these initiatives but Ayub claimed that they were of a limited nature and did not represent any fundamental change in Pakistan's foreign policy.

A formal note was sent to Beijing by the Government of Pakistan in early 1961 proposing negotiations for the demarcation of 'the boundary of China's Sinkiang and contiguous areas, the defence of which is the responsibility of the Government of Pakistan' with a view to ensuring 'the tranquillity of the border between the two countries'. India reacted by despatching a strongly worded protest note to Beijing and Islamabad. Ayub asserted that Pakistan had 'every right to ask for the demarcation of that border' as Pakistan was in 'legal occupation of territories running along the Chinese border'. Manzur Qadir explained that talks with China were continuing and demarcation of the border would be undertaken only after an agreement had been reached. Then came the news that China had agreed, in principle, to demarcate its border with Pakistan. A few days later at a luncheon given by Chancellor Adenauer in Bonn, Ayub described Pakistan's relations with China as normal and said that negotiations were intended to define the border in certain areas.[47]

Perhaps the strongest move Ayub made to encourage China to come to an agreement with Pakistan on the demarcation of the border was his public statement in Washington before coming to Bonn that it was only fair to allow Beijing to occupy its legitimate place in the United Nations and that Pakistan would vote for China's admission in future. On his return from his American trip, he told the Chinese Ambassador that he was looking forward to negotiations with China to conclude a border agreement. When the Chinese Ambassador told him that the matter was very complicated, he replied quite bluntly that China's admission to the United Nations 'was even more complicated'.[48]

It was obvious that the Chinese government wanted to move slowly so as not to get into greater difficulties with India. As events progressed it became abundantly clear that China wanted to explore all possibilities of a peaceful settlement of its border dispute with India before undertaking any negotiations with Pakistan. With characteristic patience the Chinese never rejected the Pakistan initiative, although they gave no indication of their willingness to take up the offer. By the end of 1961, China had had enough of Indian obduracy and arrogance and decided that there was merit in taking up negotiations with Pakistan on the boundary question. The Chinese note of 27 February 1962 said that history had entrusted to China and Pakistan the responsibility of demarcating the border in the disputed area.

China indicated its readiness to conclude with the Government of Pakistan 'an agreed comprehension of the location and alignment of this boundary so as to prevent the tranquillity on the border from being adversely affected on account of misunderstanding'. The note made it clear that any agreement that might be reached between China and Pakistan would be of a provisional nature on the location and alignment 'actually existing between the two countries' pending the settlement of the Kashmir dispute. On 3 May 1962, Pakistan and China formally announced their intention of defining the boundary between China's Sinkiang and the 'contiguous areas, defence of which is under actual control of Pakistan'.[49]

Negotiations started in Beijing on 12 October 1962. A joint press release issued on that day stated:

> In pursuance of the decision of the governments of the People's Republic of China and Pakistan to conduct negotiations through diplomatic channels on the question of the boundary between China's Sinkiang and the contiguous areas, the defence of which is under the control of Pakistan, the representatives of China and Pakistan began talks in Peking on 12 October 1962. During the first meeting the two parties exchanged opinions in a spirit of friendship and mutual understanding and reached agreed views on procedural matters concerning the future discussions. The talks were held in a very cordial atmosphere.

The Chinese delegation was led by the Vice Foreign Minister who in his address to the first meeting recalled that the boundary talks had been 'long under preparation' and said that the question of the boundary was one left over by history: 'This boundary has never been formally delimited or demarcated: nevertheless, there has long existed here a traditional customary boundary.' He noted with gratification that both sides had respected this traditional customary boundary and jointly preserved the tranquillity along the border ever since the founding of the People's Republic of China and the Independence of Pakistan, thus providing favourable conditions for the settlement of the boundary question through negotiations. He mentioned that the boundary was related 'to the Kashmir question regarding which the Chinese Government has throughout adhered to a stand of not getting itself involved in the India-Pakistan dispute'. In view of this the negotiations would be limited to attaining an agreed understanding of the location and alignment of the boundary between the two countries, and after the Kashmir dispute was resolved, the sovereign authorities concerned would reopen negotiations with the Chinese government on the question of the boundary of Kashmir, so as to sign a formal boundary treaty to replace the previous agreement.[50] He mentioned the successful conclusion of boundary agreements between China and Nepal and between China and Burma, omitting all reference to the difficulties which China was having with India, though he did not fail to recall the five principles of peaceful co-existence and the ten principles of the Bandung Conference, to which both China and India were signatories. In his report to Ayub (24 October 1962), the Pakistan Ambassador gave his evaluation of the position China was likely to adopt during the boundary talks. The Chinese, he indicated, would treat the traditional customary boundary as the *de facto* boundary line.[51]

These talks were taking place precisely at the time when China was at war with India. Throughout the war the two delegations continued to discuss minute details of the boundary agreement. When the Chinese declared a unilateral cease-fire, the Chinese Ambassador in Islamabad saw Ayub and explained China's position *vis-à-vis* India. The Chinese understanding at that time was that the Indians would not settle their boundary dispute with China through peaceful negotiations despite repeated Chinese offers. Having made considerable progress in the industrial field the Indians wanted to concentrate on developing their military strength. This they could achieve only if they kept up the tension with China to induce Western powers to give them military assistance. According to the Chinese reckoning, India could not bring more than about seven brigades against China over the whole front. The Chinese estimate was that it would take India a year or two to develop the necessary capability to resume war with China. The Chinese had no intention whatever of provoking a fight but they would hit back hard in self-defence. The Chinese Ambassador assured Ayub that China had no desire to create any difficulties in the settlement of the Kashmir dispute.

Ayub told the Chinese Ambassador that China's premature declaration of cease-fire had increased Pakistan's military problems: 'If you had continued fighting with India for another week or so, I have no doubt in my mind that Nehru would have been ousted and our problems would have been satisfactorily solved.' Instead, India had been able to cash in on its conflict with China to obtain massive military aid both from the West and the Soviet Union. Pakistan knew that India could not use this military strength against China: 'They will use it against their smaller neighbours in Asia.' China had quite unintentionally added to Pakistan's military hazards: 'I wish the Chinese had consulted us before they ordered the cease-fire and in future, too, I hope that before they take any precipitate steps they will consult us, as we may be able to give them sound advice.' The question of the signing of the border agreement was raised by the Chinese Ambassador, and Ayub said: 'So far as we are concerned we have given our word of honour and it is as good as our signature on the official document.' Ayub promised to send his Foreign Minister to sign the agreement. The Chinese Ambassador warmly appreciated this gesture. The Sino-Pakistan agreement, in principle, on the demarcation of the border was announced on 27 December 1962, the day the first round of Indo-Pakistan talks on Kashmir opened in Rawalpindi. Ayub had seen the leader of the Indian delegation and received the Chinese Ambassador later in the evening. Ayub congratulated the Chinese Ambassador on his contribution to the agreement. The Chinese Ambassador told Ayub that he had known General Thimaya of the Indian Army and had also seen the Indian Army units around Delhi: 'They may be good ceremonial troops but had very little conception of modern mobile warfare.' He also commented on the poor quality of the

Indian Army's leadership. Ayub tried to ascertain the strength of the Chinese troops in Tibet. Ayub wrote in his diary that the Chinese Ambassador was 'very boastful' of the effectiveness of Chinese troops.[52]

Ayub and the Chinese Ambassador then talked about Sino-Soviet relations. The Ambassador left Ayub in no doubt that the rift between China and the Soviet Union was increasing and hardly any Russian technician or engineer was stationed in China. The Chinese Ambassador wanted to make sure that Pakistan would not use the boundary agreement 'merely as a lever to gain advantage over India'. Ayub assured him that it was Pakistan's firm policy to remain on the friendliest terms with all its neighbours, especially China, and that this was also the basis of Pakistan's approach to India.[53]

Pakistan's boundary agreement with China shocked the Americans but it helped Ayub to retrieve his political position at home. Ayub had always regarded his alliance with the West as reciprocal. Pakistan had become America's ally at a time when neutralism and non-alignment were the most distrusted concepts in the West. Ayub was shocked that the West should be abandoning its allies and wooing neutrals like India who were amongst its sharpest critics. The Americans found it difficult to believe that Ayub was so naïve as to imagine that their policy of cultivating certain selected countries as allies was dictated by some sort of idealism and not by self-interest alone. Once the Americans had pulled the ideological rug from under his feet, geographical imperatives assumed critical importance in Ayub's formulation of Pakistan's regional strategy. With antagonistic neighbours like India and Afghanistan, both enjoying the support of the USSR, and Pakistan's Western allies redefining the purpose of their regional pacts and the limits of their assistance, Ayub was left with no alternative but to grasp China's hand of friendship.

On 29 August, three months after the collapse of India-Pakistan talks, Pakistan and China signed an Air Agreement in Karachi 'for airlines of the two countries to operate over each other's territory' and for the provision of 'all facilities necessary to ensure the smooth flow of traffic at all specified points situated in their respective territories'. India was incensed. Nehru said that he would not allow Chinese aircraft to fly over Indian territory in pursuance of the Sino-Pakistan Air Agreement. The US government registered its displeasure by postponing the signing of a loan agreement of $4,300,000 for improvements to Dhaka Airport. In Washington the Sino-Pakistan Air Agreement was called 'an unfortunate breach of free world solidarity'. The unthinkable had happened; Ayub had 'opened a window on the world' for the air-locked Chinese.[54]

George Ball lands up in Pakistan

Five days after the signing of the Air Agreement, George Ball, the US Secretary of State, was in Islamabad for talks with Ayub (3-5 September 1963). On 2 September Ayub wrote a memorandum in his own hand: 'Answers to probable points Mr George Ball may raise.' The memorandum read like a personal balance sheet: 'You have been good friends and helped us in many ways, but we too have been very good friends and in doing so incurred lots of risks and odium.' Ayub made a particular point of 'the facility provided to the Americans to establish a major satellite and rocket launching centre in Badaber which exposed Pakistan to the wrath of the Russians'.[55] He also noted the transit facilities provided to American aircraft and personnel supporting the Khamba rebellion in Tibet which the Chinese came to know about from a story published in the American Press. 'A most awkward situation was created by Gary Cooper (sic) and the Russians had not forgiven Pakistan for that.'[56]

Ayub took up the position that he had been forced to settle the border problem with China 'to save ourselves from a serious military situation' and to save 'our American friends' from getting embroiled in it. The fact that Pakistan's negotiations with China reached their culmination after the Sino-Indian border clashes was a mere coincidence: 'Too much should not be read into this.' The Air Agreement with China was a 'purely commercial transaction'. Ayub could not see why any politics should be brought into that:

It is a mistake to think that this will give the Chinese an outlet to the outside world. One, you cannot bottle up 700 million virile people, and two, the British and some others were only too anxious to have an Air Agreement with the Chinese. We have no intention of jeopardizing American interests. *On the contrary, we may be of some assistance in bringing about a rapprochement should the Americans at some stage so desire.'* [Emphasis added].[57]

Ayub laid great emphasis on Pakistan's geographical position. It was:

...[a] country divided in two and surrounded by three mighty powers on the Eurasian land mass, one of them was openly hostile to Pakistan and the other two believed in an ideology which was diametrically opposed to Pakistan's ideology. It was a vital requirement for Pakistan to normalize her relations with them and to bring her military and political commitments within her means. With the menacing Indian military buildup this requirement had become imperative. This was the aim of Pakistan's border settlement with China and some trade arrangements.

Pakistan hoped to have similar economic arrangements with the Soviet Union which 'should not be misunderstood'. Ayub put the US government on notice that Pakistan was no longer available for any 'military or political commitment' beyond its means. The maximum that Pakistan could guarantee was that it would do nothing against US interests. The US government had chosen, as part of its global strategy, to strengthen India's military capacity to combat communism. For Pakistan, this was a direct threat. The Chinese had no immediate plans for expansion in the region. India was in no position to extend her border clashes with China into an all-out war against communism but it would certainly use them to enhance its military strength in order to dominate its smaller neighbours. All the talk of an 'imminent Chinese attack' was, according to Ayub, 'a smoke-screen' aimed at keeping Nehru in power and getting as much military aid as possible from the West and the USSR. India wanted to equip two armies, one ostensibly for China and the other for Pakistan. Once it had obtained sufficient arms it would come to some accommodation with China and then move against its smaller neighbours. Pakistan was the first on its list. Eventually India would want to get rid of US influence—this was a 'political and psychological compulsion' with her. 'Americans will then feel the need for someone to hold India.' The Americans had it in their power to bring about a disengagement between India and Pakistan, instead they had encouraged the Indian government to become more intransigent by delinking their military aid from the settlement of the Kashmir dispute. The people of Pakistan were naturally incensed: they were giving expression to grief and anger not to anti-Americanism. People, whose survival was at stake, could not be expected to remain philosophical. Ayub categorically rejected the US proposal for the expansion of US communication centres in Pakistan which had been given to him by the US Ambassador before Ball's arrival. 'In the present political climate it was out of the question. People just won't take it.'

Here was Pakistan talking to the US as nation to nation. Ayub's logic was not easy to fault, but George Ball had not come to chop logic, but to find out for Kennedy whether Pakistan would form a front with India against China.

Summing up his talks with George Ball, Ayub wrote on 5 September 1963 that 'US policy is that arms aid to India will continue and they cannot link arms aid to a Kashmir settlement.'

On the eve of George Ball's visit, the US Information Service in Rawalpindi had issued a press release describing the Sino-Pakistan boundary agreement as the latest and most important of a 'series of pinpricks, none of them fundamentally important in itself, that have indicated Pakistan's drift toward Communist China.' No communiqué was issued at the end of the talks; Ball said he had not come 'on a negotiating mission, but to talk in depth', and concluded that there had been 'an excellent conversation between friends in the interest of better understanding'. A Pakistani source claimed the same day: 'We are still loyal members of the military alliances with the US. We have not changed sides in the cold war.'[58]

George Ball's visit marked a historic turning point, if not a break, in Pakistan's relations with the USA. Pakistan had not changed sides in the cold war, but its presence in SEATO and CENTO had now become purely symbolic. If Pakistan did not leave the pacts it was to avoid giving a public affront to the USA. A new dimension had been added to Pakistan's international relations—a dimension which clearly cut across the US strategy in the region.

Throughout this difficult period Ayub played his hand close to the chest, handling the negotiations personally without relying on any aide—he would write his own brief and keep the minutes of the meetings himself. His Foreign Minister, Bogra, was too unwell to be of any assistance. Ayub anticipated the American and the Indian moves with remarkable insight and prepared his response in a firm and pragmatic manner, never for a moment over-estimating his own strength or under-estimating the power and influence of the United States. He used the moral card with great dexterity and purpose to divert the American thrusts. Never for a moment did he allow any personal political consideration to dictate his tactics. Ayub extracted the maximum advantage for Pakistan from a complex and explosive situation and emerged from the ordeal with great confidence which won him the respect of world leaders. Even his bitterest critics at home knew in their hearts, though they never acknowledged it in public, that he had served the cause of Pakistan with great patience, moderation and foresight. Had he succumbed to American pressure, he would have exposed Pakistan to China's hostility without winning the friendship of India; and if he had opted for the course which some of his more emotional associates and many of the politicians were advocating, and moved into Kashmir when India was wavering under the Chinese onslaught, he would have put Pakistan's survival at risk.

President Kennedy was assassinated on 22 November 1963. The following month General Maxwell Taylor, Chairman of the US Joint Chiefs of Staff, arrived in Pakistan 'to make an assessment of the general security position in the area, which would include the extent of Chinese capabilities as also the Indian threat and disposition of forces in the area'. The US Ambassador sought an interview with Ayub to enquire whether it would cause any embarrassment to Pakistan if General Taylor went on to India from Rawalpindi 'to review the general situation there from the military point of view'. Ayub said: 'General Taylor can go

wherever he wants.' Ayub gave the Ambassador a note containing
his assessment of the threat in the area. The Ambassador said that
the original intention was for Secretary McNamara and Under-
Secretary Ball to accompany General Taylor but it was now felt
that 'such visits should be spread out.' General Taylor, he
explained, would bring with him some ideas about the extent of
additional deterrents, restraints and safeguards that could be
provided to meet 'Pakistan's fear of threat from India'. The
Ambassador hinted that there was now a possibility of a stronger
US military presence in the area. The Ambassador also told Ayub
that Harriman had called on the Indian Ambassador in Washington
and taken him 'to task' for the steps taken by his Government for
the merger of Kashmir with India. Kennedy, he said, had been
concerned about Pakistan's advances toward China, and some of
its recent moves had caused misunderstanding in the US Congress.
Most Congressmen considered Pakistan's action inconsistent
with its position as a staunch ally, and found it difficult to
reconcile what Ayub had told the Congress in July 1961 with what
was happening today. 'Pakistan's word of honour has not changed,'
Ayub assured the Ambassador. Any change in Pakistan's position
was the result of changes in US policy: 'Those Congressmen who
find it difficult to understand the change should look at the record
of their government in the area.' The Ambassador asked whether
Pakistan intended to move still closer to China. Ayub replied:
'That depends on how much the US presses us to the wall.'[59]

General Taylor came to Pakistan after first visiting Delhi. He
met Ayub on 20 December 1963 and asked for his appreciation of
the problems affecting the region and the US-Pakistan relationship.
Ayub went over familiar ground but spoke much more frankly
than he had done with George Ball. 'Pakistan,' he said, 'is facing
a tragic predicament in which loyalty to our own country is
coming into increasing conflict with loyalty to our friends.' The
people of Pakistan were gravely concerned and disappointed that
the 'United States should come to regard our security so cheaply'.
By building up India, it was compelling smaller countries in the
region to seek Chinese protection. A major conflict between
China and India, according to Ayub, was 'inconceivable'. General

Taylor said he had just had an opportunity to study the Indian situation at first hand. He agreed that the Chinese had no intention of embarking on a direct massive invasion of India. Such a move would be 'imprudent, unnecessary and fatal for China'. The Chinese knew that the US would not remain passive in such an eventuality. But this could not hold true for all times to come and, at any rate, 'India, after the humiliating defeat, was anxious to build up military strength to deter any future Chinese incursion.' The US government was in full agreement with this objective, although it had 'reservations about the actual level of military build up needed to achieve it'. The Indians, in the first flush of defeat, had an exaggerated notion of their arms requirements but a more realistic programme was now being evolved. India wanted sixteen divisions, with an additional five territorial divisions, involving a total manpower of 866,000. According to the US view twelve divisions should be enough. The Indians were planning forty-five squadrons of all types of aircraft as against forty-one existing squadrons. They had no present plans for the expansion of their navy. Funds were a severely limiting factor. The US contribution would be modest, first because it was not easy to get Congressional approval and, second, because US assistance would have to be related to a careful assessment of the real Indian requirements. The UK was not in a position to make any substantial contribution, and the USSR, because of its economic difficulties and commitments elsewhere, would treat any Indian request with caution. General Taylor summed up: 'Any runaway programme of military build-up by India with American contribution was not a practical proposition.' Ayub asked for more specific information. General Taylor told him that military equipment valued at $60 million would be provided to India under the current assistance programme. This level of assistance could be maintained if India continued to behave and accepted the responsibility for defence against China. 'This was a worthwhile price,' General Taylor said, 'for detaching India from the communist orbit.' General Taylor was convinced that 'the Southern flank in Asia would remain exposed to danger so long as India and Pakistan did not come together.' Pakistan's security was a matter of genuine concern to the US government, and its planners had been developing strategic mobility to come to the aid of friends in an emergency. He referred to joint exercises in which elements of all three services would be involved to demonstrate the US capacity for rapid and timely deployment of forces in support of Pakistan in the event of aggression from any quarter. This would cover all frontiers of Pakistan and entail determination of central points from which plans of action could be evolved against attack from India, Afghanistan and even China. The United States was considering stocking equipment and material at suitable points from Cairo to Thailand for use by US forces in aid of a friendly country subjected to an attack from outside.

Ayub said Pakistan did not have to be convinced of US ability to move its forces rapidly in any part of the world. Any special exercise to demonstrate that was unnecessary. The crucial point was to understand the threat to Pakistan arising from the provision of US arms to India, which had seriously aggravated an already tense situation in the subcontinent. The primary aim of US policy should be to reduce that tension. It was natural for Pakistan to want to be in a position itself to deter any aggression from India. General Taylor said it was beyond Pakistan's physical resources to acquire such capacity. Ayub continued to insist that Pakistan must have the capacity to defend its frontiers rather than place a burden on the US to come to its assistance from far off lands—a commitment that world events might not permit the US government to fulfil in Pakistan's hour of need. Pakistan must have the confidence and the capability to bear the first onslaught and this could be done by strengthening and modernizing the existing forces, and improving their weapons and equipment rather than by enlarging its armed forces. General Taylor then mentioned the projected patrolling of the Indian and Arabian oceans by a Task Force from the Seventh Fleet in the Pacific. The idea had been under consideration for some time. Ayub said that he had given careful thought to it and had also sounded out some representatives of the countries likely to be affected by the move. He was constrained to point out as a friend that smaller nations in the region saw it as 'a revival of gunboat diplomacy'. The Task Force would not have much political or military value. Military problems from Vietnam to Iran were basically land and air problems and the extension of the Seventh Fleet into the region could not materially advance US strategic interests. Such a step taken in the context of SEATO and CENTO might have gone down better with many countries. General Taylor explained that no decision had been taken and tried to assure Ayub that the US had every intention of consulting its allies, especially Pakistan, before deciding on sending a Task Force on a regular basis to the Indian and Arabian oceans. Unfortunately the news had been leaked prematurely and this had made the situation difficult. The US Ambassador, who was present at the meeting, asked whether the Task Force would not give Pakistan a greater sense of security against India. Ayub replied emphatically: 'No. It is a military gimmick.'

Ayub concluded by repeating to General Taylor a remark he had heard from an American visitor: 'American policy has a set order of priorities: first comes the appeasement of the enemies, then the wooing of neutrals, and, if there is time, a nod to friends.' General Maxwell Taylor recorded a memorandum about his conversation with Ayub on 20 December 1963. According to this memorandum, parts of which are still classified, General Taylor told Ayub,

> …could we not accept the existence of an honest difference of view as to the rightness of US military aid to India, cease the recriminations which have been souring our relations and move forward together toward common objectives? On the US side we have nothing to apologize for our course of action. The decision has been taken after careful thought and close attention to the views of the Pakistan Government.

General Taylor expressed concern about the coming visit of Zhou Enlai to Karachi and said that, 'Ayub in close company with him on every TV in the world' would be to the detriment of US-Pak relations.[60]

The Americans gave up on Ayub after General Maxwell Taylor's visit. Few people in Pakistan knew what Ayub had gone through, and what he had achieved. Unfortunately his political party—the Convention Muslim League—had little contact with the people, and there was no other mediatory agency or institution which could have communicated to the people the gravity and immensity of the pressures which Ayub had resisted with resolution and courage to uphold and maintain the prestige of the country. Ayub's success made his administration even more arrogant and extended the gap between the officials and the people. The government-controlled media would recite Ayub's achievements with relentless repetition and exaggeration to no purpose. What nobody in the government, least of all Ayub himself, seemed to realize was that the people, having been deprived of all sense of participation in the whole process of decision-making, could hardly be expected to take pride or rejoice in Ayub's triumphs in the field of foreign affairs. The vocal sections of the people did not fail to suggest that acknowledging or applauding Ayub's success in any venture would only strengthen and prolong his personal rule. Ayub would dismiss any criticism that came to his notice as the work of the wretched politicians. Not familiar with the 'magic of the street' Ayub did not know how to establish any rapport with the masses. Oratory and rabble-rousing were not Ayub's forte. Nor did he believe in the people, whose outbursts of emotion he treated as no more than an effervescent phenomenon. Emotion had no role in Ayub's orderly and rational scheme of things. For him the exercise of power in a competent fashion was its own reward and justification. Ayub's opponents, though they had been politically marginalized, refused to concede him an inch of ground and continued to harp on the authoritarian character of his regime. They kept grumbling that he had failed to take advantage of India's vulnerability in Kashmir during the India-China War. All this made Ayub despise the politicians even more. A section of the Press, particularly some right wing journals and magazines, blamed Ayub for alienating the Americans without any benefit to Pakistan. Ayub reacted angrily and decided to impose stringent restrictions on the Press by promulgating the Press and Publications Ordinance in September 1963.

Ayub's domestic problems and worries receded into the background as events in Kashmir took a wholly unexpected and dramatic turn toward the end of the year.

NOTES

1. Confidential Memorandum, NEA/PAB:RKMcKEE:gn dated 23-5-77, US National Security Archives.
2. Ayub Khan, op. cit., pp. 125-9.
3. *See* Ayub Khan, op. cit., pp. 125-9, and Dr Aftab Ahmed's thesis: 'The Indus Basin Project and the World Bank', Lahore, University of the Punjab, 1967 (unpublished), pp. 107-13.
4. Ayub Khan, op. cit., pp. 107-13.
5. Neville Maxwell, *India's China War,* London, Jonathan Cape, 1970, p. 229.
6. Ibid., p. 239.
7. Ibid., p. 342.
8. Ibid., p. 229.
9. Ayub Khan, op. cit., pp. 141-3.
10. J.K. Galbraith, *Ambassador's Journal*, London, Hamish Hamilton, 1969, pp. 441-5.
11. Ayub Khan, op. cit., p.137.
12. The Kennedy letter of 29 October 1962, which McConaughy was to deliver to Ayub Khan, did not amount to consultation with the Pakistan government about military aid to India. The letter only said: 'We now intend to give the Indians such help as we can for their immediate needs.'
13. The discussion between McConaughy and the Pakistan Foreign Minister did not contain any hint of consultation.
14. J. K. Galbraith, op. cit., p. 137.
15. According to Galbraith: 'The meeting of minor bureaucrats, including Talbot, in London has composed mild and pleasant documents which assume that the Chinese have no disagreeable intentions.' (16 November 1962, *Ambassador's Journal*, p. 478).
16. Ibid., p. 486.
17. Ibid., p. 487.
18. Ibid., p. 489.
19. Before joining Ayub's Cabinet as Finance Minister M. Shoaib had a meeting with the Acting Secretary of State on 10 November 1958 in which 'The Acting Secretary wished Mr Shoaib every success in his new position...' US Department of State, Memorandum of Conversation, XR 790d. 13 National Archives, Washington.
20. Neville Maxwell, op. cit., p. 417, 'Astonishment almost blots out relief at the sudden Chinese decision'—quoting *The Times*.
21. J.K Galbraith, op. cit., p. 490; Galbraith who was asleep at the time noted, 'Yesterday, like a thief in the night, peace arrived.'
22. *Dawn,* 22 November 1962.
23. Ayub's personal papers.
24. J. K. Galbraith op. cit., p. 437.
25. Ibid., p. 434. He told Washington: 'Next time I question some shipment of new arms to Pakistan, it will not be so easy to send me the usual reminder that this is important for defence against communism.'
26. Ibid., p. 441. Galbraith added a footnote: 'This, not the merits of the Kashmir question, being of course the issue.'
27. Ibid., 28 October 1962, p. 442. The word 'assurance' occurs six times in one paragraph.
28. Ayub was most upset by the mounting US military supplies to India. The US

maintained that necessary assurances had been given to Pakistan after due consultation. These assurances consisted of a copy of the press release containing the text of the notes dated 14 November 1962 exchanged between the US and India, a copy of the press release issued by the State Department about the exchange of these notes, and a copy of the Secretary of State's letter to the Foreign Minister. The Pakistan Ambassador told Talbot that these assurances would not be considered adequate by Pakistan. In a statement on 20 November, Kennedy said: 'In providing military assistance to India, we are mindful of our alliance with Pakistan. All of our aid to India is for the purpose of defeating Chinese communist subversion…our help to India in no way diminishes or qualifies our commitment to Pakistan, and we have made this clear to both Governments as well.' The following statement was issued on 17 November 1962:

> The Department of State released today the text of Exchange of Notes concerning the provision of defence assistance by the Government of the United States of America to the Government of India. In the exchange of notes it is stated that the assistance will be furnished for the purpose of defence against outright Chinese communist aggression now facing India. In 1954 when the US decided to extend military aid to Pakistan, the Government of India was assured that if our aid to any country, including Pakistan, was misused and directed against another in aggression, the US would undertake immediately, in accordance with constitutional authority, appropriate action both within and without the United Nations to thwart such aggression. The Government of the United States of America had similarly assured the Government of Pakistan that, if our assistance to India should be misused and directed against another in aggression, the United States would undertake immediately, in accordance with constitutional authority, appropriate action both within and without the United Nations to thwart such aggression. Needless to say, in giving these assurances the United States is confident that neither of the countries which it aids harbours aggressive designs.

The statement caused great disappointment in Pakistan. No one believed that the Americans had given a commitment to come to Pakistan's assistance if she were attacked by India. The United States had put Pakistan at the same level as India in her relations. The American undertaking to thwart aggression was given to the two countries in identical language, in fact the paragraph relating to India preceded the one concerning Pakistan. Worse still, America had asserted that India did not harbour any aggressive designs against Pakistan.

29. J. K. Galbraith, op. cit., p. 434.
30. Ibid., p. 484. Galbraith noted on 18 November 1962: 'A trip to India by Duncan Sandys to discuss the Kashmir issue is, I think, being postponed. Ayub does not want to see him. If he came to Delhi alone, he would seem to be confining his pressure to the Indians with bad effect.' Galbraith was as dismissive of Duncan Sandys as of any other official who ventured into his domain. Commenting on his earlier visit in June 1962 he said: 'He is not popular with Nehru. He is exceedingly self-confident and reminds the Prime Minister, I fear, of the kind of Englishman who put him in jail.' If Ayub did not even want to see Duncan Sandys, and he reminded Nehru of British gaolers, it is remarkable that it less than a week he should have persuaded both Nehru and Ayub to make a fresh start on Kashmir.

31. *Keesing's Archives* p. 19541. Column 2 (1963-4).
32. There is nothing on record to substantiate this claim.
33. *Keesing's Archives* p. 19541. Column 2 (1963-4).
34. *Dawn,* Karachi, 2 December 1962.
35. Ayub Khan's papers.
36. Ibid.: Ayub had come to know that Galbraith was totally opposed to the US exercising any pressure on Nehru on Kashmir.
37. Morrice James *Pakistan Chronicle* p. 138. Oxford University Press, Karachi, 1993.
38. Ayub Khan's papers.
39. Ibid.
40. Author's notes.
41. J. K. Galbraith, op. cit., pp. 534-6. Galbraith recalls meeting Bhutto on the morning of 16 January before the talks opened, and noted: 'He is an intelligent man of conciliatory mood, I think. I braced him on the importance of keeping the talks with India going, not walking out in frustration.' He later recorded on 19 January:

> The talks between India and Pakistan resemble badminton. The arrangement was to talk a few days first in Pakistan, now a few days in India. The thing is to get the shuttle back in the other court; so I have concentrated my efforts to get through these three days without disaster and to get out a communiqué promising another meeting. So much I have achieved. A few minutes ago the negotiators announced that they would meet again early next month in Karachi. I must invent some way of carrying things a step further before they assemble again. Although the Department won't like it, perhaps we could come up with some proposal and perhaps also somebody who would act as mediator. Deep in my heart I know nothing will come of the effort, although new pressure from the Chinese might have some effect.

43. Ayub Khan's papers.
44. *The Nehru Letters;* Appendix 1.
45. *Keesing's Archives* 1963-4, p. 19544.
46. As Commissioner of Karachi Municipal Corporation, the author presented the address of welcome to Premier Zhou Enlai on behalf of the citizens of Karachi at a civic reception attended by over 10,000 people on the lawns of Frere Hall. The address contained a reference to Iqbal's verses where the poet says: 'Pull down the citadels of power and burn those cornfields which produce nothing but hunger for the cultivator.' Zhou Enlai warmly applauded these verses.
47. Ayub's personal papers.
48. Ayub Khan, op. cit., p. 162.
49. Ayub's personal papers.
50. The Vice-Foreign Minister used the words 'sovereign authorities', thus recognizing that more than one authority might be left in sovereign control of Jammu and Kashmir after the settlement.
51. Ayub's personal papers.
52. Ayub's diary, 28 October 1962.
53. Ibid.
54. *Dawn,* Karachi, 24, 25, 26 August 1963.

55. Near Peshawar in the North-West Frontier Province.
56. Ayub meant Captain Francis Gary Powers who was the pilot of the US aircraft which took off from Peshawar and was shot down by the Russians on 1 May 1960.
57. The Americans dismissed the suggestion at the time but some seven years later Pakistan was used as a diplomatic cover and a 'refuelling station' for Kissinger's secret trip to China.
58. *Dawn,* Karachi, 7 September 1963.
59. Ayub's personal papers.
60. Document SM 462-75, OJCS dated 20 December 1963, Lyndon B. Johnson Library.

CHAPTER 5

The Kashmir Situation—1964

While India was trying to tighten its stranglehold on the occupied territories in Jammu and Kashmir, conditions inside the Valley were fast deteriorating. A serious incident occurred at a mosque at Hazratbal near Srinagar, the capital of the state, on 26 December 1963. What was believed to be a hair of Prophet Muhammad (PBUH) kept as a sacred relic in a small glass tube in a wooden box, disappeared. 'The Hindus must have stolen it,' was the spontaneous Muslim suspicion. The general belief was that the government had a hand in this sacrilege and that the motive was to humiliate the Muslims and to bring the state into India's secular fold. This belief gained strength from the measures the Government of India had been taking before the Hazratbal incident to convert the disputed accession of the state to India into a permanent legal reality.

On 3 October 1963, three months before the Hazratbal incident, the Kashmiri Prime Minister, Bakhshi Ghulam Mohammed, who was generally regarded by the Muslims in Kashmir as a minion of the ruling Indian National Congress, announced in the state legislative assembly that the head of the Kashmir state would, in future, be called Chief Minister rather than Prime Minister. This would bring Kashmir in line with the other states of the Indian Union. Moreover, the representatives of Kashmir in the Indian Parliament would be directly elected instead of being nominated by the state legislature. He also indicated that amendments to the state's Constitution would be made in February 1964 to make its accession to the Indian union 'final and irrevocable'.[1] Article 370 of the Indian Constitution which accorded a special status to Kashmir, would remain temporarily in force. But Nehru himself forecast that the article would undergo 'gradual erosion'. India would not take the initiative to rescind the article: 'The initiative should come from the state government and the people of Kashmir,' Nehru told the Lok Sabha on 27 November 1963.[2] Pakistan strongly condemned the proposed changes as 'clearly illegal' and 'in flagrant violation of India's commitments'.[3]

The proposed changes in the status of Kashmir had caused deep resentment among the people of Jammu and Kashmir which turned into violent confrontation with the government when the theft of the holy relic was reported. The state was engulfed by a public disorder of unprecedented intensity. Huge processions paraded the streets every day, defying the state police and the Indian Army. The submissive Kashmiris appeared to have risen in open revolt. The administration was paralysed while thousands of Kashmiris vowed that they would not submit to Indian domination.

The Indians were quick to put the blame for the disturbances on Pakistan. An influential section of the Indian Press saw the revolt in the Valley as the work of Pakistani agents. The disturbed situation in the Valley enabled the intelligence agencies in Pakistan to establish contacts with the leaders of the movement and obtain information about the internal situation in Kashmir. Senior officials in the Pakistan foreign office soon convinced themselves that the Indians were in a highly vulnerable position: a little help from Pakistan and the brave Kashmiris would drive out the Indian forces from Kashmir. By the end of December 1963, the whole of occupied Kashmir was under curfew. Public meetings and processions were banned. The administration had indeed collapsed and Kashmir was in the grip of the worst political crisis since 1947.

On 1 January 1964 Bhutto, who had taken over the portfolio of Foreign Affairs, claimed that the theft of the relic had been

...permitted by the Indian occupation authorities and their agents as part of India's plan to reduce the Muslim majority in Jammu and Kashmir to a minority, by bringing home to its Muslim population the feeling that the lives, honour and religion of Muslims were not safe, and that, therefore, they must leave the state.[4]

Public opinion in Pakistan was expressing itself in mass demonstrations in major cities and the crowds were being harangued to prepare for *jihad*. Many senior army officers felt that the time had come to liberate Kashmir, a job that had been left unfinished in 1947. The relic reappeared as mysteriously as it had disappeared. But the Kashmir Action Committee, under Maulana Mohammed Syed Masoodi, which had taken control of public life in Srinagar, declared that the recovered relic would not be accepted as genuine until it had been examined by a committee of experts. The Committee demanded that all those arrested since the theft of the relic should be released and a judicial enquiry held into the incident.

The unrest did not subside. Every new outburst of violence was blamed by the Indian Government on Pakistani *agents provocateurs* and this provided fresh opportunities to the intelligence agencies in Pakistan to bask in the limelight of public approbation. A situation was reached in which the agencies started claiming in official circles in Pakistan that they, indeed, were masterminding the agitation in Kashmir.

The Kashmir Action Committee now demanded that fresh elections must be held to determine the future of the State. The Government of India decided that the only way to restore order was to release Sheikh Mohammed Abdullah, the most popular Kashmiri leader, whose influence had been greatly enhanced by his prolonged incarceration—he had been in prison since April 1954, and on trial for ten years. On 8 April 1964, the Sheikh was released after the prosecution formally withdrew all charges against him. His release was seen as the victory of the Kashmiri people: unarmed civilians had humbled the mighty Indian Army. Given some arms and training could they not expel the Indians permanently and achieve their cherished goal of freedom?

Ayub was impressed by what the Kashmiris had managed to achieve but he did not share the wild-eyed enthusiasm of his Foreign Minister. Despite the failure of six rounds of talks with India to resolve the Kashmir problem Ayub was still adhering to the path of negotiations. He was not prepared to risk Pakistan for the sake of Kashmir.

After his release, Sheikh Abdullah announced that he regarded the accession of Kashmir to India as provisional. At a press conference on 9 April 1964, he said that he could not offer a precise solution of the Kashmir problem until he had discussed the matter with his friends, particularly his 'dearest comrade and colleague, Mr Nehru'.[5] He rejected the suggestion that the state might be partitioned and declared that the Kashmir problem must be solved through a negotiated settlement between India and Pakistan on the basis of the right of self-determination of the Kashmiri people. The Nehru government was alarmed. One of the ministers said in the Lok Sabha: 'There can be no freedom to preach some kind of independence,' while another warned that if Sheikh Abdullah advocated the secession of Kashmir, 'the law will take its course.'[6]

Sheikh Abdullah in Pakistan

Sheikh Abdullah arrived in New Delhi on 29 April, and had a private meeting with Nehru. Two days later he received a formal invitation to visit Pakistan. Accepting the invitation, he informed Pakistan: 'No solution will be lasting until it has the approval of all the parties, namely India, Pakistan, and the people of Kashmir.'[7] This was to reassure Ayub, who had written separately to Sheikh Abdullah warning him that 'no settlement should be reached without due consultation and agreement with us.'[8]

There was much excitement in Pakistan about the first ever visit of Sheikh Abdullah—'Sher-e-Kashmir' (The Tiger of Kashmir). His critics preferred to call him the 'leopard of Kashmir' who had finally changed his spots. What was India's game in allowing Sheikh Abdullah to visit Pakistan? Had there been a real change in Nehru's position or was he merely using 'the tiger' as a stalking horse to buy time and get over his current difficulties in Kashmir? The accepted view in official circles in Pakistan was that Nehru had no intention of resolving the Kashmir dispute on the basis of a free and fair plebiscite, and whatever else Sheikh Abdullah might bring in the way of gifts, a schedule for the holding of a plebiscite in Kashmir would not be among them.[9]

Sheikh Abdullah played his cards with caution after his release. While he dissociated himself from the claim that Kashmir's accession to India was irrevocable and denounced the three elections held in the state as rigged, he did not yield to the demand that Kashmir must join Pakistan, although such a demand had been voiced in public rallies in the Valley. He also opposed any solution that might entail the migration of non-Muslims from the Valley and thus planted himself as the third party in the dispute, the one who had the right to speak for the people of Kashmir. He was there to be wooed by India and Pakistan. The Indians were following a two-track strategy: while some Cabinet ministers were taking a tough line others were telling the Sheikh that with his impeccable credentials as a secularist, he had an excellent chance of succeeding Nehru. All he had to do was to agree to Kashmir becoming an integral part of India enjoying as much autonomy as the Sheikh might ask for, indeed grant, as the prospective Prime Minister of India. Sheikh Abdullah brought for Nehru and his daughter Indira Gandhi, honey, almonds, saffron and lilies of the valley and an American journalist traced 'the allusion to the Old Testament's Song of Solomon as an apparent rebuke to Nehru's conscience for jailing his old friend for the previous 15 years'.[10] While the Sheikh was immersed in negotiations in Delhi, Indira Gandhi left for New York where she lost no time in declaring: 'There can be no major change in India's policy on Kashmir. The whole stability of India depends on it.'[11] Bhutto, too, was in New York at the time, trying to persuade the UN Secretary-General to intervene in the Kashmir situation which, he said, was completely out of control. Bhutto wanted Sheikh Abdullah to be invited to the UN as an observer to explain the developments in Kashmir. When Pakistan pressed for Sheikh Abdullah to be invited to take part in the debate on Kashmir, in the UN Security Council, the Indian representative Muhammad Ali Chagla, India's Minister of Education, said: 'I am here to speak for India, Mr Bhutto for Pakistan, and there is no need for others. If the Council once opens the way for individuals to come and speak there will be no end to it.'[12]

Neither Ayub Khan nor any of his ministers and governors knew Sheikh Abdullah personally. For them, as for most people in Pakistan, he was remembered as the man who had defied Jinnah and opposed the Pakistan Movement. Many of them recalled the statements Sheikh Abdullah had made when the Muslims of India were engaged in their struggle against Hindu domination. Even after the creation of Pakistan he had criticized Jinnah's two-nation theory. In a public speech in Srinagar in October 1947 he said: 'I never believed in the slogan for Pakistan. It is my firm belief that the slogan will bring misery for all. I do not believe in the two-nation theory.'[13] On 7 July 1948 he said: 'India is our motherland, Kashmir cannot be separated from India, nor can India be separated from Kashmir.'[14] The official view in Islamabad was that while Sheikh Abdullah should be given a warm reception, it should not be too effusive. The suggestion that Ayub should receive him at the airport was turned down, as was the proposal that the Muslim League, the ruling party, should host civic receptions for him in major cities. Nevertheless, an elaborate programme was drawn up to take Sheikh Abdullah to all the industrial centres so that he could see for himself the progress that Pakistan had made since Independence.

Sheikh Abdullah arrived in Lahore on 24 May, where he received a rousing welcome. The whole city came out to have a look at the great Kashmiri leader. Most of the ministers, and in particular the Provincial Governor, the Nawab of Kalabagh, who did not have much time for Kashmiris, were a little put out by the spontaneous outpouring of public emotion, but there was little they could do to stem the popular tide which swept the whole of the Punjab.[15]

Sheikh Abdullah had his first meeting with Ayub on 25 May in Rawalpindi. An impressive man, he spoke to Ayub with deference but made his points forcefully. Ayub took to him immediately. Sheikh Abdullah told Ayub that he had met Nehru after eleven years and wanted to find out whether his thinking on Kashmir had undergone any change. His impression was that it had. Nehru now wanted to resolve the Kashmir dispute, and recognized that no solution would work unless it was acceptable to Pakistan.

President Ayub at a Governor's Conference Rawalpindi; November 1963.

Ayub Khan recording an interview for Friends Not Masters. Also present is
N.A. Faruqi, Principal Secretary to the President; Murree 1964.

Ayub Khan, Zhou Enlai and Zulfikar Ali Bhutto in Beijing; March 1965.

Author with Chairman Mao in Beijing; March 1965.

The President a day after the elections. Also present are Altaf Gauhar and
M. H. Shah, Commissioner Rawalpindi Division; January 1965.

President Ayub with the Mufti of Tashkent; March 1965.

Zulfikar Ali Bhutto and Chairman Mikoyan in Moscow; March 1965.

Altaf Gauhar with Premier Zhou Enlai at the Great Wall; March 1965.

The President a day after the elections. Also present are Altaf Gauhar and M. H. Shah, Commissioner Rawalpindi Division; January 1965.

President Ayub with the Mufti of Tashkent; March 1965.

Zulfikar Ali Bhutto and Chairman Mikoyan in Moscow; March 1965.

Altaf Gauhar with Premier Zhou Enlai at the Great Wall;
March 1965.

Author at a meeting chaired by President Ayub Khan. Also present are Nawab of Kalabagh and Masroor Hassan Khan, Commissioner Peshawar Division; Peshawar 1965.

Altaf Gauhar with General Sarfaraz. Also in the picture is Tajammul Hossein; Lahore Front; September 1965.

Ayub Khan with Mr and Mrs Liu Shao Chi at Chaklala Airport; 26 March 1966.

President Ayub and Premier Aleksei Kosygin, President's House, Rawalpindi; 17 April, 1968.

Author at a meeting chaired by President Ayub Khan. Also present are Nawab of Kalabagh and Masroor Hassan Khan, Commissioner Peshawar Division; Peshawar 1965.

Altaf Gauhar with General Sarfaraz. Also in the picture is Tajammul Hossein; Lahore Front; September 1965.

Ayub Khan with Mr and Mrs Liu Shao Chi at Chaklala Airport; 26 March 1966.

President Ayub and Premier Aleksei Kosygin, President's House, Rawalpindi; 17 April, 1968.

Ayub Khan's last official act, decorating Altaf Gauhar with Hilal-i-Quaid-i-Azam. President's House, Rawalpindi; 25 March 1968.

President's farewell lunch for Altaf Gauhar and family (L-R) Raana, Naveed, Altaf Gauhar, Ayub Khan, Begum Ayub, Zarina, Humayun; President's House, Rawalpindi; 25 March 1969.

Altaf Gauhar with Manzur Qadir, coming out of High Court of Sindh and Balochistan after hearing a habeas corpus petition; Karachi 1972.

He had asked Nehru bluntly whether he wanted good neighbourly relations with Pakistan. If that were so India must come to terms with Pakistan and with the people of Kashmir to resolve the Kashmir dispute. The solution might not be wholly satisfactory to all the parties but a reasonable settlement would eliminate much of the prevailing tension in the subcontinent. Ayub's face brightened because Sheikh Abdullah was echoing his own views.

About the Hindu minority in Kashmir, Sheikh Abdullah's view was that if the holding of a plebiscite was likely to lead to the migration of Hindus from the state, which might create a refugee problem and result in communal rioting in India, then other ways of reaching a solution could be found. 'Plebiscite', he said, 'was no more than the mechanics of ascertaining the wishes of the people.' It should be possible 'to find some other way of satisfying public opinion.' He assured Ayub that if he had not seen a distinct change in the political climate of India he would not have come to Pakistan.

Ayub lauded the sacrifices made by Sheikh Abdullah and expressed appreciation of the mission that had brought him to Pakistan. He recalled that when Nehru came to Pakistan in 1962, he told him that India was the natural focal point for the whole of Asia. But to play the role of a leader, India must establish good relations with its neighbours and, in particular, with Pakistan. The world would judge India by its conduct in Kashmir, its treatment of the minorities, and its relations with its neighbours. But Nehru did not seem to have any need for Pakistan's friendship. Ayub mentioned the enormous defence expenditure that India and Pakistan were incurring. According to Field Marshal Claude Auchinleck, the subcontinent did not need more than $100 million for its defence. Yet, India was already spending about $450 million annually to build a massive military force. Pakistan, too, had to incur heavy defence expenditure. If the two armies were disengaged they could effectively check any aggressor, however strong. Even without a settlement of the border problem with China, India could reduce its defence expenditure by $250 million or more if only it would resolve the Kashmir dispute and normalize relations with Pakistan. Both India and Pakistan should then be able to devote most of what they were spending on defence to the amelioration of the lot of their people.

'There was no question of Pakistan invading and conquering India,' Ayub said. Surrounded by enemies, including Afghanistan, it was of the greatest importance for Pakistan to remove the threat from India. He assured Sheikh Abdullah that he would not hesitate to come to an agreement with India on reasonable and honourable terms. But Pakistan would not allow India to annex Kashmir nor would it allow the Indian Army to remain in occupation of Jammu and Kashmir. The reason was perfectly clear. Since three of the western rivers allocated to Pakistan under the Indus Basin Settlement passed through Jammu and Kashmir and the northern areas, Pakistan had a legitimate and vital interest in those areas.

An independent Kashmir was a non-starter, nor would any kind of a condominium work in practice. The interests of India and Pakistan would clash and so would the two armies, if they were put together within the state. An independent Kashmir would become the hotbed of international intrigue and subversion, and would not be viable financially or militarily. Ayub ruled out the idea of a confederation between India, Pakistan and Kashmir as totally unacceptable.

When Sheikh Abdullah met Ayub Khan the next day he spoke without reserve. He had no regrets about the position he had taken up with successive governments in Pakistan and made out quite a case against some of them. He explained how his differences with Jinnah had developed. He had started his political movement under the National Conference to enable the Muslims of Jammu and Kashmir to exercise their right of self-determination. The movement was directed against the Maharaja of Kashmir and Dogra rule. The Maharaja had the support of the British, and the Muslim League was at that time not prepared to take up any position against the British. The Indian National Congress, on the other hand, was carrying on a people's struggle against the British as well as the rulers of the princely states. A close affinity naturally developed between the Congress and Sheikh Abdullah's

National Conference. Jinnah wanted Sheikh Abdullah to merge his National Conference with the Muslim Conference of Chaudhri Ghulam Abbas, which was essentially a communal organization, and advised Sheikh Abdullah to remain loyal to the Maharaja when the National Conference was actually engaged in the 'Quit Kashmir' movement against the Dogra ruler. The basic difference was that the Muslim League was concerned with the problems of the Muslim minority in India whereas Sheikh Abdullah was fighting for the future of Muslims in Jammu and Kashmir where they were in a majority. Another difference lay in the fact that whereas the Muslim League was aligned with the rulers of the states in its fight against Hindu majority, the fight of Kashmiri Muslims was wholly against the ruler of Kashmir. In its composition and character, too, the Muslim League was different from the National Conference: the League was dominated by landlords and other elitist elements, while the National Conference drew all its strength from the masses. But once Pakistan was established, Sheikh Abdullah had recognized that a strong Pakistan would be in the interest of Kashmir.

The Maharaja wanted Kashmir to remain independent but events forced his hands. Immediately after Partition there were disturbances in Poonch and then suddenly the tribesmen from Pakistan appeared in the Kashmir Valley. They began to kill and loot indiscriminately. This had the effect of alienating the Kashmiris from Pakistan. Had the tribesmen gone to Jammu province, which was predominantly a Hindu area, and blown up the railway line from Sialkot to Jammu they would have had greater success. Unfortunately Khan Abdul Qayyum Khan, Chief Minister of Pakistan's North-West Frontier Province, who had organized the whole operation, was much more interested in grabbing the Valley where, he thought, he would be able to establish his little kingdom. He had given his tribesmen a list of persons who were to be eliminated once the Valley was secured and that list included the names of Sheikh Abdullah and his associates.

Sheikh Abdullah said that when the accession of the State was being discussed in New Delhi in 1947, he had told Lord

Mountbatten and Nehru that such an accession by the Maharaja would never be recognized by the people of Jammu and Kashmir, who must be allowed to exercise their right of self-determination. It was at his insistence that the clause relating to the right of self-determination was included in the announcement. When the matter went to the UN Security Council Sheikh Abdullah was in New York, where he tried to contact the Pakistani representatives. However, there was such arrogance and hostility towards him that the Pakistani delegates would not even talk to him. They were so confident of the support of the Americans and the British that they thought they could do without his co-operation. When he went to the Security Council the second time, he did meet Chaudhri Mohammad Ali and told him that the only way to get the Indians out of Kashmir was to agree to the independence of the State. He argued that the British and the Americans would never support Pakistan at the risk of alienating India but the Pakistanis found his line of reasoning unacceptable.

Sheikh Abdullah expressed grave doubts about the competence of the intelligence agencies in Pakistan who had no real contacts in the Valley and often acted on the basis of insufficient or misleading information about developments in Kashmir. The result was that Pakistan, for some time pursued a course of action which did not help the cause of Kashmir. Pakistan had missed a great opportunity when it refused to come to terms with India over the evacuation of Indian troops and kept wrangling about the number of soldiers to be left in the State—the difference was about 5,000 soldiers. Nehru had later offered to confine the Indian forces to the barracks without withdrawing them from the State, which would have sealed off the Indian Army in three or four places. Pakistan rejected that offer too. But the most distressing failure of policy occurred in August 1953. The State was then in the grip of a popular agitation and a little pressure from Pakistan would have helped the resistance movement, but Pakistani Prime Minister, Bogra, decided to fly to New Delhi and embrace Nehru as his 'Big Brother', little realizing that the Indians were in a particularly vulnerable position at that time and needed to come to a show of understanding with Pakistan to demoralize the Kashmiris. Pakistan fell into that trap.

Sheikh Abdullah said that whatever might be thought of Nehru he was in command and it was necessary to deal with him. He was emotionally attached to the Valley and there was a circle of Kashmiri pundits around him who had considerable influence on him. The encouraging thing was that he seemed to realize the need for settling India's differences with Pakistan while he was still in office. Vinoba Bhave, the Indian leader with a mass following, had considerable influence among the Hindus and his view was that the best solution was for India and Pakistan to agree to form a confederation with Kashmir.

Ayub replied somewhat impatiently that confederation was the one solution totally unacceptable to Pakistan. Any kind of confederal arrangement would undo the partition and place the Hindu majority in a dominant and decisive position in respect of the confederal subjects i.e. foreign affairs, defence, and finance. All federations come to be dominated by the major partner. In any case Pakistan could neither align herself with some of India's misconceived policies nor accept the legacy of India's political blunders. Another problem was that a confederal arrangement would generate strong pressures in East Pakistan to merge with West Bengal, and for Bengal as a whole to join the confederation as an independent member. Similarly South India, Rajasthan and even the Sikhs would want to become autonomous members of the proposed confederation. Sheikh Abdullah promised to apprise the Indians of these possibilities so that they understood the reasons for Pakistan's rejection of the proposal of confederation. Ayub suddenly got up and said that he was getting a little fed up with the variety of solutions that were on offer and told Sheikh Abdullah to forget about Pakistan and come to any settlement he wanted with India. A little taken aback, Sheikh Abdullah exclaimed that there could be no settlement without Pakistan: 'The future of the Kashmiris lies with Pakistan.' Ayub Khan relaxed. Sheikh Abdullah suggested that Ayub should visit New Delhi to discuss the different possibilities with Nehru who was now in a more reasonable frame of mind. This would give Ayub a chance to talk to other Indian leaders such as Raja Gopalachari, Jai Prakash Narain and the Indian President Radha Krishnan. These leaders could prod Nehru to come to a settlement with Pakistan. Ayub said he would be willing to undertake the visit for Sheikh Abdullah's sake.

Everything changed the next day, 27 May. Nehru died and the whole exercise undertaken by Sheikh Abdullah with the concurrence of Nehru lost its purpose. After addressing a mammoth public meeting in Rawalpindi Sheikh Abdullah had gone to Muzaffarabad in Azad Kashmir where he received the news of Nehru's death. The Indian journalists accompanying him advised him against appearing at any public meeting in Muzaffarabad. Nevertheless, he converted the occasion into a huge condolence meeting where he spoke for about fifteen minutes. Cutting short his stay in Pakistan Sheikh Abdullah flew back to New Delhi. Bhutto went to New Delhi to attend Nehru's funeral and assured the Indian leaders that Pakistan would observe a moratorium on Kashmir.

Ayub was greatly impressed by Sheikh Abdullah. After their second meeting he said: 'I wish I had someone like him with me.'[16] In his last private conversation with Sheikh Abdullah Ayub advised him to 'move slowly and allow events to take their own course.' He should let the squabbling end before getting personally involved. Ayub told Sheikh Abdullah not to fall for the bait of accepting the role of a messiah of Hindu-Muslim unity: 'Such a move would neutralize you. But you must avoid any head-on collision at all costs.' Ayub forecast that parochial and regional tendencies would soon develop in India. The provinces would get more assertive and the central government would weaken. The brahmin and the banya (the merchant class), the traditional rulers of India, would come into their own. Ayub saw Nehru with his secular outlook as someone who had interrupted the natural course of Hindu history. That course would lead to the emergence of a strong revivalist movement. Such a movement would be cloaked in secular idiom but its aim would be to establish the ascendancy of the brahmin. The result would be growing pressures for provincial autonomy to isolate the Gangetic culture—the heart of Indian civilization: 'India can be kept together only by some supra-provincial ideal or military force. Since no such ideal was available, and force wasn't a viable option in the present age, the inevitable result will be growth of separatism.'

In a broadcast after Nehru's death, Ayub called for an end to the 'bitterness and recrimination' that had marred relations between the two countries: 'India and Pakistan are neighbours for better or worse. Why let it be for worse, and not try the alternative of living together for better?' Referring to Sheikh Abdullah's visit, he said: 'I was deeply impressed by Sheikh Abdullah's sincerity and determination to see the Kashmir dispute resolved in a manner which would not harm Pakistan's vital interests, and bring about happier relations between India and Pakistan.'[17]

Responding to Ayub's appeal, Lal Bahadur Shastri, who took over as Prime Minister after Nehru, said, 'India and Pakistan are two great countries linked together by common history and tradition. It is their natural destiny to be friends with one another and to enter into close co-operation in many fields.'[18] Shastri praised Ayub for his wisdom and understanding but made no mention of Kashmir.

Ayub's dilemma

Nehru's death created a vacuum and Ayub was once more confronted with the question: What should Pakistan do about Kashmir? The Inter-Services Intelligence agency, headed by Brigadier Riaz Hussain, had convinced itself that the moment for decisive intervention had arrived. Bhutto, too, was trying to impress upon Ayub that India was facing a leadership crisis and the growing agitation in Kashmir offered Pakistan an opportunity to act. Bhutto found a loyal ally in his Foreign Secretary, Aziz Ahmed, a rigid bureaucrat who shared Bhutto's belligerence towards India. Together they would impress on Ayub that, with Nehru gone, the world expected him to assume the role of a leader of the subcontinent, indeed the role of de Gaulle in South Asia. The view was gaining ground that if Pakistan were to make a decisive move in Kashmir, India would not be able to resist it. Ayub remained unmoved. He issued instructions that inflammatory propaganda on Azad Kashmir Radio should be cut down. He was clearly worried that public opinion might get too worked up against India, making it difficult for him to pursue the path of negotiations to which he was still firmly committed. For Ayub the more immediate problem was the possibility of all US aid being cut off in the not too distant future. He thought it highly unrealistic for Pakistan to think of fighting India without assured sources of supply of military arms. Ayub saw with anguish the snapping of his old ties with the Americans. Again and again he would say that under Kennedy the US government had abandoned all moral principles in its dealings with old friends. US foreign policy had become thoroughly opportunistic, lacking all idealism. Ayub was still clinging to the naïve belief that the Americans had originally built up their regional alliances out of some altruistic philosophy which had been abandoned by Kennedy. He told an American journalist that the Americans had no scruples: 'They do not want allies, they want lackeys.'[19] Ayub did not favour any aggressive move against India. More than anything else he wanted to avoid getting into an arms race with India: 'We should exert political and diplomatic pressure against India and not do anything which might unite India.'

Ayub did not have a high opinion of the Indian Army; it had expanded too rapidly, and lacked disciplined leadership. Still, it represented an overwhelming threat to Pakistan. Ayub did not share the view that India might embark on some military adventure to divert public opinion from problems at home. Any aggressive move in Azad Kashmir would be expensive for India: 'It will be a general war when it comes. An isolated war confined to one area was not possible.'[20] Ayub had no doubt that India would not go to war with Pakistan as long as the Chinese threat persisted.

Ayub was aware of the concern in GHQ about the Indian Army stationed along Pakistan's borders. 'It was causing a great strain' and Ayub was worried that his boys 'might take some jittery desperate action'. To pacify the hawks around him Ayub would say: 'Let us continue to lean on India. If our borders are violated let us hit hard. The Hindu has no fight in him.' Ayub was worried about the Muslim minority in India. But the Indians must know that if they were to try and drive them out 'we will shut our eyes and go to war. This we must make quite clear to India and to our friends.'[21]

Bhutto wanted Pakistan to review its membership of SEATO which was a source of irritation to the Chinese. Such a move, Ayub thought, would only dramatize the growing distance between the US and Pakistan and bring no particular benefit to Pakistan. Ayub was agonizing over every step that was taking him away from the Americans. He did not expect the Russians to come to Pakistan's assistance: 'The Russians will never want to annoy the Indians.' Ayub's real fear was that if Pakistan went too far the US government might 'do something stupid'. The Chinese were not in a position to pick up the tab. Pakistan must not go to the breaking point with the US: 'But we must tell our western friends not to push us too hard.' Ayub thought that closer contacts with the Afro-Asian community would 'give us standing'.[22]

Before Ayub could find an answer to his dilemma he was overtaken by events at home. His first term was coming to an end and he had to prepare for the pressures and rigours of a presidential election before too long. Ayub Khan regarded elections as an unavoidable nuisance but he wanted to put them behind his back to be able to get on with his job.

NOTES

1. *Dawn,* 5 October 1963.
2. Ibid., 29 November 1963.
3. Ibid., 1 December 1963.
4. Ibid., 2 January 1964.
5. Ibid., 10 April 1964.
6. Lok Sabha proceedings, April 1964.
7. Ayub's personal papers.
8. Ibid.
9. Author's notes.
10. *The Washington Evening Star,* 1 May 1964.
11. Ayub Khan's papers.
12. *Dawn,* 24 April 1964.
13. *The Statesman,* Calcutta, 5 October 1947.
14. *The National Herald,* New Delhi, 8 July 1948.

15. The account that follows is based on the Foreign Office minutes of Sheikh Abdullah's meetings with Ayub, and the author's notes.
16. Conversation with the author.
17. *Dawn,* 2 June 1964.
18. Ayub's personal papers.
19. Author's notes, July 1964. This was the sentence which suggested the title *Friends Not Masters* for Ayub's autobiography.
20. Author's notes.
21. Ibid.
22. Ibid.

CHAPTER 6

Presidential Election

While Ayub's image was beginning to glisten in the region as a result of Pakistan's blossoming friendship with the People's Republic of China, his domestic outlook was looking quite murky. His Constitution had disappointed the people and his political party had no support among the masses. Through indirect elections the party had secured a majority in the national and provincial legislatures in 1962 but there were powerful opposition elements that not only questioned the democratic character of the Constitution but also Ayub's right to promulgate a Constitution at all. The Press which had remained subservient and aphonic under martial law, suddenly recovered its freedom and started to voice strong nationalistic demands.

But Ayub was too deeply involved in international affairs. Even as late as September 1964, when the election campaign had already started, he was having a meeting with the Sarvodaya leader from India, J.P. Narayan, in Rawalpindi. He was still exploring the possibilities of resolving the Kashmir dispute through negotiations; his hope was that with Nehru out of the way, the Indians might see the benefit of normalizing relations with Pakistan. On his return to Delhi J.P. Narayan gave a statement that Pakistan's attitude toward the Kashmir question was not inflexible and there was scope for 'meaningful negotiations'.[1] A month later, on 12 October 1964, Ayub met the Indian Prime Minister, Lal Bahadur Shastri, when he passed through Karachi on his way back from the non-aligned conference in Cairo. A joint communiqué stated:

The President of Pakistan and the Prime Minister of India had a general discussion on relations between their two countries. They were both firmly of the view that these relations needed to be improved and continued to their mutual benefit as good neighbours. They agreed that it was necessary to promote a better understanding between the two countries and to settle outstanding problems and disputes on an honourable, equitable basis.[2]

The presidential election was certainly not on top of Ayub's agenda in the first half of 1964. It was not difficult to forecast that the election would be strongly contested and candidates would have to go to the masses from the start, though under the Constitution candidates were required only to appear before the members of the electoral college to put across their programme and to answer any questions that members might ask. Having elected the Basic Democrats, the people were not required to take any part in the presidential election. Ayub's associates believed that the Opposition would be too divided to put up any candidate on a unanimous basis and there would be no contest. They assured him that given his achievements and his prominent international status there really was no one in the country who could pose a challenge to him. Ayub and his ministers were, therefore, taken by surprise when on 18 September the Combined Opposition Parties (COP) announced that Miss Fatima Jinnah had 'graciously accepted their request for nomination as a candidate for the Presidential elections'.[3] Miss Jinnah, sister of the Quaid-i-Azam, was a venerable lady, deeply respected throughout the country. No one could quite fathom how the opposition parties had managed to sink their differences and agree on a single candidate. The Law Minister, Sheikh Khurshid Ahmed, who had been baiting the Opposition in the National Assembly to come out with the name of their candidate, was quite crestfallen. The two provincial governors, who had maintained law and order with an iron hand and snuffed out all dissent, were bewildered by the ecstatic manner in which the people celebrated Miss Jinnah's decision to fight their hero, the soldier-statesman Ayub. She had no experience of government, no knowledge of administration and no contact with world leaders. Nevertheless, she was the idol of the people and wherever she appeared hundreds of thousands of people would gather only to catch a glimpse of her. She was frail and elderly and could hardly speak any of the national languages but her charisma was irresistible. She was seen by the crowds as the only person who could bring down Ayub's authoritarian rule and restore the democratic rights of the people.

The ruling political party was in complete disarray. It had no cadres and no organization, only a clutch of paid employees. The Secretary General of the party, Abdul Waheed Khan, a pusillanimous character, was almost paralysed by the appearance of Miss Jinnah on the political scene. He continued to insist that presidential candidates must not be allowed to hold public meetings; they must wait for the emergence of the electoral college to put their case before the BDs. The Constitution did not envisage any electoral campaign at the popular level but it did not forbid a presidential candidate from going to the people directly and organizing public rallies to acquaint the masses with various political issues. The possibility of promulgating an ordinance forbidding the candidates from addressing public meetings was considered, but it was realized that the size of the crowds Miss Jinnah was attracting would make it impossible for the administration to enforce such a measure.

The campaign trail

The first phase of the campaign started on 18 September 1964 and continued until the end of October when Miss Jinnah finished her tour of the major cities of West Pakistan. The halo around her brightened with each public appearance. The ruling political party maintained a discreet silence during this period because no one in the government had the courage to utter a word of criticism against Miss Jinnah. Ayub was fuming because he could not understand how a campaign could be conducted when not a word of criticism could be uttered against his rival. He repeatedly urged his associates to expose Miss Jinnah's political record, and draw the attention of the people to her lack of experience and her old age. All that Ayub's associates could manage was to criticize the political advisors around Miss Jinnah and attack their bona fides.

Ayub finally decided to take up the challenge himself and started addressing public meetings. He addressed his first public meeting in Peshawar on 13 October. The local administration had lassoed a large crowd into the meeting ground but Ayub did not have Miss Jinnah's charisma and he had no experience of public speaking. His knowledge of Urdu, which was the only common language the crowds in West Pakistan understood, was limited. But he learnt quickly and after the first three or four public meetings, started speaking with greater confidence. He was handicapped by the fact that he could not criticize Miss Jinnah because attacking an old lady would be considered unbecoming of a gentleman. While his own party was getting more and more demoralized and succumbing to internal differences, the five feuding opposition parties had succeeded in forging a powerful combination. The real problem of Ayub's associates was that they were all convinced that he would never allow the situation to reach a point where he might lose the election. They were certain that if things went too far he would call upon the army to put an end to popular hysteria. Only Ayub knew that he had no choice but to go through the process he had himself initiated. If he were to become the victim of the process the armed forces would not come to his rescue, since they too could see the crowds that daily paraded the streets denouncing Ayub and his Constitution.

After finishing one round of public meetings in West Pakistan, Miss Jinnah proceeded to East Pakistan where the Awami League, led by Sheikh Mujibur Rahman, was carrying on a crusade against the Ayub regime. The people in East Pakistan felt that they had been deprived of all their rights and that the province was no better than a colony of Islamabad. Miss Jinnah was seen as the only hope of changing an unjust and oppressive system. The crowds that greeted her in East Pakistan were even larger than those in West Pakistan.

In her speeches Miss Jinnah criticized Ayub mercilessly, portraying him as an interloper and a dictator, and alleging that his ministers and governors were his lackeys who had no real power.

She attacked Ayub and his family for corruption. One minister whom she singled out for personal condemnation was Bhutto. She called him an 'inebriate and a philanderer' in a speech in Hyderabad. Ayub could take it no more and, at a press conference in Lahore, he said that Miss Jinnah had been leading an 'unnatural' life, a reference to her spinsterhood, and was surrounded by 'perverts'.[4] Everyone in the government was totally stunned, but somehow Ayub survived, mainly because the campaign rhetoric had already sunk to a low level and rival parties were freely exchanging invective and abuse.

The campaign raised serious questions about Ayub's style of government. Allegations of corruption against Ayub's family, particularly his son Gohar Ayub, were openly levelled and widely believed. Gohar, a retired Captain from the army, had acquired an assembly plant from General Motors (to which he gave the name Gandhara Motors) through the influence of his father. Throughout the campaign 'Gandhara' was used as the ultimate proof of nepotism against Ayub. The Opposition adopted 'Gandhara' as a slogan, which they used with devastating effect, and people from Peshawar to Chittagong came to treat it as the ultimate symbol of corruption in Ayub's government and in his own family. Nothing destroyed Ayub's prestige and credibility more than 'Gandhara'. Even his reforms came in for a lot of criticism. His land reforms were seen as an elaborate design to consolidate the power of landlords and bureaucrats and his Islamic reforms, especially the family laws, were criticized as a deviation from the Sunnah.

Ayub was persuaded by his party to use the religious card against Miss Jinnah. A *fatwa* (religious decree) was obtained from some *ulema* to the effect that a woman could not become the head of a Muslim State. The Opposition organized an even larger set of *ulema* to produce an equally authoritative *fatwa* in support of Miss Jinnah. They discovered from the writings of various Muslim jurists that a woman could become the ruler under exceptional circumstances. And who could deny, asked the Opposition, that Pakistan was going through exceptional circumstances? The weapon of religious decrees worked against Ayub throughout the campaign.

But the most damaging effect of the campaign for Ayub was that it affected the ability of his administration to influence the Basic Democrats. The assumption all along had been that BD elections would be completed in the first phase and the presidential campaign would then begin as a separate exercise. As it turned out the presidential campaign swept the country well before the BD elections. The ruling party had first decided that it would nominate its candidates for BD elections and issue them with party tickets. As the campaign progressed the ruling party lost confidence in its ability to get a majority of its candidates elected. It was, therefore, decided that there should be no officially nominated party candidate and each candidate should fight the election as an independent. The Combined Opposition Parties (COP) also decided not to issue party tickets. This reopened the possibility that the administration might be able to persuade or pressurize elected candidates into giving support to Ayub. Had COP put up candidates throughout the country there would have been a distinct possibility that it could have won a majority of seats in the electoral college. The real reason why COP could not follow such a strategy was that while its leadership had been able to agree on a single presidential candidate, it could not agree on 80,000 candidates for the electoral college and contending claims proved irreconcilable.

The elections of Basic Democrats ended on 19 November 1964 with both sides claiming an overwhelming victory. The Muslim League declared that eighty per cent of the elected members were Ayub supporters and COP claimed that ninety per cent of the members were pledged to vote for Miss Jinnah. The administration did its own research, compiling and analysing the antecedents of each one of the elected members. The Intelligence Bureau gave Ayub the cheerful message that seventy-five per cent of the members would support him. The governors now proceeded to obtain a formal oath of allegiance from the elected members. Divisional commissioners and district magistrates were then assigned the task of ensuring that the elected members did not deviate from their oath. There followed a competition among district magistrates, each trying to bring the largest number of BDs to Ayub's side, knowing that high scorers would earn special recognition for initiative and dedication to duty. The whole election was now reduced to an administrative exercise to ensure Ayub's victory.

Ayub gets re-elected

Ayub still had to fix a date for the election of the President. His term was expiring on 23 March 1965 and under the Constitution the election to the office of the President had to be completed at least twenty days before that. Ayub was advised by his governors and many of his ministers that he should fix the date as close to 23 March as possible. But he had seen how ineffectual his party had been and instinctively knew that time was on Miss Jinnah's side. If she were to undertake another round of public meetings, gruelling though such an exercise would be for her, COP might manage to frighten the members of the electoral college into submission. The Opposition would certainly use all means of winning over the members. Already pressures were building even in the countryside, and elected members were complaining to district officers that if they did not vote for Miss Jinnah COP activists would burn down their houses and destroy their property and crops. The district officers were themselves under so much pressure that they wanted the election to be wrapped up as soon as possible. Ayub finally decided that the election should be held on 2 January 1965.

The decision took COP by surprise. The first round of the campaign had clearly gone in favour of Miss Jinnah. She had demolished the ruling party, leaving Ayub to fight a lonely battle against her. She now undertook a second round of public meetings in West Pakistan during which she started to question Ayub's performance as President. She claimed that he had bartered away Pakistan's waters by signing the Indus Basin Waters Treaty with India. She revived the controversy about the offer Ayub made to Nehru in 1959 to enter into a joint defence pact with India against China. She referred to a meeting that Ayub had with the Aga Khan in Nice in 1951, soon after the assassination of Liaquat Ali Khan, during the course of which the Aga Khan said to him: 'You have got Pakistan after great sacrifices. You do not want to lose it. But if parliamentary system is the one you are going to follow then you will lose Pakistan. I have called you here to tell you that you will lose it this way, and that you are the one person who can save it.'[5] She used this incident to show that he was planning to overthrow the civilian government long before the *coup d'etat* in 1958. Much as the ruling party tried to defend Ayub, Miss Jinnah succeeded in creating serious doubts in the public mind about Ayub's reforms and his achievements in the field of international affairs. The only mistake she made was to refer to the United States in one of her speeches as Pakistan's 'only friend', which upset many of her 'left-leaning' associates, but she soon retracted that statement.

While Miss Jinnah's charisma continued to captivate the masses, COP, seeing success within reach, started quarrelling about political issues on which they had conflicting, even contradictory, positions. The leaders of the Opposition parties also began to resent the way Miss Jinnah treated them. She had adopted the aloof and domineering style of her brother, and would not allow any of the political veterans around her to say anything. Nor would she follow their advice on the election strategy. The Opposition had carefully analysed the results of the election of Basic Democrats and had noticed that thirty-seven per cent of old members had been returned in West Pakistan, and forty-five per cent in East Pakistan. Of the old chairmen of the councils of Basic Democrats nearly seventy per cent had been returned in East Pakistan and sixty per cent in East Pakistan. Few of the members had any education or an assured source of income. Fewer still had any political experience. Their influence was primarily local and they were not accountable to any political party. Once the BDs were elected, the vulnerability of the electoral system to administrative pressures and counter-pressures began to be exposed. The government set out to buy as many of the elected members as possible, while blaming the Opposition for disturbing the peace.

The final phase of the campaign was marked by a series of confrontation meetings. Presidential candidates would appear before the members of the electoral college in principal towns and, after making an opening statement, answer the questions put to them by members of the electoral college. These meetings were presided over by judges of different High Courts and questions were all deposited in a box. The presiding officer would draw out a question and read it aloud and then ask the candidate to answer the question. The ruling party managed to put a very large number of questions into the box so that when the presiding officer put his hand in the box the likelihood was that he would draw out a question of the ruling party's preference. Some of the presiding judges were amenable to government pressure, others were more than willing to show their loyalty to Ayub Khan: they rejected questions they thought would be considered offensive by Ayub. An Ordinance was issued debarring the public from attending these meetings and the election commission decided to keep the two candidates apart; Ayub would appear before the members in the morning and Miss Jinnah in the afternoon or vice versa.

Miss Jinnah was on her own in these confrontation meetings and her lack of political experience and irascible temperament started to show. The first meeting was in Rawalpindi and she was led to believe by some of her workers that the government had decided, in collusion with the election commission, to keep all the elected members away from the meeting. The night before the meeting she wrote a letter to the commission alleging collusion and demanding a change in the time of the meeting. The commission declined to make any change, and the members of the electoral college started gathering at the venue of the meeting early in the morning. By nine o'clock in the morning the place was packed to capacity. The ruling party had indeed tried to prevent the members from coming to the meeting but had completely failed. Miss Jinnah turned up at the appointed time and in a brief speech attacked the commission for its failure to bring the members of the electoral college to the meeting. The members who were all present, were perplexed by Miss Jinnah's speech. The judge who was presiding over the meeting had only to point out that all the members invited to the meeting were sitting there to show that Miss Jinnah's charge was baseless. She lost many of her supporters that day. By comparison, when Ayub appeared before the members in the afternoon he was enthusiastically greeted and his speech was quite warmly applauded.

The question-answer sessions which were broadcast by Radio Pakistan, after careful editing to ensure that nothing damaging to Ayub was put on the air, also went badly for Miss Jinnah. There was hardly a question to which she could give a clear and coherent answer. Some questions she did not even understand. Others she understood, but she avoided taking a clear position lest she should alienate any of the constituent parties of the COP. By avoiding all difficult and crucial issues she did manage to keep COP united, but her constant hedging cost her the support of many members of the electoral college. As the confrontation meetings proceeded, the war of pamphlets, posters, and advertisements also reached its peak. In this COP had an edge over the ruling party because it could manufacture a variety of rumours and slanders against Ayub. It also started issuing threats to businessmen and bureaucrats to maintain pressure on the members. Towards the end of the campaign COP started a wild rumour that Ayub was planning to pack his bags and leave the country before the polling day. The rumour hit East Pakistan with particular force because there was greater willingness among the Bengalis to believe that Ayub had lost his nerve and would soon quit the field. On 25 December, Ayub issued a statement denying the rumour and told the pressmen at the Dhaka Airport that 'a section of the Press has said that I am packing up and leaving. Let me tell them through you that I will fight these enemies of the country to the last.'[6] Ayub was beginning to wonder whether the Opposition had really come to believe that they would win the election.

The polling took place on 2 January 1965, in a peaceful environment. The COP strategy of harassing the members was effectively neutralized by the measures taken by the government to maintain a calm atmosphere at the polling stations. The Opposition wanted the results of the election to be determined at street corners and not at polling stations which they knew were under the control of the government. The government moved in the army in aid of civil authorities thus frustrating the COP strategy of attacking the voters. A few days before the polling, the

COP steering committee issued a statement in which it threatened to launch a country-wide disobedience movement if the results did not go in favour of Miss Jinnah. Ayub ignored the hysteria of the Opposition and waited for the election day and did not yield to the pressure from his party to adopt such desperate measures as imposing pre-censorship on newspapers.

On the day of polling, both sides appeared equally confident although the Opposition was much more demonstrative than the ruling party. Heavy polling was reported in the morning and results started coming in after 1 p.m. Arrangements had been made that the results should be announced by Radio Pakistan as they were issued by the presiding officers at the polling stations. This was to ensure that the Opposition did not level any charges of administrative tampering with the ballot boxes.

The first results came from Dhaka and looked bad for Ayub. Next came Karachi and that too went against Ayub. Lahore provided considerable relief because it was generally believed that Lahore always went with the Opposition. Throughout the country people were glued to their radio sets. In Dhaka, the Opposition started celebrating its victory after hearing the local results. By the evening however, COP had collapsed. Miss Jinnah could not be reached and the gates of her Karachi residence, Flagstaff House, were bolted and barred. The Chief Election Commissioner announced the results, which gave a clear majority to Ayub.

Ayub was to go on the air at 10. p.m. But by 7 p.m. Ayub, who had been a lonely figure of some weeks was once again surrounded by a host of sycophants and admirers who were all submitting suggestions about what he should say in his 'victory' speech. The speech had already been drafted by the Information Secretary and Ayub, still in a dazed state, read it out into the microphone without any feeling. The dazed look did not leave Ayub's face for several hours. What had shaken him completely was the knowledge that he had come so close to defeat and his Constitution and his reforms had been so comprehensively rejected by the people. Out of 80,000 members of electoral college, 49,951 voted for Ayub, and 28,691 for Miss Jinnah. But in East Pakistan the gap was much narrower—Miss Jinnah had 18,434 votes against Ayub's 21,012 giving him a winning margin of only 2,578 votes. In West Pakistan, Ayub won in all the divisions and districts except Karachi, but in East Pakistan he won in only two divisions, Rajshahi and Khulna, and lost in Dhaka and Chittagong. Out of seventeen districts in East Pakistan he lost in four: Dhaka, Noakhali, Sylhet, and Comilla. The loss of Karachi caused consternation. It demonstrated the strong support Miss Jinnah enjoyed among the refugees. In many other towns of Sindh also, the refugee vote went against Ayub.

No lessons learnt

Ayub asked the Information Secretary, who had accompanied him during the campaign, to carry out a detailed analysis of the election campaign and its results.[7] The analysis showed that the demand for democracy had been Miss Jinnah's main source of popularity, and had won her the support of the intelligentsia. The government had suffered because of allegations of corruption, and it was widely known that the administrative machinery had been used to swing the members of the electoral college in Ayub's favour. COP suffered because of internal conflicts and the poor performance of Miss Jinnah in the projection meetings. While her magic worked in public rallies and processions, in the orderly atmosphere of meetings organized by the election commission her appeal plummeted.

The analysis brought out the deep feelings of alienation among the people who had been denied any meaningful participation in the affairs of the state since Independence. The BD system had further increased the isolation of the people. The ruling party was seen as a haven for opportunists and time-servers dominated by Ayub's minions and stooges. It was true that the crowds had gone to see Miss Jinnah out of curiosity but they had also decisively registered their protest against the government and its policies.

It would be unfortunate, the analysis suggested, if the strength and intensity of the protest was doubted or attributed to the machinations of politicians or enemy agents. What people needed most was a sense of belonging and participation. This was completely lacking, and if remedial measures were not adopted popular resentment would explode whenever an opportunity offered itself.

The President, the governors, and ministers should all declare their assets before the commencement of the next term. All allegations of corruption should be thoroughly investigated and dealt with. But above all the system of Basic Democracies must be made acceptable to the people. If the demand for direct elections was not acceptable to the government then the size of the electoral college must be sufficiently enlarged to put it beyond the reach of the administration.

This analysis was put on the agenda of the Governors' Conference a few weeks later. By then the ruling party had convinced Ayub that he had scored a convincing victory and the Opposition had been thoroughly trounced. Instead of taking any decision on the points made out in the analysis, the Governors' Conference decided to set up a 'patronage committee' to reward all those lawyers and teachers who had worked for Ayub during the campaign. The ruling party had obviously learnt no lesson from the opposition campaign or from the results of the election. Ayub briefly considered the possibility of enlarging the size of the electoral college but decided not to tinker with the system.

It did not take Ayub long to get back into the warm waters of international affairs leaving his feuding opponents bogged in the quagmire of domestic bitterness.

NOTES

1. Ayub Khan's papers.
2. *Dawn*, 13 October 1964.
3. Ibid., 19 September 1964.
4. Author's notes.
5. Ayub Khan, op. cit., p. 193.
6. *Dawn*, 26 December 1961.
7. Summary for Governor's Conference submitted by Information Secretary; January 1965.

CHAPTER 7

Back on the International Trail

Ayub Khan decided to put his domestic problems on the back burner. All the outpouring of popular resentment was attributed to the machinations of disgruntled politicians who had misled the innocent people during the heat of the campaign.

As messages of congratulations poured in from all sides, including tributes from heads of governments, the bitterness of the election campaign was all forgotten. Ayub's ministers, in particular Zulfikar Ali Bhutto, who was worried that he might lose his seat in the Cabinet or the portfolio of foreign affairs, soon convinced him that the election results meant a popular endorsement of his Constitution and any change or modification would be seen as a sign of weakness and a concession to the wily politicians.

Ayub goes to Beijing

As if to celebrate his victory Ayub accepted an invitation from the Chinese government to visit the People's Republic of China from 2 to 9 March 1965. The reception that he received exceeded all expectations. No foreign dignitary had ever been accorded a more enthusiastic welcome. From the airport to the city of Beijing, there was a mass of humanity marshalled along the road, singing patriotic songs, while Ayub, accompanied by Zhou Enlai, stood in an open car waving to ecstatic crowds lost in a vast pageant of colour and music. Already he was beginning to look like a great leader of South Asia. Television audiences throughout the world saw Ayub acclaimed by the Chinese leaders as a friend and a hero.

Perhaps the most important result of the visit was the signing of the boundary protocol which gave details of the demarcation work jointly undertaken by the two countries on the basis of ground surveys and aerial photography. As a gesture of friendship Zhou Enlai allowed some grazing areas to be placed on the Pakistani side of the border. Ayub was deeply moved by this because Pakistan had given up its claim to those areas during the negotiations. India delivered a bellicose protest note on 10 March 1965 asserting that Pakistan and China had no common border and that Pakistan's presence in North Kashmir was based on aggression and illegal occupation. The protest note said that the Chinese motives in concluding the border agreement was to share the fruits of aggression with Pakistan and to exploit Indo-Pakistan differences in pursuit of its own aggressive designs on India.

Ayub's China visit transformed the political climate in Pakistan. All opposition to Ayub literally melted away. The people felt elevated by the knowledge that China had become Pakistan's friend and ally against India. The National Assembly elections were held on 21 March. Nearly 700 candidates contested the 150 National Assembly seats. Ayub's Muslim League secured 118 seats while Miss Jinnah's COP could muster no more than nine seats. A number of prominent opposition leaders from East Pakistan were defeated. Ayub was sworn in as President for a five-year term on 23 March 1965. Ayub decided to reappoint both the existing provincial governors: the Nawab of Kalabagh in West Pakistan and Monem Khan in East Pakistan. A few days before the new Cabinet was sworn in Bhutto had seen Ayub and written him a letter assuring him of his loyalty and devotion. He had offered his services in any capacity, without concealing his preference for Foreign Affairs. Bhutto knew that certain people in the government, in particular the Nawab of Kalabagh, were keen to see him eliminated, but he had the support of some of the Secretaries to the government, in particular the Information Secretary, and was able to persuade Ayub to retain his services and let him keep the portfolio of Foreign Affairs. Some of the old ministers were dropped and five new ones were brought into the Cabinet.

On to Moscow

Ayub's next visit was to the Soviet Union. No Pakistani head of government had ever been to Moscow.[1]

Ayub and his entourage landed at the Moscow Airport on 3 April on a bitterly cold morning. Prime Minister Kosygin received Ayub and the delegation was taken to the Kremlin. Along the route there were no cheering crowds, nor any flags or festoons, to welcome the guests. The contrast with the Beijing reception was stark and depressing. After lunch Ayub went to the Prime Minister's office for his first formal meeting with Kosygin and his Foreign Minister, Andrei Gromyko. Ayub knew that it was going to be a difficult meeting: the Russians were bound to bring up the question of the American military base in Pakistan to which he had no answer. Ayub started by recognizing the contribution that the Soviet Union was making towards the cause of world peace and then touched upon different conflict areas, in particular the growing differences between the United States and China. Turning to Indo-Pakistan relations he said that the growing convergence of US and Soviet policies in the region was aggravating Pakistan's strained relations with India.

Kosygin reacted to this at once. He told Ayub that there had been no convergence of Soviet and US interests in Asia: 'We entertain no interest in Asia which could coincide with the United States. They are pursuing a policy of enslaving the people of Asia. The present tensions between India and Pakistan and India and China are all the result of past imperialist domination and current capitalist designs.' The Soviet Union believed in resolving its disputes through peaceful means. Kosygin must have felt that he had spoken a little too sharply. He smiled and leaning forward said: 'I am not talking to you as one diplomat to another; I am talking to you very openly, frankly, and honestly.'

What had started as a meeting between strangers now turned into a frank exchange of views between two individuals who seemed to understand each other. Ayub told Kosygin about Pakistan's problems with India. 'The unhappy fact', Ayub said, 'is that India's relations with all its neighbours are strained and unhappy.' India was busy enlarging its armed forces and securing vast quantities of American arms on the pretext that China was about to attack India again. 'Does that make military sense?' asked Ayub. While millions of people were starving in India, a large proportion of Indian national resources was being consumed by military hardware. Ayub explained that for the last six years he had tried to establish normal, neighbourly relations, but every overture had been spurned by India.

> The Muslims of Kashmir, under Indian control, were no better than hostages. They had no rights, no freedom. Over half a million Muslims had been driven out of India because of the policies of the Indian government. India was able to do all this because it had the support of the Soviet Union and now military assistance from the United States.

Kashmir, Ayub said, was the one problem that was responsible for the current state of relations between India and Pakistan. 'We do look up to you to help resolve this problem. You occupy a special position and you will lose nothing by trying to resolve this problem.' Ayub went on to press Kosygin to reconsider his stand on Kashmir. 'You have been bailing India out with your veto in the Security Council. Once the armies of the two countries are disengaged, India could reduce her military budget by fifty per cent and that would be an act of friendship and mercy to the people of India.' Ayub put all this across in a mixture of high praise for the Soviet Union and a hard hitting, and what must have seemed to the Russians a highly partisan, critique of Indian policies.

Kosygin looked perplexed, his face a little drawn and his broad brow deeply knitted. Kashmir, he said, was a complicated matter that must be discussed but the cause did not lie in the quantity of arms acquired by India. The real causes of the present tension could only be identified and remedied by India and Pakistan. Unless these causes were eliminated the arms build up would continue. But, he insisted, the Soviet Union had not seen any signs of belligerence in India toward Pakistan. 'The Soviet Union,' and now Kosygin made his first attacking move, 'saw Pakistan acting as an instrument of American policies in the region.' He hastened to add that he was not saying this in a spirit of recrimination but the fact was that Pakistan was a member of two Western alliances—SEATO and CENTO—which were under US command. The U2 incident was an act of provocation and had caused mistrust between Pakistan and the Soviet Union. He repeated that the Soviet delivery of arms was not the cause of Indo-Pakistan tension: 'If we were to stop the supply of arms the United States would take our place and fan the conflict further.' Ayub asked: 'Then why not pool the efforts of Pakistan, India and the USSR to put out the flames of tension in Kashmir?' He conceded that the Soviet Union had a legitimate reason to complain about Pakistan's participation in Western alliances but pointed out that Pakistan had been forced to join these pacts when it found itself exposed to aggression from all sides. He assured Kosygin that there was no military life left in the pacts and Pakistan would never serve as an instrument of US policy in the region. He mentioned that the US government had tried very hard to persuade Pakistan to send some troops or even a medical team to Vietnam but Pakistan did not agree to do that. The U2 incident had come as a shock, as much to Pakistan as to the Soviet Union, but he admitted that Pakistan was at fault. 'If there is no life in the pacts why not bury them?' asked Kosygin. Ayub replied that Pakistan's membership of the pacts did not hurt the Soviet Union. 'Nor do they give us any pleasure,' rejoined Kosygin. Ayub assured Kosygin that he would never allow any American offensive weapons to be put at the Badaber communication base which had become an 'eyesore'.

Reverting to Kashmir, Ayub again urged Kosygin to reconsider the Soviet stand: 'I am not asking for a snap decision, all I ask for is reconsideration.' Kosygin put both his hands on the table and heaved a deep sigh. 'Well I can assure you that we will do nothing to fan this dispute. We shall do our level best to bring it to an end.' As Kosygin started folding his papers Ayub said: 'I wish we had met earlier.' Kosygin replied, 'We shall remedy that situation. Not the past, but the future.' Ayub invited Kosygin and Gromyko to visit Pakistan. Bhutto, speaking for the first time, said that Gromyko had been to the East and the West but never to Pakistan. Gromyko replied with a laugh: 'I always keep ahead of U2.'

Ayub came out of the meeting completely exhausted. It had been a gruelling encounter. Bhutto and Aziz Ahmad were full of admiration for Ayub and felt that he had analysed India-Pakistan relations with great courage and clarity even though parts of it were obviously unacceptable to the Soviet leaders.

A clay pigeon shoot

The next day, 5 April, Ayub along with his delegation was taken to a dacha on the bank of the Moscow River in a picturesque pine and birch forest. Everything was covered in snow. There was to be an interlude of clay pigeon shooting before the resumption of formal talks. Ayub, Bhutto and some others in the Pakistan delegation, who had devoted every weekend of their working life to pre-arranged official duck shoots, were very excited. They were confident that they would give the elderly Russians a lesson or two in shooting down mechanically released saucers. But it turned out to be a one-sided affair, with the Russians smashing every saucer that appeared on the horizon and the Pakistanis missing everything that came their way. The best scores were Gromyko nine out of ten and Ayub one out of ten. Bhutto and the rest of the Pakistani sharp-shooters each bagged a duck!

After this tournament, the two delegations went into the dacha, where the main hall had been converted into a conference room. Kosygin was joined by Brezhnev and Podgorny, the two other members of the triumvirate that ruled the Soviet Union at the time. It was obvious that the Soviet leaders, having evaluated the previous day's discussion, had come to the conclusion that the time had come for them to take up clear positions on some of the issues raised by Ayub. The fact that Ayub had indicated his willingness to reconsider Pakistan's membership of SEATO and CENTO, and more than hinted at the possibility of not renewing the lease of the US communications base in Pakistan, had clearly persuaded the Soviet leaders to review their own position on Kashmir. As soon as the participants were seated, Ayub started talking about the growth of nuclear weapons and how the world order had undergone a fundamental change as a result. He said that blocs and alliances were becoming obsolete because of the emergence of China as a major nuclear power. The confrontation between the United States and the USSR was becoming less direct and Europe was acquiring greater unity and strength. He thanked Kosygin for the frank statement of Soviet position on the previous day and said that he was particularly grateful that Kosygin had taken him into confidence. Nevertheless, there were one or two points that needed clarification. The first was the problem of excessive rearmament going on in India. As the Soviet Union agreed with Pakistan that there was no danger of China attacking India, there was no need for India to arm itself far beyond the level of its legitimate requirements. As India's next door neighbour, Pakistan was worried about India's expansionist policies. Ayub quoted influential Indian writers, particularly K.M. Panikkar, who were of the opinion that India must establish its control from the Oxus to Sinkiang, regardless of existing national boundaries. Ayub mentioned the message he had received from Islamabad about the bellicose statements that the governor of Rajasthan was making about the Rann of Kutch, where the Indians were trying to establish new posts beyond their area of control.

The Soviet Union may be right in its view that India had no immediate intention of invading Pakistan, but intentions could always change with the development of capability. The US government had entered into a bilateral military aid agreement with India and, as a result, they had lost their influence among India's neighbours.[2] Ayub warned that Soviet influence too, might suffer if India's neighbours felt they could not expect help from the Soviet Union in the event of Indian aggression. India's neighbours were being left with no choice but to turn to China for their security. To expect Pakistan to eradicate the causes of tensions in India-Pakistan relations amounted to asking it to surrender to India. Pakistan would never accept such a position: 'We are willing to live as honourable and reliable friends and neighbours, not as satellites. We will not take orders from anybody.' Ayub's exposition lasted well over thirty minutes. Kosygin, Brezhnev, and Podgorny listened with their faces drawn. Kosygin said that Kashmir was a problem that no one but India and Pakistan could solve. He repeated that arms were not the real cause but added that the Soviet Union was against the arming of any nation. If frontier conflicts and ideological tensions were removed, arms would create no problem. Kosygin said that the Soviet Union had come to realize that one had to learn to co-exist with different ideologies. No two ideologies could be more incompatible than communism and capitalism, but the Soviet Union had accepted the principle of co-existence in practice. He was not persuaded that India was committed to a policy of expansionism. He again questioned Ayub's statement that the interests of the Soviet Union had come to converge with those of the United States in the region: 'Such a thought must have been planted in your mind by someone who is our enemy.' Kosygin went on to recount how the Soviet Union had supplied arms to Vietnam and Indonesia to fight against the imperialists: 'We have never provided arms for wars between neighbouring states.'

Ayub could restrain himself no longer and leaned forward to ask: 'What imperialist power is India fighting against?' He hastened to add that he did not wish to contradict the Soviet Premier nor was he trying to score a point, but if the Soviet government wanted to help the people who were exposed to the threat of aggression and foreign domination then it should be helping Pakistan. The thought about the convergence of Soviet and American interests had not been put into his head by anybody. It was his own idea but he did not wish to press the point any further.

At that tense moment Brezhnev broke into the discussion and said in a rough voice with some impatience: 'It is a pity India is not here. She too has a long list of complaints and would have a great deal to say about Pakistan's behaviour.' He asserted that India was a neutral and non-aligned country and he did not believe that Indian policies could lead to war. Ayub was not impressed by this outburst. He retorted: 'India is more aligned than any other country. Only a blind person would call India non-aligned. She uses this as a pretext to mislead the world.' He went on to claim that India had sought the nuclear umbrella from the United States during its conflict with China: 'If this is non-alignment then it is a wonderful concept.' Kosygin changed the subject and said that it was possible that the Soviet Union did not fully understand the problem between India and Pakistan. But Pakistan could not justify US presence in its territory. Ayub let that pass and continued to insist that it was a mistake to regard India as non-aligned. If the Indian government genuinely believed in non-alignment it would have fulfilled its obligations in Kashmir. He repeated that there was no justification for the Soviet Union using its UN veto to support India. It was the Soviet veto that was giving India the opportunity to refuse to come to any settlement on Kashmir. Kosygin and Gromyko got into a huddle at this point and Kosygin said that the Soviet Union had not used its veto against the original Kashmir resolutions under which India was obliged to hold a free and fair plebiscite in the State. Bhutto intervened to explain that the Soviet Union had not vetoed the two original resolutions in August 1948 and January 1949, but the veto had been exercised on Kashmir resolutions in 1954 and 1962.

Brezhnev now took over. He was shuffling two pencils in his right hand, one blue and one red. He had dropped his earlier rough manner and was speaking softly, almost philosophically. 'The Kashmir problem,' he said, 'cannot be solved here and now.' He explained that the Soviet Union treated India as a non-aligned country because it was not a member of any bloc. Nor, he argued, had it been the first to wage war, and was in favour of general disarmament. He thought Ayub's appraisal was 'too rigid and tough'. He was impressed by Ayub's sincere and fervent desire to improve Pakistan's relations with the Soviet Union and assured him that 'the Soviet Union would reciprocate his desire all down the line'. He felt that good relations could develop despite Pakistan's membership of Western pacts. Ayub's statement that Pakistan would not allow its territory to be used for military bases or for the dissemination of nuclear weapons was particularly reassuring. If Pakistan would limit or end military co-operation within the blocs that would be a great contribution to the improvement of Pakistan-Soviet relations.

Ayub said that so far as the blocs were concerned they should be treated as obsolescent: 'These pacts are dead but we are not in a position to bury them.' Pakistan was no longer interested in the pacts: 'You can be assured of our bona fides and we would like to be assured of your bona fides, if I may put it very bluntly.' Ayub added that if the Soviet Union was really concerned about US bases in Pakistan, just as Pakistan was worried about the Soviet veto on Kashmir, 'the matter could be negotiated and the two sides could come to a reasonable arrangement.' Almost with a sigh of relief Brezhnev said: 'That already is a good step.' There was Ayub offering to swap the US bases in Pakistan for a Soviet promise not to use its veto on Kashmir.

The discussion then turned to specific areas of co-operation. Ayub thanked the Soviet Union for a loan of $30,000,000 and a credit of $11,000,000 for machinery. He expressed great satisfaction that mutual problems had been discussed with candour. Ayub said that he had come to Moscow before going to Washington because he was looking for Soviet friendship. He repeated the point that if only the Soviet Union would decline to use its veto in the Security Council on Kashmir the attitude of the Pakistani people would immediately change: 'We are not ungrateful people. Once you help us we will not forget it.' Brezhnev put his hand in his right pocket and pulled it out saying, 'See, I have kept nothing in my pocket. Everything here is above-board.' He said that the Soviet Union attached 'paramount importance' to Ayub's visit. There was no superficiality or demagoguery in the talks, which had proceeded on the right lines. The relations between the two countries could be improved, trade expanded, visits exchanged, and technical know-how provided by the Soviet Union. It was time to discuss specific details of co-operation. Again he said, 'Mr President you can look into my pocket, I have nothing but a comb.' And he proceeded to brandish a small brown comb. Ayub responded by showing him his pocket, saying that he too had nothing there: 'I wear my heart on my sleeve.' Brezhnev repeated that there were many ways to improve bilateral relations. In particular he mentioned the possibility of cultural exchanges. He concluded: 'I say all this because all my comrades uphold this policy. These are not mere words but the policy of the party. That is the best assurance I can give you.'

Kosygin said the two sides had achieved positive results in less than twenty-four hours and Brezhnev added: 'Because we are working without protocol, though not ignoring our Foreign Ministers.' It was already well past lunch time. Kosygin said: 'In one day we have achieved more than what others take years and, sometimes, fail to achieve.' He said the meeting would prove historic: 'A turning point which will lead to further exchanges of views and to big decisions in the interest of our two countries.' The trade treaty was ready, as was the credit agreement on oil prospecting. This was but a small portion of what could be achieved to strengthen mutual co-operation.

Back in Moscow, Ayub confided to the Information Secretary that he was expecting substantial Soviet military aid.[3] He seemed quite excited. Obviously both Brezhnev and Kosygin had given him some indication of this during lunch. Later that afternoon a cable was received from Islamabad saying that Indian forces had trespassed into the disputed territory of the Rann of Kutch and necessary defensive measures were being taken by the Pakistan Army. Ayub said to the Information Secretary, 'These fellows have started a war on their own.'

The next day, 6 April, Ayub had a meeting with the Acting Chairman, Anastas Mikoyan. After a brief exchange of courtesies, Mikoyan said that his first contact with Pakistan was when Bhutto came to see him.

He congratulated Ayub on selecting such a capable and vigorous person as his Foreign Minister: 'He is a very able man—very insistent on upholding his country's point of view.' He said the Soviet Union attached great importance to Ayub's visit: 'We are aware of your own great role and we recognize you as the architect of an active foreign policy. This is something which we value very highly.' Ayub replied, 'We intend pursuing that course.'

When Ayub returned to the Kremlin after his meeting with Mikoyan he received a signal that President Johnson had decided to 'reschedule' Ayub's visit to Washington because of the pressure of events! It was like a bombshell which shattered Ayub's whole game plan. He was looking forward to his visit to Washington where he thought he would be able to explain the rationale behind Pakistan's change of policy towards its socialist neighbours and allay American fears and misgivings. But the postponement of Ayub's visit to Washington had the unforeseen advantage of convincing the Soviet leaders of Ayub's sincerity of purpose. This became evident the next day when he went to Leningrad and received a colourful and enthusiastic welcome in complete contrast to the bleak reception accorded to him in Moscow on his arrival.

The Indian lobby in Moscow, too, became extremely active. The Soviet Ambassador in New Delhi, Benedictov, who was present in Moscow told Ayub's Information Secretary that it was of the utmost importance that nothing should be done to upset India. Moscow's commitment to New Delhi, he said, was firm and it would help the growth of Pakistan-Soviet relations if the Indians were kept in the picture. Benedictov was clearly feeling left out and seemed anxious that his views should be conveyed to Ayub. By now Ayub had developed warm personal relations with both Brezhnev and Kosygin and while the experts were discussing specific areas of co-operation the leaders were having separate meetings without the assistance of any of their ministers.

Ayub left for Tashkent on 9 April in an Ilyushin plane. It was a long flight. The delegation was put up at an austere rest house. Ayub had a long meeting with Madam Nasirednov, Chairman of the Uzbekistan Republic, a woman of great presence. She had a broad forehead and Mongol features and spoke in a very soft voice. She was accompanied by her Prime Minister Kurbanov. She explained that the Republic had been established in 1924 and had its own Constitution, and its own national anthem and flag. Before the October revolution the population of 10,000,000 was almost completely illiterate. The Republic had now achieved full literacy and was a truly multinational Republic in which people of one hundred nationalities lived as equal citizens.

Ayub thanked the Uzbek leaders for the welcome that the people of Tashkent had accorded him: 'For me it was an emotional event. Our history has been so closely inter-connected, our culture and our way of life so similar. It was unfortunate that

through the machinations of the British our two countries lost
contact with each other.' Bidding farewell to Ayub, Madam
Nasirednov said: 'We look forward to your return to Tashkent.
Our people would be so happy to see you again.' Little did she or
Ayub know at that time how soon he would be back in Tashkent
and in what circumstances.

NOTES

1. The author accompanied Ayub Khan on this visit and the quotations in this section are
   from his notes.
2. Ayub did not know that the aid agreement was, in fact, a formal military alliance
   between India and the US against China. It was this alliance which impelled the US
   to cut off military aid to Pakistan in 1965. *See* Appendix I.
3. Author's notes.

PART II

CHAPTER 8

Pakistan's Adventure in Kashmir

The gathering storm

On his return from Tashkent on 10 April 1965 Ayub went to the General Headquarters in Rawalpindi where a group of senior army officers briefed him on the situation in the Rann of Kutch on the border of Sindh. The brigadiers and colonels were all quite excited about the way the Indians had abandoned their positions and retreated in total disarray. Now was the opportunity for Pakistan to pursue the enemy deep into his territory. Senior officers repeatedly made the point that the Indians had come in great strength after making full preparations, but they took to their heels at first contact with the Pakistani forces lead by their intrepid commanders. Ayub must have felt that left to itself GHQ, supported by a hawkish Foreign Office, might unnecessarily enlarge the area of conflict. Already the situation was taking a menacing turn and official propaganda about the way the Indians were trounced in the Kutch was creating a jingoistic mood among the people. Ayub could rely on his Commander-in-Chief, General Muhammad Musa, to act with discretion, but there was always the possibility that the brigadiers around him might swing him to their more aggressive point of view. Ayub decided to take personal control of the operations. There was one last engagement between the two armies on 26 April 1965 which resulted in a further retreat of the Indian forces. There was great excitement in the country, and the military establishment was now in a state of euphoria. A few minor skirmishes were projected as a war in which the Indians were as thoroughly defeated as in their war against China in 1962.

It was this little skirmish in the Rann of Kutch which took Pakistan to war with India six months later.

The area called the Rann of Kutch is a deserted inland lake situated between the former province of Sindh in West Pakistan and the former princely State of Kutch. The area was incorporated in the Indian State of Gujarat after Partition. Pakistan claimed the northern 3,500 square miles along latitude 240 in the disputed area. The Indians claimed the whole 8,400 square mile area of the Rann. Since the border remained undemarcated, villagers from both sides used the grasslands called *bets* for grazing purposes. The Indian border forces drove the Pakistani villagers out of one of these *bets* in 1956 and impounded their cattle. Pakistan used its army to expel the Indians from the area. Thereafter the *status quo* remained undisturbed. In January 1965, the Indians started obstructing the movement of Pakistani border patrols south of Kanjarkot, a half-ruined fort lying in the wilderness. Despite Pakistan's protests, the Indians continued to obstruct the Pakistani patrols. Towards the end of March the Indians established new posts opposite the Pakistani posts and moved an infantry brigade into the area. Trenches were dug and on 27 March the Indian high command started a joint exercise code-named Arrow Head involving a brigade group, INS *Vikrant,* and several destroyers and frigates in the Gulf of Kutch. On 7 April, the Indian Home Minister announced in parliament that necessary measures would be taken to put an end to Pakistan's intrusions in the area. The next day Indian troops, entrenched in their newly occupied positions, opened fire to eliminate long-established Pakistani posts. An encounter took place on 10 April in which Pakistan's 51 Brigade was involved. The battle was not decisive but the Indians abandoned Sardar Post which was under attack. Pakistan decided to move the whole of 8 Division and plans were finalized on 17 April to launch a major attack in the area. The aim was to dominate the area, first denying the Indians the use of lateral tracks inside the disputed territory and then mounting an assault on two key enemy positions—Chhad Bet and Karim Shahi. The major offensive was entrusted to Brigadier Eftikhar Khan Janjua. The move began on 26 April. Two tanks of 24 Cavalry got bogged down and the squadron was left with eight tanks. Brigadier Eftikhar, who was riding in one of the tanks, decided to launch the attack without waiting for the infantry. The main encounter took place in Biar Bet, which was captured on 26 April. The Indians had crossed over the inlet from the sea, having constructed a causeway with empty 44-gallon drums, and Pakistan could block their only route of return by destroying the causeway. Ayub disallowed this action, and the commander was told to consolidate his position and not pursue the enemy any further.

When the Indian attack on Kanjarkot was reported on 11 April, the Foreign Office handed over a note to the Indian High Commissioner categorically rejecting the Indian charge of aggression and calling upon India to put an immediate and unconditional end to the fighting in the area. In a statement issued on 15 April Bhutto said: 'The Rann of Kutch situation is the latest example of Indian chauvinism' and warned India that if it persisted in the use of force, it alone would 'be responsible for the consequences which must follow'.[1] Bhutto was responding to the threat given by the Indian Prime Minister Shastri in the Lok Sabha that appropriate action would be taken against Pakistan 'when the time and circumstances are right.'[2]

There was great pressure on Shastri to take firm action against Pakistan. U.M. Trivedi, leader of the Jan Sangh group in the Lok Sabha, called on the government to send its forces 'right up to Lahore to bring Pakistan to its senses'. A socialist leader, Dr R.M. Lohia, declared that East Pakistan could be overrun by India in a matter of days. An independent member, P.V. Shastri, said that the proper course for India was to march on Karachi. After a long debate in the House on 28 April a motion was unanimously adopted affirming 'the firm resolve of the Indian people to drive out the aggressor from the sacred soil of India'.[3]

The dispute goes to arbitration

By now the British and the US governments were getting seriously concerned about the situation. Harold Wilson expressed Britain's readiness to help establish an early cease-fire. The British High Commissioner in Pakistan, Sir Morrice James, and the British High Commissioner in India, John Freeman, persuaded Shastri and Ayub to agree to a cease-fire and talks on restoring the *status quo ante,* as it existed on 1 January 1965, followed by negotiations on the border dispute. Both India and Pakistan rejected the proposal. Morrice James played an important role in persuading Ayub and Bhutto to agree to a cease-fire because he could see that the Indians were deeply upset over the setback they had received in the Rann and there was 'a very real risk that they would decide to retaliate elsewhere'.[4] He made more than one trip to New Delhi and finally told Ayub on 1 May that 'a solution could be reached without a war.'[5] As a result of these efforts a *de facto* cease-fire was established on 6 June.

Ayub and Shastri were both in London for the Commonwealth Prime Ministers Conference from 17-25 June. They had separate talks with Harold Wilson and the Commonwealth Relations Secretary, Arthur Bottomley. Following these discussions an agreement was signed by India and Pakistan on 29 June which provided for the establishment of cease-fire from 1 July, the withdrawal of all troops within seven days, the restoration of the *status quo* as of 1 January, ministerial discussions on the demarcation of the border, and if these were unsuccessful, the reference of the question to an impartial tribunal whose decision would be final. The Congress parliamentary party approved the agreement on 12 July, after Shastri had made it clear that the agreement would not create a precedent automatically applicable to other India-Pakistan disputes and that each dispute would be dealt with separately. The Lok Sabha approved the agreement on 18 August by 269 votes to twenty-eight, with twenty-three abstentions. On 29 July 1965, it was agreed that the Foreign Ministers of India and Pakistan should meet in New Delhi on 20 August to discuss the dispute and if they failed to reach an agreement, it should be referred to a tribunal by the end of October. On 18 August Shastri announced in the Lok Sabha that a message had been sent to Pakistan suggesting that in view of the deteriorating relations between the two countries there was little likelihood of reaching an agreement on the Rann of Kutch and that the question should be referred at once to a tribunal. Pakistan accepted the proposal.

Ayub was reasonably confident that the Rann of Kutch accord might serve as a model for the settlement of the Kashmir dispute. He, in fact, declared that 'in all cases where peaceful means of settling the Indo-Pakistan dispute prove unavailing, the sensible answer is to have recourse to independent arbitration.'[6] Ayub was probably encouraged in this belief by Harold Wilson with whom he discussed the possibility of resolving the Kashmir dispute through arbitration during his stay in London.

The feeling in army circles in Pakistan was summed up by Gul Hassan, then director of military operations:

> The setback in Kutch proved immeasurably disconcerting to the Indian Army. As a result the government of India was in a quandary. On the other hand ours was in a state of euphoria. The high command of our army was intoxicated by our showing and our morale could not possibly have been higher. We were ready for any task that may be assigned to us and without any question.[7]

In senior army circles and in the Foreign Office, Ayub Khan came under criticism for letting the Indians off the hook. There was great disappointment in GHQ that when the Indians were withdrawing, their retreat could have been easily cut off but unfortunately Ayub Khan did not allow it.

For all his realism and prudence, Ayub's judgement did get impaired by the Rann of Kutch in one respect: his old prejudice that 'the Hindu has no stomach for a fight' turned into belief, if not a military doctrine, which had the decisive effect on the course of events.

Operation Gibraltar gets under way

How did Ayub Khan blunder into war with India in 1965? A cautious man by temperament, Ayub never lost sight of the real issues even in a crisis, and could make a realistic assessment of

any situation and come to a rational judgement, however grave
and compelling the circumstances. As President his major concern
had been to normalize relations with India and to resolve the
Kashmir dispute through negotiations. After the Rann of Kutch he
kept impressing upon his ministers and generals that while Pakistan
should go on leaning against India, it must not do anything
provocative which might invite armed retaliation. Kashmir was
of vital importance but Pakistan could not put its own survival at
risk for the sake of Kashmir. As Supreme Commander of the
armed forces Ayub firmly believed that any armed engagement
between India and Pakistan would not remain limited to a particular
sector but would lead to a general war. After Nehru's death when
India faced a serious leadership crisis, Bhutto and Aziz Ahmed
both started trying hard to persuade Ayub to take advantage of
India's vulnerability, but he refused to deviate from the path of
negotiations. Indeed, even after the fighting had erupted in the
Rann of Kutch he affirmed his commitment to a peaceful resolution
of Pakistan's disputes with India during his talks with the Soviet
leaders in April 1965.

By April 1965 the agitation inside Kashmir following the
Hazratbal incident had quietened down and the wave of protests
that followed the arrest of Sheikh Abdullah in May, when he
returned from a tour abroad where he had a meeting with Zhou
Enlai, had been ruthlessly put down by the Indian security forces.
In these circumstances how was Ayub Khan persuaded to embark
on a perilous course which, in the event of even limited success,
could take Pakistan to the brink of war? The decision to send
'freedom fighters' (*mujahids* for Pakistan and armed infiltrators
for the Indians) across the cease-fire line to start a guerilla war in
the Indian-held part of Kashmir, where there was no evidence of
any popular stirring at the time, made no military sense. The
Foreign Office and the military intelligence agencies were churning
out reports of an insurrection in Kashmir but Ayub always treated
these reports with great scepticism. He used to complain that the
intelligence agencies were completely out of date: they were
addicted to the old methods of police investigation, and intelligence
was a field with which they were not familiar. Sheikh Abdullah

had warned him about the limited contacts of his intelligence services with the people of Kashmir during his visit to Pakistan in 1964.

The Pakistan Army had no experience of guerrilla warfare. Its first venture in this field in early 1964 had ended in a fiasco when it trained and despatched its first group of *mujahids* to carry out sabotage activities across the cease-fire line following the Hazratbal incident. They were all netted by the Indian security guards within a few days. How could Ayub authorize a major military operation based on the same flawed pattern? He must have known that the adventure would plunge Pakistan into a crisis and destroy all his work and career. Was it Ayub's own decision or did he become, despite being in full command, an unwitting victim of some conspiracy hatched by his Foreign Office and GHQ? A brief account of the events as they unfolded should help answer this question.

A *de facto* cease-fire was established in the Rann of Kutch on 6 June 1965, though it formally came into effect on 1 July, and the dispute was referred to the International Court of Justice at the Hague. Pakistan's relations with India now reverted to their normal level of quiet antagonism. Pakistan's forces along the borders were occupying defensive positions and were under no pressure. Some of the Pakistani generals, who owned large tracts of land along the international boundary in Punjab, started complaining that the mines laid on their fields had become a nuisance and a hinderance to the harvesting of their crops. The mines had been laid all along the Punjab border to forestall any possible advance by Indian troops. On the intervention of the Defence Secretary, Nazir Ahmed, GHQ agreed to the removal of the mines from the border areas on the pretext that the mines were getting damaged by heavy rains though, according to the metrological record, the rainfall in the months of June and July 1965 was negligible. The real purpose was to save the generals from any loss of tax-free agricultural income. That the Indians might launch an attack across the international border in pursuance of Prime Minister Shastri's threat that India would fight Pakistan at a time and place of its own choosing was obviously being treated as no more than a bluff by those in charge of military operations and intelligence in GHQ.

The first indication that some movement across the cease-fire line in Kashmir was in progress was given by Ayub at a Cabinet-Committee meeting on 24 July. It was a humid summer afternoon and the Military Secretary's room, where the Information Secretary was waiting to see Ayub, was buzzing with telephone calls as messengers walked in and out with files and documents, making the air-conditioning an unnecessary pretence. After a long wait he was ushered into the Cabinet room. The meeting appeared to have concluded its business and Ayub was standing with a big folder under his arm. Ayub said to the Information Secretary, 'A great deal will depend on how we handle the propaganda front.' The significance of the remark was not immediately grasped by the propaganda chief. Ayub left after asking Bhutto to take the chair and the meeting restarted. Bhutto, looking unusually stern, gave a brief account of what he called 'a popular revolt' that was sweeping the whole of Indian-held Kashmir. The people of the Valley, he said, were locked in a life-and-death struggle. Large bands of volunteers were crossing the cease-fire line to join their Kashmiri brethren in a war of liberation against the Indian warlords. History would never forgive Pakistan if it remained an idle spectator. The government had decided to extend all reasonable moral and material support to the 'freedom fighters'. Bhutto said he would not allow any questions to be asked in the interest of secrecy. 'The Information Ministry,' he said, 'will have an important role to play, and a close liaison must be maintained between Information and Military Intelligence. That would be all, gentlemen.'[8] With that he got up and left the room and the meeting came to an abrupt end. Bhutto obviously wanted everyone to know that he was in command. General Musa and his top advisers sat throughout in reverential silence. Outside the meeting Brigadier Irshad, Director of Military Intelligence, asked for two Kashmiri-speaking broadcasters to be assigned to his network to maintain communications with the freedom fighters. The Information Secretary asked where they would be stationed. Irshad laughed, 'Allah Jané' [God knows]. But he promised that he would alert the Information Ministry at least twenty-four hours before 'the curtain goes up'.

On the morning of 8 August 1965 a distraught Brigadier Irshad conveyed to the Information Secretary that the 'operation' had begun and that he was sorry for not giving him the promised twenty-four-hour notice. But now he was in dire need of the Ministry's assistance to get over an unforeseen hurdle: the mobile transmitter which the army had specially acquired to broadcast the Voice of Kashmir had conked out! Could the Ministry make some alternative arrangement and take over the responsibility of propagating the cause of freedom fighters. Brigadier Irshad had a genius for simplifying disaster. How could the Ministry of Information assume the responsibility of running the Voice of Kashmir without knowing anything about the nature and purpose of the operation? 'That is the beauty of it. Even I know very little about the operation,' was the Brigadier's hearty response. He proceeded to confide that each of the persons involved in the play knew only the part assigned to him. That was meant to ensure that the enemy should never be able to discover the whole plan. And with a sudden burst of rustic confidence the Brigadier promised, 'In less than twenty-four hours some important targets will be captured by the freedom fighters and I will give you all the news you want to keep the world humming.' The search for a spare transmitter proved futile. The Information Ministry had no other option but to put the Voice of Kashmir on the same frequency on which the government-controlled Azad Kashmir Radio had been broadcasting for many years. The Indians must have discovered the hoax within a few hours. The Ministry was then put in touch with Brigadier Riaz Husain, head of the Inter-Services Intelligence Directorate (ISI). Brigadier Riaz was even more upbeat than Irshad. He had a whole range of equipment which, he claimed, would keep him in touch with every development inside Jammu and Kashmir: 'I shall flood you with information. We have our contacts.' The next day a crestfallen Riaz Husain would tell the Information Secretary that he had lost all his contacts: 'They have all gone underground.' The army transmitter was down, the ISI out, but the operation was on.

The only source which the Ministry of Information could now rely upon was the monitoring unit in Radio Pakistan. The unit was put on the alert. The first report came at 10 o'clock at night on 8 August, the day the operation commenced according to Brigadier Irshad. In its nine o'clock news, All India Radio claimed that four Pakistani soldiers had been captured by Indian troops in Kashmir and their interviews would be broadcast after the news bulletin. Half an hour later the captives gave an account of what they called Operation Gibraltar, in which they were engaged, and provided details of their assignments. The Information Secretary immediately drove up to Muzaffarabad, the capital of Azad Kashmir, to ask Brigadier Irshad whether he had heard the interviews of the captured soldiers. He had not. When he was given a summary of what the soldiers had told their interviewer, Irshad slumped into his chair: 'Oh my God, the bastards have spilled the beans.' In less than twenty-four hours the details of Operation Gibraltar, which had been kept secret even from those officials in Pakistan who were to be directly involved in its execution, were in the possession of the enemy while the people of Pakistan were still in the dark. Those who heard the news bulletin and the interviews on All India Radio dismissed it as enemy propaganda.

Operation Gibraltar: its genesis and execution

Some time after Sheikh Abdullah's visit to Pakistan in 1964 Ayub authorized the Foreign Office to prepare a plan in consultation with GHQ to 'defreeze' the Kashmir issue. A secret Kashmir cell (called the Kashmir Publicity Committee) consisting of the Secretaries of Foreign Affairs and Defence, Director Intelligence Bureau, Chief of General Staff and the Director of Military Operations, was set up to keep the Kashmir situation under constant review.[9] The Foreign Secretary, Aziz Ahmed, was the Chairman of the Committee. The meetings of the cell used to be held at the house of the Education Secretary in Satellite Town, Rawalpindi, to protect the proceedings from bureaucratic curiosity. Dogmatic, highly secretive and assertive, Aziz Ahmed would never allow the members of the cell to know whether the ideas he was floating from time to time were his own or were directives from the President. Nor would the President know whether the proposals coming from Aziz Ahmed represented the recommendations of the cell or were just his own ideas. According to Gul Hassan the cell was informed by Aziz Ahmed sometime in 1964 that the 'President had ordered GHQ' to prepare two plans, one to encourage sabotage activities across the cease-fire line and the other to provide 'all-out support for guerrillas to be inducted into Kashmir'. The responsibility for preparing the two plans and for training the personnel was assigned by GHQ to 12 Division which had its headquarters in Murree.[10]

Aziz Ahmed had convinced himself that Pakistan was in a position to dislodge the Indians from Kashmir. Once trained Pakistani soldiers went into Kashmir, the people of the Valley would spontaneously rise in revolt. The fear of China would prevent the Indians from provoking an all-out war and that would give the Pakistan Army the opportunity to drive the Indian forces out of Kashmir just as it had done in the Rann of Kutch. It was on these wishful assumptions that a plan of action was drawn up by the Foreign Office and the ISI directorate, supposedly on the recommendation of the Kashmir Cell, and submitted to Ayub Khan toward the end of December 1964 in Dhaka, when he was immersed in his election campaign. The plan sought his approval for inducting groups of armed men, disguised as freedom fighters, into Kashmir to carry out a sustained campaign of sabotage in the territories under Indian occupation. Ayub asked his Principal Secretary and the Information Secretary, who were accompanying him on that tour, to examine the plan. Both found the plan odd in its timing and adventurous in its intent. 'Quixotic' was how the Information Secretary described it as he reminded Ayub that the plan did not differ very much from the one which, as Commander-in-Chief, he had dismissed as 'amateurish'. After Ayub's re-election as President, the plan was placed before the intelligence committee of the Cabinet sometime in the second week of February 1965. General Musa and his senior aides were all there as were Bhutto and Aziz Ahmed. The Commanders-in-Chief of the Air

Force and the Navy were not invited. A large blackboard was set up in the Cabinet room and T.S. Jan, Deputy Director of ISI, an eloquent officer, explained the details of the plan on a map. When he had finished, Ayub asked the participants for their views. It was now Aziz Ahmed's turn to dilate upon the international implications of the plan. India, he said, was in a highly vulnerable situation, as it suffered from lack of leadership, and its position in Kashmir had become indefensible: a popular revolt was sweeping the Valley, and if Indian forces were diverted by sabotage, and subjected to a campaign of armed harassment by trained soldiers, Kashmir could soon be liberated. The most powerful factor in Pakistan's favour was its growing friendship with China which would stop India from invading Pakistan, even if it was driven out of Kashmir. All the time that Aziz Ahmed was speaking, Ayub kept writing on a notebook before him. After he had finished Ayub looked up and asked if anybody else had any comments to offer. The Commander-in-Chief and other senior army officers did not utter a word. Ayub said, 'If there are no more comments, let me ask: Who authorized the Foreign Office and the ISI to draw up such a plan? It is not their job. All I asked them was to keep the situation in Kashmir under review. They can't force a campaign of military action on the Government.' Ayub spoke quite sternly and everybody looked a little embarrassed. Bhutto was in a vulnerable position at that time because he did not know whether Ayub would include him in his new Cabinet. He kept quiet to suggest that he had no hand in whatever his Foreign Secretary had been designing for the liberation of Kashmir. That was the end of the plan or so one thought.

Following this meeting, Ayub went to China where no mention of the plan was made to any of the Chinese leaders. Had it been his intention to start some kind of guerrilla warfare in Kashmir, which relied on Chinese support for its success, Ayub would have certainly taken the Chinese leaders into confidence. He knew more than anyone else in his government that the Chinese expected their friends to be straightforward in their dealings.[11]

It is now possible to reconstruct the events between the rejection of the plan at the Intelligence Committee meeting in February

1965, its subsequent adoption in complete secrecy, and its commencement on 24 July 1965. Ayub went to Murree on 13 May 1965, six weeks before the cease-fire in the Rann of Kutch became effective, to examine the plan that had been prepared by General Akhtar Malik, General Officer Commanding 12 Division, to launch guerrilla operations in Kashmir. General Malik, a tall handsome officer, highly respected by his colleagues and popular among his men, explained the details of Operation Gibraltar on a sand-table. Bhutto, General Musa and some other senior army officers were present at the briefing which went on for over an hour. Towards the end Ayub put his finger on Akhnur, an important town of great strategic value, and asked, 'But why don't you go for the jugular?' 'That would require a lot more men and money,' replied General Malik. After some discussion Ayub sanctioned additional funds and told the Commander-in-Chief to provide the necessary manpower. Thus was Akhnur introduced into the operation which was shown as a red flag in General Malik's plan. The assault on Akhnur was later given the code-name Grand Slam. The timing of Grand Slam was not discussed but everyone admired Ayub for giving the operation a real edge and a new dimension. Operation Gibraltar, it was understood, would remain a secret and even the Corps Commanders would not be told about it at that stage. No civil official except the Foreign Secretary and the Defence Secretary were taken into confidence nor was the air force brought into joint planning as they were not considered sufficiently security-minded.[12]

A day before Operation Gibraltar was approved, Bhutto who had been re-appointed as Foreign Minister, wrote a letter to Ayub in which he advised him that India was '...at present in no position to risk a general war of unlimited duration for the annihilation of Pakistan'. According to him Pakistan 'enjoyed relative superiority...in terms of quality and equipment'. For Pakistan there were two alternatives: (1) 'to react now boldly and courageously in self-defence or (2) allow the initiative to move irrevocably to India, who would then proceed to launch her final attack for the liquidation of Pakistan subsequently at a place and time of her own choosing'. Bhutto strongly urged Ayub to opt for the first alternative: 'This is our hour of decision and may God guide us on the right path.'[13] Bhutto obviously wrote the letter to swing Ayub in favour of the plan which was to be shown to him the next day. Bhutto used to meet General Akhtar Malik and some other army officers at his house quite regularly to impress upon them 'the indispensability of launching raids [in Kashmir] as soon as possible'.[14] These meetings were a relaxed affair where army officers would pour out their hearts in response to Bhutto's eloquence and passion. Musa would later complain to Ayub that Bhutto used these meetings to 'brainwash' his officers. The job that Aziz Ahmed used to perform as Chairman of the Kashmir Cell was now taken over by Bhutto, but by now senior army officers, under the Rann of Kutch euphoria, were rearing to go and found a wonderful ally in the Foreign Minister. Bhutto's major concern was to assure Ayub that the risk of India unleashing a war on Pakistan, in retaliation of Pakistani raids in Kashmir, was negligible and could certainly be contained by Pakistan's diplomatic skill and military superiority. Musa found himself surrounded by Bhutto converts in GHQ and they all urged him to bite the bullet. It was under these conditions of strict secrecy and a state of tension between the Commander-in-Chief and some of his senior aides that plans for the launching of the operation in Kashmir were given their final shape.

Operation Gibraltar was entrusted to five forces, Tariq, Qasim, Khalid, Salahuddin and Ghaznavi, all named after legendary Muslim conquerors, supported by a subsidiary operation called Nusrat (the name happily coinciding with that of Bhutto's wife). All the forces started moving to the forward concentration areas on 24 July and reached their destination by 28 July. From there they infiltrated across the cease-fire line and made their way to other operational positions inside Kashmir territory under Indian control.

Tariq moved over the Himalayan Range at heights reaching 17,000 ft. The force commander and twenty-one men died due to lack of acclimatization. The force was then withdrawn. Qasim established its base north of Bandipura and demolished several bridges. But by the third week of August the force found it impossible to live off the land. As the Indians started tightening their noose, the force, caught between the necessity of survival and enemy attacks, decided to withdraw on 4 September.

Khalid launched a raid on an enemy battalion at Trahagan but the commander lost control of the companies and the force made its way back in small groups.

Salahuddin commanded by Major Mansha Khan, who was reputed to have a great deal of experience and knowledge of the Srinagar Valley, moved over the snow-covered Pir Punjal Range and reached Tosha Maidan, which was to be its base camp, only to discover an Indian battalion engaged in a field firing exercise. Mansha Khan decided to descend from the Punjal heights and found himself in the thick of meadows (margs) on the western slopes of the range, which were swarming with shepherds. Mansha's plan was to infiltrate into Srinagar by mixing with the local population, who would be celebrating the anniversary of a Saint (Pir Dastagir) on 8 August. But on 5 August, a shepherd boy, Muhammad Din, reported to the police in Tanmarg the presence of 'strangers' who had tried to bribe him to get information. The Indians reacted immediately. Guided by the shepherds they attacked Mansha Khan's base camp. By 18 August, Major Mansha Khan had lost control over his force, which withdrew from the area in disorder. The force met with no significant success as the Srinagar Air Force base was well-guarded, the Banihal Pass well-defended, and the ammunition dumps fully secured.

Ghaznavi established its base camp in Budhil area by 6 August. The Indians attacked this force but it stood its ground, inflicting heavy casualties on the enemy. By 18 August, Ghaznavi was in virtual control of Budhil and a large number of local inhabitants volunteered to join it. Ghaznavi continued to dominate the wide region in western and south-western Jammu throughout the war and was not withdrawn until after the cease-fire.

Nusrat groups were to operate in the immediate rear of enemy positions along the cease-fire line and attack enemy communication centres, gun positions, and supply dumps. The operation was to last for about fifteen days and, depending on its outcome, the force was to merge with Gibraltar. None of the Nusrat groups succeeded in making any impact on enemy positions. By the third week of August, both Gibraltar and Nusrat were spent forces. Operation Gibraltar had ended in complete disarray by the third week of August, leaving Ghaznavi as the only force which succeeded in maintaining its hold on Budhil and certain adjoining areas and managing to get the support of the local people.

Contrary to the information of the Pakistan Foreign Office and the intelligence services, the Indians had been taking effective and ruthless measures to control the unrest in the occupied territory. Shortly before Gibraltar was launched the Indians had taken into custody all political activists. When Gibraltar forces descended on the Valley they were met by a frightened, hostile population which knew nothing about Gibraltar or its purpose. The local people were scared of making any contact with the forces for fear of Indian reprisals. By 16 August the Indians had neutralized the infiltrators and started retaliatory operations by occupying two important posts in Uri Sector.

On the night of 24-25 August an Indian battalion, guided by a local villager, followed a track that brought it opposite Pakistan's 16 AK Battalion at Danna. Preceded by an hour-long artillery operation, the Indians captured Danna before daybreak and then without losing time pushed on to capture Pir Sahaba on 25 August. Nothing now stood between them and Muzaffarabad other than the Battalion Headquarters of 16 AK.

The Indians now launched their biggest operation against Bedori Bulge, which separated Uri from Poonchh. On 28 August the Indians occupied Haji Pir Pass which left Gibraltar forces in a critical situation. General Musa rushed to Bhutto's house, along with one of his aides, and putting a map on the table, started explaining how the loss of Haji Pir Pass had left the Pakistani forces at the mercy of the Indians. He shouted in considerable distress: 'My boys have nothing but stones to fight with.' He had been to Murree to discuss the situation with General Malik, who was in dire straits and was desperately insisting that Grand Slam must be launched immediately otherwise everything would be lost. The problem was that Grand Slam would require the Pakistani forces to move across a small section of the international frontier between Sialkot and Jammu. The Information Secretary was present at this meeting when General Musa was urging Bhutto to obtain Ayub's approval to launch Grand Slam. It was obvious that Bhutto and Aziz Ahmad were now in a hopeless situation; they knew that Gibraltar had collapsed and their whole plan had come apart. Akhnur looked like the proverbial last throw of a gambler but there was no other way to retrieve the situation. Perhaps the Indians would not notice the minor transgression of the international boundary. Bhutto decided that it was a gamble worth taking.

Just after Musa left, the Chinese Ambassador came in and Bhutto explained the situation to him. The Ambassador talked at some length about the Chinese experience of guerrilla warfare. He explained how highly trained volunteers were inducted into different villages where they lived as cultivators and craftsmen, merging with the community. The population of the village would be put through an intensive course of training before any guerrilla operation was undertaken. The village served as the base and no guerrilla fighter remained away from the base for more than twenty-four hours. Bhutto listened to all this knowing that Gibraltar forces had been trained in less than six weeks, and had no contact with the people of the villages where they would turn up disguised as 'freedom fighters'. Bhutto asked the Ambassador whether retaliation against Indian attacks should remain within Kashmir or go beyond the international boundary, if necessary. The Ambassador gave no reply but he must have understood the import of the question.

Operation Grand Slam

The purpose of Grand Slam was never clearly defined. If the objective was the capture of Akhnur to cut off the only rail link between India and Kashmir, to isolate the five Indian divisions stationed in Kashmir from their logistic and supply links in India, the logical thing would have been to launch Grand Slam in the very first phase of Gibraltar to surprise and overwhelm the enemy. Ayub's remark, 'Why don't you go for the jugular' clearly meant that Akhnur represented the most potent threat to the Indians in Kashmir. If Grand Slam was to be kept on hold, the only rational explanation could be that the threat to Akhnur was meant to keep the enemy under pressure while Gibraltar forces would enlarge their area of occupation and consolidate their influence in Kashmir, without letting the operation escalate into a general war. Grand Slam was never visualized as a desperate salvage operation after the collapse of Gibraltar. To go for the enemy's jugular when one's knees were wilting, made no military sense.

For some inexplicable reason Ayub left for Swat immediately after Gibraltar was launched. Bhutto flew to Swat and returned with a directive signed by Ayub on 29 August 1965. The directive was addressed to the Foreign Minister and the Commander-in-Chief and bore the title: 'Political Aim for Struggle in Kashmir.' The aim was

> ...to take such action that will defreeze the Kashmir problem, weaken Indian resolve, and bring her to the conference table *without* provoking a general war [emphasis added]. However the element of escalation is always present in such struggles. So whilst confining our action to the Kashmir area we must not be unmindful that India may in desperation involve us in a general war or violate Pakistani territory where we are weak. We must, therefore, be prepared for such a contingency. To expect quick results in this struggle, when India has much larger forces than us, would be unrealistic. Therefore, our action should be such that can be sustained over a long period. As a general rule Hindu morale would not stand more than a couple of hard blows at the right time and place. Such opportunities should, therefore, be sought and exploited.

This directive is the most revealing document of the war. It shows conclusively that Ayub did not know, even on 29 August, nine days before the war started, that Gibraltar had failed, that not one of its major objectives had been achieved, and that enemy forces were in a commanding position with Muzaffarabad, the capital of Azad Kashmir, within their reach. Ayub had gone to the hills on two earlier occasions to camouflage his real intent; once when Iskander Mirza was about to abrogate the Constitution, and again when the border war between India and China started in

1962. On both occasions he had put certain plans into action and returned to Rawalpindi to take advantage of the denouement. Having given the go-ahead to Gibraltar he removed himself to Swat hoping to keep the Indians in ignorance of the scope and purpose of the operation. He did not realize that this time he would become the victim of his own stratagem. His absence from the capital gave Bhutto and Aziz Ahmed the freedom to take control of Gibraltar, not only in the context of Foreign Affairs, but also in the field of military planning and manœuvers. They could, and did pretend whenever necessary, to be acting under the instructions of the President. How else can one explain the Commander-in-Chief asking Bhutto to get him the permission of the President to launch Grand Slam? Perhaps Ayub was not the only one who didn't know the exact fate of Gibraltar. GHQ itself had a highly coloured picture of events on the ground. According to Gul Hassan some of the formations were sending highly dubious and exaggerated reports: 'Self-delusion had become a code with us replacing conscience.'[15] The colonels would put an optimistic glow on the reports sent to them by their field officers and the brigadiers would remove any hint of failure and by the time the reports reached GHQ they read like an account of a triumphal procession. But the Commander-in-Chief knew; he was constantly visiting the forward areas and it was his responsibility to keep his Supreme Commander informed of the true state of affairs.

The directive also shows that Ayub's mind was still tuned to some pre-Gilbraltar number. After having fired all his shots he was still living in a make-believe world dreaming about taking 'such action that will defreeze the Kashmir problem, weaken Indian resolve and bring her to the conference table without provoking a general war'. He did not 'expect quick results' and was thinking in terms of action 'that can be sustained over a long period' not knowing that his Foreign Office and GHQ had already taken all the action behind his back. He was still fantasizing about the general rule that 'Hindu morale would not stand more than a couple of hard blows at the right time and place'. That was why he did not give a clear directive to his forces to launch an offensive on Akhnur and left it to his Foreign Minister and his Commander-in-Chief to choose the right time and place to deliver 'a couple of hard blows' to the Hindu. Ayub Khan, the decision-maker, was acting like an adviser, whose responsibility did not go beyond suggesting the guidelines for action.

Bhutto could not have asked for a more helpful directive which put him in a pre-eminent position: no other minister could challenge his authority and the Commander-in-Chief had to rely on him to interpret the terms of the directive. Bhutto must have assured General Musa that Ayub had authorized the launching of Grand Slam in the full knowledge that the operation would involve the transgression of the international boundary.

The preparations for Grand Slam were all completed by 30 August and the operation itself was launched on 31 August. It met with unexpectedly fierce resistance and ground to a halt in one sector, and in another sector its advance was inexplicably delayed. By the morning of 2 September the operation was in shambles and later that afternoon General Akhtar Malik was ordered to hand over command of the operation to General Yahya Khan. It is not easy to reconstruct the story of the failure of Grand Slam because the details are still shrouded in a haze of confusion, indecision, and loss of communications. According to a study carried out by the Staff College, Quetta, based on war diaries and operational records, there was a breakdown of communications between General Malik and his commanders in the early hours of 2 September. General Malik's staff officer, Brigadier Iqbal Ahmed Shamim, recorded in his diary, 'Headquarters and the commander of 10 Brigade both went off the air' just when the Brigade was supposed to go into action in a vital area. Headquarters 10 Brigade had been split into two and its operational part was being shifted from one place to another aggravating the operational problems. According to General Musa, 'There was no proper articulation of command and grouping of forces.'[16]

Grand Slam was based on the assumption that the Indians were in a highly exposed position in Akhnur and had insufficient forces. But the Indians had been building up their strength for the defence of Munawwar Gap through which Pakistan could attack Akhnur. They had also moved headquarters 10 Infantry Division from Bangalore to take charge of the Akhnur sector. While the Indians had been re-grouping, the General Headquarters in Pakistan had been doing the reverse. 7 Division commanded by General Agha Muhammad Yahya Khan had been stripped of all its brigades: its armoured regiments and reconnaissance and support battalions, 10 and 25 Brigades were transferred to 12 Division while 14 Para Brigade was sent to 15 Division. 7 Division itself was assigned the task of protecting the line of communication of 12 Division from Gujrat to Akhnur.

The news of the change of command spread like wildfire throughout Pakistan. The people had been swallowing stories of the triumphal progress of the 'freedom fighters', purveyed out to them by a euphoric Press. Independent newspapers were vying with the official media in projecting the exploits of their heroes in Kashmir. Radio Pakistan, which normally inspired only boredom and scepticism, became compulsive listening. General Malik, following in the footsteps of the great Muslim hero, Tariq, who burnt his boats before he conquered Spain, was seen poised to inflict a crushing defeat on the enemy. Why had he been relieved of command at such a crucial moment? Few people knew that GHQ had been feeding the Press with highly exaggerated stories of imaginary victories against fictitious foes. Within the government there was no arrangement to check or verify these stories. Whether it was an advanced form of camouflage, self-delusion, or prevarication by common consent to boost one another's morale and prospects, conscience had certainly yielded place to wilful fabrication.

Ayub Khan must have developed some misgivings about the operation because he was no longer getting the kind of euphoric messages with which GHQ flooded the President's House during the Rann of Kutch. He returned to Rawalpindi on 30 August, the day after he signed the fateful directive. He wanted to go to the forward areas but was advised against it. It would unnecessarily alarm the Indians and might provoke retaliation, advised Bhutto. General Musa had still not briefed his Supreme Commander about the real situation on the ground. He had told Ayub that though Gibraltar had suffered a few reverses the operation was still on course. When the spectacular breakthrough expected from Grand Slam did not materialize the picture looked hopeless, despite the capture of one or two important enemy posts. Ayub summoned Bhutto and Musa and demanded the truth. Musa admitted, at last, that Gibraltar had been a complete failure and Grand Slam was frozen in its tracks. After some discussion it was decided that the time had come to cut the losses and wind up the operation. Hopefully, the Indians would get the message and avoid any further escalation. General Malik, had by now lost all credibility with the high command. His enthusiasm had got the better of his judgement and he had launched Gibraltar, a guerrilla operation, for which he had neither the right type of manpower nor any support among the villagers in Kashmir. The task of winding up the operation was entrusted to General Yahya Khan, who was hitting the bottle because he had been given a marginal role in Gibraltar.

The change of command

General Musa went to the Headquarters of 7 Division which was under General Yahya's command. General Malik was also summoned there. After reviewing the situation General Musa asked Yahya Khan to assume control of operation Grand Slam with immediate effect (1300 hours, 2 September). The decision was confirmed by a flash message from GHQ which said: '7 Division assume control of operation Grand Slam with immediate effect.... Further orders to be issued by 7 Division in accordance [with] plans discussed by Commander-in-Chief with commander 7 Division.' The operational records of General Yahya's headquarters provide no clue to these plans. The war diary of GHQ 10 Brigade records:

GOC 7 Division [General Yahya] explained that there was a shift in plans from offensive to defensive. He ordered that on 2 September we [10 Brigade] would only establish a bridge-head across Tawi and at the same time organize a defensive position on Tawi with 102 Brigade in the north and 10 Brigade in the south.... When asked by commander 10 Brigade whether he could advance at first light on 3 September [from the bridge-head], GOC 7 Division said that he would issue orders for the next day at our Headquarters on the morning of 3 September. GOC also mentioned that H hour at 0400 hours [to cross Tawi] had been postponed because the Commander-in-Chief feared that our armour and other echelons may get caught by enemy air while crossing the obstacle [Tawi].

Before Yahya Khan could give Gibraltar and Grand Slam a decent burial, the Indians launched an attack on Lahore, the heart of Pakistan, in the early hours of 6 September 1965. Ayub woke up to find himself at war with India.

Much would be made of the decision to relieve General Akhtar Malik of the command of Grand Slam. The prevailing view in GHQ was that Ayub had lost his nerve. Just when the Pakistani forces were poised to capture Akhnur and inflict a crushing defeat on India, Ayub decided to call off the operation because he did not want to provoke a general war with India. Later, Bhutto would contribute to this belief to malign Ayub. The truth is that General Malik was a broken man because he knew better than anyone else that his mission had failed. He met the Information Secretary in Rawalpindi on 4 September and burst into tears. 'I don't know what to say to my children,' was all he could manage to mumble. He did not say a word against anyone. The change of command was used by GHQ and the Foreign Office as a cover to hide their own incompetence and indiscretions. Both Bhutto and Musa had been guilty of grave errors of judgement, which they tried to conceal in a culpable and deceitful manner, and they relied on the Grand Slam myth to exonerate themselves from blame.

NOTES

1. *Dawn,* 16 April 1965.
2. Ibid.
3. Ibid., 29 April, 1965.
4. *See* Morrice James, op. cit.
5. Ibid.
6. *Dawn,* 20 August 1965.

7. Gul Hassan; *Memoirs*. Oxford University Press, Karachi, 1993.
8. From the author's notes of the meeting. Few persons knew that A.B. Awan, who was Director Intelligence Bureau at the time, had met Sheikh Abdullah in Saudi Arabia in March 1965. During this meeting Sheikh Abdullah suggested that if Pakistan was planning some guerrilla action in Kashmir, arrangements should be made for him to stay either in the northern areas in Pakistan, or somewhere in Europe from where he could support and encourage the liberation movement in occupied Kashmir. The proposal was, unfortunately, not taken up by the Foreign Office.
9. Gul Hassan, op. cit.
10. Ibid.
11. Author's notes.
12. Gul Hassan, op. cit.
13. White Paper, Ministry of Foreign Affairs, Government of Pakistan, January 1977.
14. General Muhammad Musa, *My Version,* Wajidalis, Lahore 1983, p. 24.
15. Gul Hassan, op. cit.
16. General M. Musa, op. cit. p. 25.

CHAPTER 9

The War

When India attacked Pakistan the most surprised person was Ayub Khan. His surprise was shared by the Commander-in-Chief of the Pakistan Army. Both of them had assumed that with the winding down of Grand Slam the Indians would relax, but they did not realize that the Indian military intelligence agencies were perhaps as tardy as their Pakistani counterparts. Bhutto and Aziz Ahmed were temporarily halted in their tracks. All their forecasts and assurances about the Indian military intentions, based as they claimed at the time, on unimpeachable sources, had proved utterly fallacious. They could not even claim that they had not received any warning of the coming Indian attack.

On the evening of 3 September, the Indian Prime Minister, Lal Bahadur Shastri, in a speech on All India Radio, had called upon his people to do their duty in 'this hour of serious crisis', and warned them of the 'hard days ahead' during which they may have to 'suffer damage from air raids'.[1] After listening to that speech nobody should have been left in any doubt that India had decided to launch an attack on Pakistan territory, except the General Headquarters and the Foreign Office in Pakistan, where no one seemed to have taken much notice of Shastri's bluster.

The Pakistan High Commissioner in New Delhi, Mian Arshad Hussain, had sent a cypher message through the Turkish embassy to the Foreign Office in Islamabad that India was planning to launch an attack on Pakistan territory on 6 September. The message was duly received on the evening of 4 September and this was communicated by the Turkish Ambassador to Mian Arshad Hussain. As a rule, copies of all cypher messages from envoys abroad are required to be submitted to the President. This particular message was not passed on to the President. Nor did the Foreign Office think it necessary to take any action on it. It would later transpire that Bhutto and Aziz Ahmed decided to suppress the message because they thought that Arshad Hussain, known for his nervous temperament, had panicked as usual.

Ayub was woken up at 4 o'clock in the morning on 6 September and given the news of the Indian advance towards Lahore by an officer of the air force on reconnaissance duty. Ayub telephoned General Musa who said he had also heard the news but was waiting for confirmation!

Ayub was now facing the moment of truth. He called a Cabinet meeting and told his colleagues that the Indian challenge would be met with full force. He decided that he must take the people into confidence without delay. Bhutto and Agha Shahi, Additional Secretary in the Ministry of Foreign Affairs, produced a draft statement which Ayub found unsatisfactory. Ayub called the Information Secretary, who had become his principal speech-writer, to prepare an alternative draft. He told him about his meeting with the US Ambassador a couple of hours earlier. The Ambassador started by telling him, 'Mr President, the Indians have got you by the throat.' Ayub said: 'Any hands on Pakistan's throat will be cut off.' While he was giving the Information Secretary the points he wanted to make in his speech, Ayub said: 'The Indians don't know what people they have taken on.' For the speech-writer that was enough. In less than an hour he presented the alternative draft to Ayub. Ayub made only one change in the text. The draft said 'We are virtually at war,' Ayub scored out the word 'virtually'. Almost as an afterthought, he said 'I think I should also speak in Urdu.' Ayub made his speech in English at 12 o'clock and then in Urdu at 3 o'clock. It was the finest speech of his life. He spoke with great passion and made a tremendous impact. The whole nation was electrified and the hundred million people of Pakistan were welded into a united force. It was Pakistan against India: all differences disappeared, all disputes were forgotten. Ayub the dictator had become the nation's hero— the great leader who had accepted the Indian challenge and had come out to lead the people in their hour of trial.

It was decided that the media should not be subjected to any kind of pre-censorship. Even the scrutiny of scripts before broadcast, a procedure which had been rigidly followed since the British days, was dispensed with. All those lists under which successive governments had debarred certain political activists, poets, and writers from broadcasting were withdrawn. Almost instantaneously the official information network was transformed into the voice of the nation. The people were glued to their radio and television sets enthralled by patriotic songs and poems. It was the sudden outburst of creative energy which kept the people spellbound.

The enemy forces had come within a few miles of Lahore but their advance had been halted. The BBC, relying on a British correspondent in New Delhi, announced in their news bulletin that Lahore had fallen to the Indian forces. This caused great alarm in Dhaka. The people in West Pakistan were furious that the BBC should have acted in such an irresponsible manner. The BBC did not recover its credibility until after the war. This alerted Radio Pakistan to the importance of carefully checking the accuracy of all items of news broadcasts. Some precautions were taken to scrutinize the despatches prepared by the Inter-Services Public Relations department (ISPR) but they continued to transmit highly exaggerated and false stories from every front. The willingness of the people to believe anything which put their heroic armed forces in a favourable light was limitless. They considered it unpatriotic to publish or broadcast anything which might give comfort to the enemy.

On 7 September came the news that 11 Division, under General Hamid, had established a bridgehead across the Rohi Nullah near the Kasur-Khem Karan road. The stage was now set for Pakistan to launch its counter-offensive, Mailed Fist, to capture Amritsar. There was much excitement in the President's House, where the Cabinet and its sub-committees were in constant session. General Musa and Air Marshal Nur Khan would put in an appearance every now and then to confer with Ayub. Air Marshal Asghar Khan, the man who had raised the Pakistan Air Force (PAF) from scratch and put it into a state of battle-readiness, had been

surprisingly allowed to retire on 23 July, a day before Gibraltar
went into action, and Nur Khan, who had left the air force to
become Chairman of Pakistan International Airlines, a commercial
concern under government control, and whose major preoccupation
at the time was to build a chain of hotels to attract tourists, was
recalled and appointed as Commander-in-Chief of the PAF.
Asghar Khan was never consulted or taken into confidence about
Gibraltar. This was not done, as noted earlier, because the PAF
was not considered security-minded!

A day after the war started, Ayub decided to invite all the
political leaders for consultation. Unfortunately, no one from
East Pakistan could come as there were no flights from Dhaka.
Chaudhri Muhammad Ali, Maulana Abul A'la Maudoodi, Sardar
Shaukat Hayat, Chaudhry Ghulam Abbas and Mohammad Safdar
responded to the invitation. As he was going into the meeting,
Ayub said to the Information Secretary, 'So you have collected all
my enemies.' Inside the meeting he met enthusiastic friends, all
pledging their full support. Ghulam Abbas almost broke down in
tears saying that nobody in Pakistan had done for Kashmir what
Ayub had done.

Khem Karan, an important Indian village across the border,
was captured on 8 September and the Foreign Office was back in
business. Aziz Ahmad demanded propaganda leaflets to be printed
in millions for the air force to drop over Amritsar to reassure the
Sikhs that Pakistan had come to liberate them from Hindu
domination. Bhutto wanted a survey of all the ethnic groups in
Kashmir to determine their relationship with their brethren in the
adjoining districts of Punjab and NWFP. Bhutto said that after the
referendum in Jammu and Kashmir, district boundaries would
need to be redrawn.

The ninth of September passed without any news about Mailed
Fist. The Indians tried to regain some ground in Khem Karan but
their attacks were repulsed. Large bands of tribesmen from the
NWFP were invited by GHQ to proceed toward the Lahore border
to provide support to the men on the front. The tribesmen looted
whatever shops came their way along the route to the front but the
administration treated these incidents as part of the customary

exuberance of tribesmen in pursuit of their foe. The tribesmen were to become a serious nuisance to General Hamid because he could not find them any hilly terrain along the Punjab border where they could hide and display their traditional skills. They refused to expose themselves to air attacks in an area where clouds of dust were their only cover. General Hamid had to forcibly repatriate them to their tribal sanctuaries.

The United Nations passed two resolutions on 4 and 6 September calling for an immediate cease-fire. The Secretary General, U Thant, came to Pakistan. He had a meeting with Ayub, who told him that by trying to bring about a cease-fire without resolving the Kashmir dispute the UN would only be laying the foundations of another war. Ayub's impression was that U Thant had 'yielded to India's pressure'. During a meeting on 8 September, Ayub said, 'America is doing everything conceivable to help India.'[2] King Faisal of Saudi Arabia offered some financial aid, and there was a possibility of getting superior aircraft from Indonesia but Ayub feared that the Russians might block that. The French agreed to provide thirty aircraft, ten to be delivered immediately. It was doubtful whether Turkey would supply any ammunition, although there was a bilateral treaty between Turkey and Pakistan. Ayub told the Cabinet on 9 September that any advance by Pakistan would be very heavily resisted by the Indian forces: 'The Hindu protects himself in bunkers, pillboxes, and behind barbed wires and keeps a firing distance of 2,000 yards.'[3] It was obvious from what Ayub said that Mailed Fist had run into difficulties.

The US Ambassador, Walter P. McConaughy, met Bhutto at his residence on 9 September. It was an unpleasant meeting. The Ambassador told Bhutto that the Congress had decided to stop all military aid to Pakistan and India. But the decision, said the Ambassador, was 'not in any sense a punitive action; it was meant only to lend support to the UN Secretary General's efforts to attain a peaceful settlement'. Bhutto was indignant. Here was Pakistan, a friend and an ally, fighting for its survival and the United States was plunging a dagger in its back. He warned that this would damage Pakistan's relations with America. When Bhutto said that Pakistan's cities were being bombed, McConaughy asked him whether this had not been foreseen: 'It was a fateful decision you took to plan and organize the Mujahid operation.' Bhutto flatly denied that Pakistan had been involved in any such operation but conceded that the Mujahids had the support of Pakistan. Bhutto claimed: 'It is India that has committed aggression and we are fighting for our honour.'[4]

By now the country was getting used to the routine of daily black-outs and air attacks on civilian targets. A large number of people were leaving Lahore and withdrawing into the interior. This seriously impeded the movement of troops along the Grand Trunk Road. The Indian Air Force dropped bombs on Lahore, Peshawar, Rawalpindi, Sialkot and Sargodha, causing a number of civilian casualties. In East Pakistan, too, the Indians bombed civilian targets in Dhaka and Chittagong.

Secretaries of the Ministries of Foreign Affairs, Defence, Finance and Information had a meeting with representatives of GHQ to review the situation on 10 September. One of the decisions taken at this meeting was that both the Foreign Office and the Information Ministry should 'examine the question of our political objectives in the present war with India and to prepare a paper'. The question had obviously not been addressed when the Foreign Office was planning Gibraltar. A thoroughly subdued Aziz Ahmad could no longer explain why the country had been pushed into the war. Considerable anxiety was also expressed about the dwindling stocks of petroleum and other essential supplies. Messages were sent to the Pakistan Ambassador in Paris to expedite the purchase of French fighter aircraft, and to the Ambassador in Ankara to persuade Turkey to supply aircraft spare parts immediately. Largely on his own initiative, but with Ayub's approval, Asghar Khan had gone to China, Indonesia, Turkey, and Iran to secure aircraft, ammunition, and explosives. The Defence Secretary was assigned the task of examining 'the question of the duration and length of the present conflict with India and how Pakistan's defence needs could be met'. No one explained why attention had not been paid to these critical issues earlier.[5]

Ayub had another meeting with U Thant on 10 September. Once again, he explained to him the genesis of the war and argued that a simple cease-fire, which did not simultaneously establish a self-executing machinery to resolve the Kashmir dispute, according to the UN resolutions, would be an exercise in futility. The people of Kashmir had been suffering for ten years and India was annexing the state by force. He explained that there were Muslims living on both sides of the cease-fire line and when the people in Muzaffarabad were asked for help they had provided it without hesitation. Ayub admitted: 'We too gave them arms. It was perfectly natural and human because people must have the means to defend themselves.' He said that India was bent upon aggression against Pakistan and had concentrated its armies on the international border to pounce upon West Pakistan. Ayub felt that U Thant was visibly impressed by this argument: 'He is a weak man.' An official statement issued at the time said that Pakistan had read the report, which U Thant had submitted to the Security Council on 4 September 1965, 'with dismay'. U Thant 'had been given a wholly one-sided and inaccurate account of the happenings in the state by the UN observers'. The statement recalled that the Prime Minister of India had threatened during the Rann of Kutch crisis that India would choose its own time and place for attacking Pakistan.[6]

11 September was a fateful day. At 9 o'clock in the morning Ayub recorded a broadcast to mark the anniversary of the death of Quaid-i-Azam. After the recording, he took the Information Secretary to his office and showed him on a map how the counter-offensive in the Khem Karan sector was developing. He had personally approved that offensive and was extremely optimistic about its outcome. While Ayub was explaining the details of the operation, his Military Secretary, General Rafi walked into the room in a state of great agitation and almost shouted that the Indians had breached the Madhapur canal. Ayub forgot about the briefing. He wanted to know how long it would take the area to get inundated. GHQ had no idea. The Information Secretary rang up Ghulam Ishaq Khan, who was then Chairman of the Water and Power Development Authority in West Pakistan, and he calculated, on the basis of some old irrigation records, that the area would get submerged in about eight hours. Ayub discovered to his dismay that General Nasir, the commander of the operation, had relied on old survey maps and a large number of tanks

had been bogged down in a waterlogged terrain. The Indians claimed that Khem Karan had been turned into a graveyard of Pakistani tanks. The Khem Karan counter-offensive ran aground on 11 September, and with that collapsed Pakistan's entire military strategy. For Pakistan the war was over.

The army and the air force were now experiencing acute shortage of spare parts, ammunition and petroleum, and desperate efforts were being made to secure additional supplies from friendly countries. On the evening of 11 September, Nazir Ahmed told Ayub Khan that neither Turkey nor Iran was willing to provide armour-piercing ammunition. Ayub was mortified. He turned on him: 'Nazir, I am going to hold you responsible for this.' Since major tank battles were developing on the Sialkot front the Pakistan Army desperately needed armour piercing ammunition. Ayub Khan was stunned to find that GHQ had been importing the wrong kind of ammunition. Instead of armour-piercing (AP) ammunition they had been piling up highly-explosive (HE) ammunition which was of no use.

Briefing the Cabinet on 13 September, Ayub said that the enemy was broadening his base to get across the Sialkot border but the Pakistan Air Force was in full control and satellite air fields were in operation. He complained that there was no pressure on India at the international level. The US Ambassador to the United Nations had hinted at the possibility of sanctions being applied against Pakistan. Harold Wilson, the British Prime Minister, having initially condemned Indian aggression, was now pressing Pakistan to accept the 6 September Security Council Resolution. The West, it seemed, had only one worry and that was the fear of Chinese intervention. Ayub said that the Americans and the British wanted a subdued Pakistan and their major anxiety was to forestall any Chinese intervention. Ayub was talking as if the war was already over. He was counting his gains: 'We have fought and held our position and the world can't take us for granted.' He said: 'As Commander-in-Chief I always believed that we must wait for a positive moment.' Already he was regretting the moment he had chosen. He then talked about the growing tension between the US and China: 'This tension will continue to grow for another fifteen years. The US cannot destroy the determination of China where 700 million people are united like one man.' He mentioned how little assistance Pakistan could hope to get from sources other than the US. The Information Secretary wrote in his diary, 'It looks like a surrender meeting.'[7]

Later that day Ayub was sitting in a cane sofa on the lawn with a book in his lap and the Information Secretary, now his constant companion, was with him: 'These days I read about military strategy. The lesson is that one blunder and the whole operation is lost.' He then started talking about the cease-fire and asked whether the people would accept the cease-fire as the only way to save Pakistan, 'How do you think the people will react?' The Information Secretary, who had been in a state of anguish since the Cabinet meeting in the morning, almost shouted, 'Cease-fire without any settlement of the Kashmir problem would be a disaster. I hope I will not be alive on that day.' Ayub fell back in his chair and said, 'You feel like that?' The Information Secretary reminded him of his own argument, which he had been pressing on the people, that India was bound to attack Pakistan by 1970, when Pakistan would be in no position to resist it effectively. He had chosen the moment himself and the nation was behind him. 'We have been let down by the Americans,' Ayub said, 'but they are frightened of Chinese involvement.' 'And that, Mr President, is now the only card in your hands,' said the Information Secretary. Ayub sat up and, putting the book down on the table, said : 'Then let us use that card.' He picked up the telephone and asked General Rafi to summon all the Cabinet members for an emergency meeting. In less than an hour they had all assembled in the Cabinet room. Ayub came in looking very confident and told the Cabinet that if Pakistan were to accept the cease-fire on less than honourable terms the people would regard it as a surrender. He added: 'Our best card is the China card. We have to decide at what stage should Chinese aid be obtained. Our dealings with the Chinese must be frank and above-board. We should not be using them, otherwise the next time they will say we also know how to play tricks.'[8]

Ayub thought the time had come to tell the Security Council that Pakistan would prefer a prolonged struggle to a cease-fire that did not guarantee the resolution of the Kashmir dispute through negotiations and, if necessary, arbitration. In Ayub's judgement India had exhausted its major offensive, so had Pakistan: 'From now on ding-dong battles will take place here and there.' Bhutto added:

> The Chinese position is pivotal. East Pakistan has been left out of the war because of China. A defeated Pakistan would be against the Chinese interest. Kashmir under Pakistan is what the Chinese want. The real deterrent is the Chinese threat. The US is not itching to provoke the Chinese and that is why they want a cease-fire.

Ayub told General Musa, 'We must ensure that we are in and the Indians are out before we agree to a cease-fire.' Indian bridgeheads must be dissolved and there should be no agreement to withdraw the forces from their forward positions before a plebiscite is held in Jammu and Kashmir. And then quite casually, Ayub asked whether it would not be better to move out of the Security Council which was dominated by the big powers and added that: 'Fighting must go on whether it lasts for four to six weeks or three months. We must press against the UN. The diplomatic position is not against us.'[9]

China's support to Pakistan

The Chinese government had been giving full support to Pakistan. The Chinese Foreign Minister, Marshal Chen Yi, had a meeting with Bhutto in Karachi on 4 September, during which he said that China supported the 'just action taken by Pakistan to repel the Indian armed provocation' in Kashmir. On 7 September China condemned India's 'criminal aggression' as 'another exposure of the chauvinist and expansionist features of its ruling circles'. The statement added that 'the Indian government probably believes that since it had the backing of the US imperialists and the modern revisionists it can bully its neighbours, defy public opinion and do whatever it likes.' Earlier, in a note of 27 August, the Chinese government had accused the Indian Army of committing 'acts of aggression and provocation' on the border of Sikkim and Tibet. The Indians rejected the Chinese note on 2 September and China warned India on 8 September that if it did not end its 'frenzied provocation activities' it would have to 'bear the responsibility for all its consequences'. India denied the Chinese allegations and proposed that an independent and neutral observer should visit the Sikkim border to look into China's complaints. On 12 September, China rejected the Indian proposal as 'pretentious' and gave India an ultimatum that unless the Indian government 'dismantled all military works on the Chinese side of the border within three days', stopped intrusions into China, returned Chinese livestock and kidnapped civilians, and pledged to stop further cross-border raids it would have to 'bear the full responsibility for all consequences'.[10]

The Chinese ultimatum, while reaffirming its policy of 'non-involvement' in the Kashmir dispute, stated that non-involvement 'absolutely does not mean that China can approve of depriving the Kashmiri people of their right of self-determination or that she can approve of Indian aggression against Pakistan.' The Indians, now thoroughly alarmed, urged the USSR, USA and Britain to issue a joint declaration warning China against any attack on India. In Moscow, Kosygin promised the Indian Ambassador, T.N. Kaul that the Soviet Union would continue its regular arms supplies to India. In Washington, Dean Rusk assured B.K. Nehru that if India were attacked by China the United States would carry out its commitment of extending military aid to India. Britain, too, expressed understanding of Indian anxiety and the British Prime Minister, Harold Wilson, issued a statement that if the Chinese were to intervene in the war, Britain and the US would be bound to assist India.[11] The Indians, however, did not succeed in getting a joint three-power declaration. Neither Ayub nor the Foreign Office knew the details of the agreement between India and the US worked out in 1962, that in the event of war between India and China the United States would provide full military support to India.

On 18 September Indian sources reported that Chinese troops had moved nearer to the border both on the Sikkim frontier and in the Demchok area of Ladakh, and had advanced on the following day to within 500 yards of the Indian positions in the Daulat Beg Oldi area of Ladakh. An Indian military spokesman said on 20 September that the Chinese had fired a few shots along both borders but the Indian forces had not returned the fire. Shastri said in Lok Sabha that day:

> It is clear that what China is looking for is not redress of grievances, real or imaginary, but some excuse to start its aggressive activities again, this time acting in collusion with its ally, Pakistan. The extension of the time limit for the ultimatum was in our view no more than a device to gain time to watch what comes out of the discussions in the Security Council.[12]

Some 300 foreign correspondents had descended on Pakistan during the war. Ayub decided to address a press conference on 15 September. A detailed brief was prepared for him by the Information Secretary anticipating the likely questions. The brief was based on the position that Pakistan would not accept the cease-fire unless a self-executing machinery was established to solve the Kashmir problem. Pakistan was determined to fight to the bitter end. It was arranged that Ayub would come to the press conference in Field Marshal's uniform, but he turned up in a drab grey suit looking pale and sombre. Ignoring the brief, which he had approved a few hours earlier, he made an appeal to President Johnson to establish peace in the region. It transpired later that just before the press conference he had a meeting with the Commanders-in-Chief of the Army and the Air Force where the Defence Secretary had given him a report on the position of defence stores and supplies. The two Commanders-in-Chief had apparently persuaded him to immediately ask for American assistance. The foreign correspondents were completely surprised by this sudden reversal of Pakistan's position. The next day the *Daily Telegraph* (London) reported that there was 'obvious anxiety to reach agreement with India' on Ayub's part. The *Guardian* (London) said Ayub's statement was a 'sign of real flexibility in Pakistan's stance. Rigidity ended at the hands of Ayub Khan himself.' The correspondents also noted that Ayub had mentioned China only once, and that in answer to a question. The BBC reported that Ayub 'virtually invited President Johnson to intervene directly in the dispute.' The Voice of America said Ayub would 'welcome American initiatives to end the Indo-Pakistan conflict'. Most correspondents remarked that Ayub's statement was infinitely less harsh than the previous Pakistani statements, and concluded that it must be the result of 'the apparent stalemate on the military front'.[13]

Bhutto, who was present at the press conference, was quite obviously taken aback by Ayub's appeal to President Johnson. He stopped the transmission of all press despatches from Pakistan. The journalists came rushing to the Information Secretary. He took up the matter with Ayub who summoned Bhutto for discussion. Bhutto insisted that if the despatches were allowed to be transmitted it would do incalculable harm to Pakistan. The Information Secretary explained that the world already knew what the President had said. By withholding the despatches the government would only be fooling its own people. The argument prevailed and it was decided to allow the despatches to go through uncensored.[14]

Ayub's overture to President Johnson came as a complete surprise to everyone around him. He had never given any indication that he was considering such a move. With that personal appeal to President Johnson, Ayub had put the China card back in the deck. He had obviously decided against prolonging the struggle to avoid any risk of escalation. Immediately after Ayub's press conference the Indian Foreign Minister gave a 'hands off Jammu and Kashmir' statement, and Prime Minister Shastri announced that 'in view of President Ayub's remarks, the defence operations must continue with unabated vigour.'[15]

The situation on the battlefront was not moving in Pakistan's favour. Bhutto now shifted his stance and started claiming that diplomacy could not be stronger than the military position on the ground. Bhutto and Aziz Ahmed were under attack in meetings where they would be reminded of their repeated categorical assurances that India would never cross the international borders. They would reply that the Foreign Office had only given its assessment, and not any assurance, about Indian intentions.

The cease-fire resolution was delivered to Ayub on Saturday 18 September at 10 p.m. Agha Shahi was in New York. He had been instructed to get a reference to the earlier Security Council resolutions included in the resolution and to resist the inclusion of any clause requiring the withdrawal of forces from Kashmir. The Indians wanted a simple cease-fire resolution with no reference to any previous UN resolution or to the Kashmir dispute. The resolution was moved by the Netherlands whose representative said that the Security Council was not a court and, therefore, did not have to decide who was the aggressor—India or Pakistan. Ayub decided that the resolution should be opposed, at least for the record. Bhutto was assured by the French Foreign Minister that France would not support the application of sanctions against Pakistan. On Sunday 19 September, the British High Commissioner, Morrice James delivered a letter from Harold Wilson to Ayub conveying the British assessment that 'in time Indian numbers may tell.' Wilson also wondered why the Chinese should run any risk for the sake of Pakistan. Aziz Ahmad, when given this letter by Morrice James, told him: 'If you force this resolution down our throat you will be starting a world war.'[16]

Ayub flies to Beijing

It was at this point that Ayub decided that he must discuss the whole situation directly with Zhou Enlai. He flew to Beijing from Peshawar during the night of 19/20 September, and returned the following night. The visit was a closely guarded secret and few people knew about it. In the President's House the daily routine was strictly observed—the bearer taking the morning tea to Ayub's bedroom and bringing back the tray; even the security guards did not suspect that Ayub was not in the house. Ayub was accompanied by Bhutto and they had two long meetings with Zhou Enlai and Marshal Chen Yi. Ayub explained the military situation and how the Indians, because of their superiority in numbers, were beginning to strengthen their hold, and how Western powers were giving full diplomatic support to India while persuading the Soviet Union to assume the role of a mediator. Zhou Enlai said that numerical superiority would be of no avail to the Indians in a prolonged war. Even if one or two major cities were lost, the Pakistani forces, supported by a patriotic people, could inflict crippling blows on the invaders. He recalled instances from China's long struggle for liberation to show that numerical superiority cannot prevail on the will of the people. Ayub explained that the flat terrain of Punjab was not suitable for mounting guerrilla attacks on an advancing enemy. Marshal Chen Yi intervened to say that every little canal, every bit of high ground could be used as cover. Zhou Enlai said: 'And don't forget that we will be maintaining our pressure all the time.' Ayub asked: 'How long would you maintain that pressure?' Zhou Enlai looked straight into Ayub's eyes and said, 'For as long as necessary, but you must keep fighting even if you have to withdraw to the hills.' Ayub did not know how to respond to this offer of unconditional support. He said: 'Mr Prime Minister I think you are being rash.' Zhou Enlai smiled and cautioned Ayub against succumbing to American pressure: 'And don't fall into the Russian trap. They are unreliable. You will find out the truth.' Ayub tried to reassure Zhou Enlai that Pakistan was China's friend: 'I am not going to turn like Nehru. Please convey this to Chairman Mao.' By the end it became clear that if Pakistan wanted full Chinese support it had to be prepared for a long war in which some major cities like Lahore might be lost. However, every reverse would unite the people and the Indian forces would be sucked into a quagmire of popular resistance. Neither Ayub nor Bhutto was prepared for this. The whole Foreign Office strategy was designed as a quick fix to force the Indians to the negotiating table. Ayub had never foreseen the possibility of the Indians surviving a couple of hard blows, and Bhutto had never envisaged a long drawn out people's war. Above all, the army and the air force were totally against any further prolongation of the conflict.[17]

General Musa was demoralized by the lack of ammunition and spare parts, and Air Marshal Nur Khan by the high attrition rate which was daily reducing the number of operational aircraft available to him.

On 21 September Bhutto called a meeting of senior officials to discuss the latest draft cease-fire resolution. Bhutto came under severe criticism for having driven Pakistan to a most humiliating position. Bhutto burst into tears and said, 'My political career is over. I must resign and go abroad.' With that Bhutto got up and left the room. Later that day Bhutto said to Ayub that the US wanted an immediate cease-fire because it would not permit any escalation. He advised: 'Cease-fire at this point will not mean any loss of face for Pakistan. It might, indeed, be seen as an act of statesmanship.' He said: 'Pakistan was faced with a critical choice, complete alienation from its traditional Western allies and an uncertain future.' The Information Secretary advised against the acceptance of the resolution, while Bhutto and Aziz Ahmad advocated its acceptance.[18]

Ayub invited the political leaders whom he had met immediately after the Indian advance against Lahore and asked for their advice about accepting the cease-fire resolution. They unanimously urged him to resist the resolution because the people would feel utterly betrayed if Pakistan agreed to an unconditional cease-fire.

The Soviet Ambassador delivered a message to Ayub from Prime Minister Kosygin offering the good offices of the Soviet Union for a meeting between Shastri and Ayub in Tashkent and expressing the hope that such a meeting might help produce constructive results. Ayub was doubtful about the utility of such a meeting: 'What purpose will it serve? Shastri will state his case and I will state my case.'[19]

Ayub's major worry was that India might capture Lahore. 'How many people can we take on? That is our problem,' he said in despair. He then turned to Bhutto and said: 'We must extricate ourselves from this situation.' Bhutto contacted the Chinese Ambassador who told him: 'You are having difficulties. The US is big but you must face up to the threat.' Bhutto reported this to Ayub Khan.

Ayub had a meeting with his ministers on 21 September to consider the draft resolution. As Bhutto was reading the text Ayub turned to Altaf Hussain, the Industries Minister, and said: 'Don't write editorials on this.' Altaf Hussain had been the editor of

Dawn, and would contribute the odd editorial even as minister. After Bhutto had finished reading, Altaf Hussain said, 'We must be firm,' and Ayub snapped, 'I have not lectured to you and you will not lecture to me.' General Musa was even more offended and wanted to know what the Industries Minister meant by being firm. Air Marshal Nur Khan strongly urged that both the cease-fire resolution and the Soviet invitation be accepted and when Altaf Hussain suggested that the Chinese threat had caused some jitters in the American administration, Nur Khan's face dissolved into a convulsion to register his disagreement. The Governor of West Pakistan, Nawab of Kalabagh, who had vanished from the scene after 6 September, had been specially invited to the meeting. He was the man on whom Ayub could always rely to pull the chestnuts out of the fire for him. Kalabagh strongly favoured the immediate acceptance of the resolution. He said those who were fighting and dying were people from his area. Asked for an assessment of public reaction to cease fire, the Information Secretary gave a résumé of Ayub's meeting with the political leaders and warned the government that the acceptance of the cease-fire resolution, in its present form, would invite a fierce public backlash. The question would be asked: 'Why did the government embark on this operation?' And, people would not accept the cease-fire unless there was a clear commitment by India to allow the people of Jammu and Kashmir to exercise their right of self-determination. Any attempt to sell the cease-fire resolution as a step forward to the solution of the Kashmir problem would be counter-productive. Explaining the resolution, Bhutto said that strenuous efforts had been made to persuade the Security Council to accept that India had committed aggression on 6 September and that the Jammu and Kashmir dispute must be resolved through the implementation of the earlier UNCIP resolutions. The best that Pakistan could get was a recognition that the cease-fire was 'a first step toward a peaceful settlement of the outstanding differences between the two countries on Kashmir and other related matters'. Bhutto was happy that the words 'outstanding differences' in the text had been replaced by 'outstanding difference'. The use of the singular was significant as it identified Kashmir as the only problem between the two countries. Bhutto then discussed the unfavourable aspects of the resolution and endorsed the assessment given by the Information Secretary. The reference to the date 5 August 1965, he said, would put the responsibility for 'infiltration' on Pakistan, and the fact that there was no reference to any previous UN resolution or to the right of self-determination of the people of Kashmir, was against Pakistan's interests. The clause relating to the withdrawal of forces would cover not only the armed forces but also the 'freedom fighters'. Aziz Ahmad argued that the resolution was useful as it opened the way for Pakistan to get the support of the Soviet Union. Ayub wanted the withdrawal of forces to follow the establishment of a machinery for negotiations between the two countries. Nur Khan looked visibly distressed by the long-winded debate and wanted the resolution to be accepted immediately. Ayub decided that Bhutto should go to New York and try and obtain some kind of a guarantee about the negotiating machinery. The atmosphere at this meeting was totally different from the one in the previous meeting. A few verbal changes in the draft resolution had convinced Bhutto and Aziz Ahmed that the resolution was favourable to Pakistan. Bhutto read out a telegram from the US representative to the UN, Arthur Goldberg, which said that the 'US did not want the Chinese to get involved'. Goldberg suggested that Ayub should talk to President Johnson directly. Bhutto claimed that Pakistan had secured the support of all the great powers for the settlement of the Kashmir dispute. Ayub said he had told the US Ambassador that the Americans had an alliance with Pakistan but they had failed to prevent the Indians from attacking their ally. They had now left the field to the Soviets who had seized the political initiative in the region. During the meeting Ayub received pressing messages from the President of Turkey and the Shah of Iran to accept the resolution. The deadline for accepting the resolution was Wednesday 22 September, at 12 noon, and Ayub wanted to wait until the very last minute. He still hoped that by holding out he might get India to agree to some negotiating machinery.

Ayub's speech accepting the cease-fire resolution was drafted by the Information Secretary a few hours before the expiry of the deadline. The best he could say was that cease-fire did not mean the end of war. The Urdu equivalent of cease-fire, *jang-bandi,* would have given the impression that the war was over. A new phrase, *fire-bandi,* was coined to convey that Pakistani forces would hold their fire but stay entrenched in their positions on the front.[20] The people were left with the impression that Pakistan had not submitted to US pressure and if the Indians did not yield on Kashmir, hostilities would be resumed. Despite this linguistic gambit the speech caused widespread disappointment, except in East Pakistan where the people welcomed the cessation of hostilities because they had been left totally exposed with nothing but a sense of isolation to sustain their morale. Neither General Musa, nor the Chief of General Staff or any of their deputies thought it necessary to visit East Pakistan during the seventeen-day war which left West Pakistan plunged in gloom and East Pakistan smarting under a profound sense of alienation and neglect.

NOTES

1. *The Hindu,* 4 September 1965.
2. Author's notes.
3. Ibid.
4. Ayub Khan's papers. Minutes of Bhutto's meeting with the American Ambassador prepared by the Foreign Office.
5. Author's notes of the meeting.
6. Ayub Khan's papers.
7. Author's notes of the meeting.
8. Ibid.
9. Ibid.
10. Author's diary.
11. *The Times,* London, 18 September 1965.
12. *Dawn,* 20 September 1965.
13. Press Information Department, Government of Pakistan, Monitoring Report, 16 September 1965.
14. Author's notes of meeting.
15. *Dawn,* 17 September 1965.
16. Author's notes.

17. This account is based on a long conversation that the author had with Ayub Khan soon after his return from Beijing. The relevant note in his diary reads:

> It was a distressing encounter. Ayub looked tired and depressed. He gave me a blow-by-blow account of his meetings with Chou En-lai. I took down every word. He has been wavering and vacillating. Somewhere within him is a great urge to go on fighting. But after every meeting with Musa and Nur Khan he seems to slump. I had hoped he would jump at Chou En-lai's offer. I wonder what has happened to Bhutto. Why has he chickened out? Must talk to him.

18. Author's notes of the meeting.
19. Author's notes.
20. The phrase was suggested by Zulfiqar Ali Bukhari, first Director-General of Radio Pakistan, an eminent Urdu poet and scholar.

CHAPTER 10

Road to Tashkent

The Foreign Office and GHQ washed their hands off the war leaving Ayub in the rubble to pick up the pieces. He seemed to have lost all power of decision. He continued to agonize over his own mistakes and never once thought of instituting an enquiry into the conduct of the Foreign Office and GHQ. Serious charges were being levelled against senior army officers who had removed the mines from their lands along the Wagah border on the Lahore front only a few weeks before the Indian invasion. Why was the cypher message sent by the Pakistan High Commissioner in New Delhi on 4 September about the Indian plan to attack Lahore on 6 September suppressed? Who was responsible for withholding this vital piece of information? Ayub would hear of these accusations but take no action. Ayub didn't have the politician's skill of finding a scapegoat for his failure. He knew that Gibraltar was his decision. Others might have used their positions to mislead him but there was no one in the Foreign Office or GHQ who could have forced him to act against his judgement. By the time the cease-fire resolution was accepted Ayub knew exactly who was responsible for the failure of Gibraltar, but any criticism of the army or the Foreign Office at that stage would have only encouraged the Indians to stiffen their aggressive posture and delay the withdrawal of forces. Senior army officers who had been decorated for fanciful acts of valour were left free to fabricate and broadcast stories of their triumphs on the battlefield. Ayub himself contributed to this by taking pride in the performance of his boys who had revived the legends of early Muslim heroes. The people lapped up these stories because they were not prepared to believe that the puny Hindu soldier could stand up against a

Muslim *jawan*. A point was reached where it came to be believed that the army had trounced the Indians on the battlefield, and the Foreign Office had dominated them in the arena of diplomacy, but Ayub had lost his nerve and thrown away all the gains of war.

Ayub was now being urged by General Musa to persuade the Indians to withdraw their forces from Pakistan territory because the morale of the soldiers was plunging. With the two sides in their trenches—sitting eyeball to eyeball—the pressure was beginning to tell on Pakistani forces, which were running out of supplies and ammunition. But with his Foreign Minister making provocative speeches against the Indians in every forum, Ayub could hardly bring the Indians to the negotiating table.

Attempts at mediation

Soon after the outbreak of fighting in Kashmir in August 1965, the British Commonwealth Secretary, Arthur Bottomley, had a series of meetings with the Indian and Pakistani High Commissioners in London. The Indian High Commissioner made it clear that India would not accept any kind of British mediation and proposed that Britain should ask Pakistan to desist from its activities in Kashmir. A message from Harold Wilson was delivered to Ayub and Shastri on 3 September, expressing the British government's growing concern over the fighting in Kashmir. The same day the Canadian Prime Minister, Lester Pearson, offered to go on a mission to India and Pakistan to bring about a cease-fire. President Tito of Yugoslavia and President Nasser of the UAR also offered their good offices and issued a joint appeal for a cease-fire.

On 6 September, Harold Wilson issued a statement in which he said:

> I am deeply concerned at the increasingly serious fighting now taking place between India and Pakistan and especially at the news that Indian forces have today attacked Pakistan territory across the international frontier in the Punjab. This is a distressing response to the resolution adopted by the Security Council on 4 September calling for a cease-fire.[1]

Wilson asked other Commonwealth Heads of Government to appeal to Ayub and Shastri to respond to the UN resolution calling for a cease-fire and to facilitate the work of U Thant. Wilson also emphasized that the British government would not offer any mediation nor initiate any Commonwealth action as that might undermine U Thant's mission.

The US Secretary of State, Dean Rusk, informed Congress on 8 September that all US military aid to India and Pakistan had been stopped and that no further economic aid would be given to either country without consulting Congress. Faced with Indian aggression, Pakistan invoked the CENTO agreement on 7 September. The Iranian Prime Minister, Mr Hoveida, met his Turkish counterpart and a communique was issued in which India's attack across the international frontier was condemned. The Governments of Turkey and Iran reaffirmed their solidarity with Pakistan. But Turkey declined Pakistan's request for twenty-four jet aircraft with pilots and instructors, on the excuse that any weapons or equipment supplied by NATO, or as part of US military aid, could not be diverted to Pakistan. A Turkish government spokesman, however, said on 10 September that Turkey would supply Turkish-made arms and ammunition worth $5 million to Pakistan, while Iran offered oil, medical supplies and a field hospital. Indonesia accepted Pakistan's request for aid. The only Muslim country that opposed Pakistan was Malaysia. The Malaysian Prime Minister, Tunku Abdur Rahman, said: 'Malaysia must regard her international ties as more important than her religious ties with other countries.' As a result, diplomatic relations between the two countries were broken off.

The Indian attitude hardened after the cease-fire. Shastri said, 'this time peace will be on Indian terms. We will sit tight where we are.'[2] There was much gloom in Pakistan where those who had 'helped to conceive and direct the country's policies' were suffering from a 'buried sense of failure.'[3] On 11 November it was announced that Bhutto would be visiting Moscow soon.

The Soviet offer

The Soviet Union had come into the picture at an early stage. On 20 August, the Soviet Prime Minister, Aleksei Kosygin, wrote to Ayub and Shastri asking them not to take any step which might lead to a major conflict. He wrote again on 4 September appealing for an immediate cessation of hostilities and a reciprocal withdrawal of troops behind the cease-fire line. He offered the Soviet Union's good offices in negotiating a peaceful settlement of the differences between India and Pakistan. Neither side took up the offer. In a third letter, on 17 September, the Soviet Prime Minister proposed that Ayub and Shastri should meet in Tashkent or in any other Soviet city for negotiations and offered to take part himself in the meeting, if both sides so desired. Ayub discussed the implications of the offer with his ministers for several days. He was quite disturbed that the US and the British should leave the field to the Soviet Union. The subcontinent had been traditionally the area of Western influence and the induction of the Soviet Union into the region as a mediator would only strengthen India's position. He wondered whether the superpowers had come to some understanding, allowing the Soviet Union greater room for manœuvre in the region. He was aware of the convergence of strategic and political interests of the US and the USSR because of the growing pressure of the Chinese and the difficult US position in Vietnam. Both the Soviet Union and the US wanted to build India into a strong counter-force to what they considered the Chinese threat of expansion. Ayub knew that the Soviets would not exert any pressure on India, with which they had strong friendly ties, and he could not see any purpose in going to Tashkent unless some prior understanding was reached between India and Pakistan on the question of Kashmir. The Foreign Office, now stuck in a blind alley, started supporting the idea of a Tashkent meeting. Bhutto argued that by accepting the Soviet invitation, Pakistan would get Soviet support in the Security Council. Two days after the cease-fire Ayub wrote to Kosygin that a meeting with India in Tashkent would not be productive and urged the Soviet Union to use its influence in the Security Council to adopt 'a meaningful resolution that can lead to an honourable settlement of the Kashmir dispute.'

Bhutto went to Moscow on 23 November for consultations. Shastri announced in the Upper House that he would be ready to go to Tashkent but 'he would not be prepared to talk specifically about Kashmir, but would be ready to discuss the whole range of relations between India and Pakistan—which, of course, could not exclude Kashmir'.[4] After a long meeting with Kosygin on 25 November, Bhutto told a press conference in Moscow that the prospects of a peace conference between India and Pakistan were 'fairly good'. He added that 'the ball was now entirely in India's court' and Pakistan was ready to 'discuss the whole gamut of Indo-Pakistan relations' with Mr Shastri at a meeting in the Soviet Union. He felt that the Indian Prime Minister's statement of 23 November 'does not go as far as our willingness, though it does not preclude such willingness'.[5] Bhutto indicated that 'a meeting between Pakistani and Indian leaders might take place in Tashkent towards the end of this year or early next year.' *The Statesman* (Calcutta) published Bhutto's statement, which was reproduced by *Dawn* on 27 November, that 'Pakistan had accepted Premier Aleksei Kosygin's offer for Tashkent talks *unconditionally.'* On his return to Pakistan, Bhutto twisted his statement and claimed that his Moscow talks dwelt on the entire mechanism of Soviet attempts to solve the Kashmir dispute and were extremely 'useful and profitable'.[6] Bhutto knew that no mechanism of solving the Kashmir dispute came under discussion during his talks in Moscow. The next day he told the Press that Soviet-Pakistan relations were 'based on a firm foundation and have good prospects of development'. Bhutto suggested that the Soviet Union would now find it difficult to exercise its veto in the Security Council in favour of India. He had impressed upon Gromyko the desirability of setting up a self-executing mechanism for the solution of the Kashmir dispute but was vague about Gromyko's response. Later, at a critical point during the negotiations in Tashkent, Kosygin would remind Ayub that Bhutto had given a categorical assurance to Gromyko that Pakistan would come to Tashkent with an open mind, with no preconditions, and it was on the basis of that assurance that he had secured Shastri's agreement to participate in Tashkent.[7]

Ayub meets Johnson

It was announced in Rawalpindi on 26 November that Ayub would be leaving for London on 10 December on his way to Washington to meet President Johnson. He was expected to go to Tashkent in the first week of January 1966.[8] Ayub said on 1 December that he had accepted Premier Kosygin's offer of 'good offices in settling the Kashmir dispute in all sincerity and in the hope that his efforts will bear fruit.'[9] Aziz Ahmad was exuding confidence once more and assuring the Cabinet that Pakistan could get a self-executing mechanism to resolve the Jammu and Kashmir dispute in Tashkent if it played its cards right. The least Pakistan should expect was an arbitration arrangement á la Rann of Kutch. Ayub was caught in a no-win situation. While he allowed his Foreign Minister to talk about carrying on the war to the bitter end, he was being told by his Commander-in-Chief that the Indians were continuing to improve their position in Pakistani territory by violating the cease-fire. For Ayub, Tashkent had become the only hope of military disengagement though there was always the possibility that something might turn up in Tashkent to help resolve the Kashmir problem. Bhutto and Aziz Ahmad both kept nudging him in that direction. It was not realized that the expectations that were being built up about Tashkent were not even relevant to the framework of discussion that Bhutto had accepted in Moscow. The Indians knew exactly what to expect from Tashkent because the Soviet leaders had communicated to them the unqualified assurance given by Bhutto that discussions in Tashkent would not be dependent on the two sides coming to an agreement about resolving the Kashmir dispute. Bhutto's repeated public pronouncements that Pakistan would never give up the cause of the people of Kashmir added to the general mood of optimism in West Pakistan, particularly in the Punjab, where the popular view was that the Indians, having lost the war, were desperate to settle the Kashmir dispute in Tashkent.

Ayub left for Washington on 10 December for a meeting with President Johnson. He stopped in London for a meeting with Harold Wilson on 11 December. Ayub started by telling Wilson that he would not go over all the developments leading to the Indian invasion of Pakistan. The Indians had built up a three-to-one superiority over Pakistan in armed forces and were spending over a billion dollars a year on their war machine. The West had bought the great hoax that India needed a vast army to meet the threat from China and had provided it with enormous financial and military assistance. But there was no threat from China, nor was there any possibility of India deploying such huge forces in the disputed territory between India and China. Pakistan had always known that the Indian Army was there to be used against Pakistan, and events had proved that to be true. Pakistan had halted the Indian advance and a cease-fire was established, 'because both of us lost the power of further offensive action'.

While Ayub expatiated on the theme, Wilson, pipe in mouth, his legs stretched under the table, sat quietly puffing away. Ayub said: 'The results are in the lap of the future but Pakistan has no doubt that India's hostile intentions will continue to increase.' Ayub complained that the recent conduct of the US administration had not been helpful at all: 'There are too many sloppy people in the administration who are sold out to the Hindu' and he named Chester Bowles, who had been the US Ambassador in London, as the major culprit. Pakistan could only hope that the big powers would not go on arming India: 'They must know that India will not hesitate to attack Pakistan again.' But history would bear witness to the valour of the Pakistani armed forces which had given a most praiseworthy account of themselves. He recalled the collapse of the Khem Karan bridge, which had frustrated the Pakistani offensive in that sector, and added philosophically: 'These things do happen in war.' Explaining Pakistan's relation with China, Ayub said the Chinese had given moral support and had been helpful because 'they would not like to see us go under.'

Ayub then talked of the Indian situation and remarked that 'there are divisive tendencies within India but they have not yet asserted themselves fully.' He particularly mentioned the problem of the Sikhs which, he forecast, would become acute in the future.

After Ayub had finished, Wilson nodded and leaned forward. He said: 'We agree about the senseless character of the arms race and its disastrous consequences.' He mentioned that the amount of food going to the Indian subcontinent was fifty per cent of the total US food production of 1960. There was, he felt, no point in going into the past. There had been too much mud-slinging at Britain in India and he could not really go into the merits of the Kashmir dispute. Ayub asked 'Why should you be shy to do that?' Wilson replied that the situation had become much too complicated, and then, deftly changing the subject, asked Ayub about Tashkent. Would Kosygin be there as a mediator? Ayub replied that Kosygin had indicated that he would be available for discussion but not as a mediator. Ayub hoped that Tashkent would contribute towards the settlement of Kashmir and ensure the withdrawal and demobilization of forces. Bhutto added that Tashkent talks would also cover other differences between India and Pakistan. 'Including China?' asked Wilson, to which Ayub replied, 'Maybe.' Wilson remarked that Pakistan had improved her relations with the Soviet Union and Ayub said: 'Yes, but they still suspect us.'

Wilson then broached the subject which was obviously uppermost in his mind. Weighing his words carefully, he said that as far as Britain could see, 'China's proclivity to fish in troubled waters is the real problem.' China, he said, was 'the greatest danger' in the region because it was far more expansionist than the Soviet Union or India. The West, he admitted, was deeply worried about Chinese intentions and involvement in the region. Ayub did not rise to the bait and said with an air of indifference: 'What the Chinese do is their affair.' A little put out, Wilson asked how Ayub saw his forthcoming meeting with Johnson and added with a grin that he did not want to turn the meeting into a dress rehearsal for the Ayub-Johnson encounter, which he knew was going to be tough because the Americans were quite unhappy: 'They don't like being kicked in the teeth or the belly.' They had a feeling that Pakistan had taken advantage of the 1962 India-China conflict by concluding the border treaty with China: 'That really amounted to calling in China to help solve Pakistan's dispute with India.' Ayub replied that such a view did not take into account the history of Sino-Indian relations before 1962. It was Nehru who welcomed the Chinese into Tibet. Pakistan had no means of knowing how Indo-Chinese relations would develop. India had been Pakistan's tormentor from the first day and it was unnatural to expect Pakistan to join forces with India against China. Wilson insisted that Pakistan had moved into the Chinese orbit in 1962: 'You have let the animal into your house, perhaps as a good watch-dog.' Britain certainly had no intention to be drawn into major war which would create much sharper polarization with Russia and India on one side and China and Pakistan on the other. This explained why the US and Britain had agreed to let the Russians move into the region. By casting the Soviet Union in the role of a mediator, the West was pre-empting that polarization which it feared most. Ayub reacted a little sharply and said that Pakistan was a small country and if neither the US nor Britain were willing to help while India was indulging in 'unbelievable brutality' in Kashmir, they could not expect Pakistan to do nothing to defend herself. 'This might be true,' Wilson responded, 'but a wider conflagration had to be avoided at all costs.'[10]

As the discussion seemed to be leading nowhere, Wilson asked Michael Stewart, his Foreign Secretary, for his assessment of the situation. Stewart, who had just returned from Moscow, said that the Russians saw themselves as hosts at Tashkent. In his judgement, China in its present mood was 'an extremely dangerous friend to have'. China needed a difficult and explosive world to take advantage of. The Soviet attitude was deeply influenced by this reading of Chinese intentions. Stewart said to Ayub, the Soviets are particularly 'worried about your friendship with China.' That, according to Stewart, was making them lean towards India even more. Pakistan would have to convince the Soviets that it was not positively seeking China as a friend and that the normalization of its relations with China could be helpful to the Soviets because they wanted a peaceful subcontinent in their own interest. Ignoring what Stewart had said, Ayub stated that he was going to Tashkent because the US and Britain had lost the initiative. Wilson said: 'I am sure you are right to go. Obviously you are not going with excessive hopes.' He explained that the US and Britain had lost the initiative because of the Soviet attitude in the Security Council. The Soviet Union would not allow any resolution to be adopted by the Security Council, and that left the UK and the US with no option but to allow the USSR into the region. Ayub was not persuaded. He maintained that Britain and the US must not forsake the region. Wilson was now on the defensive: 'We do not want to get the wires crossed.' Once U Thant had embarked on his mission, the US and Britain considered it necessary that the lines be kept absolutely clear. The Russians held the field and there was some advantage in allowing the Soviet Union to take up the peace-keeping role that Britain and the US were in no position to assume. He conceded that the Anglo-American position had been flip-flopping, but as the Soviet attitude became harder and clearer they had to align themselves with the Soviets. Wilson then mentioned that the coming elections in India, the first since the death of Nehru, had made the situation more difficult. Ayub dismissed that 'as a poor excuse'. Wilson assured Ayub that the British government would take another look at the situation after Tashkent. That, Ayub said, might be too late. Ayub then suggested the possibility of the Commonwealth setting up a self-executing machinery for Kashmir along the lines of the Rann of Kutch agreement. Wilson said that the Commonwealth was a multi-racial organization under great pressure because of Rhodesia, and it would not be possible to discuss Kashmir under the aegis of the Commonwealth. He narrated the proceedings of a recent meeting of the Organization of African Unity (OAU) in which Britain had been severely criticized by the African Foreign Ministers for not taking a strong enough stand on the situation in Rhodesia.[11] The British High Commissioners had been expelled and Nyerere was threatening to leave the Commonwealth. Having finished his tale of woe, Wilson looked straight at Ayub and said: 'Foreign Ministers tend to be more explosive than heads of state, particularly when they get away from home.' This was directed at Bhutto. Wilson's meaning was clear: Britain did not wish to take sides on Kashmir.

The Commonwealth Secretary, Arthur Bottomley, explained that Britain was working behind the scenes but its influence was limited because it was considered to be pro-Pakistan. One could argue in favour of Britain taking some initiative in the subcontinent but the environment was not propitious. Ayub reiterated the point that Pakistan was deeply interested in peace but would not allow itself to be liquidated in the pursuit of that goal. Wilson assured Ayub that India would get no encouragement from the United States in committing aggression against Pakistan. Ayub could criticize Britain, but he must know that 'it is the Americans who hold the key'. Wilson's concluding observation was: 'We can't really hurry the Kashmir issue, though we realize that the conflict is driving India and Pakistan to orbits we fear.'

On to Washington

Early next morning Ayub left for New York where he was due to address the United Nations General Assembly. As soon as the delegation was airborne, a mini-crisis developed. Ayub did not like the speech the Foreign Office had prepared for him. It was a turgid history of the Kashmir dispute and a dreary recital of accusations and counter-accusations. The Information Secretary was asked to redraft the speech which proved a major undertaking. He tried to rework the original draft into some shape but it crumbled in his hands. He then wrote an entirely new speech to bring out the points that the occasion demanded. He was so engrossed in the job that he did not know when the plane landed at Kennedy Airport nor when he checked into the hotel in the evening. In the process he missed the formal reception given by Pakistan's permanent representative to the UN in honour of Ayub. The rest of the night was spent in typing and retyping the speech. Ayub saw the speech after breakfast next morning and made several changes which entailed another spell of retyping. As a result Ayub arrived at the UN a few minutes after the scheduled time. The assembly chamber was packed to capacity and Ayub spoke with great feeling. The Indian delegate staged his customary walk-out when Ayub demanded, 'Let India honour her agreement as we would, to let all the people of Kashmir settle their own future through self-determination in accordance with past pledges.'[12]

Ayub arrived in Washington the following day. President Lyndon Johnson received him as he stepped out of the helicopter at the White House. After the formalities, the delegation was conducted into the White House and Johnson took Ayub by his arm and led him to a room toward the far end of the corridor. The members of the delegation sat waiting in the Cabinet room not knowing how long they would have to wait for the two Presidents to reappear. After a while George Ball, the US Secretary of State, said, 'Gentlemen, I am used to waiting for the President. It is most unlikely they will join us much before 12 o'clock.' That was around 10.30 in the morning. George Ball then suggested that perhaps the delegations might have a look at the draft communiqué prepared by the State Department. While the two Presidents were engaged in their discussion in private, the delegations started going through the draft. The very first paragraph reaffirmed the continuing interest of the United States in the maintenance of the sovereignty and territorial integrity of Pakistan. The State Department must have known that the Pakistani public would find such a reaffirmation somewhat belated if not thoroughly hypocritical. Throughout the crisis the Pakistan Foreign Office and the official media had maintained that the United States had let down Pakistan and equated her with the aggressor. The Information Secretary had a heated argument with Bhutto and Aziz Ahmad who seemed quite happy with the offensive paragraph. After some argument the paragraph was removed from the beginning of the communiqué to a position between paragraphs 3 and 4. Bhutto and Aziz Ahmad seemed extremely anxious to get the communiqué adopted without too much fuss.

By about 12.30 p.m. everyone was getting a little restive and the earlier stiff-lipped formality was beginning to dissolve into half-suppressed yawns. The two Presidents walked into the room a little after 1 o'clock and took their seats around the Cabinet table. Johnson had a coloured globe of the world before him which he kept spinning with his forefinger as he talked. He said Ayub and he had made the best possible use of every moment: 'We are very good friends and there is no one whom I admire more than Ayub and I deeply cherish his friendship.' He thought one or two more meetings between them would resolve all the problems. Johnson said Ayub had reassured him that he was deeply interested in maintaining friendship between the United States and Pakistan and that whatever tensions had appeared between the two countries could be removed. Ayub responded to Johnson's statement with no warmth at all. Almost as a formality he said he had great affection and regard for Johnson. Ayub said that there had been, unfortunately, a certain drift in the relations between the two countries but since security and peace were the common concern of both countries, any problems that were causing estrangement between the two could always be resolved. Ayub did not want to blame the US because it could be argued that the world situation changed and the pacts to which Pakistan had subscribed had lost their relevance. There had been the India-China War during which the US had come out in support of India. 'But the Kashmir problem must be resolved,' Ayub said with some emotion. He admitted that neither Pakistan nor the Kashmiri population could get all they wanted, but by the same token India too should be prepared to make reasonable concessions. First should be reduction of armed forces; the two countries should be free from mutual fear; US interests in the region would be promoted through peace in the subcontinent. If India could not comply with the United Nations resolutions then arbitration by an independent body was the only peaceful way to resolve the dispute.

Johnson put on his spectacles, which seemed a little out of shape, and gave a rambling survey of the world's trouble spots, starting with Rhodesia. He forecast the downfall of the Smith regime. The US wanted to avoid the use of force in Rhodesia. He then talked about France and said that the next vote for de Gaulle might be much smaller, and moved on to Indonesia where, he thought, a peculiar political evolution was taking place. The Indonesian Communist Party, PKI, was badly damaged as an institution but still Sukarno was necessary for the warring factions:

'To deny Sukarno would be to deny the revolution.' Johnson thought the outcome in Indonesia would depend on how the power struggle there was eventually resolved.

In the Soviet Union there had been no change in the power structure and Brezhnev was carrying on the traditional Soviet policies. Great Britain, he said, no longer had any particular influence on the general trends of policy affecting the world. The US would have to increase its defence budget substantially because of the situation in South East Asia. That was not a happy thing, but it was necessary. What had happened in Korea was a signal to the United States. In Vietnam things would get worse before they got any better. He had no doubt that public opinion in the United States was largely supportive of his policy in Vietnam but he would not deny that there was a small but articulate dissenting minority. America had no option but to honour its commitment to the people of South Vietnam. He was worried that the expression of dissent in the United States could be sending the wrong signal to Hanoi. But there was, and this he said with some passion, no failing of American resolve and there was 'not the slightest chance of our changing our position'. This was the price that had to be paid by an open society. The US would certainly not pull out of Vietnam the way the French had done. Hanoi had adopted 'a most rigid position' but the United States had no problem of contact with Beijing or Hanoi. The problem was that 'there was absolutely no sign of give on the North Vietnamese side.' The United States had 'a big reservoir of manpower and weapons' but the terrain was not particularly suitable. He admitted that the Americans were not quite clear about the long-term Chinese objectives in the region. The Soviet Union was providing arms and supplies to the North Vietnamese whereas the Chinese were providing equipment and training facilities and a number of Chinese were working on railroads. The meeting adjourned at around a quarter past two in the afternoon, to reassemble at 5.30 p.m.[13]

When the meeting reassembled, Johnson resumed his review of the world situation. He explained that if the United States developed friendship with some country it was never to the exclusion of its traditional allies. He repeated that there was no leader with whom he had greater rapport than Ayub. He hoped that Tashkent would be a success. Ayub had assured him that Pakistan would do nothing inimical to US interests and that if he found that the United States was being treated unfairly in Pakistan he would certainly take steps to stop that. The United States was a friend of all the smaller countries in South Asia, and spinning the globe, Johnson growled: 'If any big country tries to gobble up a smaller country, I will be there.' He concluded: 'President Ayub has asked for nothing and he's going back with everything we have got.' He hoped that the United States would be able to regain the brotherly love and confidence of the people of Pakistan: 'I regret that we did not meet a year or two years ago.'

Ayub was brief in his response. He said: 'Let us hope we get more comfort in future out of our alliance with the US.' Pakistan could not dictate American policy but the United States should 'understand our difficulties and our position'. He regretted that US and Soviet policy had come to coincide in India; that was why the Soviet Union was continuing to help India and the US too had allowed itself to be 'suckered' by the Indians. However, he promised that Pakistan would use its influence for moderation, and invited Johnson to visit Pakistan. As Ayub finished, Bhutto nudged the Information Secretary and whispered, 'He has given in.'[14]

The parleys in Tashkent

Ayub returned from his visit to the United States deeply disappointed. He had failed in his major objective, which was to persuade the United States and the United Kingdom not to pass on the initiative in the region to the Soviet Union. He had hoped to persuade them to exercise some pressure on India to come to an agreement about establishing some machinery to resolve the Kashmir dispute. The only response he got was that Indo-Pakistan problems had been put in the lap of the Soviet Union. He was politely but firmly told that the United States and its western allies believed that the Soviet Union alone could prevent the kind of

polarization of power, which the West dreaded most, with the
Soviet Union and India on one side and China and Pakistan on the
other. Should such polarization occur, the United States would
have to come out on the side of India and that would enlarge the
sphere of conflict. The United States was badly embroiled in the
Vietnamese War and found the prospects of engaging the Chinese
in the subcontinent alarming. The Soviet Union, too, would not
wish to get involved in a conflict with China under any
circumstances. These two considerations made the Soviet Union
the most appropriate intermediary in the situation.

Ayub had a meeting with his ministers on 31 December 1965,
in Rawalpindi, on the eve of his departure for Tashkent via Kabul.
All the ministers were present as were the Governor of West
Pakistan, Nawab Kalabagh, the Commander-in-Chief of the Army,
General Musa, and the Speaker of the National Assembly, Abdul
Jabbar. The only minister absent was Altaf Hussain, who was
away in Manila to represent Pakistan at the swearing-in ceremony
of President Marcos. Ayub started by saying that he did not know
what to expect of Tashkent. The first hurdle would be to get an
agreed agenda and that was not going to be easy. The issues of
prime importance for Pakistan were, and this was the order in
which Ayub listed them: withdrawal of forces; settlement of
Kashmir; proportionate reduction of forces, and adoption of a no-
war declaration once there was agreement on the first three items.
After that a permanent mechanism could be established to resolve
other problems. In his judgement, the Indians might agree to the
withdrawal of forces but they would not yield on Kashmir. He
asked: Where do we go from there? Should we break all contact
with India? Khwaja Shahabuddin said that the forthcoming Indian
elections would make India's position on Kashmir even more
rigid. The right-wing of the Congress party would make it
extremely difficult for Shastri to agree to any concession on
Kashmir. Nawab Kalabagh pointed out that the few Indian leaders,
who had been talking in terms of a peaceful settlement of Kashmir,
certainly did not represent the mainstream of Indian opinion. The
Finance Minister, Muhammad Shoaib, thought that Tashkent
should be used to settle other peripheral problems like enemy

property, overflights, etc. It was left to the Home Minister, Ali Akbar, to emphasize that the most important issue for Pakistan was the settlement of the Kashmir problem. General Musa interrupted him to say that India would never negotiate on the basis of Kashmir being anything other than a part of India. Ayub admitted that the chances were that the Soviet Union would apply more pressure on Pakistan than they would on India. The important thing was for Pakistan to be clear about its stand on Kashmir. He talked about the Mujahideen sometimes using the word 'infiltrators' for them. Bhutto said that his understanding of the Soviet position was that they would 'lean toward India' but he advised that Tashkent should be approached as an opportunity since it was not exclusively a Soviet initiative. It had the backing of the United States, Britain, and the UN. Ayub said: 'I know people who want to risk Pakistan for the sake of Kashmir.'[15]

Before Ayub took off from Peshawar for Kabul *en route* to Tashkent on 1 January 1966, Averell Harriman, US special envoy, called on him and conveyed a message from President Johnson wishing him good luck. Ayub told him that he was going with an open mind: 'I don't think much can come out of it. The Indians are in no mood to be reasonable.'[16] After his meeting with Ayub, Harriman went to Delhi on 2 January. It was not clear why Ayub decided to spend two days in Kabul before going to Tashkent. Perhaps because Shastri, too, was going to stop at Kabul. The stay in Kabul was devoted to the discussion of Pakistan-Afghanistan problems and although the Afghans, including the King, Mohammad Zahir Shah, were polite, there was not much enthusiasm for the Ayub mission to Tashkent. Zahir Shah said to Ayub at one point: 'General, you have to be strong.' And Ayub replied: 'Yes, in the end you have to fight your own battle.'[17]

Tashkent at last

Ayub arrived in Tashkent in bright sunlight on the afternoon of 3 January. The Soviets had taken enormous pains to give equal treatment to the Indian and Pakistan delegations. Ayub had his

own villa and the rest of the delegation was put up at the Central
Committee rest-house, which was comfortable. The Indians were
taken to their destination by a different route. Both routes were
bedecked with exactly the same number of national flags and it
appeared that the same number of people had been lined up to
cheer the two leaders on their arrival. Shastri was a short, thin
man, and the crowds were chanting 'Little Lenin' as he went past
them in an open car.

The Pakistan delegation assembled at Ayub's villa on the
afternoon of 3 January for a formal discussion. The delegates
were a little put out when they were told that the Foreign Office
had neither prepared any provisional agenda for the conference
nor the draft of Ayub's opening speech. How could Aziz Ahmad,
an extremely hardworking and punctilious person, have not
foreseen the need for preparing an opening statement for Ayub?
Perhaps the Foreign Office no longer knew what to say or it had
lost contact with Ayub. It was known that Aziz Ahmad was going
to be replaced by S.M. Yusuf, who was Ayub's Principal Secretary,
and was a member of the delegation. Ayub mentioned the points
he wanted to make in his opening statement. He thought it would
be a good idea to begin by recalling the historical links between
the people of Pakistan and the people of Tashkent, and end by
stressing that what Pakistan hoped to achieve was 'not a semblance
but substance of peace'. The root cause of the conflict should be
mentioned and the need for its resolution emphasized. He wanted
the speech to end on an optimistic note. It was suggested that the
statement must mention the Kashmir dispute as forcefully as
possible. Bhutto felt that it would not be appropriate to make a
pointed reference to Kashmir in the opening statement. Once
again the Information Secretary was assigned the task of preparing
Ayub's speech at short notice. Bhutto saw the draft and thought
that it read extremely well. The statement did mention 'the basic
problem' confronting India and Pakistan, but there was no specific
mention of Kashmir. It was only after Ayub had read the statement
at the inaugural session on 4 January that Aziz Ahmad said to the
Information Secretary: 'I shall never forgive myself for agreeing
to this omission.' The Indian Press did not fail to notice the

omission and claimed that Ayub had not uttered the words 'Jammu and Kashmir dispute' in order to avoid a strong Indian reaction.

The Information Secretary was designated as the official spokesman for Pakistan. Over 500 journalists from all over the world were in attendance, including a large contingent from India. The spokesman was required to convey to the Press that Pakistan had not come to Tashkent to abandon its historic position on Kashmir. The more convincingly he made this point the better it would serve Pakistan's negotiating strategy. More specifically, he must dispel the impression that Pakistan would sign a no-war pact with India without any understanding on Kashmir.

On the morning of 5 January, Ayub had a meeting with Shastri, while Bhutto met the Indian Foreign Minister, Swaran Singh, in the afternoon. Following that, Bhutto had a long discussion with the Soviet Foreign Minister, Andrei Gromyko. Neither after the inaugural session nor the next day did Bhutto give any indication to anyone in the delegation that he was in any way upset about the way things were going. The Press was told on 6 January that Ayub was in Tashkent to discuss 'the totality of our relationship with India' and this included the crucial question of Kashmir. The Indian Foreign Secretary, C.S. Jha, told the Press that 'Kashmir was not negotiable' while the Pakistan Information Secretary maintained that the results of Tashkent would be judged by the success that was achieved in resolving the basic problem affecting Indo-Pakistan relations. Pakistan had come to Tashkent with an open mind but that did not mean a mind open at both ends. A belligerent Indian journalist, who seemed a little worked up, started shouting that since Kashmir was not negotiable what was the point of Tashkent? He did go on a little, so the Information Secretary reminded him that according to Hindu philosophy even irreconcilables could be reconciled. He must have realized later that the saying had been made up for his benefit but, at the time, it left him leaning against the wall, a little open-mouthed and a bit lost.

On 6 January Ayub briefed the delegation at lunch about his talks with Shastri. Shastri, he said, seemed a reasonable man but kept insisting: 'General, you must appreciate my position. I have a very difficult job at home. I have stepped into the shoes of a giant and I am really too small for the job.' Ayub said he tried to humour Shastri and reminded him that history had cast him in a great role and he could make a lasting contribution to peace in the region by taking some positive step to resolve the Jammu and Kashmir dispute. But Shastri kept talking of his domestic problems and how much he was answerable to public opinion. Ayub's impression was that there was no possibility of Shastri yielding on Kashmir, despite Soviet pressure, but he would probably agree to the withdrawal of forces. When Ayub was relating how Shastri kept saying that he was answerable to the people, Bhutto interrupted him and said quite sharply: 'But you too are answerable to the people. You don't have a heavenly mandate.' That was the first indication of Bhutto's unhappiness with the way negotiations were proceeding. He was depressed about the results of his own meeting with Swaran Singh because the Indian Foreign Minister gave him no indication of India's willingness to concede any of Pakistan's demands. If anything, he had been more emphatic than his Prime Minister that there could be no question of India modifying its declared position on Kashmir. The Soviets did not find the Indian position unreasonable. They were suggesting that Pakistan should realize that Kashmir was a complicated matter and that any machinery for its resolution could not be established in Tashkent. Bhutto failed to persuade Swaran Singh even to put Kashmir on the Tashkent agenda.

On 6 January there was a meeting between Ayub and Kosygin at Ayub's villa. Bhutto, Aziz Ahmad, Iqbal Athar, who was Pakistan's Ambassador in Moscow, and the Information Secretary attended the meeting. Kosygin was accompanied by Gromyko, Marshal Malinovsky, the Defence Minister, and Lilachov, the Director of South East Asian Affairs. Kosygin said the meeting was a continuation of his talks with Ayub the previous evening. He had benefited from Ayub's counsel and would like to put forward some suggestions of his own. He mentioned his meeting with Shastri and said they had discussed all the issues that they felt should be settled for the good of both sides. He emphasized that Tashkent must leave its imprint on history. That would be in the interest of both India and Pakistan. If the meeting ended in discord, and there were signs of rupture, it would only please the enemies of India, Pakistan and the Soviet Union. On the other hand, any understanding between India and Pakistan would be a source of joy to progressive peoples all over the world. If no document of peace was adopted in Tashkent the world would be left with the impression that disputes can be settled only by force. Since the two countries had no 'organic contradiction', it would be a tragedy if they were to rely on force as the only means of solving their problems. Kosygin looked at Bhutto and said: 'I can see from the Foreign Minister's face that his meeting with the Indian Foreign Minister has not been encouraging.' He then looked at Gromyko and said: 'Our Foreign Minister is also looking glum.' Gromyko said he was quite cheerful and he had reason to be since he had not had any lunch and was looking forward to the Pakistani banquet in the evening. Kosygin then handed over the Soviet draft of what would come to be known as the Tashkent Declaration and told Ayub that he had also given a copy of it to Shastri. He did not want it to be treated as a Soviet document, and invited Ayub to suggest alternative formulations. He added, 'One can look at a document in different ways and Foreign Ministers know how a document can be drawn up or torn apart.' He indicated that Shastri had, with great difficulty, agreed to include the reference to Jammu and Kashmir in the document. He felt it would have been useful to have a reference also to some machinery to solve the Kashmir dispute but Shastri had not accepted that. The Soviet Union had exhausted its good offices, and the draft agreement he was offering was the maximum that could be achieved under the circumstances.

After Kosygin left, the draft was examined clause by clause. Bhutto was not too unhappy with the Soviet draft and said that although the Indians had not agreed to the establishment of a self-executing machinery, it was quite an achievement to have persuaded them to include a reference to Jammu and Kashmir in the document. But he agreed that it would be extremely difficult to sell the document to the people back home.[18]

On 6 January, the Chinese had given a formal warning to India that: 'The Chinese side will resolutely strike back if India continued her intrusions and provocations along their Himalayan border.' The Chinese note condemned India for her 'frenzied effort to create tension'.[19]

It was in the middle of all this tension that Bhutto mentioned to the Information Secretary that 5 January was his birthday. The Information Secretary invited his colleagues to dinner where Bhutto was given a birthday present. Bhutto wrote him a letter warmly appreciating the gesture.

On 7 January, Kosygin had more than one separate meeting with Ayub and Shastri. Ayub finally decided to reject the Soviet draft and Arshad Hussain, Pakistan's High Commissioner in Delhi, was deputed to convey Pakistan's decision to the Indian Foreign Minister. Arshad Hussain came back and reported to Ayub that when he told Swaran Singh that Pakistan could not accept the draft, he was dumbfounded and did not speak for a few moments. At lunch that day at Ayub's villa, Khwaja Shahabuddin was wearing an elegant dark suit and a natty bow-tie which gave him quite a youthful look. Bhutto was in a roguish mood. Addressing Ayub he said, 'Your Information Minister will soon be acquiring a young bride.' This caused considerable amusement and Bhutto proceeded to spin out a theory about women and how they had exploited men throughout the ages: it was part of a global conspiracy to depict women as the victims of male chauvinism.

After lunch Bhutto, Aziz Ahmad and the Information Secretary went over the Soviet draft once again. When it came to the clause relating to the resolution of disputes without the use of force, a heated argument development between Bhutto and Aziz Ahmad. The Soviet draft provided: 'The two sides will settle disputes through peaceful means without the application of force.'[20] Bhutto wrote down a revised formulation which read: 'The two sides will try and solve disputes through peaceful means.' When Bhutto handed over the paper on which he had written this Aziz Ahmad rolled it into a ball and threw it back at him. Bhutto went pale as Aziz Ahmad almost shouted: 'Let's have no nonsense about peaceful means.' The Information Secretary picked up that piece of paper and put it with his notes.

By now the hope that Tashkent might result in the setting up of a machinery for the resolution of the Kashmir dispute had been abandoned. There was a great deal of bickering and tension within the Pakistan delegation. One reason was that Aziz Ahmad was anxious that his long career in the Civil Service should not end on a note of disaster. He was, therefore, taking a particularly hard line during the negotiations, hoping to salvage something out of the wreckage of his diplomacy.

By the evening of 8 January all contact between the two delegations had ceased. Gromyko held a meeting with the two Foreign Ministers which continued during a soirée arranged by the hosts for the two delegations. At the press briefing that day the Pakistan spokesman was asked whether Pakistan would go back from Tashkent without a joint communiqué. His answer was that a communiqué was not a return ticket and the Pakistan delegation could certainly go back to Islamabad without a communiqué. Has Tashkent failed? It would be premature to say that, was his reply. It was becoming extremely difficult to maintain the pretence that the talks were continuing when, in fact, they had broken down.[21]

The Indian and Pakistani delegations were invited to a musical performance in which several Uzbek artists participated. During the performance, which went on for two hours, Kosygin sat between Ayub and Shastri. The repertoire included several Urdu and Hindi songs. The one that brought the house down carried the refrain in Hindi: *Hai Ram, mujh ko budda mil giya* (Oh god, how did I get hitched to this old man). It was during the course of this evening that Kosygin persuaded Shastri and Ayub not to abandon the hope of coming to an agreement.

Early next morning, 9 January, the Information Secretary went to Ayub's villa and found that he and Kosygin had gone somewhere outside Tashkent. The other members of the delegation were busy with their own meetings or sightseeing. When Ayub came back he invited the Information Secretary to a walk in the beautiful lawns around the villa. Kosygin had taken him to see an aircraft factory and shown him how many aircraft were produced there every month. He then mentioned the number of such factories in the Soviet Union and the total number of aircraft, tanks and guns that

were manufactured by the Soviet Union every year. Kosygin said
the days of conventional war were over. The two superpowers,
and their major allies, had developed weapons of ultimate
destruction and for countries like India and Pakistan, which could
only fight a limited war for a brief period, it was madness to
embark on the settlement of their disputes through the use of
force. He told Ayub there were still 70,000 old German tanks
embedded in Soviet soil. For Third World countries war was no
longer a means of resolving their disputes. Ayub was deeply
impressed by what Kosygin told him. 'How do you view the
prospects?' he asked the Information Secretary, who replied:
'Tashkent is an opportunity but it could turn into a trap.' He added
that public reaction in Pakistan would be one of extreme frustration
if Ayub signed any agreement that did not give the people the
feeling that Pakistan had made some substantive gain on Kashmir.[22]

A meeting was fixed for Ayub with Kosygin on the evening of
9 January. It was this meeting which decided the fate of Tashkent
and the future course of events in Pakistan. The draft declaration
was taken up once again for a clause-by-clause examination.
Much time and argument was spent in getting the right words for
the paragraph relating to the non-use of force. When Ayub kept
insisting that there must be some reference to the need for a
machinery to resolve the Kashmir dispute, Kosygin, looking quite
exhausted, turned to Ayub and said in a calm and studied manner,
'Mr President, it is too late to insist on that. Your Foreign Minister
gave us an assurance in Moscow that Kashmir will not be made
the decisive point in these negotiations.' And turning to Bhutto he
said, 'Is that not correct?' Bhutto kept quiet. He spoke only once
after that when the item about hostile propaganda by the two sides
came under discussion. As the paragraph was being read, the
Information Secretary shook his head in disagreement. Kosygin
noticed that and said to Ayub: 'Your friend does not seem to like
this.' Bhutto intervened to say that the paragraph should be
deleted. Kosygin crushed him with the retort that it would be most
unreasonable to say that the two sides wanted to have peaceful
relations but would carry on hostile propaganda against each
other.

Tashkent was over. Pakistan accepted the Declaration proposed by Kosygin with such amendments and revisions as were agreed to that evening. The Declaration was signed at a formal ceremony on 10 January. There were no secret protocols, appendices, or letters annexed to the Tashkent Declaration.

Ayub and Shastri separately met a group of Soviet journalists after signing the Declaration. Shastri said the Declaration had achieved tangible results, of which the most important was that a concrete step had been taken toward the restoration of genuinely peaceful relations between India and Pakistan. Ayub congratulated the Soviet Union on the results they had achieved in Tashkent. Asked how he would evaluate those results, he expressed the hope that the Declaration would help to normalize Indo-Pakistan relations and reduce the tensions and the temperature: 'The Declaration has not gone as far as it should have done,' he said. The solution of the Kashmir dispute should have been attempted because that was the basic problem and the real concern of the people. Once the Kashmir dispute was settled it would bring great relief to the people of India and Pakistan. One day, 'the Indian leaders will realize the value of settling the Kashmir dispute because they have a lot to gain by this'. Ayub emphasized the need for the two countries to reduce their defence expenditure so that national resources could be devoted to the welfare of the people. To the question whether the right kind of psychological climate could be created to consolidate peaceful relations between India and Pakistan, Ayub replied: 'We will genuinely play our part, let us hope India does the same, but it is not the psychological climate which will normalize relations, it is the settlement of the basic dispute.' Asked about Soviet-Pakistan relations, Ayub said: 'We are your neighbours separated by about seventeen miles of Afghan territory. The consciousness is dawning that there is need for close friendly relations between Pakistan and the Soviet Union: Pakistan had made a late start but mutual confidence was growing.'[23]

There was a farewell banquet on 10 January. Formal toasts were proposed and the banquet concluded quite early. Ayub and Shastri were standing together saying goodbye to the guests.

When the Information Secretary was saying good-night to Shastri, Ayub put his hand on his shoulder and said: 'The Prime Minister is very keen that propaganda by the two sides against each other should stop immediately.' Pakistan's Press and radio had made quite an impact on world opinion and the Indians were extremely worried about that. The Information Secretary nodded as Shastri held his hand. He would later remember the warmth of Shastri's grip. Back in the rest-house the Information Secretary joined three other officers in a game of bridge. They were sitting in a small room adjacent to the one occupied by Khwaja Shahabuddin. There was a sound of groaning coming from that room but they thought it was the minister snoring. No one suspected that the minister had suffered a heart attack and the groans were those of suffocation. After the game the Information Secretary returned to his room and soon fell asleep. He was woken up by a loud knocking. He shot out of bed and opened the door. He was confronted by a sombre-looking Asghar Khan who told him that Shastri had died of a heart attack and his body was to be flown over to India. Would he arrange to get the necessary clearance for the Indian aircraft to fly over Pakistan territory? The Information Secretary got in touch with Ayub's Military Secretary and asked him to convey the sad news to Ayub. By eight o'clock all the officials were on their way to the airport. Every single flag along the four-mile route was flying at half mast. The Soviet officials must have worked through the night to lower the flags on hundreds of ceremonial poles. The airport was a scene of mourning. At the tarmac Kosygin and Ayub were standing near Shastri's coffin. Kosygin touched Ayub's elbow and the two moved forward to help lift the coffin into the aircraft. The picture of Ayub acting as Shastri's pallbearer caused an outrage in Pakistan and the Information Secretary was blamed for not having blocked its release.

A couple of hours later the Pakistani delegation was back at the airport to board the PIA plane on their way back to Islamabad. A little before their departure Kosygin took Ayub aside and told him that the despatches of Ayub's press conference had been withheld. Kosygin felt that the publication of Ayub's criticism of the Tashkent Declaration at that moment would be extremely harmful.

Fortunately the text of Ayub's statement had been transmitted to Pakistan and most newspapers did report and comment on whatever Ayub had told the Soviet journalists. As the plane was approaching Pakistan, Ayub wanted to know what he should say on his arrival in Islamabad. A statement had been prepared for him but Bhutto and Aziz Ahmad persuaded him not to say anything on arrival. This was a most unfortunate piece of advice but Ayub accepted it. Like the foreign policy of Pakistan the publicity policy too was now in shambles. Publicity ever since Gibraltar, had been geared to the foreign policy of Pakistan, and when the foreign policy disintegrated, official propaganda turned into a burlesque.

NOTES

1. *The Times,* London, 7 September 1965. Wilson's statement came in for severe criticism in India. Later when Noel-Baker, Labour MP for Swindon, asked him why he had issued such a statement Wilson said in a letter,

   > ...the news on 6 September, that the Indian Army less four divisions, was attacking in the Punjab, suggested that India's aim was the military defeat of Pakistan. The public reaction to the news of the Indian attack demanded it. The subsequent explanation by the Indians of why they attacked does not invalidate the point. The Indian attack came immediately after the UN appeal.
   > *(The Times,* 6 January 1966).

2. Ibid., 2 November 1965.
3. Ibid., 28 October 1965. A special correspondent's report.
4. Ibid., 24 November 1965.
5. Ibid., 26 November 1965.
6. *Dawn,* 26 November 1965.
7. Author's notes.
8. Ibid., 27 November 1965.
9. *Dawn,* 2 December 1965.
10. Author's notes of the meeting.
11. The OAU Council of Ministers had called upon Britain to 'crush the rebellion and restore law and order in Southern Rhodesia preparing the way for majority government.' Author's notes and *Keesings Archives,* 1965. *The Times,* London.
12. *The Times,* London, found the speech 'remarkable for its straight-forwardness and moderation'. 14 December 1965.
13. Author's notes of the meeting.
14. Ibid.
15. Ibid.

16. Ibid.
17. Ibid.
18. Ibid.
19. *Dawn,* 8 January 1966.
20. Ibid., 9 January 1966.
21. Ibid., 8 January 1966.
22. Author's notes.
23. *Dawn,* 11 January 1966.

CHAPTER 11

Tashkent Backlash

It did not take Bhutto long to recognize the profound frustration and anger of the people and their unwillingness to accept the Tashkent Declaration. The public reaction in Punjab was far more severe than in the other provinces of West Pakistan. Only in East Pakistan, where people had experienced a terrible sense of isolation during the war, the Declaration was received with a sense of relief. Ayub's popularity plummeted from the heights it had touched before the cease-fire. Ayub asked Bhutto to issue a statement explaining the advantages of the Declaration but he wriggled out of it and came up with the astonishing suggestion that the best course would be to disclaim the Declaration! Ayub shut him up: 'There is no point in talking absolute nonsense.' For some reason Ayub continued to resist the advice that he should make a detailed statement about what had transpired in Tashkent. Bhutto left for Larkana and there he stayed for some time spreading all kinds of little canards. He talked informally to some Western journalists and hinted that the Declaration was not the only document that Ayub had signed in Tashkent and that there was a protocol to the Declaration which had been kept secret. Since these 'disclosures' were being made by the Foreign Minister himself most journalists accepted them. Bhutto knew that his days in Ayub's government were numbered so he was busy distancing himself from Tashkent. Bhutto had been fully involved in the negotiations in Tashkent. Every day he would discuss with the Information Secretary the lines on which the Press should be briefed. He had been involved in the drafting and adoption of the Declaration, and he was deliberately falsifying the record when he started suggesting that Ayub had signed some secret protocol along with the Declaration.

On 12 January Ayub called a Cabinet meeting to which the three Commanders-in-Chief were also invited. Ayub said that Tashkent was the first instance where the Soviet Union had offered its good offices to resolve any dispute between two countries. They had done so because they realized that peace in Asia depended on the normalization of relations between India and Pakistan. But their major concern was the People's Republic of China. The growing Pakistan-China friendship could create a situation where the Russians might find themselves aligned with India against China—a situation they wanted to avoid at all costs. Earlier, Afghanistan had been a kind of non-man's land between the Soviet Union and the Indian subcontinent. Now a vast network of roads had been built and enough landing strips were available to move up to ten army divisions. All these facilities had been created by the US and the Soviet Union could not ignore that a hostile force could advance from Peshawar to Tirmiz in a single day.

Ayub said that he had gone to Tashkent without any hope that the problem of Kashmir would be resolved, but there was always the possibility that Tashkent might provide an opening for co-existence with India. India might realize the cost of continuing the Kashmir dispute. There was also the belief that a meeting on Soviet soil could not remain barren and that the Indians would respond to reason. Ayub explained that Pakistan could not have walked out of Tashkent as that would have meant rebuffing the Soviet Union when the United States and all other major powers had pledged their support to the Soviet initiative. After such a rebuff the Soviet Union would have continued to block any initiative on Kashmir in the Security Council by exercising its veto. Ayub said he had told Kosygin that Kashmir was of paramount importance; all other issues were subsidiary. But India was not prepared to move an inch on Kashmir. The only kind of settlement the Indians had in mind was to adopt the cease-fire line as the international boundary between the Indian-held Kashmir and Azad Kashmir, with some minor adjustments. The choice was to break or make a compromise. The difficulty was that the responsibility for the breakdown would have been attributed to Pakistan and this would have encouraged the extremist elements in the country. Ayub said he had faced a stone wall during his meetings with Shastri. He admitted: 'Militarily we have not been able to demolish the wall. We have to wait.' He described India's growing military strength and emphasized the need for Pakistan to gain time: 'Pakistan just has to wait till India acquires an effective rival to prevent her from free-wheeling.' The Indians had come to Tashkent under the impression that Pakistan was desperate for withdrawal of forces from the borders. They wanted Pakistan to sign a no-war pact, and give a guarantee that there would be no further violation of the cease-fire line and that Pakistan would have no contact with any third power. The last point was of particular importance to them because it would have secured them an undertaking from Pakistan not to develop any further relations with China. These demands suited the Soviet Union also, and Pakistan had to fight hard to establish that unless the basic problem of Kashmir was resolved, conflict between India and Pakistan would continue. In the meantime the wisest thing for the two sides was to bring down their forces to a tolerable level. Ayub said that the reaction to Tashkent had been quite favourable in East Pakistan but there were certain elements in West Pakistan who would continue to agitate: 'We must deal with them firmly.' He knew that 'carrying out any agreement with the Hindu was not easy, but we must give Tashkent Declaration a trial. There must be no bad faith from our side'. Ayub recalled his meeting with Shastri on the day the Declaration was signed. He had asked him whether he could fly over Pakistan territory on his return journey and Ayub had agreed. Summing up his impressions of Tashkent, Ayub said that as far as Kosygin was concerned he had come to see the importance of resolving the Kashmir dispute. He quoted Kosygin as saying: 'It requires thought.'

Throughout the meeting Bhutto did not say anything though he promised to issue a statement on Tashkent at the appropriate time. Because of Bhutto's silence on the subject the impression gained ground among the people that he was most unhappy with the

Declaration because Ayub had surrendered at the negotiating table whatever the armed forces had gained on the ground. Senior army officers privately applauded Bhutto for his patriotism. GHQ was carrying on its own publicity campaign. The Commander-in-Chief of the Air Force, an aggressive self-publicist, had built up quite a reputation, not entirely undeserved, as a war hero. Everyone basked in the sun while Ayub was left out in the cold.

Agitation against Tashkent began in West Pakistan around 13 January. It soon spread to different colleges and universities. In Lahore, the police opened fire on a large group of demonstrators and two students were killed. On 14 January all educational institutions were closed. Bhutto issued his first statement on 14 January in extremely guarded terms. He denied a Press report that he had asked the students to concentrate on their studies. This was as far as he wanted to go at that stage to encourage the agitation without an open break with Ayub. His game was clear: if the administration failed to control the agitation he would join the agitators to topple the regime, and if it was suppressed he would stay on in office for as long as possible.

The agitation began gathering momentum. There were more protest meetings in Rawalpindi, Lahore and Multan and more casualties. Lahore and Tharparkar were placed under curfew and West Pakistan was buzzing with rumours of grave differences between Ayub and Bhutto. On 29 January Ayub denied these rumours. He addressed a meeting of civil and military officials at GHQ Hall. Bhutto was absent from the meeting because of 'ill health' but Mrs Bhutto was present. In his speech Ayub stressed that Tashkent was not a one-man decision. In his broadcast on 1 February Ayub focused on Tashkent and advised the people to do some cool thinking.

A few days later Ayub began his tour of Sindh which included a visit to Larkana. Ayub told Bhutto, on 5 February, that he had decided to relieve him of his position in the Cabinet. Bhutto pleaded that his immediate exit from the Cabinet would only encourage the agitation. He asked Ayub to allow him to stay on for a little while longer and promised to make a series of statements supporting the Tashkent Declaration. Ayub agreed. Bhutto could not have planned it better for himself. All he had to do was to tell stories about Tashkent which politicians, officials, and journalists accepted without hesitation because they came from such an authoritative source. They admired Bhutto for his courage because he was obviously running the risk of annoying Ayub. No one in the government knew that Ayub had told Bhutto that he had decided to expel him from the Cabinet. The impression was that Bhutto had explained everything to Ayub and there was no misunderstanding between them any more.

The right wing Opposition in West Pakistan condemned the Declaration as a humiliating document. A two-day conference of all the opposition parties, with the exception of the National Awami Party, was convened in Lahore on 5 February where a resolution moved by Maulana Maududi was unanimously adopted, condemning the Tashkent Declaration as detrimental to Pakistan's interests. The West Pakistan government imposed a black-out on the proceedings of the meeting. It was at this meeting that Sheikh Mujib presented his six-points programme. None of the Opposition leaders criticized that programme, nor did anyone dissociate himself from it. To cover their own political bankruptcy they floated a ridiculous rumour that Mujib's six-points had been drafted by the Information Secretary at the behest of Ayub to disunite the Opposition.

On 9 February Bhutto issued his second press statement as he had promised Ayub. He said that the Declaration must be judged in its totality as a means to settle the Kashmir issue. Following the statement, Nawabzada Nasrullah Khan, Malik Ghulam Jilani, Sardar Zafrullah, Khwaja M. Rafiq, and Sardar Shaukat Hayat were arrested. The following day all school and college examinations in West Pakistan were postponed for a month.

The agitation against Tashkent was now beginning to founder because it had received no support from East Pakistan. Bhutto returned to the limelight when he welcomed the US Vice-President, Hubert Humphrey in Islamabad. It was announced that Indo-Pakistan ministerial talks would start in Rawalpindi on 1 March, with Bhutto leading the Pakistani delegation. Bhutto told the Press that Kashmir would be the main issue in the talks. The

Opposition parties in East Pakistan did not condemn Tashkent but they claimed, not without justification, that the September War had thoroughly exposed the absurdity of the army's cherished doctrine that the defence of East Pakistan lay in the plains of West Pakistan. East Pakistan had been left entirely defenceless during the war. They now demanded that East Pakistan must have adequate military capability of its own to defend itself.

Friendship with China

On one point there was complete agreement among the people of East and West Pakistan. They supported Pakistan's growing friendship with the People's Republic of China and shared a profound sense of gratitude for Chinese support to Pakistan during the war. But for China's support, things could have taken a disastrous turn. The Chinese leaders were not happy with the results of Tashkent and Chinese media criticized the Declaration, but in mild terms. Ayub's problem was to convince the Chinese that Tashkent did not mean Pakistan ganging up with the Soviet Union to normalize its relations with India. Simultaneously, he had to reassure the Soviet leaders that Pakistan was fully conscious of the value of Soviet friendship. He had also to persuade the US Government that Pakistan was not about to create a situation in which the Chinese threat to India might plunge the whole region into war.

With East Pakistan demanding virtual independence and West Pakistan deeply frustrated over Tashkent, Ayub was sitting on top of a political volcano. Pakistan's national interests were driving him towards China and superpower interests were pulling him in the opposite direction. The Central Government was demoralized and divided, and Ayub was left with only one option: the option of repression. For this he had to rely on his provincial governors and they proceeded to put down the agitation by the use of indiscriminate force.

Indo-Pakistan ministerial meeting

The withdrawal of forces was proceeding apace and was expected to be completed before the Indo-Pakistan ministerial meeting in March 1966. A co-ordinating committee was established to oversee the implementation of Tashkent Declaration. Aziz Ahmad, still the Foreign Secretary, prepared a memorandum outlining the negotiating strategy for the ministerial meeting. The Indian plan, he said, was crystal clear. The Indians wanted to build up a façade of Indo-Pakistan friendship behind which they could bury the Kashmir dispute. They were desperate to convince the world that Tashkent had transformed Indo-Pakistan relations; hostility had given way to friendship and all tensions had disappeared in the benign environment of good neighbourliness. The Foreign Secretary claimed that the US was compelling India to settle the Kashmir dispute by denying it economic and military aid. This was a complete somersault because the Foreign Office had been fiercely arguing for months that the economic and military measures taken by the US against India and Pakistan were hurting Pakistan much more than India. The Foreign Secretary also claimed that countries such as the Soviet Union, France and the UK had been deeply stirred by the recent Indo-Pakistan war, but he failed to mention that the stirring was caused not by the seventeen-day war but by the fear of Chinese intervention.

The Foreign Secretary designate, S.M. Yusuf, was extremely critical of the strategy proposed by Aziz Ahmad. He said that for Pakistan to maintain the threat of renewed conflict as a negotiating lever was an exercise in futility. Pakistan had 'conceded the substance of a no-war agreement' in Tashkent, the rest was 'a matter of words'. He did not think that Pakistan's refusal either to return Indian property seized during the war or restore transit facilities through East Pakistan would create such a great crisis for the Indians that they would be forced to come to a settlement on Kashmir. Nor did he think that the world was overly concerned about the Indo-Pakistan conflict: 'The major powers have made it clear that they favour the partition of Kashmir along the cease-fire line.' In the forthcoming ministerial meeting Kashmir must be discussed 'but a deadlock should not be created if agreement was not forthcoming'. He felt it would be better to seek the restoration of normal conditions in occupied Kashmir by asking for the release of prisoners, rehabilitation of refugees and restoration of civil liberties.

The Information Secretary gave his assessment of the prevailing opinion in the country. The people had watched, with growing frustration, the government resile and retreat from its proclaimed positions. The government's initial negative response to the cease-fire resolution of 20 September was followed by the acceptance of cease-fire: the resolution first rejected as totally unacceptable was later described as a victory for Pakistan; the threat to quit the United Nations and to wage a thousand-year war was followed by the signing of the Tashkent Declaration in which Jammu and Kashmir barely received a mention. As a result the government stood discredited and isolated from the people. The fact could no longer be disputed that the war had been undertaken without proper planning and that the whole adventure was built on a series of false and fanciful assumptions. The government was now offering two reasons for its failure: the numerical superiority of the Indian armed forces, and the hostile attitude of the great powers. Surely both these factors were well known before hostilities were provoked. Instead of reducing the existing tension between the two countries, the Declaration had in fact increased mutual hostility. India was under no real compulsion to enter into any agreement, open or secret, with Pakistan on Kashmir.

March saw a number of developments. The first was the two-day meeting between the Foreign Ministers of India and Pakistan. The results of the meeting were exactly what S.M. Yusuf had forecast. Referring to Kashmir the Indian Foreign Minister said that a question that could not be resolved by Heads of State was not an appropriate subject for consideration at the level of ministers. India would need a great deal of time to prepare public opinion for any discussion of Kashmir. In the meantime the slate should be wiped clean and outstanding problems relating to the withdrawal of forces and vacation of territories, return of seized properties, and restoration of communications should be resolved, so that a new environment of understanding is created.[1]

The meeting proved sterile as did the exchange between Ayub and the Indian delegation on 1 March. Ayub described the relations between India and Pakistan as 'bad from the beginning'. Tashkent had created the possibility of reversing the trend: 'The whole world is tired of us, and they ask why can't these people live like human beings. We should have the ability to conduct our own affairs and have some measure of trust in each other.' India, he said, was a large country and could play a big role in world affairs, if only it would disengage itself from the futile dispute over Kashmir. What were the Indians gaining by sticking to their position on Kashmir? If the Kashmir dispute was resolved, Ayub said, 'we too could take care of the subcontinent. Together we can defend the subcontinent.' The Indian Foreign Minister, Swaran Singh, thanked Ayub for having deputed one of his ministers to attend the funeral rites of the late Prime Minister Shastri but did not respond to any of the points mentioned by Ayub.

In the concluding session of the ministerial meeting on 2 March, the Indian Foreign Minister characterized the Kashmir problem as 'intractable'. The final communiqué only said that the two sides had met and 'the Pakistan side pointed out the special importance of reaching a settlement of the Jammu and Kashmir dispute.' The Indian position was not stated in the communiqué. However, both sides agreed that all disputes between India and Pakistan should be resolved to promote and strengthen peace between the two countries. Whatever hopes Pakistan had, of using Tashkent to bring any pressure on India to deal with the Kashmir problem, were buried in the ministerial meeting.

Bhutto has a run of luck

Soon thereafter came the National Assembly session in Dhaka in the middle of March. Before the session, Ayub called a meeting of the Muslim League Working Committee in Karachi to discuss the post-Tashkent situation. In the meeting, Chaudhury Khaliquzzaman remarked that when the President of the Muslim League was discussing such a crucial matter, Bhutto, the Secretary-

General of the party, was relaxing in Larkana, making no effort to put across the party's point of view to the people. Ayub made no comment because he alone knew that he had put Bhutto on notice. By now Bhutto had come to see that the agitation which he had hoped would overwhelm the Ayub government was beginning to peter out. The opposition parties were caught in their own internal feuds. In West Pakistan the governor had arrested all the political activists and in East Pakistan there was no real opposition to Tashkent. Bhutto turned up in Dhaka and requested the Information Secretary to get him an interview with Ayub. When Ayub was approached he said: 'Well I have an appointment with my barber, but I suppose the Foreign Minister takes precedence.' He then said: 'I have not been idle. I have chosen someone to take over from Bhutto.' He did not disclose the identity of the person he had chosen. This was the first indication that Ayub gave to the Information Secretary of having decided to replace Bhutto.

The whole of Dhaka crowded into the Assembly building to listen to Bhutto. They wanted to know about Tashkent directly from the Foreign Minister. Bhutto explained how every clause of the Declaration was related to the Kashmir problem. He presented Tashkent as a triumph of diplomacy but did not fail to use the occasion to attack India as a predatory neighbour. He claimed there was a better understanding of Pakistan's foreign policy in the US and the Soviet position on Kashmir had appreciably changed. He was confident that one day 'the Soviet Union would have to support the right of self-determination in Kashmir'. Bhutto disclosed that the defence of East Pakistan had been guaranteed by the Chinese during the war. To the opposition's charge that Pakistan had indulged in adventurism in Kashmir and taken steps that could be construed as aggression, Bhutto replied: 'If support to the struggling people of Jammu and Kashmir constituted an aggression against India, then all those countries like China, Indonesia, and others who unstintedly supported the cause of the Kashmiris were committing aggression against India.'[2]

Bhutto then had a windfall. On 26 March the Chinese Chairman, Liu Shao Chi, accompanied by the Chinese Foreign Minister

Chen Yi, came on an official visit to Pakistan. Chairman Liu had a long meeting with Ayub in which he reiterated China's firm support for Pakistan's policies on Kashmir. The Chinese Chairman then went to Lahore where a warm welcome from the people of Punjab awaited him. Despite much persuasion by the Information Secretary, Ayub did not accompany the Chinese Chairman to Lahore. The Information Secretary tried to impress on Ayub that it was of the utmost importance for him to be seen with Liu Shao Chi in Lahore but it made no impression on him. His reply was: 'Listen, I have talked to people who have got their ear to the ground, and I am not going. I am not so irresponsible as to make political capital out of this situation. I must give the people the correct lead. These are difficult times and require cool and clear-headed thinking.' He was not swayed by the need to be with the people of Punjab at that crucial moment. He dismissed their emotional outbursts as 'soda bottle effervescence'.[3]

By giving Bhutto the opportunity to appear as a hero in Lahore in the company of the Chinese Chairman, Ayub had handed over the political initiative to Bhutto. It was a tumultuous reception. There was not an inch of empty space from the airport to Government House. Bhutto was beaming with joy and frantically waving to a hysterical mass of humanity. The people lifted the car in which Bhutto was travelling and carried in on their shoulders. Bhutto had won their hearts. In retrospect, it would appear as if Ayub had himself launched Bhutto on his political career.

NOTES

1. *Dawn,* 8 January 1966.
2. Ibid., 16 March 1966.
3. Author's notes.

CHAPTER 12

Ayub Loses Heart

Ayub waited till the Tashkent agitation had completely subsided before getting rid of some of his associates. The first to go was Bhutto in June 1966. But Ayub had given him enough time and opportunity to build himself a popular base. In this the Information Ministry had also played a role projecting Bhutto's activities and statements, particularly his highly charged speeches in the Security Council. The next to go was the Finance Minister, Shoaib, who was too closely identified with the Americans. But it was the removal of Nawab of Kalabagh from the scene, in September 1966, which deprived Ayub of his most powerful partner in West Pakistan. Kalabagh had kept a firm grip on the province and knew how to deal with the politicians. He was replaced by General Musa who proved singularly inept and ineffective.

General Yahya who had been given the responsibility of winding up the operations in Kashmir, a task which the Indians completed for him, was appointed Commander-in-Chief of the Army. It was generally believed that Ayub selected Yahya, in preference to some other generals, because Yahya, who had come to hit the bottle hard, had no time for politics and was considered a harmless and loyal person. The Federal Cabinet was now a colourless body composed of mindless persons who had no political base or influence. Sycophancy was their principal occupation. The only exception was Khwaja Shahabuddin, a man of integrity, who possessed a great deal of political experience and wisdom, but he was now a spent force and not particularly popular in East Pakistan. Monem Khan continued as Governor of East Pakistan, but that only alienated the Bengalis further because they regarded him as a minion of Ayub. All these changes enhanced the power of the Civil Servants close to Ayub on whom he came to rely for advice.

The politicians were being hounded: the more prominent among them were either under detention or on trial for anti-state activities. Governor Monem Khan used to say in official meetings that he would not allow Sheikh Mujibur Rahman to stay out of prison even for a day. 'No mother's son,' he would declare in his colourful style, 'can have the freedom to abuse my President.'

The Agartala Conspiracy

Frustration and bitterness continued to grow beneath the surface. The people were aggrieved and sullen and the administration had lost its hold and confidence. Ayub and his associates appeared and acted as if they were under siege. The intelligence agencies were busy detecting incipient conspiracies. They finally hit the jackpot—the Agartala Conspiracy.

Ayub was in East Pakistan in December 1967. He was due to visit a paper factory in Chandragona but the visit was called off because of a report that an attempt was likely to be made to blow up the President's plane. The military intelligence claimed that some civil and military officials were planning to secure the secession of East Pakistan in collaboration with Indian agents. Few senior officials around Ayub attached any importance to this claim. They had seen the work of military intelligence agencies during the war and knew how they would unearth some imaginary enemy plot and then, taking the bit between their teeth, set out to devise ways of frustrating that plot. They were essentially colonial investigation agencies who specialized in chasing suspects and extorting evidence, wholly unfamiliar with the more modern and sophisticated technique of intelligence.

On 6 January 1968, twenty-eight persons were arrested on charges of conspiring to bring about the secession of East Pakistan. Among them were three senior members of the Civil Service, Ruhul Quddus, Fazlur Rahman, and Shamsur Rahman, and a naval officer, Lieutenant Commander Muazzam Hussain, along with a number of non-commissioned officers, seamen and civilians. The military intelligence claimed that they had conspired with P.N. Ojha, First Secretary of the Indian Deputy High Commission in Dhaka, and had visited Agartala (capital of the Indian state of Tripura) to discuss their plans for East Pakistan's session from the rest of the country with two Indian officers, Lieutenant-Colonel Misra and Major Menon. None of the civilian agencies, except the Intelligence Bureau under the Home Ministry, had been taken into confidence, and the whole case was being handled by GHQ, under the direct control of General Yahya.

On 25 January 1968 the Information Secretary was called to the President's House and conducted to Ayub's bedroom. He knew it was going to be one of those relaxed sessions when Ayub would reminisce and talk about whatever came to his mind, and he would play the role of a quiet interlocutor and diarist. As the Information Secretary was walking towards the bedroom, Ayub's personal physician, Lieutenant-Colonel Mohyuddin, met him and said: 'He is much better now, he developed some pain in the back.' Ayub was lying in bed with a few books and newspapers on the side-table. He said that while taking exercise in the morning he had sprained a muscle in his back. The Information Secretary told him that the Japanese had completed the field survey for expanding the network of television in West Pakistan and soon it should be possible to link up Peshawar with Lahore. Ayub was quite excited: 'I want the people in West Pakistan to get closely knit up.' He was extremely happy that the Information Ministry had established television in the country in such a short time: 'It is going to be a major instrument of national integration. And you deserve great credit for that.' Ayub talked of his tour of Sindh from which he had returned a couple of days earlier. He had made a number of speeches in support of One Unit, and was very happy that he had not pulled any punches. He had warned the people of Sindh that he would not allow anybody to dismember One Unit. He was confident that the West Pakistanis would pull together but he was deeply worried about relations between East and West Pakistan. What disturbed him most was that Bengali Muslims saw little benefit in living together with West Pakistanis. The

Information Secretary suggested that perhaps the Bengalis had not had a fair deal, to which Ayub reacted quite angrily: 'You become quite emotional when it comes to the Bengalis.' The Information Secretary was a little taken aback but he did not give up. He argued that the Bengalis might be a highly emotional people but they had genuine grievances. Even what had been promised to them under the Constitution had not been delivered. For instance, the Constitution required that the federal legislature and its secretariat should be located in Dhaka, which was to serve as the second capital of Pakistan. What they had been given was a ghost town. All legislative work continued to be done in Islamabad where the assembly staff was permanently lodged. Ayub leaned back a little wearily: 'Listen, my dear fellow, I gave them the second capital because they are going to need it one day. They are not going to remain with us.'

Next morning, 26 January 1968, there was the usual Cabinet meeting which was delayed by about thirty minutes because the American Ambassador had obtained an urgent interview with Ayub. In the Cabinet meeting. Ayub was unusually harsh with his Bengali ministers. He said to Altaf Hussain, Minister for Industries, 'you used to lecture to the world and now don't mumble a word even in your sleep.' The prevailing situation in East Pakistan, Ayub said, was the result of propaganda which had been going on against West Pakistan for the last twenty years. As far as he could see, the choice before East Pakistan was partnership with West Pakistan or slavery: 'These are not popular things to say, but I am not looking for popularity.' He did not want to accuse any particular individual but the bitter truth was that no Bengali politician saw any benefit in remaining with Pakistan. The government was now confronted with an issue of enormous gravity: 'I don't think any one of us here can resolve it.'[1]

Ayub did not mention it but the Agartala Conspiracy was preying on his mind. His first reaction to the report that an attempt might be made on his life was: 'What rubbish, as if I care two bloody hoots for a thing like that.' But the incident had convinced him that the opposition parties in East Pakistan were engaged in hatching some conspiracy to tear East Pakistan away from West

Pakistan. The Information Secretary suggested that it would be helpful if the President undertook an extensive tour of the country and talked to the people directly. He shook his head and said: 'Don't forget I am not a young man.' He asked the Home Minister and the Industries Minister to issue a statement warning the people that the hymn of hate that was being ceaselessly chanted in East Pakistan would lead to separation if East Pakistani politicians did not make any attempt to stop it. It was a long and unpleasant meeting which left Ayub exhausted.

Later that evening, there was a banquet in honour of King Hussein of Jordan. Ayub was standing with King Hussein receiving the guests. As he shook hands with the Information Secretary he asked him whether the statement had been issued and said: 'They are thinking of secession over there. What nonsense, we will lace them.' All this while he kept holding the Information Secretary's hand who could feel that Ayub's hand was very warm, as if he was running high temperature.

While proposing the toast Ayub missed out a whole section of the written text. General Rafi confided to the Information Secretary that the President was not feeling well; he had gone to the airport on a bitterly cold morning to receive King Hussein, and had caught a chill. No one had any suspicion that they were seeing Ayub Khan in full health for the last time. Tall, handsome, elegant and energetic, he had just turned sixty-one. All his life he had been extremely careful about his diet and regular in his habits. He played golf and did not allow anything to interfere with his *shikar* schedule. No one could have imagined that his health would crumble so suddenly and so completely.

Ayub used to broadcast a speech to the people on the first of every month. The text of the speech for the month of February had been approved and it only remained to be recorded for broadcast. The recording was postponed as Ayub was not feeling too well. After that there was not a word about the President's health. All attempts to get any information from the President's personal physician proved futile. The President's House, and the area around it, were surrounded by soldiers on 29 January 1968 and nobody was allowed access even to the members of the President's secretariat.

The Information Secretary's role was now limited to receiving a daily health bulletin from the President's personal physician, and releasing it to the Press. On 6 February the bulletin said that Ayub had developed viral pneumonia in the right lung, following a touch of 'flu. The next day his temperature was reported to have subsided and he was feeling much better. On 8 February, the bulletin said, 'The clinical signs of pneumonia in the right lung have improved further and the President is much better.' On 10 February, the cough was better and the President was feeling comfortable. Within minutes of this bulletin the Information Secretary was called to the President's House. The President's son, Akhtar Ayub, met him in the porch and said: 'So, you too were locked out. I am glad to see you back.' Apart from Ayub's wife, no other member of his family had been allowed to see him. Ayub was reclining against two large pillows and had a glass of orange juice in his hand. He looked relaxed and agreed to the suggestion that he might meet some of his ministers and the governors. A large cardiac monitor was placed near his bed. The room next to his bedroom looked like a laboratory where two army doctors were monitoring the electrocardiograph. It was evident that General Yahya had taken personal control of the situation the moment he learnt that Ayub might succumb to what was obviously a serious heart attack. A *coup d'etat* had, in fact, taken place. Yahya would later claim that he had acted under Ayub's instructions.

The next day, 11 February, before any meetings could be arranged, came another message that Ayub had suffered 'a slight relapse on the night between 10 and 11 February'. It was not a slight relapse but a collapse. The bulletin on 15 February conveyed the cryptic but truthful message: 'Since the issue of the last bulletin on 10 February, the President's recovery got delayed; he developed pulmonary embolism Sunday night.' At last the people of Pakistan came to know that Ayub was suffering from pulmonary embolism and not viral pneumonia. The truth came out because Professor John Forest Goodwin of Hammersmith General Hospital, London, who had been summoned for consultation, refused to sign a medical bulletin which did not give the true picture of his patient's health. The President's physician, who had been doctoring the bulletins, was a little put out but his explanation was that he had been carrying out his Commander-in-Chief's instructions.

Ayub made an unexpected but steady recovery after that. He received Governor Musa on 16 February, and the next day, 17 February, Ayub appeared on the front pages of newspapers standing in his bedroom in a silk dressing-gown reading a newspaper. This was intended to quash the rumour that Ayub was paralysed. The silk dressing-gown in the middle of winter raised certain doubts. On 21 February, the bulletin said that Ayub was maintaining a steady recovery, and was feeling fine and comfortable. On 25 February Ayub was continuing to make very good progress. On 27 February it was announced that he would review the joint services parade on 23 March. By 28 February, Ayub had fully recovered and another picture appeared, this time in a heavy Swati coat, with the Governor of East Pakistan. The following day he met the Speaker of the National Assembly, and a two-minute film of his meeting with some of the ministers was telecast. On 1 March it was announced that Ayub would address the nation. The crisis was over. The Ministers could see the President and bureaucracy was back in business with Ayub at the helm of affairs. Yahya and his officers withdrew from the scene as quietly as they had come to dominate it. Power had eluded their grasp, but not for long, they hoped.

During this period a few Cabinet meetings were held under the chairmanship of Khwaja Shahabuddin. At none of these meetings did the Ministry of Law bring up the question of inviting the Speaker of the National Assembly to take over the functions of the President as required under the Constitution. The subject of succession was taboo because none of the ministers wanted to incur the displeasure of Ayub or the armed forces.

By the middle of March Ayub had sufficiently recovered to resume a restricted routine of work. He told the Information Secretary about the acute pain he suffered when the first incident occurred: 'It was like a red hot bar piercing through my chest.' He was being given heavy sedatives which affected his responses. Those who met him during this period could not help noticing that his reactions were rather tentative and his decisions uncertain.

Just before Ayub suffered the heart attack he had ordered the Ministry of Information to draw up a programme to celebrate the tenth anniversary of his reforms. He had convinced himself that the prevailing dissatisfaction in the country was due entirely to the fact that his reforms had not been properly explained and projected to the people. A comprehensive publicity programme was therefore drawn up, and it was approved by the Governors' Conference in November 1967. The celebrations were to commence on 1 January and end on 27 October 1968. Ayub himself was to play the leading role in the celebrations, touring various parts of the country and inviting people to join in the national debate to work out a consensus on important political issues. His illness robbed the programme of all its meaning. The programme went on for too long because there was nothing else to fill the vacuum caused by Ayub's physical absence from the scene, and every department got into the act to publicize its achievements while the newspapers encouraged them to go on with it because it boosted their advertising revenues. The celebrations were a great propaganda flop and the Information Secretary now became the target of attack by the Opposition. After Ayub recovered he wanted the celebrations to be wound up, but by then the damage had been done.

On 17 April the Soviet Prime Minister, Aleksei Kosygin, came to Pakistan on an official visit. This was the first-ever visit of a Soviet Premier and the crowds gave Kosygin a warm welcome, much to the chagrin of American officials in Islamabad. Ayub's first meeting with Kosygin was arranged in the drawing-room of his house. While TV cameras were being moved into the room the Information Secretary noticed Nawab Kalabagh's picture on the mantelpiece. If the cameras picked up that picture people might ask why the Nawab was occupying such a prominent place in Ayub's collection even after his expulsion from office. The picture was removed from the mantelpiece. But as soon as Ayub entered the room he noticed its absence and had it restored to its original place. Later, when the Information Secretary explained why the picture had been removed, Ayub recalled his friendship with Kalabagh with great affection. He said in Punjabi: '*Tandan tutian jur diyan nain* (once snapped the heart strings never mend).' He still retained great warmth for the Nawab. The rift between the two had been caused by the nomination of Khan Bahadur Habibullah, a Karachi businessman, as the ruling party candidate for a by-election in the Lyari constituency in Karachi. The Nawab despised Habibullah and supported Ghous Bukhsh Bizenjo, a prominent Balochi leader, the rival candidate. Some of the provincial ministers also actively campaigned against the official candidate. Habibullah lost the election much to the annoyance of Ayub. He felt the Nawab had let him down. This one incident was the cause of the Nawab's removal from the governorship of West Pakistan.

The meeting between Ayub and Kosygin on 18 April lasted for well over three hours. The Soviet Union signed an agreement for financing and executing the steel mill project in West Pakistan. An understanding was also reached regarding the setting up of an atomic power plant in East Pakistan. The Soviet Union offered assistance for establishing a radio relay link between Pakistan and the USSR and beyond to Europe. Prime Minister Kosygin addressed a press conference at the end of his visit. He said that relations between Pakistan and the Soviet Union would continue to improve and strengthen. His talks with Ayub had been 'a dialogue between two friends who were together in quest of ways to improve relations and co-operation'. He said that great credit was due to Ayub, who went to Moscow to establish personal contacts, and to bring about friendly relations and co-operation in all spheres between the two countries. The talks, he said, were meant to achieve 'a détente in international tensions'.[2]

The full significance of Kosygin's visit was not generally realized because few people knew, at the time, that Pakistan had given formal notice to the United States to remove their strategic military base at Badaber near Peshawar, which had been a major cause of tension and misunderstanding between Pakistan and the Soviet Union. The agreement for the base had been signed in 1959 and was due to expire in 1969. The agreement provided that the lease for the base would stand automatically renewed unless notice of termination was given twelve months in advance. Ayub gave the notice on 6 April 1968 and Kosygin arrived in Pakistan on 17 April.

Ayub had been told when he visited the Soviet Union for the first time in 1965, that the Soviet Union could not accept the position that Pakistan was not acting in a hostile manner by allowing the US to maintain a military base for electronic surveillance of strategic Soviet locations. Ayub had given an indication to the Soviet leaders that Pakistan would not renew the lease of the base without consulting them. This indication, more than anything else, was responsible for a marked improvement in Pakistan-USSR relations.

Ayub was deeply upset when the US stopped the supply of arms to Pakistan during the 1965 War, and when the Americans declined to resume military assistance in April 1967, he was left with no option but to look towards the Soviet Union for military aid and to expand Pakistan's relations with China. Ayub went on a second visit to the Soviet Union, between 25 September and 4 October 1967, to discuss the details of an agreement for the supply of Soviet arms to Pakistan. Ayub spent a couple of days with the Soviet leaders, Brezhnev, Podgorny and Kosygin, in Volgograd and Yalta, and it was there that he gave them a firm commitment that he would terminate the Badaber base lease by giving the Americans due notice at the appropriate time. To avoid any future misunderstanding, he also confided to the Soviet leaders that he was seriously thinking of co-operating with China to construct an all-weather road which would link Gilgit in northern areas with Kashgar in Chinese Sinkiang. Ten days after his return from Moscow, Ayub signed a formal agreement with China to build the road with a length of 155 miles on the Kashmir side, running along the Indus River and over the Minkata Pass in the Karakoram range. When the notice for the termination of the lease was given, the American Ambassador sought an urgent interview with Ayub to convey to him 'the great disappointment' of his government. Ayub refused to relent. In the meantime he made more changes in the Cabinet. Sharifuddin Pirzada, who had taken over from Bhutto, and the Industries Minister, Altaf Hussain, were relieved of their offices for 'private reasons'. Ayub was particularly disappointed with Pirzada, who would mumble in Cabinet meetings, and Ayub could never find out his position on any issue. Pirzada proved a resounding anticlimax after Bhutto. A useful man, who could always devise some formula to get over a legal difficulty, Ayub found him a little too crafty. He excelled in the art of obfuscation and Ayub was quite irritated by the way he would go on trimming and hedging every word, behaving like the archetypal Vicar of Bray.

Ayub came to his newly furnished office after he had recovered from his illness on 1 May 1968, in a black Rolls Royce, a gift from the Sheikh of Abu Dhabi, perhaps the first example of Gulf munificence towards Pakistani rulers. He was wearing a light grey suit and a pink rose and looked much slimmer than before. He stumbled a little as he walked up the steps but liked the new look of his office. His return to office marked the end of an agonizing phase. 'I was not worried,' he said with an air of satisfaction. When the Information Secretary said that the people had been extremely worried he wondered, 'Why? After all the administration continued to function.' He did not know that the administration had collapsed leaving the army hovering over its carcass. He started talking about the need for co-operatives in agriculture, a subject over which he had reflected a great deal during his convalescence. His ten-day stay in the Soviet Union, during September-October 1967, had convinced him that Pakistan could achieve self-sufficiency in agriculture only through co-operatives. He wanted to launch a campaign to build up public opinion in support of co-operative holdings: 'We can give the option to bigger landlords to form co-operatives of their own.'

The Agartala Conspiracy resurfaced during Ayub's convalescence. GHQ had completed its investigation and the case was ripe for trial. Yahya wanted the case to be tried by a special tribunal, but Ayub was not happy about that because of his earlier experience with the Rawalpindi conspiracy tribunal, in which a number of senior army officers were subjected to prolonged interrogation and cross-examination, which affected the morale of the services.[3] The next day Yahya convened a meeting to which the Defence Minister, the Defence Secretary, the Home Secretary, the Information Secretary, the Director of Intelligence Bureau, and several senior military officers, including the Judge Advocate-General, were invited to discuss the procedure for the trial. Yahya started by congratulating the intelligence agencies for the wonderful job they had done in unearthing the conspiracy against Pakistan engineered by Sheikh Mujibur Rahman. This was the first time the name of Sheikh Mujib was mentioned in connection with the case. Ayub wanted the civilians to be tried by ordinary courts and the defence personnel to be dealt with under court martial. But Yahya Khan was so excited with what his 'boys' had discovered that he wanted to make it a historic public trial. He insisted that the trial must be given the maximum publicity. That, the Information Secretary assured him, would not be difficult because the world Press would descend on Pakistan like vultures to tear into the proceedings. But he cautioned Yahya that if the proceedings were to be public then the whole trial must be open—not just the case for the prosecution. The government should not get upset when the defence presented its case, and the Press began highlighting the holes in the prosecution story. Yahya asked the Information Secretary not to worry: 'We have a foolproof case.' 'In that case,' said the Information Secretary, 'you will get foolproof publicity.' Yahya was a little put out by that and asked the Judge Advocate-General to give the Information Secretary the summary of evidence to relieve him of his anxiety.

The summary of evidence was loaded with assumptions and speculations. There was nothing to connect the 'Sheikh' mentioned in the summary of evidence as the main conspirator, with Sheikh Mujibur Rahman. The intelligence agencies had conveniently ignored the fact that Sheikh Mujibur Rahman had been in prison for most of the time when the alleged conspiracy was being hatched. GHQ was drafting the press note, which would appear in the newspapers the next day, 7 April 1968. After that it would be impossible to retrieve the situation. It was past the lunch hour but the Information Secretary decided to go and talk to Ayub before he retired for the afternoon. He told him about the meeting at GHQ and expressed his misgivings about involving Sheikh Mujibur Rahman in the conspiracy without solid evidence. If the prosecution could demonstrate during the trial that Sheikh Mujibur Rahman had anything to do with the conspiracy, the court could always indict him as a co-accused. Ayub was impressed by the argument that the 'Sheikh' in the summary of evidence did not necessarily mean Sheikh Mujibur Rahman. He promised to speak to the Defence Minister Admiral A. R. Khan, and the Commander-in-Chief. As a result of Ayub's intervention, Sheikh Mujibur Rahman's name was deleted from the list of the accused.

A special tribunal headed by a former Chief Justice of the Supreme Court, S.A. Rahman, was appointed. The other members of the tribunal were M.R. Khan and Maksumul Hakim, both Judges of the Dhaka High Court. Manzur Qadir had agreed to conduct the case for the prosecution. A few days later another press note was issued adding the name of Sheikh Mujibur Rahman among the accused even before the trial had opened. The President explained to the Information Secretary that Yahya had been told by his legal advisers that for the success of the case Sheikh Mujibur Rahman's name must be added to the list of the accused persons before the trial opened. It was an unfortunate decision which plunged the government into a crisis of far-reaching consequences. Yahya must have known that the case would explode like a bombshell, rob the government of whatever credibility it possessed, and alienate East Pakistan, perhaps for good.

Ayub left for London for a medical check-up and what he called 'my first real holiday in thirty years'.[4] He was examined by Professor Goodwin at the Hammersmith Hospital and given a clean bill of health. Professor Goodwin was however doubtful whether it would be advisable for Ayub to undertake another election campaign. Apart from that, he expressed full satisfaction with his progress. Ayub had a meeting with Prime Minister Harold Wilson, and after a few days in London he shifted to Croydon where the British government had made arrangements for his stay at Selsdon Park Hotel. During his stay there Ayub met the Conservative Party leader, Edward Heath, and had a long session with the historian, Arnold Toynbee, who had great admiration for Ayub's reforms. Bhutto tried to see Ayub through the mediation of Pakistan's Ambassador in West Germany, Abdul Rahman, but Ayub said, 'No; Bhutto should see me in Pakistan, not here.' Bhutto's interest in meeting Ayub must have been to ascertain the true state of his health on which depended his whole political game.

It was during his stay in London that Ayub had his first direct contact with East Pakistani Opposition groups. On the day of his arrival, a large group of students put up a big demonstration outside his hotel. It was the Agartala case which had particularly annoyed the East Pakistani students who seemed determined to carry on a struggle to save Mujibur Rahman and his associates from what looked like certain conviction. They had set up a 'Rights of East Pakistan Defence Front' and engaged Tom Williams Q.C. to go to Dhaka to join the team of lawyers defending Sheikh Mujib. The British Press, too, was unhappy about the circumstances of the case. *The Times* commented that Mujib was 'being charged with complicity in a plot alleged to have been hatched while he was behind bars'. The trial was to be held in Dhaka cantonment 'which suggests that it is to have something of a military background'.[5] The demonstrations outside Ayub's hotel became a daily routine from which he did not escape even in Croydon.

The Sinkiang Road

Another significant development during this period was the implementation of the agreement which Pakistan had signed with the People's Republic of China, to build a road through Mintaka Pass linking Sinkiang with Kashmir on the Pakistani side of the cease-fire line.[6] For the Americans the completion of the Sinkiang road was the final act of Ayub's betrayal of US geo-political interests in the region. They must have prevailed upon Yahya and other senior army officers to sabotage the plan, and while the Chinese were busy completing their part of the road, the Pakistan Army's Corps of Engineers started dragging its feet. Yahya managed to convince Ayub that there would be very heavy casualties if Pakistan went ahead with the construction of the road

during that season. A high level Chinese delegation arrived in
Rawalpindi to discuss the problem with their counterparts in
GHQ. The Foreign Secretary, S.M. Yusuf, asked the Information
Secretary to explain to Ayub that the Chinese were quite perturbed
by the objections which the Pakistani engineers were raising
about the completion of the road. He was anxious that Ayub
should meet the leader of the Chinese delegation. When the
Information Secretary raised the matter with Ayub, he said the
Engineering Corps had certain genuine difficulties which Yahya
would explain to the Chinese. The Information Secretary suggested
that if those difficulties were explained in Ayub's presence the
matter would be sorted out without any misunderstanding with
the Chinese. Ayub agreed and invited the Chinese delegation and
Yahya Khan to lunch. Yahya was most unhappy with this
development. Fortunately, the problem was resolved; the Chinese
accepted whatever difficulties were mentioned by Yahya and
volunteered to complete the Pakistan section of the road also!

Ayub now started thinking about the coming presidential
election in early 1970. He felt that the promise of greater economic
growth, combined with his independent foreign policy, would be
enough to rob the programme of his opponents of any radical
appeal. But the critical factor was his health which had already
created areas of rival leadership. One was the army. Yahya knew
that Ayub would not be able to take the strain of an election
campaign which was bound to be intense and prolonged.

The other was a group of *ulema,* and certain right wing
politicians who were deeply concerned that Pakistan was getting
too close to the socialist bloc. The government suspected that they
had the support of the Americans who were by now thoroughly
disenchanted with Ayub. The *ulema,* deeply unhappy with Ayub's
family laws, were looking for any issue which they could exploit
to fight Ayub from the pulpit. The government wanted to set up
an abattoir in Rawalpindi and the *ulema* denounced the project as
a violation of Islamic dietary laws. Popular passions were aroused
and the government was forced to abandon the project. Another
victim of the *ulema* was Dr Fazlur Rehman, head of the Islamic
Research Institute. His interpretation of *Mairaj* (the prophet's

ascent to heaven) was condemned as heresy and Dr Fazlur Rahman was forced to resign—much against Ayub's wishes. Ayub's ministers and associates were now reluctant to come out too strongly in defence of the government because they were uncertain about Ayub's future.

Zulfikar Ali Bhutto, who had been lying low since his exit from the Cabinet in June 1966, now saw his opportunity and jumped on the Opposition bandwagon. It was a poorly aligned and cumbersome vehicle. Bhutto's presence gave it purpose and direction. Here was an insider challenging and exposing Ayub's dictatorial methods regardless of personal risk. The masses, particularly in the Punjab, immediately responded to his call. Bhutto took care to cultivate senior military officers, particularly General S.G.M.M. Peerzada and General Gul Hassan, the former a dubious crawler, and the latter, a hippety-hopper. He raised the slogan of *Roti, Kapra, Makan* (bread, clothing, shelter) which electrified the poor who had not derived the same benefits as the richer classes from Ayub's economic policies.

Bhutto presented himself as the architect of Pakistan-China friendship and claimed all the credit even for the boundary agreement with China, which had been negotiated by Manzur Qadir under Ayub's direct supervision. He endeared himself to the armed forces by blaming Ayub for losing at the negotiating table all that the armed forces had gained on the battlefield during the 1965 War, and he charmed the people by presenting Ayub's economic reforms as a sinister design to make the rich richer and the poor poorer. Further ammunition was provided by the Chief Economist in Ayub's government, Dr Mahbub-ul-Haq, a World Bank protégé who having been a party to the whole process of economic planning, came out with the startling disclosure that Pakistan's economy was dominated by twenty-two families—a slogan which Bhutto and other Opposition leaders employed to devastating effect.

As a champion of the under-privileged and the exploited, Bhutto found a responsive audience in East Pakistan too where the feeling of alienation had assumed grave proportions after the 1965 War. Every success of Ayub's government was seen by the

East Pakistanis as a blow to their aspirations for autonomy. The situation had assumed a menacing complexion after the Agartala Conspiracy.

Ayub in the meantime had developed a detached and philosophic attitude. There would be the occasional spurt of activity when he would address day-to-day problems with his old vigour, followed by long spells of inertia and indifference. He seemed obsessed by threats to Pakistan's economic and political future—even its survival. More than once he said to the Information Secretary: 'The way we are going we might disintegrate and come under the domination of the Hindu. I dread that more than anything else.'

He would reminisce about the work he had done since coming to power. Progress, he said, had its own compulsions and its own momentum. He was proud that he had been able to introduce the land reforms in less than ten months. He had put his ideas in a cut-and-dried form for immediate implementation: 'What you need is talented people to execute your ideas.'

He had the uneasy feeling that he might have pushed the people too fast into the modern age, confronting them with the challenge of changing their traditional ways in response to contemporary realities. His satisfaction was that some people, at least, understood what he was trying to do, though there were many who thought that he had 'robbed them of the comfort of the old and exposed them to the hazards of the new'. He called the leaders of the Opposition '…sadists who were trying to take advantage of the gullibility of the people.'

He was conscious of the growing dissatisfaction among the students and the labour and would often suggest that some dialogue should be started with the students, and some method found for giving the workers a sense of real participation in management. He knew that the University Ordinance 1963 had alienated the students, and wanted it to be suitably amended but did not realize that the changes he was proposing were seen as too little, too late. He recalled that when General George Patton first become a second lieutenant, he thought it was the insignia on his shoulder that secured him instant obedience. Much later, he discovered that it was the quality of leadership, not insignias and medals, that made his subordinates respond to his commands with willingness and enthusiasm.

After every such session the Information Secretary would come away with the feeling that Ayub was now living in the past—the future had become a mirage. He would talk about the problems of the people with great feeling, but like most authoritarian rulers he would not recognize the people as a political entity, much less as a sovereign reality. Nor did he realize that the political structures he had created had deprived his people of the freedom of expression and participation. He continued to believe that his system was best suited to the genius of the people, and would have been accepted if it had been properly explained and propagated. Here he would blame the official media, the Press Trust, Radio Pakistan and television. He never realized that the media, too, was a political institution and could function only if it had the confidence of the people. The same was true of his political party, the Muslim League, which had become a sterile body plagued by internal squabbles. Ayub never realized the damage that his family's reputation for corruption had done to him personally and to his system of government. He was enraged when he read in a foreign publication that his son Gohar Ayub was pressing him for the allotment of a new industry called 'rumour-mongering' which was in great demand in the country. 'Why are these fellows hounding my son?' he asked the Information Secretary. 'Because, Mr President, they hold you responsible for the conduct of your children.' When a ruler is all powerful and the people have no say in the affairs of the state, any irregularity or misdemeanor on the part of the those near and dear to him reflects on his reputation and character. Ayub found this argument incomprehensible.

While Ayub was trapped in the past the domestic situation was beginning to explode, and external threats were assuming a menacing form. He could not understand how the Americans thought they could establish long-term peace in Asia with the Vietnam War dragging on. His principal worry was that the Americans would ditch Pakistan. Somehow the Americans must be made to understand the real Pakistani position. Unfortunately there was no Pakistani lobby in the United States. Before Partition, the Indians had a man like Sudhir Ghosh: 'What Pakistan needed was a glib chap in America who should project our point of view.' The Pakistani diplomats were 'rather timid'. Some way must be found to divert the United States from supporting India 'in a blindfolded fashion'. The US did not want Pakistan to get closer to the Soviet Union or China which meant that Pakistan should toe the Indian line. That was impossible. For the Americans, Pakistan's security was negotiable. He recalled that when the Americans were having problems in Laos he had expressed his willingness to send troops to Laos provided their safety was guaranteed. He still believed that Pakistan was a real friend of the US—the only power with which Pakistan could come to a long-term arrangement for its security.

The Americans were also putting pressure on Iran to restrain Pakistan from developing closer relations with China. Ayub had known the Shah of Iran since his days as Commander-in-Chief and used to admire him for his grasp of world affairs. At one stage the Shah had proposed that Iran and Pakistan should form a federation, and the two countries should have a common army. Ayub thought that the Shah was dreaming of becoming the Shahinshah of Iran and Pakistan. Iran, Turkey and Pakistan had formed a regional organization for development and co-operation in 1965, but the Shah was distrustful of the Turks, and did not allow any major regional project to be developed. When Pakistan started pursuing a course of friendship with China, the Shah was quite alarmed. He responded by cultivating India. This annoyed Ayub and he became deeply disillusioned with the Shah: 'This fellow keeps weaving grandiose designs.' Once when the Shah raised some complaint on behalf of India Ayub told him: 'Go ahead and come to an understanding with the Indians. But, I warn you, your Imperial Majesty, you will get isolated. The Arabs know you, the Turks know you, and once the Indians isolate you from Pakistan, that will be the end for you.' The USSR, according to Ayub, was using the Indians who had strong military relations with Iraq, to come to an understanding with Iraq to dominate the

Gulf area. He had gathered this from his discussion with Kosygin but 'this fool, the Shah, does not realize the Indian game'. The Iranian Ambassador in Pakistan, Pakravan, said to Ayub after Kosygin's visit in April 1968, 'His Majesty was glad to know that Kosygin did not talk about the Persian Gulf.' Ayub told him: 'That does not mean he was not thinking about it.' The Soviets, Ayub insisted, had been longing to get into this area. It seemed that the Shah was now beginning to alarm the Sheikhs. They saw him turning into the devil: 'I think his end is coming, he will get badly involved. Already he has alienated even the good Arabs.' Unfortunately, the defeat of the Arabs in the Israeli War gave the Shah a great sense of superiority and he was now parading as heir to Cyprus: 'This fellow who used to come running to me for protection is now telling me how to handle my relations with China. In Ramsar he told me "Don't put all your eggs in one basket." I retorted, "What eggs, and what basket." I was really angry. He has a swollen head and a petty mind.'[7]

In December 1968, Ayub presided over what was to be his last Governors' Conference, though no one suspected it at the time. The conference was held in the large verandah of the President's House on Hare Road in Dhaka. Ayub walked into the conference in a grey suit and silk shirt looking quite cheerful. His presence immediately gave a sense of well-being to the participants who, only a moment ago, were looking like a bunch of carpet-baggers. The first item on the agenda was the amendment of the Constitution to enlarge the electoral college. The item was postponed and the conference thereafter plunged into a long and rambling discussion on the food situation. East Pakistan must be provided with 2,500,000 tons of rice from West Pakistan. If superior varieties of rice, such as the Basmati, had limited export market, they should be released for internal consumption. There was a great deal of talk about the need for transferring autonomous public bodies to the private sector. 'Let us get rid of these white elephants,' Ayub remarked. He decided not to go to London to participate in the Commonwealth Conference: 'The commander should be where he is needed most.'[8]

The Director of Intelligence Bureau gave a detailed account of the growing agitation in the country. The Opposition was determined to go the whole hog; it had no programme but it was hell-bent on creating as much confusion as possible. Ayub directed the provincial governors to take direct control of the situation. The stationery provided to the ministers for the conference bore the ironic slogan, 'We celebrate ten years of development, 1958-68.'

On 16 December 1968 Ayub was in his study with the Information Secretary, going over the same questions again. Why had the people failed to recognize the benefits of his system? How had the discredited politicians succeeded in their designs? As he was getting up he said, 'The leader is a very lonely person. He cannot disclose his innermost feelings to anyone.' He was halfway down the corridor when he turned around and said, 'Is the *tamasha* about the decade of reforms still going on? They tell me it is not doing us much good.'[9]

NOTES

1. Author's notes.
2. *Dawn,* 19 April 1968.
3. In the Rawalpindi conspiracy case eleven army officers and four civilians were prosecuted for treason before a special tribunal at Hyderabad (Sindh) between June 1951 and January 1953. The charge was that the conspirators had planned to overthrow the civilian government of Liaquat Ali Khan and to set up a military dictatorship on the communist model. Fourteen of the accused were found guilty.
4. *The Times,* London; 23 July 1968.
5. Ibid., 1 July 1968.
6. Ibid., 14 May 1966.
7. Author's notes.
8. Ibid.
9. Ibid.

CHAPTER 13

'Bitter and ungrateful sands'

Reflecting on political developments during the Ayub years, Samuel Huntington wrote:

> The new institutions created in Pakistan after 1958 were in large part the result of conscious political planning. More than any other political leaders in a modernizing country after the Second World War, Ayub Khan came close to filling the role of a Solon or Lycurgus or 'Great Legislator' on the Platonic or Rousseauian model.[1]

These ringing words were published when the Ayub era was drawing to a close. The institutional structure he had raised with such care was under siege, and the hope of any democratic transfer of power had turned into a mirage. By the end of February 1969 Ayub's Basic Democracies, and his elaborate facade of indirect elections, were swept off the political map by a mounting wave of public indignation and consigned to oblivion along with him. Huntington should have recalled Machiavelli's perceptive observation that one who becomes head of a republic through his skill, encounters growing difficulties because of the institutions and methods he is obliged to introduce in order to found his state and his security.

> And one should bear in mind that there is nothing more difficult to execute, nor more dubious of success, nor more dangerous to administer, than to introduce a new system of things: for he who introduces it has all those who profit from the old system as his enemies, and he has only lukewarm allies in those who might profit from the new system.[2]

No one quite understood how the country was suddenly engulfed by an agitation which spread like wildfire across the land in

January 1969. Was Ayub abandoned by his lukewarm allies as they saw his system come under mounting public pressure? Was it the natural culmination of years of political suffocation? Was it the result of a conspiracy hatched by the armed forces in collusion with some politicians? Or, was the Central Intelligence Agency of the United States (CIA) responsible for Ayub's downfall? Like the scholars who would later study the period, Ayub too was haunted by these questions.

It all started with a single incident. In the first week of November 1968 a student was killed in a clash between the police and a crowd of Bhutto supporters outside a polytechnic in Rawalpindi. The student community reacted violently and curfew was imposed to keep the situation under control. A few days later, when Ayub was addressing a public meeting in Peshawar, two shots were fired at him. He escaped, but the incident sparked off widespread disturbances. Hordes of people thronged the streets and soon every section of urban society was caught in a rising wave of demonstrations against the regime. Bhutto, Wali Khan and several other leaders were arrested on 13 November, but that only added fuel to the fire. Mujib was already in military custody. The students were bringing out huge processions in Dhaka demanding the release of Mujib and the withdrawal of the conspiracy case against him.

The government was under the impression that people were demonstrating because of the shortage of certain essential commodities like sugar, which had disappeared from the cities in West Pakistan. The Commerce Minister, Abdul Ghafoor Hoti, who owned a sugar mill, earned himself the title of *Cheeni Chor* (sugar thief). He was accused of cornering the market and making huge profits through black-marketing. Ayub was incensed and wanted Hoti to resign but he refused to oblige. In one meeting on 26 November 1968 Ayub said, 'The private sector will be wiped out one of these days through the perfidy of the industrialist.' He wanted the government to guarantee the supply of foodgrains, sugar, oils and salt for at least eighteen months. He set up a committee to examine the question of linking wages with the price index and opening fair price shops. Neither Ayub nor any of his associates grasped the complexity or gravity of the problem. In moments of desperation Ayub would ask, 'What has gone wrong?' The ministers all blamed the party, which was divided against itself, and the party blamed the ministers for their ineptitude. The Information Ministry and its propaganda policies were constantly under attack. There was no recognition that the real cause was the public apprehension of one-man rule, the domination of the centre over the provinces, the inequitable allocation of resources between East and West Pakistan, the extension of bureaucratic control over every walk of life, and the denial of fundamental human rights and freedoms. Ayub himself clung to the belief that if some economic measures were taken to provide relief to the students and the working classes the agitation would die down. As a result the government did not undertake any fundamental review of its policies and left it to the administration to deal with the demonstrators.

There were daily encounters between the police and rioters in major cities often resulting in civilian casualties. Every such incident further inflamed passions against Ayub. The opposition parties which had been hibernating for ten years were in a state of disarray; the period for which most of the politicians had been disqualified from taking part in any political activity had expired. They sprang out of their hide-outs with renewed vigour and venom against Ayub. They had neither anticipated nor planned the urban fury which suddenly overwhelmed the regime. But the roar of the crowds was music to the ears of the old guard and in their embittered breasts sprang the hope that the fall of Ayub might lead to their re-emergence on the political scene. As the agitation continued to spread, political leaders of all varieties started endorsing every demand inscribed on any banner or placard hoisted by factory workers, students, teachers, low-paid government employees, shopkeepers and vendors. The helplessness of the administration was matched only by the submission of the politicians to the whims of the agitators.

Ayub was extremely unhappy with the Press and wanted to sack Aziz Ahmad who had become Chairman of the Press Trust after retirement as Foreign Secretary. On 30 November he told him that the Press Trust papers were not acting in a responsible manner and he was thinking of disbanding the Trust. 'These troubles,' Ayub said, 'could have been snuffed out in twenty-four hours but the country is surrounded by dangers and neither the Press nor the people seem to realize the stakes.'

Asghar Khan who had kept himself in the background so far now jumped into the fray and his name gave instant authority to the agitation. Ayub was stung by Asghar Khan's fierce criticism of his policies. In his more confident moments Ayub would say, 'I am always happy in battle. Anyone who thinks that I will not defend my system with everything at my command is sadly mistaken.' But in more thoughtful moments he would plead, 'The pity is that people don't seem to know that they are playing into the hands of the enemy.'

By 1 January 1969 Ayub was beginning to feel that it would not be possible to suppress the agitation by force. His judgement was strongly influenced by his concern about his health. He still wanted to contest the presidential election in 1970, but his physicians were doubtful whether he could go through another campaign. Within his own party there was no one who could succeed him because the system was not designed for that purpose, and there was little hope that the Opposition would be able to field a candidate acceptable to all parties. The Commander-in-Chief of the Army, General Yahya Khan, would insist that the problems which the government was facing were essentially political and must be resolved through political means. If the armed forces were drawn into the agitation they too might lose their credibility, which would make it extremely difficult for them to bring the country back to sanity. Ayub was in sympathy with this argument which was offered both as a piece of advice by a loyal subordinate and a veiled threat. The army was no longer prepared to pull Ayub out of his political marsh.

The atmosphere in the President's House was reminiscent of the days of Ayub's illness. The façade of government appeared solid enough, but behind the façade there was only drift and confusion and a sense of impending doom. Ayub's Cabinet Ministers and governors waited for him to assert his authority and call upon the army to come to the aid of civil power in an effective manner. But Ayub was content to leave things in a state of suspense while Yahya continued to play his cards with great deftness. He would profess loyalty to Ayub—'He is like my father' was his favourite expression—and assure every official who met him that the army was completely loyal to the regime. Ayub alone knew the price the armed forces would demand were they called upon to assume the responsibility of restoring law and order.

Five of the Opposition parties managed to unite under the banner of the Pakistan Democratic Movement (PDM) and assembled in Dhaka on 1 January 1969 to evolve a common programme of action. Neither Mujib's Awami League nor Bhutto's People's Party was represented in the PDM. The Opposition parties knew that they would never be able to agree on a detailed political agenda. East Pakistan's influential daily, *Pakistan Observer,* wrote on 3 January that it would be impossible to bring about unity on an ideological basis among the Opposition parties. Their best hope was to agree on a course of action 'for the overthrow of the regime and nothing else'. The message was clear—any attempt to think beyond the overthrow of the government would only bring out the inherent contradictions within the Opposition.

The agitation was now growing almost independently of the thinking and conduct of the political leaders, and no one in the Opposition was in a position to canalize it in any positive direction. Among PDM leaders, some of whom were no more than hoarse-throated slogan-mongers, there was much argument but no agreement about having the next elections on the basis of population (which would give East Pakistan a clear majority) or about the division of powers between the centre and the provinces. In his broadcast on 1 January, Ayub admitted that there were weaknesses and shortcomings in his system and it was the responsibility of the government to remove those shortcomings. But he maintained that the issues raised by the Opposition could only be solved in accordance with the provisions of the Constitution. The crowds scented blood. Ayub was wilting under pressure—one heave and he would fall.

While PDM leaders were trying to hammer out some common programme, Bhutto threw a spanner in the works. From prison he declared his intention to fight against Ayub in the next election. *Pakistan Observer* (4 January 1969) described Bhutto's announcement as unfortunate: 'It comes at a time when the normally squabbling Opposition parties are trying to overcome their differences and makes things difficult for the proposed unity.' Bhutto could see that if support for his party kept growing in West Pakistan, of which there was ample evidence, he would easily defeat Ayub.

The PDM agreed on 5 January to adopt 'a non-controversial programme acceptable to all parties and democratic forces' and two days later announced its decision not to participate in the forthcoming elections which they condemned as 'farcical and fraudulent'. They put forth five demands:

(1) Direct elections on the basis of universal adult franchise;
(2) Full powers to a directly-elected parliament and provincial legislatures;
(3) Immediate lifting of the state of emergency;
(4) Immediate restoration of all fundamental rights and freedoms; and
(5) Immediate release of all political prisoners and the withdrawal of all cases against them.

In response to these demands Governor Monem Khan announced that there was no question of the government being shaken by the agitation. He dismissed the Opposition's demand for parliamentary system of government as unacceptable because the people did not want to revert to the conditions of the nineteen fifties, 'when there had been six Prime Ministers and three Governors General in four years'. He warned that the path which the Opposition was following could only lead to disaster.

On 9 January the Opposition announced the formation of the Democratic Action Committee (DAC) comprising the five constituents of PDM, and three other parties—Mujib's Awami League, Jamiat-ul-Ulema-e-Islam, and Wali Khan's National Awami Party. DAC now embraced all important groups except Bhutto's People's Party and Bhashani's National Awami Party. DAC expressed its resolve to support the popular agitation and added three more demands to the five adopted by PDM: repeal of 'black laws', withdrawal of Press curbs, and restoration of the right to strike. DAC described its programme as 'the first step towards the fulfillment of the hopes and aspirations of our people'.[3]

The mass movement showed no sign of abating. One student was killed in East Pakistan on 20 January when the police opened fire on a procession. The provincial assembly was adjourned *sine die* because the government would not allow debate on the incident. Another student was killed the following day and all educational institutions in Dhaka were closed down. Militant processions were now fighting pitched battles with the police. The Dhaka High Court Bar Association condemned the atrocities committed by 'the present autocratic regime'.[4]

Ayub was seriously considering the possibility of contacting the Opposition, but he could not discover any basis for negotiations. He had come to realize that the administration was no longer in control of the situation, but the Opposition, too, was in no position to contain the demonstrations on the promise of any negotiated settlement with the government. When the Information Secretary tried to persuade him to establish contact with the Opposition, he said, 'Take my word. Any negotiations with these fellows will turn into a scuttle. The moment they come to the negotiating table they will forget their common demands and each one of them will start clamouring for concessions to advance his own interest.' Khwaja Shahabuddin played an important role at this stage by getting in touch with some members of the Opposition. He was urging them to adopt a reasonable negotiating position. DAC called a country-wide strike on 12 January. For the first time the army was called out in aid of civil power in Dhaka which was cut off from the rest of the country.

The ruling party was a sinking ship. Some Basic Democrats in East Pakistan gave a statement that 'as self-respecting citizens we cannot remain associated with a regime which has virtually been waging war against the people of the country and thereby creating new problems far from solving the existing ones.'[5] Dhaka was under curfew as were many other cities including Karachi. Two more persons were killed in Dhaka on 25 January and this time it was the army which opened fire on an unruly mob for violating the curfew. Yahya had obviously instructed the General Officer Commanding in Dhaka to take a much tougher line in East Pakistan than was being followed in West Pakistan. The students of East Pakistan called for a province-wide strike, and life in all district and sub-divisional headquarters came to a standstill.

Ayub finally made up his mind to negotiate with DAC. He was encouraged by Khwaja Shahabuddin who told him that DAC would come with a two-point agenda for negotiations: direct elections on the basis of universal adult franchise and immediate lifting of the state of emergency. The difficulty was that DAC leaders were sceptical about Ayub's real intentions. They suspected that all his conciliatory overtures were meant to divide the Opposition which was already under great strain. Bhutto and Bhashani had adopted a highly strident posture and they were claiming that any negotiations with Ayub would amount to a betrayal of the people. Ayub would use the negotiations to bring the agitation under control and after that he would forget about making any fundamental constitutional changes. The dilemma, both for Ayub and DAC, was that the agitation could not be contained without negotiations, and without the agitation the Opposition had no leverage to extract any concession from Ayub. Every time DAC made some advance, Bhutto and Bhashani would condemn it as a sign of surrender to Ayub. Rumours would be set afloat that some group in DAC had made a private deal with Ayub. The dilemma became acute when Khan A. Sabur Khan, leader of the ruling party, made an announcement in the National Assembly on 31 January that Ayub would convene a round table conference to consider any 'reasonable proposal' for settlement which might be made by the Opposition. This was immediately condemned by DAC as a hoax—they described Ayub's dialogue 'lobby within the lobby' as a 'fraudulent arrangement'.[6] A member of the Awami League termed the so-called round table conference a device designed to frustrate the current movement. A representative of the right wing Nizam-i-Islam party said that there could be dialogue with Ayub only after the people's demands had been fulfilled. By supporting the demands voiced by any disaffected group Bhutto and Bhashani had put themselves in the vanguard of the agitation.

On 1 February 1969 Ayub made a formal announcement: 'We shall have no hesitation in agreeing to any settlement that is arrived at through mutual discussion.'[7] He indicated that he would shortly invite representatives of responsible political parties for talks. The word 'responsible' was seen by the Opposition as an attempt by Ayub to divide the Opposition. The *Pakistan Observer* wrote on 2 February that Ayub's offer of dialogue should not be rejected out of hand. The offer indicated 'breaking of the ice' and there could be no harm in the Opposition examining the offer while keeping in mind their ultimate aim and duty to the country. However, for a meaningful dialogue, the air must first be cleared of all doubts, suspicions and fears.

Ayub set up a committee of officials consisting of the Deputy Chairman of the Planning Commission, the Principal Secretary to the President, the Information Secretary, and the Finance Secretary to study the problems arising out of the agitation and to make recommendations to deal with them. The committee held several meetings and the Information Secretary drafted the report of the committee which was submitted to Ayub in January 1969. The committee identified corruption as a major cause of popular disaffection: the common man is 'outraged by the knowledge that people in high places and their relations have taken advantage of their position and derived financial benefits openly and blatantly'. There was widespread disappointment with the Constitution and people had come to believe that 'under the new system the rich are getting richer and the poor poorer'. There was a general apprehension that the present Constitution did not contain any arrangement for peaceful and orderly succession and that one-man rule would be followed inevitably by chaos. The absence of an effective ruling party had made the bureaucracy 'omnipresent'. Ministers had become subservient to Civil Servants and the bureaucracy was as 'isolated from the people' as the ruling party. The administration's rigid control over all means of expression had 'added to the sense of frustration among the vocal classes.' Members of the government had become over-sensitive to Press criticism with the result that the 'Press, instead of serving as a vehicle of communication, had become a protective but ineffective instrument in the service of the government'.

The committee identified three ways of dealing with the situation: (1) use of force; (2) political response and reconciliation, and (3) maintaining the *status quo* with modifications. The committee advised against the use of force: 'We do not deny that use of force might snuff out the agitation but we are convinced that it will deepen the present resentment against the government and make the restoration of normal conditions impossible.' It recommended the course of reconciliation: 'There is today a wide generation gap and the government must take into account the attitudes, thinking and demands of the new generation.' In more specific terms, the committee suggested a step-by-step opening of dialogue with the Opposition, firm measures to curb corruption, a number of administrative changes, a new approach towards economic planning, broadening of the electoral college and other constitutional changes to ensure smooth and orderly succession.[8]

The report had the effect of convincing Ayub that he must earnestly embark on the course of negotiations. He agreed to invite the Opposition to a conference. Who should be invited? The question was debated for days. If the invitation was issued to DAC that would leave Bhutto and Bhashani out, and if they too were invited the conference would become unmanageable. On the advice of the Information Secretary, Ayub decided to leave it to DAC to choose its representatives to the conference. On 5 February Ayub invited the convener of DAC, Nawabzada Nasrullah Khan, to bring his colleagues to a Round Table Conference (RTC) on 17 February 'to mutually discuss the political problems which are agitating the people's mind' and to find a solution to those problems.[9] The invitation caused great confusion because neither DAC nor its convener had any mandate to make any negotiated settlement with Ayub on behalf of the people. DAC was essentially a pressure group which was relying on popular agitation to force concessions out of the government. Suddenly it was called upon to act as an organized political body to negotiate with the government. It had neither the structure nor any tradition to act with cohesion and discipline: and there was no agreement or consensus on any fundamental political question available to DAC for guidance.

After issuing the invitation, Ayub left for Dhaka where he announced that the government was thinking of lifting the state of emergency but certain legal complications had first to be overcome. He added that if Mujib and Bhutto were nominated by the Opposition as delegates to the RTC, their release could be arranged.[10] Nawabzada Nasrullah Khan welcomed this statement as 'a good gesture'. The Awami League, which was a member of DAC however, passed a resolution that it would not take part in the negotiations until a proper atmosphere for discussion had been created by the government, and the only way to do that was to accept certain demands which included direct elections on the basis of universal adult franchise, immediate withdrawal of the emergency, and release of all political prisoners including Bhutto and Wali Khan.[11]

On 8 February 1969, Ayub issued another statement in which he said that the Constitution could accommodate the changing moods and requirements of the people. He was ready to make such arrangements as would remove the feeling among the educated classes that the present system of elections had deprived them of the opportunity to participate in the affairs of the country. The next day the students of Dhaka, who had formed a joint action committee, declared that they would continue the agitation until their 11-point charter of demands was fully realized and 'the autocratic regime was brought to an end'.[12] This charter included the eight points of DAC and some other demands relating to the student community.

Nawabzada called on Ayub in Dhaka on 10 February. He came immaculately dressed in his customary *sherwani* and a Turkish cap—missing only was the *hookah,* his constant companion. Nawabzada had a good command of the Urdu language but his whole style was a little archaic for the occasion. It took him an hour, and several verses of Iqbal which he used to enliven his discourse, to convey to Ayub that it was not fair to expect him to nominate the delegates to the RTC. He wanted Ayub to invite

Bhutto and Bhashani to the conference but DAC would not officially nominate them or take any responsibility for the position they might adopt in the conference. After he left Ayub said, 'This man has no authority. He is a weak man and they have put him there because he has no opinion of his own.'[13]

The central committee of DAC discussed Ayub's invitation and found that the only point on which they could agree was to continue giving full support to the agitation and not to do anything which might give the impression that any member of the Opposition was weakening in his resolve to bring down the regime. Bhutto was keeping his options open. If DAC made any headway he could always find his way into the negotiations, but if DAC were to make any compromise he would go on with his own programme of confrontation.

Lahore was paralysed by processions and strikes which were drawing support from every student organization and education institution in the city. The National Students Federation in Karachi decided to launch a civil disobedience movement from 15 February if political leaders including Bhutto were not released. Speakers at the meeting criticized DAC and warned that 'anyone who is prepared to bargain away the people's rights or the people's movement for some concession can only earn the hostility of the students and the masses.'[14]

Ayub was beginning to look isolated and helpless. Many of his associates thought he had lost the will to govern. Some of his ministers and senior Civil Servants had started meeting Yahya and other senior military officers to impress upon them the need to act if they wanted to save the country. It was an action replay of what had preceded the army take-over in 1958. The Opposition wanted Ayub to demolish with his own hands the political structure he had built with such conviction. There was no section of urban society, nor any influential individual, willing to come out openly in support of Ayub. His anguish was deepened by his conviction that there were few people in the Opposition who possessed any integrity or wisdom. He knew most of them as adventurers and opportunists.

The clock was ticking away but the administrative routine ground on remorselessly. At one moment Ayub would be raving about some slanderous attack on him, at another coolly discussing a proposal to carve out a new district or build a new road. During his stay in Dhaka, Ayub would sit in the verandah of the house on Hare Road with the Information Secretary who had earlier lived in that house, beside him. The magnificent banyan tree still stood there—a picture of serenity in the midst of political chaos. The ministerial clamour around Ayub would keep competing with the crows on the lawns while Ayub would sit there with a blank look on his face. Occasionally he would shift his chair to avoid the sun. Governor Monem Khan would now reassure him, 'Things will improve my President—gradually, gradually,' and now complain about the theft of copper wire belonging to the post and telegraph department! Ayub would listen with his head bowed and his hands covering his pale and tired face.

Ayub yields ground

Back in Rawalpindi on 12 February 1969, Ayub discussed the strategy for the RTC. The Opposition might bring sixteen to thirty-two delegates. The venue would be the President's guesthouse and Khwaja Shahabuddin would be in charge of all the arrangements. He had assured Ayub that DAC would come with two agreed demands: (1) federal parliamentary system, and (2) direct elections on the basis of adult franchise. Ayub wondered whether they would be able to agree on anything. Looking a little forlorn he said, 'I am now beginning to feel that this marching up and down by the students is affecting the life of the country. Time is coming when we have to come down hard. I am just waiting for the parleys to end. A beginning has to be made in two or three cities. Today was the day to do it.' For a moment, it looked as if Ayub had made up his mind and would take command of the situation. But it was Ayub's vacillation which unnerved his ministers. One day the old decision-maker would be back in form and the next day he would withdraw into himself.

Later in the evening Ayub had a brief meeting in which he nominated the official delegation and then withdrew to his study.

He asked the Information Secretary to join him. He was in a brown suede jacket and black trousers. There were two books on the table beside him, *The Bogey Man* by Plimpton and Mayhew's *Britain's Role Tomorrow*. The army intelligence had told him that the Opposition was planning to impeach him. 'Do you think these fellows are going to be so malicious?' he asked the Information Secretary. The Information Secretary had no answer but deep down he knew that the report was another turn of the screw by Yahya Khan to convince Ayub that he must rely on the army even for his own security. For the Information Secretary that moment marked the end of the Ayub era.

Two days later Ayub decided that the state of emergency should be lifted on 17 February, 'but we must make it clear that we are not doing this under pressure'. When should Bhutto be released? The question was left hanging in the air. Ayub warned,

> Once this Constitution is unravelled, the country won't stay together. One Unit will be dissolved and there will be a loose federation with East Pakistan, if we are lucky. I cannot see the country functioning under the parliamentary system. Either you have the presidential system or give complete independence to every province.

Ayub spoke to Musa about Bhutto and decided that he should be released on 15 February. After a while he resumed his reflections: 'We may have saved the country from civil war. That is my only consolation. These political leaders did not start the agitation, they took advantage of it. I still hope we can have the elections though we may have to use force at one or two places.'

Two days before the RTC opened Ayub started working on his speech. He felt that he must speak at the opening session because 'a statement at the end would be taken as a beaten man's discourse'.[15] But he would not be a party to the dissolution of the country: 'I believe I have done my best. A lot of good has happened. History alone can judge the true merits of what has been achieved. But I get the impression that people want change. I am not anxious to hang on and would be very happy to leave at the end of my term.'[16]

Later in the evening Ayub remained closeted with Yahya for a long time. Manzur Qadir had given him a note a few days earlier in which he said that the President had served the country for ten years. Whether he had served the country well or not was, in strictly political terms, an academic question to which history alone could provide an answer in retrospect. He advised Ayub to make an announcement that he had done his duty and it was now 'for others to take over'. In the meantime he should take steps to organize elections to a new constituent assembly on the basis of direct franchise.[17] It was vintage Manzur Qadir, idealistic but totally unrealistic. He could not see that the moment Ayub announced his intention to retire he would become politically irrelevant. Leave alone organizing elections to a new assembly, he would not be able to stay in office for a day. Ayub consulted some of his close associates about the likely effects of such an announcement. Would he regain the confidence of the people? Asked for his views the Information Secretary said that it was a matter in which the President must act according to his personal judgement. But if the President should decide to make such an announcement it should be done before the start of the RTC. Ayub said he had made up his mind and asked the Information Secretary to draft the announcement.

The Opposition parties were now at loggerheads. The last DAC meeting in Lahore was lost in rumbustious confusion. The prospects of getting the delegates to conference were getting hazier by the minute.

The next day, 16 February, Ayub went through the text of his announcement which recognized the people's desire for change but insisted that change must come only through political consensus. The crucial sentence in the statement was, 'I also want to make it clear that I am not looking for a consensus to perpetuate [Ayub crossed 'perpetuate' in the draft and wrote 'continue' in its place] myself in office. Nothing is farthest from my thoughts.'[18]

As he was going through the statement, a message came from Dhaka that two Agartala under-trial prisoners had rushed the guards and one of them had been shot dead. The situation in Dhaka had become extremely tense. There was a suspicion that the whole incident had been staged by Yahya's intelligence chief in Dhaka to frustrate the RTC. Ayub received a message from DAC that Mujib should be invited to come to the conference, on parole, if necessary. They also wanted him to invite Bhashani and Bhutto. When Khwaja Shahabuddin learnt that Ayub was thinking of announcing his intention to step aside, he was most upset. He rushed to Ayub and pleaded with him not to leave the field to the extremists and the announcement was withheld at the last minute.

Over a million people joined the funeral procession of sergeant Zahurul Haq, the under-trial prisoner, who was killed in Dhaka. A section of the crowd turned violent and burnt several government offices and houses of ministers, including Khawaja Shahabuddin's house. Bhashani gave a new slogan to the mob—*gherao jalao* (besiege and burn). In utter frustration Ayub said, 'this man suffers from every kind of disease but he doesn't die.'

On 17 February Ayub consulted some of his ministers about inviting Bhashani, Bhutto, and others to the conference. Ayub's view was, 'If we decide to invite them, however distasteful it might be, we should do so as quickly as possible.' Everyone except the Law Minister, S.M. Zafar, was in favour of issuing the invitation immediately. Zafar thought this would give them unnecessary importance. Sobur suggested that DAC leaders were worried about their own position. They did not want Bhutto and Bhashani sniping at them from outside the conference.

Ayub talked to Governor Monem Khan on the phone about the worsening situation in Dhaka. Ayub asked him, 'Have you made up your mind about withdrawing the Agartala case?' The telephone line went dead. Ayub decided that invitations should be issued to Bhutto, Bhashani, Asghar Khan, General Azam, and Justice Murshid. In the meantime, at the request of the convener of DAC, the conference was postponed for a couple of days.

Both Bhutto and Bhashani declined the invitation leaving DAC to stew in its own juice. Maulvi Farid Ahmad of the Nizam-i-Islam party, a maverick politician, telephoned Ayub and urged him to withdraw the Agartala case. Ayub reacted sharply, 'Look, I will not compound felony.'

The situation in Dhaka was now completely out of control. Curfew was being openly violated and people were demanding the withdrawal of the army. Goods had disappeared from the shops and rumours were afloat that thousands of people had been killed. After talking to General Yahya and the Law Minister, Ayub decided to withdraw the Agartala case.

Ayub called an emergency Cabinet meeting on 19 February. He came into the meeting looking deathly pale. He asked the Civil Servants to leave 'since we will be talking about political matters'.[19] A little later Khwaja Sahabuddin came out of the meeting, his voice trembling with rage and his grey hair shaking like flakes of snow, and said to the Information Secretary, 'They are talking utter nonsense. Their opinion is that there is no remedy except martial law. This is betrayal.' Soon after that General Yahya walked into the Cabinet room along with his Chief of General Staff. Things were moving towards a climax.

Later that evening Ayub had a meeting with the three Commanders-in-Chief and the Law Minister. The service chiefs were of the opinion that martial law was the answer but before that an effort should be made to meet the Opposition. The Law Minister agreed, but advised that the demands of DAC should be met only in small instalments. It was decided to replace the two governors immediately. The East Pakistan Finance Minister, Nurul Huda would take over from Monem Khan and Air Marshal Nur Khan from General Musa. Nur Khan did most of the talking. Yahya said to Ayub at one point: 'Sir, the army is behind you. You give the orders and we will do the rest. These ruffians need to be sorted out.' Admiral Ahsan, a man of some sophistication, said, 'Mr President, whatever the Opposition says goes to the heart of the people.'[20]

The scene was reminiscent of the one when Ayub's three generals had gone up to Iskander Mirza's bedroom and asked for his resignation. The three service chiefs were now going through the same act but with greater guile. They wanted Ayub to pave the way for them to take over power. Yahya had put the air force chief forward to give him a sense of importance and to keep himself in Ayub's confidence. Their hope was that Ayub would himself abrogate the Constitution as Iskander Mirza had done. When they did not succeed in that Yahya changed his strategy. He told Ayub that it was not necessary for him to 'step down', all he had to do was to 'step aside', and the army would do the job of sorting out the politicians, and putting down the agitation. He could always come back and take charge of the affairs of government. Ayub never quite swallowed that line, but he found it reassuring. Somewhere at the back of his mind was the fear, which the army intelligence had planted with great subtlety, that the politicians might start demanding his impeachment.

By 21 February Ayub was convinced that he would not be able to persuade the politicians to come to any political settlement: 'It is a mad-house. If there was a chance I would take it. Changes here and there won't make any difference. I have had a lot of advice and now I have come to a decision. The decision is not open to question or discussion. I think I must quit. That is the only answer.'[21] He asked the Information Secretary to draft a statement that he had decided not to contest for the third term to enable the people to elect their representatives in a free and fair manner. It took the Information Secretary about two hours to draw up the statement. Ayub approved the statement without making any change and it was decided that it should be recorded and broadcast in the evening. Ayub read his statement in a firm voice without a trace of emotion. 'My dear countrymen: we are passing through a critical time. Agitation has assumed the form of a frenzy. Pakistan has been my passion and my whole life has been dedicated to its service…I know that whatever decision I take today will have a far-reaching effect on our future…' And then he came to the crucial sentences: 'At all times and in all difficulties I have sought guidance from God Almighty. It is in the light of my faith that I have decided to announce today that I shall not be a candidate in the next election. This decision is final and irrevocable. All doubts, suspicions and misgivings must end with this announcement.'

Ayub's statement was acclaimed by all DAC leaders in West Pakistan. Even Bhutto sent a message of appreciation. All this was part of a political pantomime because it made no difference to the agitation. The politicians knew that they had got Ayub on the run and passed the message to the mob with great jubilation.

Later Ayub explained why he had waited so long to make the announcement: 'I have not done this in a foolhardy manner. I have tried to save my position too. Martial law is coming. What else is there to replace the government. I still have some value. I can influence a better man to get in. I tell you Yahya would be the best man. All these other men are deadly poison.'[22]

The act of renunciation has something of the quality of death. The Governors were stunned by Ayub's broadcast and the ministers were devastated. Sobur said: 'He has stabbed the country in the back. The whole thing is nauseating. If he wanted to withdraw he should have done so after 1965. That would have been much more graceful.' Governor Musa said, 'The Opposition can now ask Ayub to go and let them deal with the problem.'[23]

Despite Ayub's announcement, arrangements continued to be made for holding the round table conference with the politicians. Their latest demand was that Ayub should concede direct elections and federal parliamentary system before the conference. Ayub had a meeting with Mujib a day before the conference opened. This was their first-ever meeting. Ayub treated Mujib with great consideration. Mujib promised that he would try to make the conference a success but he told Ayub that his 21 February announcement was a great mistake.[24]

The conference met on 26 February and was adjourned till 10 March. The delegates wanted to celebrate the festival of Eid with their families but the real reason was that they had not been able to get their act together. Yahya now had all the time he needed to complete his preparations for the take-over.

The Daily Telegraph, London, published a story alleging that there was a secret protocol to the Tashkent Declaration. The reporter had picked up the story from Bhutto. A contradiction was issued and Ayub instructed that libel action should be taken against the paper.

What happens if the talks fail? That was the question now nagging Ayub: 'Will I have to ensure that the National Assembly implements the proposals which I make if the conference fails?'

Ayub accepted the suggestion that if Mujib had a meeting with Yahya it might encourage him to act with moderation.

The 'Ides of March' was approaching! Ayub was still hopeful that he might be able to resurrect his political system in some form. There were moments when he seemed to forget that he could no longer influence the course of events. To all appearances he was in the driving seat but the speed and direction of everything that was still mobile in the government was being dictated by someone else.

Ayub was sitting in the back verandah of his house admiring the flowers in the lawn. He talked about the advent of early summer and the brief mild winter. He could not see any merit in the advice that he must not abandon his efforts to find a workable political solution. 'Time is running out Altaf,' he said to the Information Secretary. 'There is no administration left in East Pakistan. Trains are being attacked in Sindh. How long can this go on?' He was told about the Mujib-Yahya meeting that had been fixed for 6 March and he seized at that straw, 'That might provide an opening.'[25]

The irony of the situation was that the Opposition was still clinging to the belief that Ayub could grant them their demands. Ayub's condition reminded one of the prophet Solomon: not until the white ants had eaten through his legendary staff and he collapsed in a heap, did the people believe he was dead. Ayub, the most needed man, was no more. Neither the people nor the Opposition seemed to know this. The Opposition needed Ayub as a target to keep the agitation going, while the army wanted him to facilitate a popularly backed *coup d'etat*.

The Opposition was engaged in an endless round of meetings in Lahore trying to come to some arrangement on the demands which they should put before the conference on 10 March. On 8 March Nawabzada Nasrullah Khan, convener of DAC, informed Ayub that the Opposition would not come to the conference with an agreed set of demands and each delegate would be free to put up his own demands. Ayub's first reaction was one of disgust and he wanted to call off the conference but the Information Secretary persuaded him not to abandon the course of negotiations.

Ayub wanted to discuss his negotiating strategy with his ministers and advisers but they were no longer interested. Their view was that the whole idea of entering into negotiations with the Opposition was a mistake. Most of them wanted the state of emergency to be reimposed and all the agitators arrested. Otherwise, martial law, in their opinion, was the only alternative.

Khwaja Shahabuddin, who had been advising Ayub to enter into negotiations with the Opposition, found himself in the dock. A man of infinite civility, he was outraged by the accusations that the ministers were hurling at him. He told Ayub that he had asked him to negotiate with the Opposition to prevent bloodshed and to maintain the constitutional order. Since his advice had failed he must submit his resignation. Ayub reacted angrily, 'This is not the time to talk of resignation. We have to deal with the present situation.' Ayub recalled what Duncan Sandys had told him in 1962 that he had introduced the Constitution prematurely. 'The basic problem,' Ayub said, 'is that we are not a nation. We are not clear in our minds. We should give all that East Pakistan wants and all that the provinces in West Pakistan want.'

Ayub called Yahya Khan and told him, 'I think you have to go into action immediately. Perhaps on the 11th or 12th of April.' Yahya advised Ayub to see the Opposition leaders individually:

You will get a better picture. They will tell you their real position which may be quite different from their public posture. You must get an assurance from them that if you present them with your compromise formula they will support you. If they do not give such an assurance then you will be free to act. You will have done your best.

Ayub agreed, but his feeling was that he was not dealing with honourable people: 'How can I just sit back and talk when the country is on the brink of collapse.' There was no point in convening the National Assembly because Bhutto and Bhashani would prevent the members from coming. Yahya said, 'Your obligation is to meet the Opposition. If they don't let the Assembly meet you will be free to act. It cannot be a matter of months, maybe weeks or days. You should put the onus on them.' Yahya had now dropped his old subservient manner and spoke with authority. Ayub was worried that if the Assembly was called the whole thing might drag on for months. Yahya said, 'You complete the process and then give us the orders. We will do the job.' He added, 'The government has lost all credibility and abroad they are wondering why you are not acting. But you must go through the process. Put DAC on notice. There is very little time left.'[26]

Ayub asked Yahya and the Information Secretary to stay for dinner. Ayub was a careful eater. During dinner he kept repeating that things were getting out of control. He said that parliamentary system would be fatal for Pakistan: 'You will have weak governments, but if that is what the people want there is little that I can do.' He was convinced that for him to say that he would introduce constitutional changes to allow direct elections under the parliamentary system would be time consuming and counter-productive. 'It will make your task more difficult,' he said to Yahya. Ayub was now talking to Yahya like an ally in the military operation they were planning. After dinner Ayub opened the door leading to the back verandah. It was not his custom to go there after dinner and the servants had removed all the cushions from the cane chairs. Yahya suggested, 'The President might like to rest now.' Ayub said *'Khuda Hafiz,'* and walked down the passage toward his bedroom.

Round Table Conference

The conference opened on 10 March 1969.[27] The Opposition leaders presented two points on which they were agreed: direct elections on the basis of universal suffrage, and a federal parliamentary system under which the provinces would have complete autonomy. Speaking first, Nawabzada started in Urdu, but when Professor Muzaffar Ahmed objected that he did not understand Urdu, the proceedings were conducted in English. Mujib read out a nine-page statement repeating all his six and eleven points. He wanted a strong Pakistan but a weak centre. He was quite dogmatic about his demands. Mufti Mahmood followed.

He criticized the family laws but did not attack family planning. He took a rather mild position. Asghar Khan's main fear was that if the agitation were to subside, Ayub would reassert his position. Ayub felt that Asghar Khan's attack was most unfair. Wali Khan spoke sensibly and very well indeed, 'an extremely intelligent man who comes of a strong-willed family'. But Professor Muzaffar Ahmed, Ayub said,

> ...talked like a rabid extremist. I told him that if the provinces are given all the power you suggest, there would be no need for a central government. He was stumped. I think future relations between East and West Pakistan will have to be treaty relations. It is a hard thing to say but that is what the Bengalis want.[28]

In his opening speech Ayub had stated that his powers were coming to an end. He hoped that the Opposition leaders got the message. But Ayub's great disappointment was that no one among them was capable of looking at the problems facing the country in the national context. Everybody was consumed by parochial interests and personal concerns. Should they come to power, what would they do apart from rewarding their supporters and punishing their opponents?

In the afternoon Ayub met his advisers to review the results of the morning session. Manzur Qadir was also present. The general view was that DAC had not presented a clear and agreed definition of the federal parliamentary system. Nurul Huda, the East Pakistan Finance Minister, whose wife came from Faridpur and who had some contact with Mujib, observed that DAC agreed on the parliamentary form of government. Ayub rejoined, 'but not on the question of parity of representation between East and West Pakistan or the distribution of subjects between the centre and the provinces.'[29] Ayub felt that it would be pointless on his part to take his solution to parliament if it was not accepted by the Opposition: 'It will be thrown back in my face and people will laugh at me.' Manzur Qadir suggested that DAC should be asked to produce an agreed bill incorporating the precise definition of the federal parliamentary form of government. Ayub said that once he agreed to direct elections under the parliamentary system, it would be illogical for him to object to any definition of the system that DAC might adopt. Some East Pakistani members of the delegation, particularly Ajmal Ali and Hashimuddin, started insisting that it was futile to carry on any further negotiations and the time had come to impose martial law. Manzur Qadir argued strongly against such a course of action. Ayub said, 'I wonder how much of this will remain a secret.'

Ayub spent the whole of the next day, 11 March, in the conference. Asghar Khan picked up an argument with Admiral A.R. Khan which turned into quite a row. The Bengalis made no secret of their commitment to the six-point programme and even Nurul Amin seemed to have come round to Mujib's point of view.

Chaudhri Muhammad Ali and Maulana Maududi wanted the conference to agree on direct elections and the federal parliamentary system and leave the rest to the elected representatives of the people. The line-up was now becoming clear; the two right-wing parties, Nizam-i-Islam and Jamaat-i-Islami, were willing to support Ayub while the rest wanted all their demands to be accepted by the conference without waiting for the elections. Ayub asked the Information Secretary to prepare his closing statement.

Ayub saw the statement in the evening and approved it after making a few changes. He then invited Khwaja Shahabuddin, S.M. Zafar, and Manzur Qadir to examine the statement. Manzur Qadir had come armed with a draft of his own. Then followed a marathon debate almost exclusively between Manzur Qadir and the Information Secretary. The point at issue was whether Ayub should accept the two demands on which there was agreement in the conference and leave the rest to the elected representatives of the people, or accept all the demands of the Opposition parties without having the authority to implement them. Manzur Qadir asked Ayub to 'invite one who is acceptable to you to form a parliamentary government immediately with himself as the Prime Minister. As soon as the person of your choice has assumed office you can tender your resignation.' Manzur Qadir would not recognize that Ayub was in no position politically, or under the Constitution, to extend such an invitation to a person of his choice. During the heated discussion there were moments when Ayub seemed ready to follow Manzur Qadir's advice. Manzur Qadir told Ayub that he was in touch with the Opposition leaders and they would agree to the nomination of Sheikh Mujibur Rahman as Prime Minister. The Information Secretary said it would be a little odd for Ayub to nominate a person, who only a few days earlier had been under trial for treason, as Prime Minister of the country.

It was not until 2 o'clock in the morning that a compromise formula was hammered out in which Ayub would accept the two agreed demands and promise that if the Opposition could agree on any other demand he would take that into consideration too. He would also offer that the government and the Opposition should *jointly and collectively* deal with the problems facing the country. Such an offer might open the possibility of forming a national government. The Information Secretary drafted Ayub's statement on the basis of this formula but early in the morning Manzur came up with a draft based on his original suggestions. The Information Secretary took the two drafts to Ayub and strongly advised him against accepting Manzur's version. Ayub said to him, 'I am glad you stood up to him. He doesn't let go easily.'[30]

In his statement at the closing session, Ayub offered to take the two agreed demands to the National Assembly for approval provided the conference unanimously endorsed them. In the absence of such an endorsement it would be futile to summon the Assembly. In conclusion, he outlined the problems facing the country and said: 'These are problems for all of us, and all of us must jointly face them so that normal life in the country is restored immediately. Let us resolve to offer collective resistance to the forces of agitation and disruption.' Ayub's offer was supported by all the delegates except Mujib and Wali Khan. Several Opposition leaders congratulated Ayub and left the conference hall in the belief that DAC had scored a victory by forcing Ayub to concede to two of their major demands, and that after further bilateral consultations he would accept the rest.

Bhutto kept up his attack on the conference. He continued to insist that it had no authority to decide any constitutional issue 'when on one side of the table sat a totally rejected government and on the other side political leaders without any mandate from the masses'.[31] If neither the government nor the political parties had any authority to resolve the issues then, according to Bhutto's logic, the army was the only legitimate institution to take control of the country. Some senior army officers, particularly General S.G.M.M. Peerzada, were in close contact with Bhutto, and according to Khawaja Shahabuddin they had encouraged Bhutto to stay out of the conference. Ayub did not suspect that Yahya was doing a masterly double-deal, encouraging Ayub to go through the charade of a conference while using Bhutto to question the very basis of negotiations.

Immediately after the conference Mujib announced his dissociation from DAC because it had not supported East Pakistan's demand for autonomy, and the Nawabzada declared that DAC had served its purpose and stood dissolved. It was clear that the Opposition parties now wanted to deal with Ayub individually under the impression that they could extract further concessions from him. In the evening Mujib had dinner with Ayub at the President's House. The Information Secretary was also there. Nothing of importance was mentioned during dinner. Ayub asked Mujib about Asghar Khan and he said, 'He has made some impact in East Pakistan.'[32]

What was happening in the country could only be understood as an atavistic phenomenon. The newspapers were full of statements of DAC leaders congratulating Ayub for the success of the conference. Mahmud Ali, the spokesman of DAC, said: 'History will record the height of statesmanship of the President,' and claimed that the conference was 'a unique victory of the people'. Chaudhri Muhammad Ali said that by accepting the nation's demand for peaceful transfer of power, 'the President has shown great statesmanship and I have no doubt that history will record it as such.'[33] Nurul Amin called the conference a success and Asghar Khan said that the decision to introduce the parliamentary system was an important step. Even Bhashani expressed satisfaction that accord had been reached on at least two major questions. Bhutto alone was unhappy and said that he had always been 'sceptical' of the results of the conference.[34]

Bhutto's principal concern now was to discredit the other political leaders and become the spokesman of the masses.

The day after the conference all the Opposition leaders except Mujib called on Ayub. They talked about the election scheduled and asked Ayub to replace the two Governors and the Chief Election Commissioner. They seemed convinced that the negotiations had succeeded and everything had returned to normal. All that remained was for Ayub to summon the Assembly and hold the elections.

At Ayub's suggestion the Information Secretary arranged for Wali Khan to have a separate meeting with Ayub. Wali Khan seemed to appreciate that Ayub could not announce the dissolution of One Unit. The best he could do was to establish a commission to examine the problem. Wali Khan was with Ayub for an hour and came out looking quite depressed. He said, 'The President is not willing to go beyond the two points.' While waiting in the Military Secretary's office, before going into Ayub's room, Wali Khan narrated how Khwaja Shahabuddin had asked him on three different occasions during the conference, 'How is it that I never met a bright and able person like you when I was the Governor of NWFP for three years.' Wali Khan let it pass on the first two occasions but on the third occasion he could not restrain himself and rejoined, 'Because all those three years you kept me in prison.' He remembered how on one of his visits to London he called on Sir George and Lady Cunningham. He had trouble in his right eye and when Lady Cunningham enquired about it he told her that he had contracted a serious infection in 1943 in prison. 'In 1943,' she said, and then turning angrily to her husband said, 'George, were you not the Governor then and you put this nice young man in jail?'

On 15 March the Information Secretary had a meeting with Chaudhri Muhammad Ali under instructions from Ayub. Muhammad Ali suggested that Ayub should summon the Assembly and get the two agreed points approved. How could Ayub do that when so many members of his party, particularly from Sindh, had already defected? Ghulam Mustafa Jatoi, under Bhutto's influence, had joined hands with G.M. Syed, and was demanding autonomy for Sindh. The Sindhis were extremely unhappy about the growing presence of 'outsiders' in the towns of Sindh. The Muhajirs had taken over the whole of Karachi, the Punjab officials had acquired large tracts of barrage lands, and the Pathans had acquired a monopoly of all transport and construction business. Muhammad Ali thought these worries were all unnecessary because his government in the nineteen fifties had foreseen the problem and had planned the induction of Muhajirs into Karachi and other major towns of Sindh to forestall Sindhi nationalism. He wanted it to be conveyed to Ayub that his party and many other DAC leaders would support him, but he wanted a further discussion in Lahore to work out the full strategy.

The two new Governors were sworn in, Nurul Huda in East Pakistan and Yusuf Haroon in West Pakistan, and everyone around Ayub was waiting to see whether they would make any impact on the prevailing situation. Yusuf Haroon turned up from nowhere and managed to persuade Ayub that he had close relations with Mujibur Rahman and with most of the Opposition leaders in West Pakistan and could bring them over to his side. He had all the qualities of a political hustler but he proved utterly ineffective and irrelevant.

On 17 March Ayub had a meeting with some of his West Pakistani advisers. Yusuf Haroon was also present. Ayub wanted to discuss the procedure to introduce the proposed amendments if the Assembly was summoned. What would be the best way of dealing with the question of autonomy and the dissolution of One Unit. 'If these things have to come, let them not come in a rush,' said Ayub. Would it not be better to leave it to the house committees to deal with the more controversial issues? Ayub said, 'No East Pakistani is in a reasonable frame of mind. They are all trying to out-bid Mujib.' The Finance Secretary, Ghulam Ishaq Khan, who was all for martial law, told Ayub that the proceedings of the house committee of the National Assembly on economic parity and capital formation had been boycotted by all the East Pakistani members of the ruling party on the ground that important constitutional changes were in the offing, and since the centre will be left only with the subjects of Defence and Foreign Affairs, there may be no need to have a central legislature. The Finance Secretary was not sure whether it would be possible to get the budget passed: 'The East Pakistanis are saying we will get our rights by agreement or by force. We will go back to the 1940 resolution.' The Deputy Chairman of the Planning Commission observed:

> The members of the legislature are in a highly agitated frame of mind. If there is a deadlock in the Assembly the result will be martial law. The question is whether we should destroy the country by accepting all the extreme demands or bring the pressure of martial law to save the country. The choice is to break One Unit to save the centre and keep East and West Pakistan within the federation or keep One Unit and let East Pakistan go. The difficulty is that you cannot maintain One Unit without the help of martial law.

The Law Minister advised, 'The President should say, "I go this far and no further".' Yusuf Haroon intervened to say, 'I think we are being very pessimistic, I am a politician and I have had long discussions with Mujib. He is very keen to become the Prime Minister and he would not want to be in charge of only two subjects.' Admiral A.R. Khan warned that whatever the political outcome, law and order must be maintained and Ayub said a little impatiently, 'But you cannot suppress people's emotions and ingrained frustration'. Ayub felt that the new governors must have time to persuade the members of the National Assembly to see how important it was for the President to continue until the amendments were adopted by the legislature. In a voice choking with emotion Ayub asked, 'What are we doing today? We are undoing all that I have done and all that the previous governments have done, and we are undoing all that Jinnah had done. We should either have an effective center or separate. If people want to go to hell we can only warn them. We can't stop them.'

Ayub asked the Deputy Chairman of the Planning Commission and the Information Secretary to go to Lahore for further discussion with Chaudhri Muhammad Ali. He had obviously started thinking of summoning the Assembly and wanted to muster some political support. The two meetings with Muhammad Ali lasted for well over six hours. He had a scholarly way of analysing problems—

laborious and long-winded, but not without substance. The thrust
of his argument was that West Pakistani leaders should now meet
and publicly declare their support for the two-point formula
which Ayub had accepted. Daultana must be brought in line.
Perhaps the new Governor could help in this. In any case the
General Officer Commanding of Lahore should call Daultana and
give him a warning. Muhammad Ali was concerned that the
smaller provinces of West Pakistan might put themselves under
some binding obligation to East Pakistan and acquire a permanent
grievance against the Punjab. He emphasized that regional
autonomy made sense only under a viable centre capable of
maintaining the integrity of the country. Representation in the
National Assembly on the basis of population would destroy the
federal concept as it would disenfranchise the less populated
regions. He advised that the National Assembly should be
summoned around 8 April and the intervening period used to
bring West Pakistani leaders to a common position behind the
two-point formula and to improve the law and order situation. It
was also important to strengthen the moderate elements in East
Pakistan and the process must begin now and go on till the
elections. Muhammad Ali had expected Ayub to appoint two
generals as governors who could have taken firm action in
selected areas to curb the agitation. He mentioned that some of the
Bengali leaders were afraid of returning to Dhaka because Mujib
was criticizing them for not giving full support to East Pakistan's
demand for autonomy. He promised that at a public meeting in
Lahore on 23 March, he and the Nawabzada would demand that
the government should take stern and effective action against the
agitators, start legal proceedings against the extremists and
postpone the convening of the Assembly for some time. This
should strengthen Ayub's hands. He hoped that the Press, radio,
and television would give full coverage to the meeting.

Muhammad Ali emphasized the urgency of bringing all the
moderate elements in East Pakistan on an Islamic platform. He
felt this could be done if adequate funds were provided. He
thought one crore of rupees would be needed and DAC would
arrange with Yusuf Ali Choudhri, alias Mohan Mia of Faridpur,

to ensure that the money was properly spent and the right kind of *ulema* were brought into the field to counter Awami League propaganda. A determined effort should also be made to support the demand for creating separate provinces of North Bengal and Sylhet. He suggested the appointment of a non-political interim government at the centre and, if that was not possible, at least four or five central ministers should be dropped. The Opposition should be consulted about their replacements. He particularly wanted the government to ensure that Bhutto and Bhashani should not be given any publicity. After the meeting one was left with the impression that the old man was still living in the fifties and had little knowledge of the problems of East Pakistan. There were no prospects of effectively countering Awami League propaganda from the so-called Islamic front. It was a familiar device which had been tried in the past without success because the Bengalis were convinced that Islam was being used by the government to suppress and exploit them. Any money which the ruling party might provide to right wing parties for the purpose would be wasted. Mohan Mia, though a clever operator, had no influence with the students, who were spearheading the movement for autonomy in East Pakistan.[35]

Ayub was having his evening walk when the Information Secretary gave him the gist of Muhammad Ali's proposals on 20 March. He said, 'Thank you for all the trouble. Some of the points are useful, others are wishful. But now the time has come for martial law. A.R. Khan is saying that if we wait any longer some young colonel might get impatient.' That must have been Yahya's final turn of the screw when he saw his plans getting upset by the appointment of new governors and the likelihood of the Assembly being summoned.

Ayub had called an emergency Cabinet meeting the same evening. A.R. Khan, Minister of Defence, gave a detailed account of the law and order situation. He painted a dismal picture. The Director of Intelligence Bureau said that the situation in East Pakistan had become chaotic. He was himself *gheraoed* (besieged) in the Intelligence Bureau and bodily thrown out by an unruly mob. The police force was completely demoralized. A mob had rushed to the tarmac at Dhaka Airport and ransacked the plane by which some Bengali delegates were returning from Lahore. Ayub said that General Musa had been urging him for over a month to impose martial law. When the Communications Minister, A. Sobur, intervened to say, 'No government exists in the country today,' Ayub lost his temper and almost shouted, 'This is not the time to talk nonsense.' He wanted to know whether the people were really fed up with the situation. If that were the case they would accept martial law. Earlier they might have opposed such a decision. It seemed Ayub's main concern now was to make martial law as acceptable to the people as possible.

At 8.30 p.m. on 20 March 1969, it was finally decided to impose martial law. Ayub's civilian government had handed over the baton to the 'professionals' who would determine the logistics of the action. Every minister had become an avid supporter of military rule. Most of them had been promised some job by Yahya Khan and some of them were acting as Yahya Khan's informers and agents to advance their career. Ayub's concluding words were:

> I have done my best. I believe the country has made tremendous progress in spite of what the others might say. I have also done my best to help the Opposition to come to a political settlement but they do not command any influence. I think the army should now take over and restore normal conditions. I have not taken this decision light-heartedly or without regret. But the safety of the country comes first and it must not be jeopardized for any consideration. I know I must step aside so that the army can act freely. I hope and pray that this action, however unpleasant, will prove in the best interests of the nation.

And as everyone was getting up, Ayub said, 'I have no regrets. I am a very happy man. I hope the country survives. These people have gone mad.'[36]

The last rites

Ayub appeared to have recovered his civilian self next morning. He was obviously cheered by the morning papers and statements of several DAC leaders in his support. He thought that with the new governors in position the political climate was beginning to improve. He wondered whether the decision taken the previous night was not based on too pessimistic an assessment. He asked the Law Minister, the Minister for Defence and the Information Secretary to go and discuss the matter with Yahya Khan.

When the Information Secretary was ushered into Yahya's office in GHQ, the Ministers of Law and Defence and the Defence Secretary, Ghiasuddin Ahmad, were already there. Yahya said, 'What is this? A civilian *coup d'etat?*' The Information Secretary could feel the tension in the room. Everyone waited for him to begin. They had obviously discussed the matter between themselves before his arrival. After giving a brief account of last night's Cabinet meeting he said that the President was now of the view that the decision to impose martial law was premature as it was based on too pessimistic an assessment of the situation. The leaders of several Opposition parties were coming out in support of the formula accepted by Ayub and the new governors needed time to bring the agitation under control. There were also important legal and constitutional questions which must be addressed before any extra-constitutional step was taken. Yahya's face went red and in a voice quivering with suppressed anger he said, 'I am not a court of judgment. Surely you all know what is going on. These leaders have no influence. The mobs are under the control of Bhashani and Bhutto.' He then turned to the Defence Secretary and shouted, 'Why don't you speak up?' The Defence Secretary took the cue and started his tale of woe: the country is in a state of anarchy; the administration has collapsed; things cannot improve; action has to be taken now and for the whole country; the National Assembly can achieve nothing; the new governors have no magic wand, the President must step aside and allow the army to decide the timing and phasing of martial law. By now the Defence Secretary had worked himself into a state. His outburst ended on a rhetorical note: 'How long can you keep your army uncontaminated? Either rule out martial law or impose it now.' When the Information Secretary rebutted some of the more hysterical points made by the Defence Secretary, Yahya became

quite impatient, 'If you fellows can't make up your mind I am
ready to go to Peshawar and sit at home while the country burns.
I have to do my duty and I am not going to let anyone interfere with
that.' The Information Secretary interrupted him, 'But General,
you cannot interpret your duty according to your wishes. Your
duty is laid down in the Constitution and the rules of business and
you cannot go beyond that.' Everybody was stunned. The Defence
Secretary slumped in his chair. He mumbled something about his
blood-sugar level and passed out. That was the end of the meeting.
The Information Secretary went straight to the President's House
and gave Ayub an account of his argument with Yahya. Ayub took
it quite philosophically and praised Yahya for his loyalty: 'But for
him the army would have acted much sooner.' He then started
reminiscing about his own work over the years and hoped that
once he was gone people might discover some merit in his
Constitution. He felt that it might become necessary to break up
One Unit under the cover of martial law, but the question of
regional autonomy would need much greater examination. After
that Ayub lay back like Gulliver, all tied and laced up, at the mercy
of the Lilliputians.[37]

Everything now came to a standstill. The gloom in the
President's House was suffocating. Yet the sun was shining and
the grass slowly turning dark brown. The pretence of official
routine still went on though nobody was doing anything. Ayub
would go to sleep and wake up with the question, 'How did it all
go wrong?'

Ayub asked the Information Secretary to prepare his farewell
speech and the letter he should write to Yahya. It would not be a
letter of resignation because he would only step aside and proceed
on three months' leave. He gave no indication of the arrangements
he had made with Yahya about his own future.

Ayub studied with great care his abdication speech and the
letter to Yahya. He made a few changes and added one or two new
points. He then took up a file which was lying beside him and
pulling out a paper said to the Information Secretary, 'Here are the
guidelines I have given to Yahya.' According to the guidelines
Yahya, after taking over, would arrest all the agitators and some

of the more irresponsible political leaders and restore law and
order and take steps to revive the economic life. Ayub put down
the file and said, 'He will carry out my orders. He has promised
to sort out Bhutto, though I think Asghar Khan is more dangerous
than him.' It was clear that Yahya had led Ayub to believe that the
army would put down the agitation, eliminate his political
opponents, and put him back in power after three months. Ayub
accepted the gambit because it offered him a ray of hope in the
darkness of failure and despair. A pragmatic and hard-headed
person, Ayub was now a prisoner of fears and a victim of
delusions. He was still ruminating when the ADC announced the
arrival of Yahya Khan. They remained together for some time and
after Yahya left Ayub said, 'The poor man was crying at the
thought of his Supreme Commander leaving in such painful
circumstances.' Actually, Yahya had come to see the text of
Ayub's broadcast before it was recorded, and the letter before it
was signed and despatched. Yahya had constructed his plan with
great care and like all conspirators he was extremely nervous that
if one brick happened to fall out of place the whole façade would
come crumbling down.[38]

On the morning of 25 March a cool breeze was blowing under
a cloudy sky and the ivy was swinging along the white pillars in
the verandah. Ayub, in a light grey suit, was reading the final text
of his abdication speech and his letter to Yahya. The lines across
his forehead deepened as he went over every word with great
concentration. He approved the texts and said, 'Thank you. This
is exactly how I wanted it. I was anxious that my language should
not be sloppy.' Ayub instructed his staff to send copies of the
speech to the Speaker of the National Assembly and to all Cabinet
Ministers. He got up and started walking on the lawn, a tall, big
man, taking long strides, with his hands in his pockets, as if he
didn't have a care in the world. He suddenly looked liberated.
Around him was a mass of yellow lilies in full bloom as the grey
clouds began to descend on the President's House. The recording
unit was ready but Ayub was waiting for Yahya who did not want
to miss the historic final moments!

Ayub recorded his abdication speech in his study. Yahya sat on the sofa on one side wearing a gloomy expression. 'People of Pakistan,' Ayub began,

> This is the last time I address you as your President. The country is passing through a critical time. The mob has overwhelmed the administration and there is no one who can reason with the agitators. Those who claimed to be leaders have become abject followers of the crowd...The Round Table Conference failed because the Opposition could not agree on any democratic programme. Everyone wanted his demands to be accepted without waiting for the elected representatives of the people to examine them. Had all those demands been accepted Pakistan as a nation-state would have ceased to exist...One of my greatest ambitions was to establish the democratic tradition of peaceful and orderly transfer of power. In that I have failed. There is now no institution except the armed forces which can save the country from chaos and ruin. I have, therefore, asked the Commander-in-Chief of the Army to carry out his legal obligations...May Pakistan live for ever.

Ayub finished his speech and walked over to shake hands with Yahya whose eyes were glistening with tears. The moment Ayub and Yahya left the room a colonel in dark glasses walked in and told the members of the broadcasting unit to stay where they were. He then seized the tape recording and the rest of the equipment. All this was done quite brusquely. The instrument of power was now in Yahya's hands!

Ayub had asked the Information Secretary, his wife Zarina, and his children Humayun, Naveed and Raana to lunch. After lunch Ayub formally decorated the Information Secretary with the insignia of Hilal-i-Quaid-i-Azam. Ayub wrote a personal letter to him on 25 March in which he said:

> You have worked with me very closely for more than five years and all through you have discharged your responsibilities with great integrity, determination and humility... As I have told you personally you have done a tremendous job for your country. I am sorry that you were subjected to a great deal of unfair criticism but I admire the way you continued to perform your duties with dedication regardless of all pressures.

That afternoon Rawalpindi came under the sweep of a ferocious storm which pulled out old trees from their roots. Houses and walls in the cantonment crumbled into heaps of slush leaving the decaying bungalows marooned. The Information Secretary was told to be at GHQ where Yahya was going to record his speech. An officer met him at the gate and conducted him to the office of the Military Secretary to Yahya. There he found Yahya, and three of his generals, Hameed, Peerzada and Gul Hassan, huddled round the radio set, listening to Ayub's broadcast. They looked like a bunch of thieves bending over the booty and were a little startled as if caught red-handed. A little later Yahya came into his office and settled down with his script in front of him. His co-conspirators all stood pasted along the wall in front of him. He read the text quite well but Peerzada wanted him to re-record one sentence in which he had missed a word. After the recording Yahya leaned back in his chair and said, 'I don't know about you fellows but I definitely deserve a drink.' The wall in front of him seemed to crumble in embarrassment. The bearers arrived with the drinks but the civilians took their leave to allow the ruling junta to booze itself without any bind.

Yahya's speech did not reflect any of the guidelines that Ayub had given him. Ayub's letter authorized him to carry out his legal obligations to 'put the country back on the road to progress in a civil and constitutional manner' but he went far beyond the powers available to him under the Constitution.[39] He not only imposed martial law, he abrogated the Constitution itself.

On 26 March Ayub invited his former ministers to a farewell meeting. Ayub was in a light grey suit and was wearing dark glasses. A swarm of sparrows was noisily chirping away under the bright sun. 'I am sorry we have come to this pass,' Ayub began,

We are a very difficult country structurally. Perhaps I pushed it too hard into the modern age. We were not ready for reforms. Quite frankly, I have failed. I must admit that clearly. Our laws were for a sophisticated society. The rest of the world was beginning to look up to us but our politicians said, 'Don't be in a hurry we will show you what we really are.' We were really able to bluff the world but our own people called the bluff. I could not sign away the future of the country. I would have much rather committed suicide. We don't know the value of freedom. Our people feel exposed and unhappy in freedom. Left to ourselves we would go back to slavery. I had to step aside.

There was no other answer. I never thought our people would go mad like this. Unfortunately there is no constructive public opinion. My greatest ambition was to transfer power in a democratic manner. I would have handed over power to Bhutto or Asghar or Mujib or Bhashani. My deepest disappointment when I met the Opposition was that there was not one person among them who could rise above his self-interest. I doubt if in our political life we will have a good man for a long time. Thank God we have an army. If nothing else I have held this country together for ten years. It was like keeping a number of frogs in one basket. What sort of Pakistan will emerge is anybody's guess. There will be either force or mob rule. I hope we can find some answer between the two. Let the East Pakistanis live as they want. Meanwhile we should examine the problems of West Pakistan. The country cannot last without a viable centre. There is no future in two Pakistans. The East will last a few years and the West will drag on—just drag on. There is no communication between the two parts. Let us hope some miracle will save us from complete separation.

The atmosphere was that of a funeral service and as soon as the ritual finished everyone left quietly without saying a word.[40]

Ayub expected to stay in the President's House for three months and to retain his personal staff. The house was adjacent to the President's secretariat and every morning Yahya and his staff officers would pass by the house and find the old man sitting on the lawns. His presence was a constant reminder of their crime. The day after he seized power, Yahya issued a notification appointing three of Ayub's men, A.R. Khan, Mian Arshad Hussain and Fida Hassan, as his advisers. But the notification was immediately withdrawn because GHQ did not like carrying the dead wood of the old regime. The next day General Peerzada, who had become Yahya's Principal Staff Officer, complained that sitting in the President's House Ayub was issuing orders and signing papers. The last straw was the resignation of S.M. Zafar, the former Law Minister which, Peerzada claimed, Ayub had accepted after handing over power but had antedated his signature. Peerzada conveyed it to Ayub that his presence was causing annoyance to the people and it was in his interest to leave the city. Ayub was visibly distressed: 'So Peerzada has become the Prime Minister. He is a devious rascal. I never trusted him.'[41]

1 April was a hazy morning when Ayub left for Swat. Around the House everything was still and lifeless. Not a leaf was moving. The Information Secretary, who was the only official to have come to see off Ayub, was waiting outside the President's House with General Rafi and some other members of his staff. The President's car, with the official flag drooping along the rod, had already moved into the porch.

Ayub came out of the house and walked towards the car— slowly and sedately, looking lonely and abandoned. On his sculptured face the dark lines of emotional strain were deeply engraved. He embraced the Information Secretary and said, 'Thank you for all that you have done.' He then embraced General Rafi and warmly shook hands with the others. He did not forget to thank the official photographer who had served him all those years. Just before getting into the car he remembered something and went back to the house where he had lived for twenty years, first as Commander-in-Chief and then as President. He returned with some magazines and files which he handed over to his ADC and got into his car.

As the car moved out of the porch Ayub leaned out of the window to wave the final goodbye. The car turned left and went past the gate as the sentries stood to attention. Spotted shadows of trees were falling on the narrow road stretching into a wasteland of 'bitter and ungrateful sands'.

NOTES

1. Samuel P. Huntington, *Political Order in Changing Societies;* Yale University Press Cambridge, Massachusetts, 1967, pp. 250-1.
2. Niccolo di Bernardo Machiavelli. The Prince p.94 *The Portable Machiavelli,* Penguin Books 1979.
3. *Pakistan Observer,* 10 January 1969.
4. Ibid., 21 January 1968.
5. Ibid., 24 January 1969.
6. Ibid., 1 February 1969.
7. *Dawn,* 1 February 1968.
8. Author's notes.
9. Ibid.

10. *Pakistan Observer,* 17 February 1969.

11. Ibid., 8 February 1969.

12. Ibid., 10 February 1969.

13. Author's notes.

14. *Dawn,* 11 February 1969.

15. Author's notes.

16. Ibid.

17. Manzur Qadir papers.

18. 21 February was commemorated as martyrs' day in Dhaka in memory of the students who were killed in language riots in East Pakistan in 1952. Ayub was anxious to defuse the situation before that date.

19. Author's notes.

20. Author's notes of conversation with Ayub Khan after the meeting.

21. Author's notes.

22. Ibid.

23. Ibid.

24. Author's notes of the meeting based on his conversation with Ayub Khan and Sheikh Mujibur Rahman after the meeting.

25. Author's notes.

26. Ibid.

27. Author's notes based on his conversation with Ayub immediately after the first session of RTC.

28. Ibid.

29. According to Dr Kemal Hosain, who was defence counsel for Mujibur Rahman in the Agartala Conspiracy case and assisted Mujib during the Round Table Conference, Dr Nurul Huda maintained contact with the Awami League advisers and provided some 'inside reports' on what was going on in the government camp. (Chapter 4. The Round Table Conference p. 46, unpublished manuscript.)

30. Author's notes.

31. *Dawn,* 10 March 1969.

32. Ibid.

33. *Pakistan Observer,* 14 March, 1969.

34. Ibid.

35. Ibid.

36. Author's notes.

37. Ibid.

38. Ibid.

39. From: Field Marshal Muhammad Ayub Khan, N.Pk., H.J.

> My dear General Yahya,
>
> It is with profound regret that I have come to the conclusion that all civil administration and constitutional authority in the country has become ineffective. If the situation continues to deteriorate at the present alarming rate, all economic life, indeed, civilized existence will become impossible.
>
> I am left with no option but to step aside and leave it to the Defence Forces of Pakistan, which today represent the only effective and legal instrument, to take full control of the affairs of the country. They are by the grace of God in a position to retrieve the situation and to save the country from utter chaos and total destruction.

They alone can restore sanity and put the country back on the road to progress in a civil and constitutional manner.

The restoration and maintenance of full democracy according to the fundamental principles of our faith and the needs of our people must remain our ultimate goal. In that lies the salvation of our people who are blessed with the highest qualities of dedication and vision and who are destined to play a glorious role in the world. It is most tragic that while we were well on our way to a happy and prosperous future, we were plunged into an abyss of senseless agitation. Whatever may have been used to glorify it, time will show that this turmoil was deliberately created by well-tutored and well-backed elements. They made it impossible for the government to maintain any semblance of law and order or to protect the civil liberties, life and property of the people. Every single instrument of administration and every medium of expression of saner public opinion was subjected to inhuman pressure. Dedicated but defenceless government functionaries were subjected to ruthless public criticism or blackmail. The result is that all social and ethical norms have been destroyed and instruments of government have become inoperative and ineffective.

The economic life of the country has all but collapsed. Workers and labourers are being incited and urged to commit acts of lawlessness and brutality. While demands for higher wages, salaries and amenities are being extracted under threat of violence, production is going down. There has been a serious fall in exports and I am afraid the country may soon find itself in the grip of serious inflation.

All this is the result of the reckless conduct of those who, acting under the cover of a mass movement, struck blow after blow at the very root of the country during the last few months. The pity is that a large number of innocent but gullible people became victims of their evil designs.

I have served my people to the best of my ability under all circumstances. Mistakes there must have been but what has been achieved and accomplished is not negligible. There are some who would like to undo all that I have done and even that which was done by the governments before me. But the most tragic and heart-rending thought is that there were elements at work which would like to undo even what the Quaid-i-Azam had done, namely the creation of Pakistan.

I have exhausted all possible civil and constitutional means to resolve the present crisis. I offered to meet all those regarded as the leaders of the people. Many of them came to a conference recently but only after I had fulfilled their pre-conditions. Some declined to come for reasons best known to them. I asked these people to evolve an agreed formula. They failed to do so in spite of days of deliberations. They finally agreed on two points and I accepted both of them. I then offered that the unagreed issues should be referred to the representatives of the people after they had been elected on the basis of direct adult franchise. My argument was that the delegates in the conference who had not been elected by the people could not arrogate to themselves the authority to decide all civil and constitutional issues including those on which even they are not agreed among themselves. I thought I would call the National Assembly to consider the two agreed points but it soon became obvious that this would be an exercise in futility. The members of the Assembly are no longer free agents and there is no likelihood of the agreed two points being faithfully adopted. Indeed members are being threatened and compelled either to boycott the session or to move such amendments as would liquidate the central government, make the maintenance of the armed forces impossible, divide the economy of the country, and break up Pakistan into little bits and pieces. Calling the Assembly in such chaotic conditions can only aggravate the situation. How can anyone deliberate coolly and dispassionately on fundamental problems under threat of instant violence.

It is beyond the capacity of the civil government to deal with the present complex situation and the Defence forces must step in.

It is your legal and constitutional responsibility to defend the country not only against external aggression but also to save it from internal disorder and chaos. The nation expects you to discharge this responsibility to preserve the security and integrity of the country and to restore normal social, economic and administrative life. Let peace and happiness be brought back to this anguished land of 120 million people.

I believe you have the capacity, patriotism, dedication and imagination to deal with the formidable problems facing the country. You are the leader of a force which enjoys the respect and admiration of the whole world. Your colleagues in the Pakistan Air Force and in the Pakistan Navy are men of honour and I know that you will always have their full support. Together the armed forces of Pakistan must save Pakistan from disintegration.

I should be grateful if you would convey to every soldier, sailor and airman that I shall always be proud of having been associated with them as their Supreme Commander. Each one of them must know that in this grave hour they have to act as the custodians of Pakistan. Their conduct and actions must be inspired by the principles of Islam and by the conviction that they are serving the interests of their people.

It has been a great honour to have served the valiant and inspired people of Pakistan for so long a period. May God guide them to move toward greater prosperity and glory.

I must also record my great appreciation of your unswerving loyalty. I know that patriotism has been a constant source of inspiration for you all your life. I pray for your success and for the welfare and happiness of my people.
Khuda Hafiz,

Yours sincerely,
M. Ayub Khan

General A.M. Yahya Khan
H.Pk., H.J., C.-in-C. (Army)
General Headquarters, Rawalpindi

40. Author's notes.
41. Conversation with the author.

CHAPTER 14

Conclusion:
'What is past is a prologue'

Any objective appraisal of Ayub Khan's military rule in Pakistan
which lasted for well over ten years (1958-1969), would place
him in the medieval tradition of benevolent dictators. Ayub's
assumption and exercise of personal power was not an unusual
phenomenon in Muslim history. Among the Muslims the ruler has
long been seen as the 'shadow of God'—the ultimate source of
power. Muslim jurists regard power as 'a gift of Allah', hence its
own justification. To question the possession of power was to
invite disorder. Following the doctrine of the lesser evil they
firmly believed that personal rule, however tyrannical, was better
than lawlessness. A usurper had only to plant himself at the pulpit
and the 'believers' would render him instant allegiance. When the
Chief Justice of the Supreme Court of Pakistan declared that the
military revolution which brought Ayub to power in 1958, was its
own 'source of law', he was only following a well-established
practice in Muslim history.

Ayub had one advantage over most other military rulers. His
accession to power was generally, and quite genuinely,
acknowledged as the only way out of the mess which the politicians
had created during the first eleven years of Pakistan's existence.
The elitist classes, the feudal lords, the *ulema,* and the bureaucrats,
had all lost the right to speak for the people and this gave Ayub
direct access to the masses. He spoke to them and they listened—
he promised them reforms and they believed him.

Had Ayub remained true to the authoritarian tradition he would
have relied on the more vocal and influential religious leaders to

advocate and uphold his rule while keeping the army under his
personal command. Instead, he sent the army back to the barracks
and debarred the politicians, religious as well as secular, from
participating in the affairs of the country. His hope was that he
would take Pakistan into the modern age by dissociating himself
from the fundamentalist visions of the past.

He knew that he could not achieve his goal without the
participation of the people but he did not fully comprehend the
requirements and demands of the people's participation. He
thought that given the low level of literacy, hardly above ten per
cent, it should be enough for the people to choose their local
leaders—Basic Democrats—after which they should leave him
alone to get on with the job without undue interference. Like most
Muslim rulers, Ayub failed to realize that participation would
have no meaning unless it was based on the principles of equality
and interdependence. Equality makes the people partners in
failure, as in success, and interdependence generates a sense of
mutual obligations based on tolerance and trust. The Islamic
system of government, as generally understood, guarantees the
rights of all citizens but their rights are not equal, nor do different
communities interact with each other in a framework of
interdependence. Under Ayub's highly centralized system the
people in the provinces never had the feeling of equality nor were
the people of the country bound together in a network of collective
self-reliance. East Bengal, in particular, blamed and not without
justification, the central government for exploiting the resources
of the province and denying the people their fundamental rights.
Ayub presided over a coalition of unequal and unwilling partners.

Of greater public concern was Ayub's refusal to submit to any
transparent system of accountability. Anyone who questioned the
motives or the performance of his government was considered
ignorant or malicious. He expected the people to repose their trust
in 'the leader' in order to enjoy the munificence of his rule. Given
the resources of the country, Ayub should have known that the
beneficiaries of his system would never outnumber the deprived
among the masses. The prominence and affluence of the few
would only add to the unhappiness of the many, who were denied

even elementary opportunities of education, health and employment. That was why Ayub could never understand the disaffection of the Bengalis. He attributed their outbursts of resentment and agitation to emotionalism.

Under Ayub, Pakistan made great strides in the agricultural sector which was rapidly modernized and introduced to more efficient and productive methods of farming. The country made significant progress in the industrial field and a vibrant private sector, relieved of bureaucratic controls, came into operation. Unfortunately the hold of the big landlords on the land and the emergence of business and industrial cartels resulted in the concentration of wealth in a few hands. The 'trickle down' economics, which Ayub had embraced at the instigation of the World Bank proved a hollow slogan of development.

Ayub's detractors criticize him for disrupting the natural evolution of the democratic process in the country, his apologists blame the politicians who preceded him for corrupting the democratic institutions which Pakistan had inherited from the British at the time of Independence in 1947. Both these positions are familiar alibis used by Muslim intellectuals and social scientists to avoid addressing the fundamental problem of reconciling the Islamic doctrines, as enunciated by Muslim jurists, with the democratic concepts and demands of the modern age.

Ayub tried to move the people towards the modern age but he found every route blocked not only by the fundamentalists but even by the so-called modernists who would tentatively sneak out of their conventional habitat, survey the ground and withdraw into their shells at the first sign of opposition. In the end Ayub was left with no supporter nor any intermediary.

A quarter of a century on, the social and political problems which Ayub set out to resolve continue to haunt the people of Pakistan. If anything, they have acquired greater complexity and gravity. The nation-state remains undefined. Equality of citizens in all respects, regardless of differences of faith and gender is still an unacceptable concept. The demand for an Islamic state has assumed far greater intensity though there is still no agreed definition of an Islamic state. The Constitution, as it stands today, confers such overriding powers on an indirectly-elected President that he can command the government to act in accordance with his instructions or wishes, and if he finds the working of the government unsatisfactory he can dissolve the National Assembly and dismiss the government. The President can, and indeed does, act in much the same manner as his authoritarian predecessors did because the basic problem of division of power between the head of state and parliament remains unresolved.

Ayub introduced a range of reforms in the hope that the benefits flowing from these reforms would reach the people and they would come to recognize the merits of his system of government. Some of the reforms never got off the ground; others, like the land reforms, lost their purpose in the course of implementation. Still, the introduction of the reforms created an atmosphere of rethinking which constituted a challenge to vested interests. The *ulema* were particularly alarmed when Family Laws came into operation. These laws gave married women certain rights which acted as a restraint on male freedom to divorce at will or acquire more than one wife. While women welcomed these laws, the conservative classes considered them an assault on the Islamic structure of society. When Ayub's reforms came to be questioned he began to wonder whether he had not 'pushed the people too hard into the modern age'.

The implementation of the reforms was left to the administration. The result was a sudden expansion in the size and powers of the bureaucracy which started to intrude into every corner of life and, at the behest of the rulers, snuffed out all criticism and dissent. In the end it was the bludgeoning presence of government functionaries which incited the people to revolt against an intrusive and oppressive system of government. The revolt was essentially a secular phenomenon because it arose out of the people's refusal to accept any restrictions on their right of franchise or expression. Ayub thought that the people had 'gone mad' but he never understood the cause of their madness. The people had come to know of their democratic rights, and despite their history, they opted for 'lunacy' because sanity demanded renunciation of those rights.

The provinces, particularly East Bengal, felt that they had lost their identity in Ayub's unitary form of government. The governors of the provinces were mere agents of the President and the Provincial Assemblies were composed mostly of nominees of the administration, parading as representatives of the people. The struggle of the Bengalis for greater freedom evoked spontaneous response from the smaller provinces of West Pakistan, which were groaning under the yoke of Punjabi and Pathan domination. Towards the end Ayub came to the dismal conclusion that there was nothing to hold the country together except the fear of the Hindu. The best thing, he thought, was to 'let East Pakistan go' and give the other provinces the maximum autonomy they wanted.

Ayub had given Pakistan a system which Western social scientists had come to see as a model of development but as Ayub said towards the end, 'We managed to bluff the world but our own people called the bluff'.

Ayub was seen as an enlightened world leader, particularly among the Afro-Asian nations. His greatest contribution was the bond of friendship he established between Pakistan and the People's Republic of China. Few leaders could have withstood the tremendous pressure he came under during the India-China War of 1962. President Kennedy wanted Ayub to give India some gesture of support which would help it to repel the Chinese invasion without having to worry about its flanks. Had Ayub succumbed to this pressure the Chinese would have been permanently alienated from Pakistan. Instead, Ayub used the opportunity with great foresight and skill to negotiate a border agreement with China which established a close relationship of understanding and co-operation between the two countries. Unfortunately, the Americans did not recognize that Pakistan's friendship with China could also serve as an opening for them. Two years after Ayub's abdication the Americans would use Pakistan as a covert channel of communication with the Chinese which led to a degree of normalization of relations between the US and the People's Republic of China.

No less significant was the breakthrough which Ayub achieved with the Soviet Union. As an ally of the United States, which had provided the USA with military bases, and a member of two regional pacts opposed to Soviet interests, Ayub could hardly expect a warm response from the Soviet leaders to any overture on his part. Yet, when he visited the Soviet Union in March 1965, the first such venture by any Pakistani head of government, he succeeded in persuading the Soviet troika, Brezhnev, Podgorny and Kosygin, that the Soviet Union could rely on Pakistan as a friendly neighbour. He received a promise of military aid and economic co-operation and substantial financing for important joint projects. Ayub presented his case against India with great adroitness and secured an undertaking from the Soviet leaders to review their stand on Kashmir. In return Ayub gave a firm indication of his intention not to renew the lease of the US communications base in Pakistan. The Americans reacted angrily to Ayub's parlyes in Moscow and President Johnson cancelled Ayub's official visit to Washington. Unfortunately for Ayub, the USA had not yet realized that their regional pacts had lost all purpose and their bases in Pakistan were no longer of vital importance to them.

India was Ayub's great disappointment. He had successfully negotiated the Indus Basin treaty for the distribution of waters between India and Pakistan and hoped to resolve the Kashmir dispute through negotiations. The Indian Prime Minister, Pandit Nehru, who was reasonable on other issues, was adamant on Kashmir with which he had deep personal attachment.

How did Ayub, a man of prudence, who would take infinite pains to examine a problem and who never hesitated to take personal command of any difficult situation, get involved in Operation Gibraltar in Kashmir which made no military sense? And why did he allow the Operation to be controlled and run by a volatile Foreign Minister and an irresolute Commander-in-Chief? Hopefully this account answers these questions. The controversy about Grand Slam, which was planned as the crowning move in Operation Gibraltar, and the decision to relieve General Akhtar Malik, who had masterminded the whole operation three days before the outbreak of the war, is finally laid to rest. The prevailing view in Pakistan is that if Ayub had allowed General Malik to play his hand to the finish he would have won the game. Even sensible army officers in Pakistan rely on an Indian writer who suggested that Grand Slam, if successful, 'might have, at one stroke, lopped off the state of Jammu and Kashmir from the rest of India, militarily and politically'.[1] They ignore the proviso 'if successful' and insist that the change of command at that crucial moment was the most fateful decision of the war. The truth is that Grand Slam had no chance of success regardless of who was in command. General Akhtar Malik had lost all the tricks, none of his finesse had worked, and the trump he was holding was a rag.

There is no evidence that Ayub was the victim of any conspiracy, though there is enough to show that he was grossly misinformed about the details of the Operation and deliberately kept in the dark about its failure. He had approved Operation Gibraltar himself though he always regretted that he never set up a 'counter syndicate' to identify its flaws and weaknesses, a job which should have been done by the Commander-in-Chief in any case.

Ayub allowed his Foreign Minister to convince him that Kashmir was seething with discontent and the oppressed people of the state would rise in revolt once they saw Pakistan coming out in support of their struggle for liberation. There was no evidence whatever to support such a claim. Pakistan had in fact no contact with the leaders of Kashmir, much less with the people in the villages, where Pakistani commandos, armed to the teeth, would appear as liberators in the middle of the night only to create panic and terror. The whole Operation was based on two assumptions: (1) that the people of Kashmir would spontaneously rise in support of Pakistani soldiers coming to their liberation, and (2) that the Hindu had no stomach for a fight. The first assumption was a Foreign Office-cum-Military Intelligence contrivance, inspired by wishful thinking, and the second, was a reflection of the traditional Muslim belief in their martial superiority. Ayub subscribed to this belief. In the final order he issued before the outbreak of the war he said, 'As a general rule Hindu morale would not stand more than a couple of hard blows at the right time and place.'

Ayub was no Abraham Lincoln or Salahuddin Ayubi, as Bhutto presented him in the beginning, but he was no charlatan either, as Bhutto portrayed him in the end. Ayub's reforms in the economic field and the courageous and enlightened manner in which he faced international and domestic pressures during the India-China War made a lasting contribution to Pakistan's stability and advancement. Ayub failed because military rule is a complete negation of democratic principles and fundamental human rights. The people of Pakistan rejected Ayub's dictatorship, despite some of its material benefits, because they were not prepared to give up their democratic rights. More than any other form of personal rule, military dictatorship brings out the worst qualities in a citizen—fear, jealousy, suspicion—and turns the qualities of tolerance, trust, and self-sacrifice into unrewarding pursuits.

Ayub's greatest contribution was to continue the process which Jinnah had initiated, of reconciling the demands of the modern age with the demands of Islam. If the people of Pakistan pursue that process, with their eyes on the expanding avenues of the times, and defy the fundamentalists who would drive them back to the dark caves of the past, then the lessons of the Ayub era would serve as a prologue to the struggle that awaits the Muslims and demands of them a dynamic willingness to undertake *Ijtehad,* the highest form of creative defiance of obscurantist tradition. Without *Ijtehad* the dream of Muslim renaissance shall, for ever, remain an illusion.

NOTES

1. D.R. Mankaker, *The Twenty-Two Day War,* Lancer's Publishers, New Delhi, 1969.

APPENDIX

THE NEHRU LETTERS

The Nehru Letters

I came to learn about the two Nehru letters of 19 November 1962 to President Kennedy by accident. During a conversation with McGeorge Bundy in New York in December 1977 about the Kennedy-Ayub exchange of messages during the India-China War 1962,[1] I asked him why Ayub's assessment that the Chinese had no intention of prolonging or enlarging the war beyond eliminating Indian encroachment on their territory was rejected by the Kennedy administration. Bundy's view was that Professor J.K. Galbraith who was then US Ambassador in New Delhi, had assiduously and passionately argued that the Chinese purpose was to overwhelm India and the war would last long enough for the US to pull India into its orbit. Kennedy swallowed this line until it became quite an obsession with him and he would reject any advice which conflicted with Galbraith's forecast. I was familiar with the record of the meetings that Ayub had with General Maxwell-Taylor, military representative of President Kennedy, Walt Rostow, Special Assistant to President Kennedy, William Komer, Senior Staff Assistant White House, and Carl Kaysen, Deputy Special Assistant to the President of National Security Affairs, all of whom had visited him in Rawalpindi. Ayub had told them that he was in touch with the Chinese and his understanding was that the Chinese had no intention to penetrate into India, and their sole objective was to throw the Indian forces out of the disputed territory.

In a public statement on 5 November 1962, Ayub had said,

We believe that the scope of this conflict, because of the terrain over which it is being run, can perforce be limited. If it were otherwise then the contestants would have started it with a considerable campaigning period ahead of them. It was no time to start it in October when the weather conditions will progressively bring military operations to a halt.[2]

Bundy told me that his major preoccupation at the time was the Cuban missile crisis: 'Carl Kaysen was given the rest of the world and the India-China affair was Carl's war.' He suggested that perhaps the American Ambassador in Pakistan, Walter McConaughy, was not as persuasive as Galbraith who was a good friend of Kennedy. Galbraith, he said, was 'red hot when the Chinese came into India though that is not the period he would want to dilate upon'.[3] Bundy was good enough to arrange for me to meet Carl Kaysen in Cambridge, Massachusetts on Wednesday, 14 December 1977. We talked for over two hours. Kaysen started by saying, 'Since everybody else was involved in bigger things, I was allowed to take all the decisions during the India-China War.'

The Americans, he said, did not have a precise idea of Chinese intentions nor were they aware of the depth of Sino-Soviet differences. A major hurdle was the presence of Krishna Menon in the Indian government, and the prevailing view in the US administration was that if arms were supplied to India, while Menon was still in charge of Defence, the Russians would garner all the benefits. It was the administration's belief that military aid should serve a dual purpose: create friendly ties between the US and India and exacerbate Sino-Soviet tensions. An allied purpose was to alert the Indian upper classes to the communist danger. But nothing much came of it, said Kaysen, as the Indian forces just collapsed: 'The rout was startling. Had the war gone on a little longer, the US objectives would have been easily achieved.'

It was at this point that he mentioned the two Nehru letters which, he said, 'arrived in quick succession on the same day'. The first letter had been delivered by the Indian Ambassador B.K. Nehru in the morning, and in the afternoon he was seeking permission to deliver another 'most urgent' communication from his Prime Minister to President Kennedy. Kaysen knew that President Kennedy had a dinner engagement that evening but he agreed to take the letter to the White House.

He recalled: 'The President was standing in the hall having a glass of milk while Mrs Kennedy was drinking wine.' Kaysen had not had dinner and accepted a glass of wine which, he said, he should not have done on an empty stomach. Kennedy read the seven-page letter from Nehru and handed it over page by page to Mrs Kennedy who was clearly astonished by what she read: 'I thought he was a ballet dancer, he is turning into a warrior.' Kaysen's own judgement was, 'It was a hysterical letter; a silly letter asking us to bomb China.'

Even today, few people in India are aware of the existence of these letters which are treated as top secret by the US administration. The two letters were written less than forty-eight hours before the Chinese declared cease-fire on 21 November 1962.

The first disclosure came from Sudhir Ghosh.[4] In a speech in the Indian Parliament on 15 March 1965, Ghosh said that when India was overwhelmed by the power of communist China, in October-November 1962, Nehru 'the father of non-alignment asked for American air protection' and the American President ordered 'one of the American aircraft carriers to proceed to the Bay of Bengal'. Ghosh was surprised by the 'political storm of extraordinary ferocity which raged in the lobbies of Parliament and in the Press for a couple of weeks' after his statement in Parliament. Ghosh's statement was seen as a slur on Nehru's memory and there were demands for his expulsion from the Congress Party. Ghosh himself argued that Nehru 'loved India more than anything else in the world and when India was in mortal danger he was prepared to throw away anything, including his favourite policy of non-alignment, for the sake of India's survival.'[5]

The Indian Prime Minister Shastri called Ghosh to his office in Parliament House and told him that he might have made a mistake and perhaps he was talking about the 'omnibus letter' that Nehru had written to all friendly governments on 20 October 1962 asking for assistance from wherever it was available. Ghosh replied that he was referring to 'something quite different'. He was talking about 'a very special communication addressed to the President of the United States on 19 November 1962'.[6]

Ghosh claimed he had heard about it from President Kennedy when he saw him in March 1963. He advised Shastri to ask his Foreign Secretary to check the facts with the American Ambassador before making any statement in Parliament. But the pressure was so great that Shastri was forced to state in the house that Nehru did not ask for an American aircraft carrier. The American Ambassador, Chester Bowles, confirmed that 'The US government did have the document [Panditji's appeal to President Kennedy for air protection]: the document was in Washington and it could be produced if the Government of India so desired.'

Sorensen and Schlessinger published their memoirs in 1965. Schlessinger made only an oblique reference to the two letters:[7]

> Nehru, forgetting the virtues of non-alignment, sent a desperate appeal for help. With Kennedy's strong backing, Galbraith too saw the opportunity to consolidate the American friendship with India. Acting with great sense and skill, and after the usual arguments with the dilatory department, he succeeded in working out *air defence arrangements* [emphasis added] and otherwise making it clear that, in case the war intensified India could expect American assistance.

Sorensen[8] made no specific reference to the letters. He wrote that Nehru, stung by the lack of support from the Soviet Union and other Afro-Asian nations, 'admitted that India had been living in a dream world; and on October 26 he turned for help to the United States and John Kennedy'. This was, according to Sorensen, the first of some fifteen letters which Nehru and Kennedy exchanged during the next six months. The first letter asked for 'sympathy' and 'support'. His kinsman and Ambassador to Washington, B.K. Nehru, explained to the President when delivering it in person that afternoon, that the Prime Minister, after all these years in the neutralist pacifist camp, found it difficult to make a direct request for armaments from the United States. He was hoping instead, that the President in his reply would offer 'support' instead of 'military assistance' on the basis of 'sympathy' instead of an 'alliance'. Kennedy replied that he had no wish to take advantage of India's misfortune to coerce her into a pact. 'The United States would offer support out of sympathy—and our representatives could translate those terms into the military specifics.' (Speaking unofficially, he added Nehru ought to make Krushchev 'put up or shut up' on an earlier promise of MIGs and military equipment). Sorensen recalled that Nehru's reluctance to mention military specifics was temporary: 'Pleas for a vast arsenal of American armaments began to pour in and Kennedy promptly responded with substantial amount of light weapons, mortars, ammunition and other items. Within a few days he despatched a high level survey team under Averell Harriman to report how America could be most useful without driving Pakistan into Red China's arms. To the President's great satisfaction, and as the inadequacies of India's army became apparent, the acidly anti-American Krishna Menon was out as Nehru's Minister of Defence. As younger and more pro-Western men gained strength in his government, Nehru's policy of non-alignment became at least temporarily more realistic. The United States and Great Britain (who also sent military aid) were true friends, he said, 'The Chinese were never to be trusted again. The Indian people cheered all signs of US aid'.[9]

Four years later Galbraith published his *Ambassador's Journal*.[10] In his entry under 19 November Galbraith said 'not one but two pleas for help are coming to us, the second one of them still highly confidential.' A footnote under the entry said,

> These requests, which sought full defensive intervention by our Air Force, were transmitted through the Indian Embassy in Washington. My notice from Desai enabled me to warn Washington that they were coming— especially the second and more serious request for *air intervention*. The non-alignment I was asked about at lunch is far out of date; the Indians are pleading for military association.

Here was the first specific reference to 'two pleas' sent by Nehru to Kennedy on 'a day of unbelievably dismal developments' when there was 'ultimate panic in Delhi' in Galbraith's words. This was the first time he had 'ever witnessed the disintegration of public morale'.[11]

A year later appeared Neville Maxwell's definitive account of the war.[12] He recorded the landing of American jet transports in India during the first week of November at the rate of eight flights a day.[13] In response to the 'omnibus' letter which Nehru had written to friendly governments, the US provided military equipment 'on terms to be negotiated later'. The British contribution was an outright gift. The French supplies were strictly commercial. India had approached Israel with whom it had no diplomatic relations, and suggested that Israeli supplies should be 'delivered in ships that did not fly the Israeli flag'. Ben Gurion replied: 'No flag, no weapons,' and when a shipment of heavy mortars did arrive in Bombay it came in an Israeli ship.

Tracing the events of the war, Maxwell concluded that the Indian Army had been completely routed by 20 November: 'Militarily the Chinese victory was complete, the Indian defeat absolute.' Late on the night of 20 November…

> Nehru made an urgent, open appeal for the intervention of the United States with bomber and fighter squadrons to go into action against the Chinese. His idea was that American aircraft would undertake strikes against Chinese troops on Indian territory if they continued to advance, and would also provide cover for Indian cities in case the Chinese Air Force tried to raid them. The appeal was detailed, even specifying the number of squadrons required—fifteen. This suggests that Nehru had taken some service advice but he neither consulted nor informed his cabinet colleagues. The only copy of this appeal was kept in the Prime Minister's secretariat, instead of being sent to the Ministry of External Affairs in the usual way.

Commenting on Maxwell's version, Michael Brecher pointed out that the appeal was made on 19 not 20 November. It was secret, not open. Brecher claimed 'The US air intervention was to integrate, that is, to enable Indian Air Force planes to attack the advancing Chinese. Nor was it Nehru's idea that American planes would strike against Chinese troops on Chinese territory.'[14]

In December 1977 when I met McGeorge Bundy and Carl Kaysen, all I knew was that there was this 'omnibus' letter which Nehru wrote to friendly countries between 26-29 October 1962 asking for military assistance; that American planes were landing in India in the first week of November with military equipment; that Nehru had asked Kennedy for 'air protection', and an American aircraft carrier had been ordered by President Kennedy to proceed to the Bay of Bengal. Apart from that there was Galbraith's tantalizing reference to Nehru's two pleas for help, of which the second one was 'still highly confidential', and Maxwell's reference to Nehru's 'urgent open appeal for the intervention of the United States'.

On the basis of this information, I wrote to Walt Rostow in September 1977 that the Americans had not only assumed but intended that the India-China War should develop in scope and intensity to enable the Americans to establish a military alliance with India to deal with the Chinese threat. I did mention to him that by 20 November the Indian government was willing to accept any condition that the Americans might dictate for such a military alliance with the US. Galbraith had recorded 'they [the Indians] want our Air Force to back them up so that they can employ theirs tactically without leaving their cities unprotected. I am not sure that there is any useful conception at the back of this. I would think it would be very unwise for them to initiate any air action.'[15] In his reply, Rostow said that he found my suggestion 'unrecognizable'. By then I had come to question the veracity of Galbraith's account. I had heard from one of his colleagues in Harvard that by 20 November Galbraith had established a war office of his own in New Delhi and was virtually running the Indian government, if not the war itself. It was not inconceivable that the 'two pleas' that the Indian Prime Minister sent to President Kennedy were cleared, if not actually suggested, by him.

On 16 December 1977, I had a fruitful meeting with James C. Thompson Jr., (Curator, Nieman Foundation, Harvard University, Cambridge), who was holding a senior position in the State Department during the India-China War. Thompson told me that the American aim at that time was to have 'enough war' to bring India into a warm embrace. One of the problems was the American Ambassador, Walter McConaughy, in Pakistan who was a stranger to the Kennedys. Thompson remembered how the State Department had arranged that when Mrs Kennedy went to Pakistan she should give the impression that Walter was an old friend of the Kennedys. As Mrs Kennedy stepped out of the plane in Rawalpindi, she said, kissing the Ambassador on the cheek, 'Hello Walter, how nice to see you again,' and Walter, slow but honest, said, 'I don't think we have ever met before.' I told Thompson about the reply I had received from Rostow and he remarked: 'Anything that does not accord with Rostow's ideas is unrecognizable.' Thompson explained that the impression in the White House was that here was China spilling over to expand into the world, and there was poor India invaded by Genghis Khan. The Americans wanted a permanent Indian friend: 'Here was an opportunity which could be realized if there was enough war.'

This meeting with Thompson was arranged for me by Professor Jerome Cohen who was then Associate Dean of the Harvard Law School. He told me that the US was not ready for the kind of initiative that might have been taken in 1962 to come to a real understanding with China. He cautioned me against accepting any version of the events during the India-China War given to me by the Kennedy officials: 'These people rationalize to evade accusations.' He remarked wryly that Carl Kaysen would put the India-China War on his tombstone. He said that he was aware of the Sino-Soviet rifts in 1962 and that was the time when a breakthrough with China could have been achieved but American opinion was not ready for that. President Kennedy did offer food aid to China to which the Chinese reaction was, 'Here comes the god of disease with some vaccine'.

Professor Edward Mason, who was the head of the Harvard Advisory Group in Pakistan in the early nineteen sixties and was an admirer of Ayub, told me that he had flown in an American aeroplane to Laddakh during the period at Galbraith's instance. He had spent one month with Galbraith in India at the time of the crisis though the Galbraith *Journal* makes no mention of it.

In 1984 appeared the third volume of *Jawaharlal Nehru, A Biography* by Sarvepathi Gopal.[16] According to Gopal, Nehru told Krishna Menon in July 1962 that the whole essence of non-alignment was not to lose the goodwill of Russia or that of the United States. If India were to lose the goodwill of either of the two superpowers it would be 'driven into an aligned position'. In the first week of October 1962 Nehru told General Kaul

…that India had tolerated Chinese incursions into her territory for far too long and a stage had come when she should take—or appear to take—a strong stand irrespective of consequences. India should contest, by whatever means at her disposal, the claim which the Chinese were making in the Eastern sector by intruding into Dhola.

Nehru hoped that the Chinese would see reason and withdraw, but if they did not, India would have no option but to expel them 'or at least try to do so to the best of our ability'. If the Government failed to take such action, they would 'forfeit public confidence completely'.

On 12 October 1962 Nehru told the Press: 'Our instructions are to free our territory…I cannot fix the date, that is entirely for the army.' On 20 October 1962 the Chinese made an advance in the western and eastern sectors. Nehru's reaction was 'there can, of course, be no surrender to this kind of thing. But we must be prepared for losses from time to time…We have a very difficult task, but we shall face it with a stout heart. We must realize, however, that this is going to be a long, drawn-out affair. I see no near end to it.'

The Soviet Union urged India to accept an immediate cease-fire. Most of the other non-aligned leaders endorsed this position. Nasser, in particular, wanted to see the hostilities ended as quickly as possible. I learnt from a reliable source that Nasser conveyed to Nehru a cease-fire proposal which was discussed by the Indian Cabinet and accepted. But contrary to the Cabinet decision, the Indian Foreign Secretary, M.J. Desai, instructed the Indian Ambassador to UAR who had brought the proposal, to return to Cairo and tell Nasser that India could not possibly accept the terms of the cease-fire contained in the Nasser proposal. On 25 October Nehru told a conference of Information Ministers of the States: 'We are getting out of touch with reality in the modern world and we were living in an artificial atmosphere of our own creation. We have been shocked out of it, all of us, whether it is the government or the people; some might have felt it less and some more.' He said that China and the world had betrayed India and forced her, much against her will, to take to war. India's efforts at peace had been knocked on the head.

As noted earlier, Nehru had made a direct request for US military aid on 29 October. Two days later he relieved Kṛiṣhna Menon of the Defence portfolio. India was now preparing for a counter-offensive. Harold Macmillan observed that Nehru transformed himself 'from an imitation of George Lansbury into a parody of Churchill'. Nehru told his Cabinet colleagues, 'I will fight them [the Chinese] with a stick!' brandishing a swaggerstick which he always carried. On 12 November Nehru told a group of American journalists that that he had requested the United States to provide equipment for the manufacturing of arms. The Indian counter-offensive was launched on 14 November, Nehru's birthday, but it ended in a rout within a few hours. On 17 November General Kaul sent a message from the eastern front that 'foreign troops should be asked to come to India's aid'. By 19 November India's defeat was complete.[17]

According to Gopal, Nehru, apparently without consulting any of his Cabinet colleagues or officials, apart from the Foreign Secretary, wrote two letters to Kennedy describing the situation as 'really desperate' and requesting the immediate despatch of a minimum of twelve squadrons of supersonic all-weather fighters and the setting up of radar communications. American personnel would have to man these fighters and installations and protect Indian cities from air attacks by the Chinese till Indian personnel had been trained. If possible, the United States should also send planes flown by American personnel to assist the Indian Air Force in any battles with the Chinese in Indian air space: but aerial action by India elsewhere would be the responsibility of the Indian Air Force. Nehru also asked for 'two B-47 bomber squadrons to enable India to strike at Chinese bases and airfields: but to learn to fly these planes, Indian pilots and technicians would be sent immediately for training in the United States.' All such assistance and equipment would be utilized solely against the Chinese. As an immediate response Galbraith asked that units of the Seventh Fleet should move into the Bay of Bengal. Gopal stated that Nehru's two letters to Kennedy were dated 19 November 1962.[18]

Considering the controversy surrounding the contents of the two letters one would have expected Gopal to reproduce the full text of the letters. Instead he chose to summarize the contents of two long letters in six sentences leaving it open to question whether the summary was accurate and faithful. Indeed Gopal's version raises certain awkward questions. If Indian pilots were not trained to fly B-47 bomber squadrons, which India required to strike at the Chinese bases and air fields, who was to fly these planes in the moment of India's need? The training of Indian pilots might have taken several months but India wanted to strike at the Chinese bases and airfields immediately. Did Nehru really insist on the point that American personnel flying American planes should assist the Indian Air Force in battles 'in Indian air space'. Even more worrying, Gopal's version does not remotely resemble Kaysen's recollection that the second Nehru letter was 'silly and hysterical'.

Efforts to obtain copies of the two Nehru letters from the Kennedy library have not proved successful so far. Still, some useful information has become available. Of the relevant documents in the Kennedy library, four State Department documents consisting of five pages in case NLK 77-474 and five documents consisting of fifteen pages in case 77-475 are still classified. In the first case, four of the documents are secret and in the second case one document of three pages is marked 'secret'. Two documents of five pages are secret, one document of six pages is confidential and one document of one page is unmarked. Of the documents which have been declassified, the first is a State Department telegram dated 28 October 1962. It is addressed to the US Ambassador in New Delhi and repeated for information to Karachi and London. Below is the text of the telegram:

1. When you deliver President's reply to Nehru's letter of October 26, you may wish reinforce approach reported Embtel 1436 by telling him that President believes letter from Nehru to Ayub would strengthen President's hand in persuading Ayub to act in helpful way in sub-continent's hour of crisis.
2. Re President's message to Nehru, remember that control of timing and content of approaches designed to identify specifics of our support is in your hands. We in no way think US should be in position running after Nehru to offer aid but we wish to be as responsive as appropriate to his needs. We think you have been striking the right note.
3. We are working urgently on suggestions in US-ARMA's 271240Z and para 8 Embtel 1433.

The telegram was declassified on 12 July 1977. It is clear that there were two issues foremost in the mind of the US President at the time. One, to bring about an understanding between Nehru and Ayub—to persuade Ayub 'to act in a helpful way in subcontinent's hour of crisis'; the other was to take the maximum advantage of the situation and manœuver India into a position where it would be compelled to seek US military assistance on US terms. Galbraith was given the authority to control the 'timing and content of approaches' to identify specifics of US support in India. But in no case was the US to appear to be running after Nehru to offer him aid and Galbraith was told that he had been 'striking the right note'. While these diplomatic moves were in progress the administration was 'working urgently on specific suggestions with regard to armaments'.

The second letter dated 28 October 1962 is President Kennedy's reply to Nehru's letter delivered to the White House by the Indian Ambassador, B.K. Nehru on 26 October. This letter was declassified on 12 May 1978. The text of the letter is as follows:

Dear Mr Prime Minister:

Your Ambassador handed me your letter last night. The occasion of it is a difficult and painful one for you and a sad one for the whole world. Yet there is a sense in which I welcome your letter, because it permits me to say to you what has been in my mind since the Chinese Communists have begun to press their aggressive attack into Indian territory. I know I can speak for my whole country, when I say that our sympathy in this situation is wholeheartedly with you. You have displayed an impressive degree of forbearance and patience in dealing with the Chinese. You have put into practice what all great religious teachers have urged and so few of their followers have been able to do. Alas, this teaching seems to be effective only when it is shared by both sides in a dispute.

I want to give you support as well as sympathy. This is a practical matter and, if you wish, my Ambassador in New Delhi can discuss with you and the officials of your government what we can do to translate our support into terms that are practically most useful to you as soon as possible.

With all sympathy for India and warmest personal good wishes.

Sincerely,

Signed

John F. Kennedy

Nehru's letter to Kennedy unfortunately is still classified but its contents provided Kennedy with an opportunity to congratulate

Nehru for displaying forebearance and patience in the face of Chinese communist aggression into Indian territory. It also gave Kennedy a chance to remind Nehru of 'great religious teachers' and chide him for his one-sided moral posturing. The letter confirmed that the practical aspects of American support would be determined by the American Ambassador in New Delhi.

Earlier, on 22 October 1962, Kennedy had written to Nehru about the Cuban Crisis. This letter was declassified on 12 May 1978. The text is as follows:

Dear Prime Minister:

I am asking Ambassador Galbraith to deliver to you personally a copy of a speech I am making tonight, concerning the dangerous developments in Cuba and the action I have authorised.

The new Soviet actions in Cuba came at the very moment that the Chinese communists have launched their aggressive attacks on your forces. Our thoughts are with you in your hour of trial. As to Cuba, the evidence that offensive nuclear missile bases have been installed in Cuba by the Soviet Government is accurate beyond question. Your Ambassador here will be fully briefed on the details. This Soviet action is being taken in direct contradiction of Mr. Khrushchev's statements, confirmed to me personally even a few days ago by Foreign Minister Gromyko, that only defensive weapons were being supplied to Cuba.

You will recall that I stated publicly a month ago that 'If at any time the Communist buildup in Cuba were to…become an offensive military base of significant capacity for the Soviet Union, then this country would do whatever must be done to protect its own security and that of its allies.' An immediate quarantine, therefore, is necessary to prevent further offensive missile installations by the Soviet Government in Cuba. [Three lines after this are classified].

I have told Mr. Khrushchev that I hope that his Government will refrain from any action which will deepen this crisis and that we can agree to resume the path of peaceful negotiations.

I am also requesting an urgent meeting of the United Nations Security Council. I have asked Ambassador Stevenson to present on behalf of the United States a resolution calling for the withdrawal of missile bases and other offensive weapons in Cuba under the supervision of United Nations observers. This would make it possible for the United States to lift its quarantine. I hope that you will instruct your representative in New York to work actively with us and speak forthrightly in support of the above program in the United Nations.

The Department of State has given your Ambassador full information and I assure you we will keep you fully informed of all developments.

The fact that Nehru also wrote two letters about Cuba which are different from the ones that he wrote to Kennedy is proved by William H. Brubeck's memorandum to McGeorge Bundy which reads as follows:

Subject: Letter to Prime Minister Nehru. Enclosed is a draft of a letter from the President to Prime Minister Nehru in reply to two recent letters, which came in close succession on Cuba. In our suggested reply, we have taken the opportunity to take up United States military assistance to India and India's relations with Pakistan, in addition to commenting briefly on Cuba.

The letters were received telegraphically by the Indian Ambassador in Washington who delivered them to President Kennedy on 29 October 1962. Only one of the two letters, a specimen of 'babu' draft, has been declassified and it reads as follows:

New Delhi
29 October, 1962

Dear Mr. President,

We have been deeply relieved, Mr. President, by the happier turn of events in regard to Cuba. Your own restraint and wisdom, as Mr. Khrushchev has also recognised, have helped to bring about this change. I would like to express our warm appreciation of your statesmanship. We wish you all success in your efforts to ensure peace and to save humanity from the disaster of war.
Warm regards
Yours sincerely,
Signed
Jawaharlal Nehru

The second letter on Cuba remains classified.

On 29 October Galbraith sent a telegram No. 1687 to Secretary of State (Action Department 1443) saying 'Nehru made definite request for US military assistance'. A whole paragraph after that ecstatic announcement remains classified. Galbraith promised to send a full telegram within the next hour but that telegram too has not yet been declassified. But Galbraith advised 'Most important that department's comments to Press stress that request for US military assistance was made by Prime Minister Nehru personally. Embassay taking same line here with Press.'

From a reliable Indian source I have gathered that the Indian Ambassador, B.K. Nehru delivered the first Nehru letter to President Kennedy on the morning of 20 November 1962. When he returned to his office he found a long cypher telegram waiting for him. It took nearly two hours to decode the message. When he read the message, the Ambassador was 'dumbfounded'. He called Phil Talbot who was Assistant Secretary of State and told him that he had received another letter from his Prime Minister which he must immediately deliver to President Kennedy. Talbot told him that the President was leaving that evening but if the letter was important he would call Carl Kaysen to take it to the President. The letter contained a detailed description of the disposition of the Indian armed forces, and urged the Americans to carry out aerial attacks on targets on the Chinese mainland. The targets were specified and the appeal for attacking those targets was made in unambiguous terms.

The Nehru letters remain classified. Why? The only answer is that these letters together with President Kennedy's response to them constitute an alliance between the US and the Government of India to take joint military action against China. The alliance would become operative in case India felt itself threatened by China. Pakistan was not aware of the terms of the alliance in 1965. That is why Ayub could never understand the reasons that compelled the US to come out in support of India during the Indo-Pakistan War of 1965. Pakistan had the support of China which made the US an ally of India. Had the terms of this alliance been known to Ayub he may never have authorized Operation Gibraltar.

NOTES

1. Bundy was Special Assistant for National Security Affairs (1961-6). He was President of the Ford Foundation when the author met him in 1977.
2. K. Arif, *China-Pakistani Relations 1947-80,* Vanguard Books, Lahore, 1984, p.28.

3. He was right. Despite all efforts it has not been possible to get any response from Professor Galbraith on specific enquiries relating to this period.

4. Sudhir Ghosh, *Gandhi's Emissary,* Houghton Mifflin Company, Boston 1967, pp. 326-38. The concluding part of Ghosh's statement is important.

> There are others who believe that Bertrand Russell, the distinguished philosopher, sent a telegraph to Mr Chou En-lai to point out that it was not nice to worry a good man like Jawaharlal Nehru and that therefore the Chinese decided to go back. There are still others who believe that our good friend, Mr Krushchev gave some good advice to Mr Mao Tse-tung, with whom he had very affectionate relations, and as a result of that good advice the Chinese decided to go home. But it is not widely known that in those dark days of India's peril there was standing just outside Calcutta, near the mouth of the Hooghly River, about a couple of miles outside our territorial waters, one of the largest and newest aircraft carriers of the United States Navy, fitted with a full complement of supersonic aircraft and all the latest gadgets of destruction, sufficient to pulverize an advancing Chinese Army, however large. One great power knows how to give a signal to another great power, and it is not widely known that a signal was given by one side to the other that, if they advanced any further, they would be forcing the hands of the President of the United States. The American aircraft carrier with all its means of destruction was there, not on the initiative of the American President; it was there at the request of Prime Minister Nehru of India, who had asked for American air protection, which was provided by President Kennedy. In the hour of our danger so proud a man as our former Prime Minister, realized that in the last analysis, it was not a practical proposition to defend India from the military might of Communist China without using the military might of the United States. That was the background of the Prime Minister's famous remarks that there was going to be no non-alignment where China was concerned.

5. Ibid. p. 331.

6. Ibid. p. 332.

7. Arthur M. Schlessinger Jr: *A Thousand Days: John F. Kennedy in the White House,* Houghton Mifflin, Boston, 1965, p. 331.

8. Theodore C. Sorenson: *Kennedy;* Hodder and Stoughton, London, 1965, p. 662. Sorenson was special counsel to President Kennedy.

9. Ibid., p. 663.

10. J.K. Galbraith, op. cit., p. 486.

11. Ibid. p. 487.

12. Neville Maxwell, op. cit., pp. 384-5.

13. Ibid., p. 410.

14. Michael Brecher, *Pacific Affairs 52* (4), Winter, 1979-80, p. 620.

15. J.K. Galbraith, op. cit, p. 486.

16. Sarvepathi Gopal: *Jawaharlal Nehru,* Oxford University Press, London, pp. 214-31.

17. Neville Maxwell, op. cit., p.394.

18. Sarvepathi Gopal, *Nehru: A Biography, Volume III, 1956-64.* Oxford University Press, London 1975, p. 229.

Sources and Bibliography

SOURCES

(a) Author's Notes are based on official documents of the Government of Pakistan to which the author was provided access when he assisted Ayub Khan in writing his autobiography *Friends Not Masters* in 1994. Proceedings of cabinet meetings and the governor's conferences are also reflected in these notes. The author participated in those meetings in his official capacity between September, 1963 and March 1969.

(b) Mr Manzur Qadir's personal files which he gave to the author in 1973. Manzur Qadir, an eminent lawyer of Lahore, was foreign minister (1958-1962), and was closely associated with Ayub Khan in framing the 1962 constitution. He was engaged by the government in the Agartala sedition case against Sheikh Mujibur Rehman, leader of the East Pakistan Awami League. During the last few months of the Ayub regime he was closely in touch with Ayub Khan and his papers provide important insight into developments of that period. These papers are with the author.

BIBLIOGRAPHY

Ahmad, Justice Masud (Retd.). *Pakistan — A Study of its Constitutional History (1957-1975),* Research Society of Pakistan, Lahore 1978.

Ahmed, Dr Aftab. The Indus Basin Project and the World Bank. Unpublished thesis, University of the Punjab, Lahore 1967.

Ali, Chaudhri Muhammad. *The Emergence of Pakistan,* Nafees Printers, Lahore 1973.

_____, *The Emergence of Pakistan,* Columbia University Press, New York 1967.

_____, *The Task Before Us.* Research Society of Pakistan, Lahore 1974.

Arif, K. *China-Pakistan Relations, 1947-80.* Vanguard Books, Lahore 1984.

Azad, Maulana Abul Kalam. *India wins Freedom,* Vol. III. Sangam Books, London 1968.

_____, *Indian Wins Freedom,* Orient Longman 1959.

Aziz K. K. *Party Politics in Pakistan,* National Commission for Historical and Cultural Research, Islamabad 1976.

Basic Constitutional Documents. The West Pakistan (Establishment) Order, (1955),

Governor-General's Order No. 4. Printing Corporation of Pakistan Press, Islamabad 1979.

Brecher, Michael. *In the Pacific Affairs*, Winter, 1982, 1979-80.

Carlyle. *A History of Medieval Political Theory in the West*, cited by Larson, Arthur (1965). *Sovereignty Within the Law*, Dobb Ferry, New York 1950.

Chaudhri, M. A. *Government and Politics in Pakistan*, Puthigar, Dacca.

Choudhry, G. W. (ed.) *Documents and Speeches on the Constitution of Pakistan*. Green Book House, Dacca. 1967.

Dawn, Karachi.

Foreign Relations of the United States, (1955-1957) (1987). *South Asia; Department of State Washington, Vol. VIII*, US Govt. Press, Washington.

Galbraith, J. K. *Ambassador's Journal*. Hamish Hamilton, London 1969.

Ghosh, Sudhir. *Gandhi's Emissary*, Houghton Mifflin, Boston 1967.

Gopal, Sarvepathi. *Nehru: A Biography 1956-64, Vol. III*. Oxford University Press, London 1975.

Hassan, Gul. *Memoirs of Lt. General Gul Hassan Khan*, Oxford University Press, 1993.

Huntington, Samuel P. *Political Order in Changing Societies*, Yale University Press, 1968.

Jennings, Sir Ivor. *Constitutional Problems in Pakistan*, Cambridge University Press, 1957.

Jinnah Speeches. Sang-e-Meel Publications, Lahore 1989.

Keesing's Archives (1963-64).

Khan, Mohammad Ayub. *Friends not Masters, A Political Biography*. Oxford University Press, New York 1967.

Mansergh, N. (ed.) *The Transfer of Power, 1942-47, Vol. VIII*. Her Majesty's Stationery Officer, London 1977.

Maududi, Abul A'la. *The Islamic Law and Constitution*. Islamic Publications, Lahore 1955.

Maxwell, Neville. *India's China War*. Jonathan Cape, London 1970.

Machiavelli, Niccolo di Bernada. *The Prince. The Portable Machiavelli*, Penguin Books, London 1979.

Morrice, James. *Pakistan Chronicle*, Oxford University Press, Karachi 1993.

Monitoring Report (16 Sep. 65). Press Information Department, Government of Pakistan.

Musa, General Mohammed. *My Version, India-Pakistan War 1965*, Wajidalis, Lahore 1983.

Moon, Penderel (ed.). *Wavell: The Viceroy's Journal*. Oxford University Press, Karachi 1974.

Nehru Letters. State Department documents. Washington 1962.

Pakistan Observer, Dacca.

Parliamentary Debates. House of Commons, 1946-47, Vol. DXXIV, Her Majesty's Stationery Office, London.

Pirzada Sharifuddin (1970). *Foundation of Pakistan, Vol. II*. National Publishing Houses, Karachi.

The Pakistan Times, Lahore.

Qadir, Manzur papers (see sources above).

Rehman, Inamur. *Public Opinion and Political Development in Pakistan*, Oxford University Press, Karachi 1982.

Report of the Court of Enquiry into Punjab Disturbances of 1953 Government Printing Press, Lahore 1954.

Report of the Constitution Commission. Government of Pakistan 1961.

Schlesinger, Arthur M. Jr. *A Thousand Days: John F Kennedy in the White House*. Houghton Mifflin, Boston 1965.

Sorenson, Theodore C. *Kennedy* Hodder and Stoughton, London 1965.

Statesman, Calcutta.

The Hindu, Delhi.

The National Herald, Karachi.

The Statesman, New Delhi.

The Times, London.

The Washington Evening Star, Washington.

The Round Table Conference, Chapter 4. Unpublished manuscript.

Transfer of Power Documents, Vol. III. Her Majesty's Stationery Office, London 1979.

White paper. Ministry of Foreign Affairs, Government of Pakistan 1977.

Woodruff, Phillip. *The Men Who Ruled India: The Guardians*. St. Martin's Press, London 1954.

Index